A Record of the Descendants of Isaac Ross and Jean Brown

Annie Julia Mims

BIBLIOBAZAAR

ANNE MIMS WRIGHT
(MRS. WILLIAM R.)
WILLIAR PATRICIA WRIGHT
ANNE ROBERT WRIGHT   CLARA MIMS WRIGH.

A RECORD OF THE DESCENDANTS

—of—

ISAAC ROSS and JEAN BROWN

And the Allied Families of

ALEXANDER, CONGER, HARRIS, HILL, KING, KILLINGSWORTH, MACKEY, MOORES, SIMS, WADE, ETC.

Compiled by
ANNE MIMS WRIGHT
(Mrs. William R.)

A Member of
The National Genealogical Association of Washington, D. C.,
And Through Descent From the Above Families a Member
of Society of Colonial Dames of America; Daughters of
the American Revolution; United States Daughters
of 1812; United Daughters of the Confederacy.

Press of
Consumers Stationery and Printing Co
Jackson, Miss., 1911

TO THE MEMORY OF MY GRANDMOTHER, WHO
FIRST INSPIRED IN ME A LOVE OF MY ANCES-
TORS; TO MY MOTHER, WHO HAS ENCOUR-
AGED ME AND MADE POSSIBLE THIS WORK; TO
MY CHILDREN—MAY THEY EMULATE THE GOOD
DEEDS OF THEIR ANTECEDENTS; AND TO
EVERY DESCENDANT OF THESE, OUR PIONEER
ANCESTORS, THIS VOLUMN IS LOVINGLY
DEDICATED.

ANCESTRY.

When first I began my search to see,
What I could learn of my Ancestry,
They seemed to me so far away
As if they had lived in Cæsar's day.
But my interest grew, and great pains I took,
To find *my own* in each history's book.
As their names and deeds came to the light,
The ages vanished like mists of the night.
As they came so near I seemed to see
My beloved, forgotten, Ancestry,

Now I have them with me with their powdered hair,
Wearing beruffled shirts so debonair,
Their pleated coats and flowered vests,
The signet rings with their jeweled crests,
The satin breeches that fit so tight,
Begemmed knee clasps shining bright,
Long, silk stockings and polished shoe,
With their buckles of brightened silver, too,
They seemed so near and dear to me,
My new found friends, my *Ancestry.*

—*Josephine Powell Segal.*

INTRODUCTORY LETTER.

DEAR COUSINS:

This volumn is a "labor of love." The records it contains represent many years of research, at first with no object in view except for my own enjoyment. As one note book after another became filled with priceless records which I had gathered, and my endeavors met with such encouragement and willing assistance from members of the family all over the United States, I decided to share the results of my investigations with you, and this book is the result of that decision.

I have tried earnestly to complete each branch of the various families, an undertaking that few genealogists accomplish. In some branches I have failed on account of lack of interest, and in others because it has been impossible to locate any of the descendants. The records here given are correct as far as I know. There may be errors. but they will be correeected in future editions, if my attention is called to them.

I have undertaken to give all of the information about each branch that I could procure. The same opportunity has been given all to send items, sketches, war records, etc., therefore where no sketches are given of members of the older generations, the fault lies with their descendants.

I have never seen a genealogy arranged in the form that I have chosen. This arrangement, while original, is a very simple way of tracing from the present to any past generation. Genealogies, in the narative form, are confusing and the numbered genealogies are tedious to trace. You will find your parents' names about an inch to the left and above your name; your grandparents about an inch to the left and above your parents, and on in the same way to the head of the branch to which you belong. The families treated of in this volumn have intermarried so frequently that it was not as difficult to write a history of them all combined as to write of just one of the families. Where intermarriages have occurred between the families embraced in this work you will find the children of such marriages given only on the line of the father as there would be a repetition if given on both lines and confusion would be the result. For example: Rebecca G. Sims married Jacob K. Hill, you will find their children in the Hill chapter, not in the Sims chapter.

It is my desire that interest be aroused in family research and a closer bond of love be established between those of the same blood, and that further investigation be made leading to more knowledge of our earlier ancestors. It is not my aim to encourage false pride in, or dependence on the deeds of our ancestors, but that we may try to live our lives worthily. emulating the good and in constant warfare with any evil tendencies we may have inherited. My object in giving to you these records is so well understood by the writer of the letter given below, that I am going to let this kinsman, for whose opinion I have great respect, speak for me.

I assure you of my appreciation of your assistance and interest.

Your Cousin.

DEAR COUSIN:—

That you are Scotch-Irish I have not the least doubt. Your Scotch blood is shown by your tenacity of purpose; your Irish humor and tact is shown in permitting me to believe that you construed my apparent discourtesy in not replying to your several communications not to a want of courtesy to a lady, and kinswoman. but to the fact that your letters addressed to Capt, C. B. Richardson, Ihrie, Miss., went astray for want of proper address, so you addressed your last communication to Mr. Cabell Richardson, Fayette, Miss., thus lowering the bars for me to escape and open communication with you by (on my part) deception rather than by an honest confession, which is always good for the soul. Should I have done so I should have merited only your contempt. I want it otherwise, I believe you to be a bright and amiable lady, a kinswoman worthy of highest regard and I desire your respect.

On my father's side I am English, straight out, and you know the English and the Irish do not love each other very much—never did—although the Irish did help the English to subjugate the Scotch, and our Scotch blood—yours and mine—does not love the Irish very much for that, but should your Irish blood and my English blood fall out, I think the mutual tie of consanguinity our canny Scotch blood, will take the matter up and teach your Irish blood to sing "The Battle of the Boyne" and my English blood will sing "The Wearing of the Green" and thus get matters satisfactorily arranged in this Scotch-Irish-English family.

You got my address correct at your first writing, all except the prefix "Captain." which was an error, I did not get higher than 1st Lieutenant in a battery of field artillery and am not entitled to the the prefix of "Captain." The fact is there are so many official titles in our times that it is a real luxury to be called "Mister."

As you seem to have your heart set on the accomplishment of the work you have undertaken and have spent much time and faithful work and no little money in its pursuit I will subordinate my judgement—giving yours the preference—and give you the benefit of any information I may have which, though traditional, is of just such material as histories are usually compiled. I have not been in sympathy with you in this matter, nor am I much inclined to take that view of it now, and this is not from prejudice but after reasonable consideration. I was never an admirer of a man or a woman with a pedigree. It has too much the appearance of one trying to take credit to himself or herself for what his or her ancestors have accomplished. The real question to be brought home and seriously pondered is: "What have I, myself, done in that station in life to which it has pleased God to call me? Have I so lived as to be a credit to my ancestors or have I so fallen from the high estate and good name they left me as a heritage as to reflect discredit on the name I bear and cause people to quote, 'the sins of the fathers are visited upon the children unto the third and fourth generation.'"

There is no living soul who believes more strongly in heredity than I do. I know something about pedigree in the animal kingdom and man is placed in this kingdom by scientists, belonging to that type of animal classified as Vertebrate Mammals, and is therefore responsible for the laws governing the animal kingdom. He has also, which the brute animal has not, a spiritual being which is just as responsive to the laws governing the moral universe. Pedigree (like begets like nature repeating itself in endless succession) rules almost supreme in this complex being with a dual nature just as it does in the lower animal or brute creation, by the artifice of man himself it is sometimes improved, sometimes injured, this applies to his own as well as the brute type of the animal kingdom.

The best that can be done is to, intelligently, assist evolution, any other course is setting ourself in opposition to Nature's laws which are God's laws. The result of such action leads to ignominous failure, and in the case of man's dealing with his own species whether as an individual or collectively (society) to certain punishment.

To argue that a man, or a woman, *without* the benefit of the cultivation, physical and moral, inherited from generations of good forebears would stand a better chance (or equally as good) to become a good man or a good woman than with it, would be as falacious as to argue that the condition of mind most receptive and best suited to retain happiness is that of total ignorance. Alas, poor me, if you think I do not appreciate being descended from good people. But let us use this knowledge only to encourage (which I'm sure is your purpose) the weak ones of the clan who, without such uplifting and sustaining suggestion, are prone to bemean themselves and sell their birthright for a mess of potttage, an abominable mess it often is. This heritage of ours is a gift from the good God transmitted to us through our ancestors. Let us receive it not boastfully, but humbly and thankfully cherish it and try to live up to it. The man who "sits down on it" as you express it is bad enough, but the one who boastfully props himself up on it is far more— he is "the man with a a pedigree" and as a rule when you size him up, you find no man at all— only a pedigreed runt.

People who think, believe strongly in heredity. It behooves us all then, to lead lives worthy of our ancestors and hold fast to the good name they have left us. This we can do without becoming hero or ancestor worshipers as are the pagan Chinese. Black sheep will crop out from time to time, this is an inevitable law of nature and cannot be guarded against or avoided. Such ones are "freaks," we cannot get rid of them, but (as a cross) we can bear with them "being to their faults a little blind and to their virtues very kind." Emmerson has told us: "The past we cannot recall; the future we cannot secure; today (only) is ours." Let us then, day by day, try to so live as to be a credit rather than a discredit to our forefathers and by so doing raise unto their memories living memorials of far more worth than monuments of marble and statues of bronze and leave, for our children to follow through life "foot prints on the sands of time" leading, if possible, to higher levels, *not to lower depths.*

Do not, from any misconstruction of my meaning, think that I have placed you in my mental list of people with a pedigree, or that you desire to become one. I understand pretty well what you have set out to do and that you do it, not so much as a work of pride, but delight in it as a work of love, You wish to unite in one homogeneus body in friendship and sympathy. the descendants (in direct line and various branches) of Isaac Ross and his wife Jean Brown. These people are scattered over a large scope of this country, have from generation to generation mingled their blood by marriage with that of other peoples and nations foreign to the original parent stock? They have grown up under different conditions, with different environments, with hopes and aspirations along different lines, some of which are widely divergent rather than concentrated and tending to homogenity. Swinging on different rungs of the social ladder, with different facilities for education and cultivation, with totally different views of life and its duties whether viewed from a social, civil or religious stand point, entirely out of sympathy with each other and with a total lack of congeniality. They may be all of the good old stock but have wandered away from clanship and its ties too long and too far, I'm afraid, to be ever reclaimed.

I hope you may succeed but whether you do or not there is one of your clansmen who thinks he understands you and will ever give you credit for the best motives and will sincerely regret, on your account, should you fail to make of this undestaking as complete a success as it is your heart's desire to do.

It has been (from my point of view) the impracticability of this undertaking that has been worrying me. It hurts me to treat you rudely and ignore your application for sympathy and such aid as I might be able to give you and yet I know that I should have to be candid should I answer at all. I regretted then, and do now, having to express myself unfavorably, not as to the motive, but as to the chances of success and therefore the inexpediency of the attempt.

With sincere wishes for your well being and happiness through life, and for success in your undertaking, I am.   CABELL B. RICHARDSON

INTRODUCTION.

THE SCOTCH-IRISH.

The Scottish highlanders were of the ancient Celtic race which remained unconquered for many years. They successfully opposed the Romans. Being free from invasion they remained a pure race, with habits and customs distinctly their own, unaffected by other nations.

The plaids or tartans which each clan wore to distinguish it from other clans, was of ancient origin. While not extensively worn, these clan plaids are still in use. and shawls, scarfs and cloth of the various clans can be procured in the shops of Scotland today.

James First induced imigration into the northern part of Ireland and it was at that time that a large number of highlanders removed to that country, where they remained until. on account of religious persecution, they came to the American colonies in pursuit of the religious freedom they were denied in Ireland. These people were called Scotch-Irish and they were the progenitors of many of America's foremost families, The Scotch-Irish, in large numbers. came to America during the early part of the eighteenth century. They ,settled in New Jersey, New York, Pennsylvania, Maryland and finally in North Carolina and South Carolina.

The history of the settlement of this part of Ireland. by James I, is one of interest to the descendants of these people. There were three classes of settlers who moved to these lands—English, Scotch and Irish. The Scotch predominated and were considered the most desirable citizens. Among the English families who took up their residence in Ireland at that time were the Hills, Leslies, Ellises and Langfords. The Scotch families mentioned were Hamiltons, Stewarts, Maxwells. Rosses, Barclays, Moores, etc.

After living In Ireland for about 100 years the persecution became so great that, unable to bear it longer, colonies of these people determined to seek a land of freedom. This determination meant more than planning for a journey today. The trials endured by these emigrants is well related by Rev. John Livingston, the leader of the first colony that ventured to the new world, and it is descriptive of the many journeys that followed.

"We had much toil in our preparation, many hinderances in our outsetting, and both sad and glad hearts in taking leave of our friends. At last, about the month of September, 1636, we loosed from Lockfergus, but were detained some time with contrary winds in Lock Regan in

Scotland, and grounded the ship to search for some leaks in the keel of the boat. Yet thereafter, we set to sea, and for some space had fair winds, till we were between three and four hundred leagues from Ireland, and no nearer the banks of Newfoundland than any place in Europe. But if ever the Lord spoke by his winds and other dispensations, it was made evident to us, that it was not his will that we should go to New England. For we met with a mighty heavy rain from the northwest, which did break our rudder, which we got mended by the skill and courage of Captain Andrew Agnew, a godly passenger; and tore our foresail, five or six of our champlets, and a great beam under the gunner's room door broke. Seas came in over the round house, and broke a plank or two on the deck, and wet all that were between the decks. We sprung a leake, that gave us seven hundred, in the two pumps, in the half hour glass. Yet we lay at hull a long time to beat out the storm, till the master and company came one morning and told us that it was impossible to hold out any longer, and although we beat out that storm, we might be sure in that season of the year, we would foregather with one or two more of that sort before we could reach New England·

"During all this time, amidst such fears and dangers, the most part of the passengers were very cheerful and confident; yea, some in prayer had expressed such hopes, that rather than the Lord would suffer such a company to perish, if the ship should break, he would put wings to our shoulders, and carry us safe ashore. I never in my life found the day so short, as at all that time, although I slept some nights not above two hours, and some not at all, but stood most part in the gallery astern the great cabin, where Mr. Blair and I and our families lay. For in the morning, by the time every one had been some time alone, and then at prayer in their several societies, and then at public prayer in the ship, it was time to go to dinner; after that we would visit our friends or any that were sick, and then public prayer would come, and after that, supper and family exercises. Mr. Blair was much of the time sickly, and lay in the time of storms. I was sometimes sick, and then brother McClelland only performed duty in the ship. Several of those between deck, being thronged, were sickly; an aged person and one child died, and were buried in the sea. One woman, the wife of Michael Calver, of Killinchy parish, brought forth a child in the ship. I baptized it on Sabbath following, and called him Seaborn."

After the trials of such a journey, the master's report filled them with distress, storms were before them. After much prayer and consultation they decided to return to Ireland where they remained for three-quarters of a century. About 1700, ship load after shipload of men and their families left the adopted country and sought other homes in the new world. Many were the trials they endured. but they soon made new homes, established their religion and furnished the men who were the progenitors of the families herein given.

THE SETTLEMENT OF NORTH CAROLINA.

The progenitors of the families treated of in this volume were among the pioneer settlers of North Carolina, therefore the history of the settlement of that state will be of interest to their descendants.

There were several classes of settlers attracted by the genial climate, rich plains and rugged mountains of this new country. Adventurers from Virginia and the other older colonies tiring of the growing civilization around them, found North Carolina an attractive land. New Jersey furnished a large number of settlers to the region between the Catawba and Yadkin rivers. Mecklenberg county was at one time called Jersey county. This territory also became the home of many of the Scotch-Irish who came in colonies from Ireland, some settled on the shores of North Carolina, others came through Pennsylvania, Maryland or Virginia and the majority of the settlers to this valley were the persecuted Scotch-Irish. There were in the confines of the present state of North Carolina several German and Huguenot settlements and numerous detached settlers. Burk's Peerage mentions the settlement in North Carolina of John Alexander, who came before 1700. This leads us to believe that there were many others here at this early period

At one time two thirds of the white population of Mecklenberg county were Harrises and Alexanders. This adds to the difficulty of tracing the descendents of these families. New Jersey furnished the Conger family, Virginia the Hills and Killingsworths, and possibly the Wades. The Harris family came from Pennsylvania, the Ross family was, possibly, native Scotch-Irish and the Moores were English. Thus we see that our ancestors brought many customs of many lands with them to this new country but they were all originally from the British Isles.

Ross

CHAPTER I.

THE ROSS CLAN OF SCOTLAND.

The Ross clan is a very ancient one. This clan furnished most of the family of that name in America. While some may have come from England and other countries the clan in Scotland originated the name and all Ross families trace back to that clan.

The tartan of the Ross clan is a very attractive design, it is of dark blue, red and green and arranged in broad and narrow stripes.

The following from "Scottish Clans and Their Tartans" gives a history of the Ross Clan:

This clan is designated by the Highlanders as 'Clan Anrias,' which is altogether different from their name, as in similar manner the Robertsons are called 'Clan Donnachie.' In the ancient genealogical history they were 'Clan Anrias,' and it begins with PAUL MACTIRE, to whom William, Earl of Ross and Lord of Skye, granted a charter for the lands of Gairloch in 1366, witnessed by Alexander, Bishop of Ross; Hergone, brother of Earl William; Henry, the Seneschal, and others.

Robertson mentions that in the Earl of Haddington's collections he met with an entry in the reign of Alexander II; dated about 1220, a "Charter to Ferquhard Ross, of the Earldom of Ross." This Ferquhard, he adds, was called Macant-Sagart, or the Priest's son, and has, with reason, been supposed to be the son of GILE-ANRIAS, from whom the clan took its name.

He founded the Abbey of Fearn, in Ross-shire, in the reign of Alexander II. His son, Earl William, was one of the Scottish nobles who, under Alexander III, bound themselves to make no peace with England in which the Prince and Chiefs of Wales were not included. This line ended with Euphemia, Countess of Ross, who became a nun, and resigned the Earldom of Ross to her uncle, John, Earl of Buchan.

The ROSSES of BELNAGOWAN were a very ancient line, as they sprang from WILLIAM, Earl of Ross, a great patriot and friend of Robert I.

WILLIAM'S son, EARL HUGH, was killed at Halidon Hill, fighting for his king and country, in 1333.

The ancient Rosses, of Balnagowan, failed and the estate, by an unusual circumstance, came by purchase to another family of the same name, the LORDS ROSS, of Hawkhead, and old and very honorable branch of the clan which failed at the death of GEORGE, twelfth LORD ROSS, in 1754, at Ross House, and of his son the Master, at Mount Teviot, when his titles went to the Earls of Glasgow.

The line of Balnagowan is thus given in 1729 by George Crawford, Historiographer of Scotland, and other authorities.

HUGH ROSS, second son of HUGH, Earl of Ross, married the heiress of Balnagowan, and was succeeded by WILLIAM, second Laird of Balnagowan, who married a daughter of Lord

Livingstone. Their son WILLIAM married Catharine, the daughter of PAUL MACTIRE, she was the heiress of Strathcarron, Strathoykel and Fostay.

HUGH, 3rd Laird of Balnagowan, married Lady Janet, daughter of the Earl of Sutherland, their children were; JOHN, his heir, and WILLIAM ROSS, of Little Allan and Coulnaki, who was the predecessor of the ROSSES of SHANDWICK.

JOHN, 4th Laird of Balnagowan, married a daughter of Torquil LacLeod, of the Lewes. Their son, ALEXANDER, married a lady of the Duffus family, and had "SIR DAVID ROSS," who married Helen, of Iverugie, daughter of Marischal's predecessor, by whom he had WALTER, his son and heir, and WILLIAM, who was the root of Rosses of Ivercarron and its branches. The said WALTER married Mary, daughter of James Grant, of Frenchy, Laird of Grant.

Their son ALEXANDER was twice married. First to Jean, daughter of George, Earl of Caithness, by whom he had GEORGE his successor. Second, to Katherine, daughter of McKenzie, of Kintail, by whom he had a son, Nicholas, the first of the line of Pitcalnie. He died in 1591.

GEORGE 6th. of Balangowan married Marjorie, daughter of Sir John Campbell, of Cawdor, with "a tocher of 3,000 merkes" in 1572. They had a daughter married to Lord Kintail and a son, "DAVID, THE LOYAL" who married Mary, Lord Lovat's daughter. He died at Winsor castle after the restoration and Charles II bestowed on him and his heirs forever a pension of 4,000 merks, yearly.

DAVID, the last Laird of Balnagowan married Lady Ann Stewart, daughter of the Earl of Murray, and dying without issue, conveyed his estate to Brigadier General CHARLES ROSS, son of George Ross, tenth Lord Ross, of Hawkshead, by his second wife, Lady Jean Ramsay, daughter to the Earl of Dalhousie.

The Brigadier General was an officer of high military reputation, and in 1729 was Colonel of the 5th Royal Irish Horse, raised in 1688 and disbanded after the rebellion of 1798.

Ross, of Pitcaline is supposed to represent the ancient line of Balnagowan, the present Baronets of Balnagowan being in reality Lockharts.

In 1745 the fighting force of the clan was 500 men.

The obituary notices for August 1884 contained the death of Mr. George Ross, of Pitclaine, in Rossshire and Arnot in Kincardine, aged 81. Deceased was the last representative of the ancient Earls of Ross, and was chief of the Clan of Ross. He was succeeded by his grandnephew.

THE ROSS CLAN IN AMERICA.

Probably the first mention of the Ross family in America is that of Thomas Rosse, one of the early settlers on the James river in Virginia. After the massacre of 1622 he was reported dead and leaving a wife and two children. Some years later St. Peter's church, New Kent, gives the following eutries:

Wm. Ross, son of William Ross. baptized March 3, 1687-8.

Lydia, daughter of William Ross, baptized Nov. 11, 1694.

Ruth, daughter to William Ross, baptized Nov. 6, 1698,

William, son of William Ross, baptized June 15. 1801.

Eiizabeth, daughter to Richard Ross, baptized Dec. 17, 1710.

William, son of Richard Ross, baptized 1711.

Anne, daughter of Richard Ross, baptized Jan. 27, 1714.

In Elizabeth county the name of Hugh Ross appears in 1690.

Will of Margaret Priest. dated March 19, 1719. mentions her children. 1. Hugh Ross. 2. Francis Ross and William Ross. Her first husband was Hugh Ross.

1. Hugh Ross lived in Martin county, North Carolina. 2. Francis. whose wife was Anne, lived in Buford county, North Carolina. 3. William lived in Martin county.

John Ross, whose father died about 1712, moved to Edmonton, N. C., in 1742. from Virginia.

Rev. Geo. Ross came from Scotland to Deleware about 1703. His son George was one of the signers of the Declaration of Independence.

John Ross, with his family, left Scotland and settled in Ireland in 1689. His son John came to America in 1706, and in 1708 bought land in Chester county, Pa., which was known as Ross Common.

George Ross, a descendant of this family, was governor of Pennsylvania. This family were Presbyterians The branch of the Ross family to which we belong was probably descended from this Pennsylvania family.

According to the census of 1790, there were in North Carolina 67 families bearing the Ross name, in South Carolina there were 38. There were also numerous families in New Jersey, Pennsylvania, New York and Maryland.

The above early Ross families, while they do not include many that had settled in the colonies, are given to show that the Ross clan gave its quota of citizens to the settlement of the new world.

ISAAC ROSS, SR., was born about 1710. The place of his birth is not known tho he was probably born in Ireland of Scotch parents, with whom he came to America. His parents were possibly among the large number of Scotch-Irish Presbyterians who fled to America on occount of religious persecution and settled in Pennsylvania, Maryland and Virginia and later in North Carolina along the Yadkin river, finally drifting westward to the Catawba valley in Mecklenberg county. These people were strong in body and mind, intensely patriotic and altogether desirable citizens for this country which was destined to furnish some of the bravest soldiers, greatest statesmen and godliest ministers of coming ages.

The Ross family of Virginia, is not known to be connected with the family under discussion, but it is probable that they were related "on the other side of the water," for we find many of the same given names in both families On account of the meagre records left by the Scotch-Irish their history is not easily traced.

Isaac Ross married Elizabeth Fraz or (or Frazer) in 1731. Their son, Isaac Ross, 2nd, was born Nov. 9, 1732 and their daughter, Euphemy, was born Sept. 15, 1739. There is no record of any other children of this union nor have we any further record of the daughter, Euphemy.

Isaac Ross, 2nd., lived at "Stony Hill," N. C. and he was called "Stony Hill Isaac" to distinguish him from another brother by the second marriage of his father. The home *"Stony Hill" was possibly in Mecklenberg county. "Stony Hill Isaac" removed to South Carolina about 1750-60 and settled in what was then Orangeburg county. He was Collector for his district in 1764. (See Salley's History of Orangeburg County.) Nothing more is known of him except that he married Eliza Cheek and that some of his children moved to Tennessee and Mississippi during the early history of these states. Two of his sons were Isaac and Samuel. Isaac lived near his uncles, A. B. and Capt. Isaac

---

*Mrs. Lydia Harris Craig, of Charlotte, N. C., once lived at an old Ross place near Charlotte. It was situated on a high, stony hill and could easily have been called "Stony Hill" from its surroundings. Whether or not this was the home of Isaac is not known.

Ross in Kershaw, or Richland county, and is mentioned in the census of 1790 as having in family one male over 21, one under 16 and 2 females. Samuel Ross lived with A. B. Ross during the year 1800, but nothing further is recorded of him. (See Diary, A. B. Ross.)

Isaac Ross, Sr., after the death of Elizabeth Frazor, married Jean Brown, about 1742-3. She was also a Scotch lassie and lived in the Catawba valley near Charlotte.

Jean Brown Ross' parentage is yet unknown, she named her first son Arthur Brown Ross—a name that has come down through each generation—and her oldest daughter Elizabeth, inference is made that her parents bore these names.

Isaac Ross, Sr., had a brother, *Nicolas Ross, who early settled on the Yadkin river, in Rowan county, and married Elizabeth (Lizzie) Conger, daughter of John Conger. They had two daughters. (See chapter 6.) This brother Nicolas is the only brother of Isaac Ross that can be positively identified. As large families were the rule rather than the exception in those days, it is very probable that there were other sisters and brothers whom we may yet be able to trace.

Isaac Ross died about 1762 and his widow, Jean Brown Ross was married a few years later to Aaron Alexander and by this union there were two children, only one of whom survived to manhood. John Brown Alexander was born in 1765. (See chapter 9.) The date of the death of Jean Brown Ross Alexander was about 1766. Aaron Alexander married again to Mary ———. (See his line, chapter 9.) He died in 1772.

What manner of people these our first known Ross ancestors were, can only be estimated by the traits of character they handed down to their children. While there has not been found record of large land grants or great wealth possessed by Isaac Ross, Sr., he must have been a prominent man and one beloved by a large connection who did him honor by naming many sons for him, and his name lives today, having been handed down from generation to generation through the various branches of the Ross, Moores, Alexander, Conger and other families. We likewise find the name Jean Brown a prominent one in all of the allied families up to the present time. Jean in some instances having been changed to Jane. This custom of keeping alive the names of ancestors who as pioneers in a new land, made possible the civilization we have today, is one that should be encouraged.

It is the hope of the writer that we may yet learn more of Isaac Ross and Jean Brown through records we have not had access to in the past.

Isaac Ross and Jean Brown Ross had the following children:
Elizabeth Ross; born April 15, 1744; (no records.)
Arthur Brown Ross; born August 9, 1746.
Abagail Ross; born November 13, 1748.
Mary Ross; born Jan. 28, 1751, married John Conger, (see Conger family.)
Isabel Ross; born. Jan 28, 1754.
Jean Ross; born ——— 1757; married Henry Moores, see chapter 4.
Isaac Ross, 3rd; born January 5, 1760.

---

*In the old Ross Bible there is an entry of the birth of Nicolas Ross, 1774. This Nicolas was evidently a grandson of Isaac Ross, Sr.

ARTHUR BROWN ROSS, son of Isaac Ross and Jean Brown, his wife, was born, probably, near Charlotte, N. C., Aug. 9, 1746. His parents lived in North Carolina and there his father died about 1762, his mother married Aaron Alexander and it was after this time (Jan. 1769) that he married Hannah Conger, daughter of John Conger, of Rowan county, North Carolina, and removed to South Carolina. In 1774 he lived at Rocky Mount, S. C. (see map.) The following account dates it that period.

October 17, 1774.

"Mr. Orman Morgan, Dr.
    To A. B. Ross, for sundries at Rocky Mount, to the amount of £19.19.6."
(The original bill was in the possession of John I. W. Ross, 2nd.)

The first land grant he received in South Carolina was in 1774 (see maps.)
His brother "Stony Hill Isaac" Ross patented land in Kershaw county as early as 1765 and it is very probable that A. B. Ross followed his half brother to South Carolina. Arthur B. Ross received a number of land grants in South Carolina dating 1774, 1786, 1797 and 1799. In 1800 he patented 177 acres in Rowan county North Carolina on Abbots creek and conveyed this by deed to his brother-in-law John Conger in 1801. (See diary and map for location of different lands.) He moved his family in the summer to what he called his "Green Spring place" and back to the plantation in winter. He called his plantations, besides the one mentioned, "Comfort Hill," "Sand Hill" and "The Plantation."

Arthur B. Ross, his son Ely Ross, nephew Samuel Ross and brother Isaac, signed a petition to the legislature in 1788 in regard to McCord's ferry. McCord's ferry was on the Congaree river in Saxa Gotha township of the original Orangeburg county which at one time embraced about one-third of the state of South Carolina, afterward a number of counties were cut off from Orangeburg, Kershaw and Richland being among the number.

Arthur Brown Ross served in the war of 1776, although there has not yet been found official record of his service. He was living at Rocky Mount when the battle that bears that name was fought. We know that he was an ardent Whig and as such he must have participated, not only in that battle but in many others. There is now in the possession of one of his descendants, his old bullet mould that he used in the Revolutionary war. His sentiments expressed in his diary when he heard of the death of General Washington proves that he was one of the patriot army. He participated in all of the Fourth of July celebrations and described them in his diary. In the M. S. sketch by his grandson, John I. W. Ross, 2nd., the statement is made that "Arthur Brown Ross served in the Revolutionary War." The records in Columbia are not yet catalogued, when they are there will very probably be found the name of A. B. Ross as a revolutionary soldier.

A. B. Ross was a man of affairs in the community in which he lived. He was Justice of the Quorum, an office of importance at that time. He had tried before him many cases from minor to serious offenses: a trying office, since many of the offenders were friends and neighbors. His vocation brought him in contact with the prominent men of the state, many of whom were his personal friends. As a farmer, merchant and justice his persuits were varied. In the very interesting diary he has left us, he gives in detail the performance of the duties of each day. He filled any place on his farm when needed, never objecting to the most menial service if it fell to his lot.

His home life must have been very happy, his constant companion was his wife whom he affectionately called "the old lady." She accompanied him from one plantation to another, sometimes both rode in the "chair" and often times on horseback. He was fond of his children and grand children. He enjoyed the sports with his boys and, while he was not as successful a hunter as "Brown" or "Jacky," he often brought down a fat doe or wild turkey. His ferry on the Wateree was the center for gatherings to discuss politics and his fisheries on the same stream attracted the best people of Camden who drove there in the afternoons to procure fresh shad. James Kershaw, in 1798, notes in diary. "Rode to Ross' Fishery. Large party there." (See "Historic Camden.")

Arthur B. Ross was a sober man for those times. He indulged in "cherry bounce" and liked a "hot dram" early in the morning, but his brain never became dulled to the extent of drunkenness. Horse races at Camden attracted him thither and there he heard the news and discussed politics. He was honest in his dealings, he kept an accurate account of his expenditures and met his debts promptly. He was a subscriber to the Orphan's Society and was charitable to the down trodden. As a strict church member he failed. He often attended service at the "Widow Martin's" and remembered the text, to write in his diary, but he did not keep the Sabbath as our idea of Sunday observance is today. The day was spent in visiting, looking up lost cattle, attending services about once a month and entertaining his family and friends. He and his wife were kind and generous neighbors, freely sharing the good things they had with their children and neighbors.

About 1803 he spent much time surveying land and on those surveying trips was often accompanied by Mr. McWillie, father of Ex-Gov. McWillie, of Mississippi, and with his good friend and neighbor. Major Whitaker. His son, "Brown" was also a surveyor and assisted his father in that capacity.

It must have caused many heart aches to break the home ties in South Carolina and go to Mississippi, but when we consider that his children were scattered, some in Mississippi, Ely in Tennessee and Elizabeth in another part of South Carolina, it must have been a happy journey in view of the reunion in the new country. Ely K. Ross and Elizabeth Ross Sims and their families with the sons, John I. W. Ross and Isaac A. B. Ross went to Mississippi with their parents in 1805, leaving behind Sarah Conger Ross O'Quin who bid farewell with her parents never more to see them in this world.

This company settled along Cole's creek, in Jefferson county. Miss. They patented rich tracts of land and there settled in this new country to make new homes and rear their children as pioneers, enduring many privations that such a life necessitates. The country in which they settled fast became the center of culture and refinement in Mississippi and our pioneers became men of influence and were blessed by bountiful harvests.

Arthur Brown Ross knew and admired Lorenzo Dow, the early missionary and one of the pricelsss possessions of the family today is an old stiletto given by Dow to his son John I. W. Ross. The stiletto has "Lorenzo Dow" engraved on the handle. A. B. Ross did not live long to enjoy the new home, his death oecured in 1805 and his body rests in old "Beech Hill" cemetery, about two miles from Red Lick station, Jefferson county, Miss. This cemetery is in the center of a refined country community, made up of the descendants of the Ross, Wade, Sims, Hill, O'Quinn, Killingsworth and kindred families. Possibly no where in Mississippi are the old time customs and ideas of living kept up in a more perfect regime than in this part of Jefferson county.

The majority of the travelers who pass "Beach Hill" can point to the Ross plot and say: "There lie my ancestors." A feeling beyond power of description overwhelmed the writer, a great, great, great granddaughter of A. B. Ross and his wife, Hannah C. Ross, when she stood beside the graves of Arthur B. Ross and the "Old Lady," Hannah C. Ross.

Hannah Conger Ross survived her husband 16 years. She lived most of that time with her youngest son, John I. W. Ross, and he it was, who had inscribed on her tombstone:

"And she is gone, whose lovely face,
Is of her charms, her smallest grace."

Children of Arthur Brown Ross and Hannah Conger Ross:
1. Elizabeth Ross. born in North Carolina. Sept. 30, 1769; married Thomas Sims.
2. Sarah Conger Ross; born in South Carolina Sept. 23. 1771, married John O'Quin.
3. Ely Kershaw Ross. born in South Carolina Oct. 6, 1773; married, 1st, Elizabeth Hill; 2nd. Mrs. Collier; 3rd. Mrs. Henderson.
4. Abigail Gibson Ross;born in South Carolina Nov. 6, 1775; married David Sims.
5. John Isaac Gates Ross, born in South Carolina April 19, 1778; name of wife unknown.
6. Isaac Arthur Brown Ross, born in South Carolina April 30, 1782; married Jane Oliphant Hill.
7. John Isaac Wayne Ross, born in South Carolina March 4, 1785; married 1st, Jane Patterson Bisland; 2nd. Jane Brown Ross Wade. widow of Daniel Wade.

FIRST CHILD OF A. B. AND H. C. ROSS.

ELIZABETH ROSS occupied the responsible position of oldest child in her family. The deep regard her family had for her is made known to us from the old diary which has given us so much information about the family relations.

Elizabeth and her husband, Thomas Sims. lived near the Pee Dee river, forty or fifty miles from her father's home on the Wateree, but they made frequent visits back home and little "Brown," their son, spent much time with his grand parents.

Thomas Sims, James Sims and David Sims were brothers, who their parents were is yet a conjecture but their father was probably James Sims and their mother Rebecca Sims. Thomas Sims and his family came to Mississippi about 1805. He patented 250 acres of land on Cole's creek in Jefferson county in the same vicinity with the brothers James and David.

Elizabeth Sims inherited the frugal habits of her parents and she and her husband prospered in this world's goods. They were devout christians, following the Presbyterian faith.

The exact date of Thos. Sims' death is not known but he died several

See diary and pictures of tombs. Also map of Camden, etc.

years before his wife. leaving her with the management of affairs and the training of her children. She lived many years to be a blessing to her children and grandchildren. (See letters.)

LETTER FROM ELIZABETH ROSS, DAUGHTER OF ARTHUR BROWN ROSS, TO HER

DAGHTER SARAH GREENLEE.

February 3, 1843,

My Dear Children:—

I sat down this morning through a great deal of weekness to write a few lines to you as we have not heard from you since by yonr sons and we have not heard from them since thcy got home. I came home from Mr. O'Quinn's with the intention of going home with them but Divine Goodness over rules all things, I was taken that night with a difficulty of breathing and every night since, till last night I rested some better but am not able this morning to make up my bed. I am weaker than you could imagine from my former health and strength.

I should have written you before this time but have not strength to write. All my desire is to serve my children of temporal things. I have not seen Hannah since I left her but she is better, all the rest of the family are as well as common. My health is such as will not let me think I will ever be able to come and see you. Am very glad my dear grandchildren came to see us when they did for Elizabeth and Eliza were much satisfaction to us all but the boys were so sick that they had no comfort for themselves and we were so sorry for them that none of us enjoyed ourselves but I hope they are now well and hope you will write to me soon.

Kiss my dear little Margaret, tell Franklin I hope he has gotten rid of the ague. Tell Mr. Greenlee that we have been looking for him for some time but when you and he can spare the time we shall be glad to see you.　　　　　　　　　　　　　　　　　　Elizabeth Ross Sims.

LETTER FROM ELIZABETH ROSS SIMS TO HER GRAND DAUGHTER, ELIZABETH HILL,

DAUGHTER OF JACOB K. HILL AND REBECCA SIMS.

Miss Elizabeth:—

I have nothing particular to write this morning. We are all enjoying moderate health but myself. I am particularly afflicted with some say asthma but I think not for I think it is weakness and old age but be that as it may, without some relief it will terminate in death. I was much alarmed when I was first taken but my cousin from Tennessee told of their grandmother being afflicted in the same way, or else we would have sent for my children for I shall never be more certain that I am dying or more willing to go. I believe that pain will check the fear of death but I do not desire to live any longer than my dear Redeemer intends for me to.　-

I think my reason is weaker than my body but all is most spent. I have a great desire to see your father and mother and dear little Rebecca. If your uncle comes up and I feel able to ride I will come to see you with him as I feel better this morning, perhaps I may get better.

We write by mail but they fail so often or I would write separately. I am in hope that you will write to us soon as we are anxious to hear from you.

Please to give my love to your father, tell him I would thank him to write a kind and affectionate letter to your aunt Malinda for me, he will not write for himself. Tell her if I ever am able to write to her I will for I feel a great love for her and all the family. Remember me in warm wishes for your good grandmother and inquiring friends and accept my warmest wishes for yourself. Tell your brothers and sisters I love them, tell them to be good. Tell your father and mother I remain their affcctionate mother and want to see them very much.

Elizabeth Ross Sims.

Arthur Brown Ross gives the following in his diary under date of May, 1802. "I wrote a long letter to my sister, Euphemy Conger, she lives in Ligan county."

FIRST CHILD OF A. B. AND H. C. ROSS.

ELIZABETH ROSS, oldest child of Arthur Brown Ross and Hannah Conger, was b in South Carolina Sept: 30, 1769, d in 1834 in Mississippi. She m Thomas Sims, a brother of James and David Sims. (See Sims line.) Issue:—

(1.) ISAAC A. SIMS, m ‡Eliza K., she was b Dec. 20, 1814, d Sept. 17, 1841.

*BROWN SIMS, m Jane O'Quin, his first cousin. She was the daughter of Sarah Ross and John O'Quin. Issue:—

Martha Sims, m Henderson Frisby. Issue:—

†Rosalie Frisby, m 1872 James McMaster. Issue:—

Jessie McMaster.
Lilly McMaster.
Juliette McMaster.
Clara McMaster.
Nettie McMaster.

Brown Sims, m second Hannah Powell. Issue:—

Margaret Sims, b Sept. 1841, m Joseph Stephens. She d six months after her marriage.

Mary Sims, b Oct. 4, 1843, m John McPherson, d 1897. Issue:—

Brown Sims McPherson, b 1868, m 1889 to Emma Shirley. He was killed by a train Feb. 28, 1904. Issue:—

Mattie McPherson, b 1890 m 1910 to Aubrey Silas Ashley.
Mary Emma McPherson, b 1893.
Brown Shirley McPherson, b 1895.
Willie Shuler McPherson, b 1897.
Amelia Elizabeth McPherson, b 1900.
Robert Edgar McPherson, b 1903.

Mary Sims m 2nd Joe Dunbar. Issue:—

Orien Dunbar, b 1870, d 1889.

(3.) REBECCA G SIMS, b Jan 29, 1797, m Jacob Killingsworth Hill May 16,, 1816, d May 8, 1860. (See Hill line.) (See picture.)

HANNAH SIMS, b 1805, d April 7, 1837, m Ross O'Quin, her first cousin. (See O'Quin line.) (See Ross O'Quin diary.)

ALEXANDER SIMS, m Eliza Middleton. Issue—

(2.) Judith Sims, m Sam Hughes. Issue:—

§Sam Hughes, m Miss Tolbert, had several children.

LIZZIE SIMS, died the night her sister Hannah married.

(4.) LOUIS HOBBS SIMS, b April 14, 1814, d Aug. 7, 1857, m May 24, 1837 to Eliza Shaw, daughter of ‖Thompson and Mary Shaw. Issue:—

¶Mary Elizabeth Sims, b Jan. 25, 1840, m 1866 to W. H. Watson, son of John Watson and Margaret Mikel. Issue:—

---

*Both Brown Sims and James O'Quin are mentioned many times in the diary of their grandfather, A. B. Ross. They accompanied their grandparents on many visits to the neighbors, through the farm and to Camden. This is one of the many instances of marriage of first cousins in this family.

†Mrs. Rosa McMaster was reared by her relatives after the death of her parents. She has been a widow 15 years and has, by her industry and good management, educated her five daughters who are ornaments to society and are fitted to meet the responsibilities of life.

‡Buried in old Sims Grave Yard, 2 miles from Harriston, Miss. Tombstone bears this verse:
"Weep not for me, my husband dear,
I am not dead, but sleeping here."
(See picture of tombstone.)

§Last heard of in Texas.

¶Mrs. Mary Sims Watson lives with her daughter, Mrs. John Bedker, at 214 Magnolia street, Jackson, Miss. Here she is sunshine in the lives of her daughter and little grandchildren.

‖Both Shaws but not related by blood.

—23—

Sims Watson, b 1867, m 1903 to Annie Louise Phillips, daughter of David A. Phillips and Eunice Wasden, of Ga.

Joe Watson, b 1868, m 1888 Louela Godbold, daughter of Blue Godbold and Dona Gilmer. Issue—
   Boyce Watson, b 1902.
   Josie Watson, h 1907.
   Orville Watson, b and d 1899.

Maggie Watson, b 1870, m 1901 to John Bodker, son of Henry P, Bodker and Hattie Pinkston. Issue:—
   Robert Alexander Bodker, b and d 1902.
   Edole Watson, b 1907.
   William Grant Watson, b 1910.

Sidney Watson, b 1872, m 1894 to Kate Douglas, daughter of Tim Douglas and Mary Bufkin. Issue:—
   Bessie Watson, b 1902.
   Nel Watson, b 1904.
   Mildred Watson, 1906.
   Paul Watson, b 1907.
   Marvin Frank Watson, 1909.
   Sidney Watson, b 1910.

Marvin Watson, b 1877, m Katie Applewhite daughter of Seth Applewhite and Candie Alred. Issue:—
   Edith Watson, b 1906.
   Carroll Watson, b 1907.
   Helen Watson, b 1911.

¶Hannah Josephine Sims, b Jan. 13, 1842, m March 21, 1875, to *W. H. Freeman, son of W. H. Freeman and Louisa Ann Guice. Issue:—
(9.) Lewis Hobbs Freeman, b Feb. 6, 1876.
   Dumont Sidney Freeman, b Dec. 10, 1878, m May 13, 1906 to his cousin Olive O'Quin, daughter of T. J. O'Quin. (See his line.) Issue:—
      Josie Mae Freeman, b April 14, 1906.
      Louberta Freeman, b May 1, 1908.
      Sidney Dumont Freeman, b Nov. 5, 1910.
   Clarinne Ernestine Freeman, b May 1, 1880.
   Carline Louberta Freeman, b Jan. 11, 1882.
   Avery Lemoyn Freeman, b May 30, 1884, m Lessie Stevens Nov. 10, 1907. Issue:—
      Avery Lewis Freeman, b Sept. 3, 1898.

†Lewis Hobbs Sims, b Oct. 19, 1844, d May 10, 1864.

William Thomas Sims, b Aug. 24, 1846, m March 28, 1883. to ‡Mary Sanders who was b April 3, 1859. She is the daughter of Joseph Sanders and Mary Lammons. Issue:—
   Thomas Sims, b March 28, 1883.
   Sinai Sims, b Jan. 29, 1884, m June 30, 1908, to Dr. Jesse Havis Riley.
   Mary Sims, b March 20, 1886.

Julia Eliza Sims, b Aug. 1848, m Jan. 18, 1868 to Julienne H. Hulbert. He d Oct. 18, 1880. Issue:—

---

†Killed at battle of Spotsylvania.

‡Mrs. Mary Sims lives with her daughter, Mrs. Riley, at Haddock, Ga., where Dr. Riley is a prominent physician

*Company A, 7th Miss. Reg. Tenn. Army, enlisted at the beginning and served throughout the war.

¶Mrs Josephine Freeman, who lives near Fayette, Miss , has been the genealogist of this family for many years and has given the writer valuable assistance. Mrs. Julia Hurlbert writes beautiful reminiscences of the older generation. Her impression of my grandmother, Rebecca Hill Sims will be found in notes.

MRS. MALINDA GREENLEE
WILSON
See Page 27

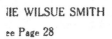

IIE WILSUE SMITH
ee Page 28

Graves of HANNAH CONGER ROSS and ARTHUR BROWN ROSS, in the Beech
Hill Cemetery, Jefferson County, Mississippi

The grave to the left is that of JANE ALLISON ROSS, wife of
CAPT. ISAAC ROSS.

Graves of DAVID SIMS and his wife, ABIGAIL GIBSON ROSS SIMS.
She was the first person buried in the Beech Hill Cemetery.

Grave to the right is that of JANE OLIPHANT HILL ROSS,
wife of ISAAC A. B. ROSS

REV. AND MRS. JOHN JONES
See Page 43.

Paul Clifford Hulbert, b Dec 25, 1868, m Dec. 19, 1896 to Jennie Landers. Issue:—

    Irwin Hulbert, b Feb. 14, 1898.

    Annie Pearl Hulbert, b Oct. 22, 1900.

    Myrtle Alberta Hulbert, b Oct. 22, 1902.

    Rosalie Hulbert, b Oct. 22, 1905, d Sept. 27, 1910.

    Mildred Hulbert, b March 22, 1910.

Ward Hulbert, b July 18, 1871, m Dec. 18, 1891, to Gueilma Doughty, she died Sept. 22, 1905. Issue:—

    Clara Alberta Hulbert, b 1893.

    Clarence Hulbert, b 1895.

    Abby Hulbert, b 1897.

    Doughty Hulbert, b 1889.

    Irene Hulbert, b 1903.

Ward Hulbert m 2nd Orrie Lee Lanstrum Aug. 21, 1911,

Clara Alberta Hulbert, b July 28, 1873, m Dr. Bert Stuart Smith, of Memphis.

Catherine Anne Sims, b Sept. 10, 1850, m Feb. 21, 1877, to William Devine Dennis. Issue:—

    William Devine Dennis, b Jan. 13, 1878, m April 16, 1902, to Idessa Stephens. Issue:—

        Willie Sue Dennis, b Feb. 23, 1904.

        Hazel Dennis, b March 8, 1905.

        Mona Dennis, b Nov, 13, 1907, d May 15, 1907.

        Charles Chamberlain Dennis, b Nov. 15, 1907

        Elizabeth Morris Dennis, b Aug. 30, 1879.

        Perry Leon Johnson (Dennis) b Oct. 25, 1881, m Dec. 30, 1907. Issue:—

            Perry Mark Johnson, b Sept. 29, 1908.

            Minnie Amanda Johnson, b Feb. 25, 1909.

        Addie Josephine Dennis, b Oct. 18, 1884.

        Eliza Alberta Dennis, b March 3, 1887.

        Catherine Marie Dennis, b April 22, 1892.

(5.) Addie Sims, b May 10, 1852, m Dec. 20, 1870 to Bolls Johnson. She d Dec. 15, 1910. No issue. She adopted Perry Dennis.

Clara Alberta Sims, b Sept. 21, 1854, d March 12. 1887, unmarried.

Armstrong Everett Sims, b Sept. 22, 1856, m Dec. 17, 1890, d Nov 7, 1910. Issue:—

    Mary Blanch Sims, b April 17, 1893.

    Adelaide Sims, b Aug. 5, 1895

    Albert Paul Sims, b May 3, 1907.

    Ursula Sumtha Sims, b Oct. 18, 1900.

    Armond Everett Sims, b Oct. 18, 1901.

    Richard Alfonso Sims, b June 27, 1903.

(5.) Sidney Sims, d unmarried.

SARAH SIMS, daughter of Elizabeth Ross and Thomas Sims, b in 1801, m Feb. 4, 1819 to (7.) Elisha Greenlee at Red Lick, Jefferson county, Miss. Elisha Greenlee was b (6.) June 1, 1795 and d Nov. 28, 1844. Sarah A. Greenlee d Sept. 2, 1856. Issue:—

James A. Greenlee, b Jan. 14, 1820, m Aug. 27, 1848, to Angeline Stovall, issue:—6 children, all d young, in La., except Sarah Greenlee.

William Alexander Greenlee, b in Jefferson county, Miss., Oct. 15, 1821, m Mary Jane Scott May 16, 1843. Issue—

James Saxon Greenlee, b Ded. ?, 1848, m Dec. 23, 1897 to
    Florence Martin Young. She was b Aug. 18, 1875.
    Issue:—
        Willie Y. Greenlee (girl,) b Oct. 12, 1898
        Laura J. Greenlee, b Jan. 32, 1900.
        James S. Greenlee, b Nov. 22, 1901.
        Thomas S. Greenlee, b Dec. 4, 1908.
        Robert Alex. Greenlee, b June 6, 1911.
Mary Eva Greenlee, b Oct 15, 1851, m Jan 31, 1878 to *Andrew
    Jackson McEwen d Nov. 15, 1908. He was b Feb. 10, 1842.
    d Sept. 25, 1893. Issue:—
        (Mary Eva McEwen
        (Elizabeth Margaret McEwen, twins, b Oct. 11, 1878
        M. E. McEwen and D. V. Herlong m Dec 1.
        1900, Issue:—
            Robert C. Herlong b Nov. 1, 1901.
            Gladys Herlong, b May 8, 1903.
            Daniel Victor Herlong, b July 1909.
    Andrew Jackson McEwen
    (Annie Belle McEwen
    (Fannie Pearl McEwen, twins, b Feb 18, 1881. F.
        P. McEwen m G. C Scott, m 10, 1910. No
        issue. A. B. McEwen m May 27, 1905 to
        R. N Gill. Issue:—
            Robert Bertram Gill, b March 9, 1906
            Clinton Gill, b Nov. 16, 1908.
    Willie M. McEwen. b June 5, 1883 m June 19, 1910
        to Baxter Johnson.
    Robert Carden McEwen, b Nov, 1885
    Ida Lou McEwen, b 1887.
    (Louna McEwen (girl)
    (Joddie Samuel McEwen, twins, b March 1891.
Dr. William Greenlee, b March 27, 1856, m Mrs Annie La.
    dell. Issue:—
    Wren Greenlee, m John Weil or Bridger.
Hannah Elizabeth Greenlee, b Feb. 17, 1824, m April 30, 1844, to Milton
H. Foster. Issue:—
    Sarah Elizabeth Foster, daughter of Hannah Elizabeth Green
    lee and Milton H. Foster, b Sept. 8, 1845, in Union
    county, Ark., m July 29, 1863 to George Speed who was
    b July 15, 1844, d Nov. 26, 1872. Issue:—
        W. M. Speed, b Aug. 12, 1859, m June 18, 1892 to
        Ida Crews, b Sept. 25, 1864. Issue:—
            J. C. Speed, b Aug. 5, 1894,
            Rosalie Speed, b March 1, 1896.
            Ida Belle Speed, b March 25, 1903.
        R. F. Speed, b Nov. 22, 1869,, d Aug. 22, 1906, m
        Aug. 6, 1896 to Serena Scott. Issue:—
            Marion Speed, b May 8, 1897.
            Serena Speed, b May 31, 1898.
        R. F. Speed, m 2nd Lydia Simrall, Oct. 1900. Issue.
        George Graham Speed, b Oct. 1901.

---

*A. J. McEwen joined company E, 4thMiss. cavalry, July 28, 1862. He served in Logan's cavalry at Port Hudson
1898, Maybe's brigade; Forrest's Cavalry Corps in Tenn.. Miss. and Ala. Paroled at Gainsville, Ala.: May, 1865. Mr. and
Mrs. A. J. McEwen lived on the farm where they reared and educated their children, six daughters of whom are teachers
and all are good citizens. A. J. McEwen was superintendent of the Methodist Sunday School for many years. After his
death, by frugal management, Mrs. McEwen succeeded in keeping her family together and completing their education

Polly Speed, May, 1903.

Charles Speed, b April 12, 1871.

S. E. Speed m 2nd, Oct 15, 1882 to Charlie Pierce. Issue:—
Nannie E. Pierce, b in Copiah county, Miss. Oct 3, 1883, m Oct. 16, 1906 to Hugh A, Cary, he was b in Maples, Ind. Sept. 1, 1877.

John W. Pierce, b in Copiah county, Oct. 31, 1885, d Nov. 26, 1908.

French Bascum Pierce, b Oct 31, 1887.

Robert Elisha Foster, b Nov. 25, 1851, in Copiah county, Miss., m Nannie E. Heath, daughter of John Heath, of Issa-quena county, Miss., Jan. 22, 1867. Issue:—
Annie Eliza Foster, b Dec. 11, 1877, m John S. Ellis. Issue:—
John R. Ellis, b March 22, 1901.

Donovan F. Ellis, b April 27, 1904.

Alfred D. Ellis, b Nov. 14, 1906.

*Robert Heath Foster, b Sept 13, 1885.

†Mary Lurline Foster, b Aug. 20, 1887.

Milton Foster, b March 10, 1854, m Dec. 23, 1879, to Lizzie Florence Crews. Issue:—
Mollie Ida Foster, b Nov. 25, 1880, m Oct. 10, 1903 to James Stanford. Issue:—
Mollie Stanford, b April 15, 1906.

Randolph Stanford, b Dec. 3, 1907.

Milton Crews Foster, b Oct. 2, 1884, m Dec. 4, 1906, to Irene Torrey.

Ruby Elizabeth Foster, b Nov. 20, 1885, m Oct. 27, 1910 to William Lee Davis.

Mary Etta Foster b Dec. 14, 1856, m Jan 28, 1876, to §W. G. Herrington. Issue:—
W. B. Herrington, b Nov. 3, 1877, m Nov. 5, 1905 to Ella M. Ross.

Lizzie A. Herrington, b Aug. 6, 1880.

Robert Preston Herrington, b Sept. 4, 1884.

Mabel Ella Herrington, b Sept. 2, 1894.

Elisha E. Greenlee, b Sept. 3, 1825, m April 4, 1848, to Jane C. Foster,

John H. Greenlee, b Oct. 3, 1830.

(8.) *Robert Brown Greenlee, b in Copiah county, Miss., Sept. 14, 1834. m Jan. 13, 1859 to Annie Trim, d July 2, 1862. Issue:—
Robert B. Greenlee, b Jan. 24, 1860, m Nov. 26, 1891 to Lucy Trim. Issue:—
Willie F. Greenlee (daughter,) b July 22, 1893.

Kathelien Greenlee, b Nov. 22, 1896.

Willie E. Greenlee (son,) b March 28, 1861, d Aug 15, 1876.

†Sarah Malinda Greenlee, b Dec. 12, 1838, m John P. Wilson. Issue—, Sarah Artie Wilson, b Nov. 6, 1858, d June 1862.

Mary Elizabeth Wilson, b Oct. 25, 1861, m Nov. 16, 1880 to P. J. Flowers. Issue:—
Annie Flowers, m Hegle. Issue:—
Edgar Flowers.

---

*Robert Brown Greenlee entered the Confederate Army in 1862 enlisting in the 39th Miss. Reg. He was wounded in the battle of Shiloh and was brought home where he died July 2, 1872.

§W. G. Herrington enlisted April 18, 1861. Captain Jenkins, Jasper Light Infantry, a company 104 strong, was at battle of Manassas, then commanded by General Jones. Later joined Company E. 25th Va., Battalion, Capt. W. L. Meals, Co. He was 1st Sergeant, 2nd Lieutenant, was captured and imprisoned at Washington City, had a thrilling experience throughout the war. Was one of the immortal 600 sent to Charleston. S. C.

Minnie Flowers.

John Patrick Wilson, b Dec. 8, 1866, d Aug. 25, 1899, unmarried

†Fannie B. Wilson, b Sept. 13, 1870, m Dec. 15, 1897 to Charlie L. Will, of New Orleans.

†Nannie E. Wilson, b June 30, 1874, m Mr. Smith, now a widow.

Thaddeus Hobbs Greenlee, b Nov. 18, 1840, d at about 8 years of age.

Albert Lane Greenlee, b Nov. 30, 1842, d infant.

FROM SARAH SIMS GREENLEE TO HER MOTHER ELIZABETH ROSS SIMS.

Dear Mother:—

I now comply with your request in writing to you the melancholy scene that is almost spread on the countenance of every one that you see. for we all feel that we are only sojourners. Your children are all tolerably well and there has been nothing very serious the matter with us since you left us. R has been a good deal sick, and Martha too, but not dangerously.

Mrs. R. Dunbar has been unfortunate enough to loose three daughters; illness which has caused this sore affliction. Mr. Goodrum lost three children Sunday night and expected that the fourth could not survive till last night. Mrs. Camberlain lost her two eldest children on Thursday last, one or two days before the death of Hellen, she departed this life Friday morning about half past six. The corpse left here at half past three o'clock Saturday morning with Mr. and Mrs. Dunbar. They have not returned yet.

I heard from the Harrison settlement yesterday. They are all well and are still setting apart days for feasting. Too often becomes the place of mourning and it is to be dreaded, with them I hope it will be a turn for the saving of their souls. I have not received a letter from any friend since you were here. Sister Hannah says she will be very glad to see you though she wants you to stay where you are till you make your visit out.

I do not know when I can be up for we have two sick negroes and they have been dangerously sick though we are all spared as yet for a short time. Nothing more at present,

Yours with respect, etc.

Sarah Greenlee.

FROM SARAH GREENLEE TO HER NEICE HANNAH ELIZABETH A. HILL.

Miss H. A. E. Hill.

Dear Niece:—

I was very desirous to see you when I was up there. Though I was glad that you were at school. Your aunt says you are still very wild. We know that your age and youth would not justify you in being otherwise for you are not entirely settled in your mind does not argue that you have to cherish any sin in your youth more than in your old age. The youthful mind is naturally active so let it be active in some good work that you may be rewarded in your old age, and not be like the almost disconsolate parents of Hellen, know no place of happiness than the one they are now in. O! my dear niece. if you could only have seen the grief of the sorely afflicted parents and they knew not how to be comforted for they have lived in sin and folly all the days of their lives. Had they known the right sort of religion they would have known what to have done for they would have rejoiced and been happy though they might have grieved for the separation. It would only have been for but a short time, though this separation may be final. So it is that the sinner finds nothing to console the mind in this world and only constant afflictions to look forward beyond the grave makes this sinful life worse than it is without reflection. When we consider a well spent life, it gives pleasure and contentment. I assure you that there is no pleasure in a wicked youth's life and if you do not believe me you can try it. There is more pleasure in pursuit of eternal happiness than there is in possession of the whole world and I am sure that the possession of so great a prize is inestimable.

Your most affectionate aunt,

Sarah Greenlee.

---

†Mrs. Wilson and Mrs. Smith live at Hermanville and it was this writer's pleasure recently to visit them in their hospitable home. (See pictures.)

‡Have adopted a little boy now aged 9 years. This little boy comes from prominent Mississippi families and bids fair to be a son that will bring much comfort and pleasure to his adopted parents. Mr. and Mrs. Will live at the old Wilson home at Wilsonville, Miss.

FROM ISAAC A. SIMS TO JACOB K. HILL.

Mr. Jacob K. Hill.

Dear Brother:—

I write you to let you know that we are all well. We are all moving on about as usual with the exception of L. H. Sims who has been on his way to Texas since Sunday week in company with V. S. Buck.

Ross O'Quin sold to T. B. Shaw yesterday for $17,000. Brown, I expect, will remain at the same place the coming year as times are hard and the purchaser poor.

I have many things to write that I have not time to submit to you at present. There has been no property sold here this week at sheriff's sale as yet.

Give my love to all the family and particularly to sister and friends and receive for yourself the same. As I remain in truth,

Isaac A. Sims.

I shall be at your house the 9th or 10th night in January 1839 and go with you to Jackson. Say to Elizabeth I shall expect her to accompany me home.

———————

(3.)   Baskin, La., May 30th.

Dear Cousin:—

Your esteemed favor to hand. I've an exalted sense of appreciation. Not to comply with your request would be discourteous.

The drift of time brings changes. Tis said "all times when old are good." You ask of my impressions of your gr-grandmother Hill. She was small, quite active, a fluent talker, had an intense love for her kindred, next she loved her old time friends. When she visited my father she always must see her relatives and friends. One cherished friend was Rev. Bro. Johnson, near Fayette, who was often sent by request on the Burtontown Circuit. She entertained him at her home. The friendship was very beautiful, when they met it was a benediction. Bro. J. would read his favorite portion of Scripture, the 14th chapter of St. John, "Let not your heart be troubled," then they would sing "Jesus Lover of My Soul," "How Firm a Foundation." Father J. has long since joined the old friends on "That Beautiful Shore" to sing the sweet songs as of old.   Julia E. Hulbert.

*   *

(5.)

His father lost a son in the late war, a promising young man, a college graduate, who died in a hospital in Richmond, Va., another son married my sister, Addie Sims, another son, Labe, married Venie, a sister of Major Millsaps, the famous philanthrophist of Jackson. Osborne J. belonged to the 19th Mississippi regiment, company D, Capt. Ambrose Gergohagan's company, of Fayette, Miss., who left at the outbreak of the war with a company of 110 men, served four years in northern Virginia, came home after the surrender with only ten left. They were near all killed in the battle of The Wilderness in Virginia. I lost a brother in that battle even his resting place is unknown (Lewis Sims.) Another brother, Sidney, joined the Jefferson Artillery, he joined just before the battle of Corinth, Miss., was taken sick, came home and died of typhoid fever. He was a prominent Mason and was buried with masonic honors. After the war he and three of the order were buried in effigy and a monument erected. He was buried near Harriston, Miss., in the family cemetery where my father's mother rests. Those were sad days that visited us with their blight, like a sorrowful night.   J. E. Hulbert.

(2.) Judith Sims, after the death of her parents, Alexander Sims and Eliza Middleton Sims, lived with a wealthy bachelor uncle, Henry Middleton, ten miles from Natchez (Cannonsburg.) It is a grand old place, a country home. She married Captain Hughes who was killed in Virginia, in a battle early in the war. She remained with her uncle till 1866, after his death she, with her son Sam, about five years old, went to Texas. She often visited us at my father's home. She was a very beautiful woman. I cannot give any account of her or her son.

From Julia E. Hulbert.

The following letter was written by James Greenlee to his uncle, Jacob K. Hill, husband of Rebecca G. Sims, his aunt.

Sweet Home, 22nd March, 1848.
Jacob K. Hill, Sen.

Dear Uncle;—Your very kind and affectionate letter of 19th February last was handed me on 20th inst. and I hasten an answer to it as it afforded great pleasure in its perusal, coming as it did from one whom I know to be one of my best friends and who, I am satisfied, wishes me well in both temporal and spiritual affairs. Its perusal brought to my mind the things that were in the days of yore   *   *   *   When it came to hand I was rather in a peculiar mood of mind, having just returned from closing the eyes (in death) of one of my best friends, and my feelings wrought up to their highest, with condoling with the bereaft family and friends, but they mourn not as those who have no hope. I have pretty near filled out this sheet without noticing anything in yours, but will say when I see you we will take our leisure in a social confab. Relative to the affairs of the nation let me now acknowledge my thanks to you for the papers sent me from your capitol. I trust you will be able to furnish me with a copy of the proceedings of your late legislature when I come over. Yours found me and family enjoying that inestimable blessing health. There are but few cases of sickness on our bayou at present and they are principally colds, some chills and fevers. I am done planting corn and have a fine stand in all my first planting, and did intend commencing planting cotton this morning but had on yesterday a pretty heavy rain which kept us from commencing until tomorrow morning. I want to get two-thirds planted in this month, which will be upwards of sixty acres. I have all my old land for cotton in readiness and will during next week get the new, which I cleared this winter, ready for the seed. I am planting this year for 125 bales, I think I shall grow 1,500 pounds, if I have intervention of Providence in my behalf. I sometime since received the brown seed from Mr. J. N. Catthnys and design giving them a fair show in rich land. The seed you and Mr. Miller promised me have not been received yet.

My sheet is nearly filled and I must close by saying I think I will be at your house on 7th May in time to accompany you to P. Hill to church, it being 1st Sabbath. Give my love to the family and my friends and receive a due proportion for yourself from your affectionate nephew, and may the Lord continue to shower down His choicest blessings on you and yours and all mankind is the prayer of   James.

(9,.) The story of the success of L. Hobbs Freeman, is a remarkable one. His success in life has been due to his own efforts and to the fine traits of character he has inherited. He is today the leading merchant of Fayette, Miss., and a man of high principles and fine morals.

(4.) NOTE—Louis Hobbs Sims was reared near the old Simms graveyard, about two miles from Harriston. The old home is not standing but it was the writer's privilege to visit the old grave yard and site of the old home. L. H. Sims was a man of influence. He was a large slave owner and planter. After his marriage he built a home several miles from the old home and here surrounded himself with the best that the times could afford. He gave his children good educational advantages, which fitted them for lives of usefulness.

Mrs. Josephine Freeman now lives near the site of her childhood home, and has in cultivation part of the land once owned by her father.

(8.) Robert Greenlee was wounded at the battle of Corinth, Miss., in 1864. A ball lodged in his head and the best medical skill was of no avail to save his life. He lingered six weeks and during that time his mind was constantly on the battlefield. In his uncouscious moments he would say, "I am coming." When arroused and querried by loved ones he would reply, "I thought I was with my company" and it was his all absorbing thought during his illuess to get well and once more join his command and fight for the Southland he loved so well.

(7.) Elisha Greenlee and his wife, Sarah, gave the land and helped build the first Methodist Church at Pleasant Hill, Miss. (Old deed in my possession.) He requested that he be buried there and now his body sleeps in the spot he loved so well. Both Mr. and Mrs. Greenlee were noted for their piety and charity and were much beloved by all who knew them. He served for many years as Justice of the Peace. In the war of 1812, between the United States and England; he served as private.

(7.) Elisha Greenlee and his wife were among the first pioneers of Copiah county. They erected a rough cottage, the logs of which were hewn in that county and the chimney was a rudely constructed one. They were surrounded by a wilderness and bears, wild cats, deer and other native animals were to be found in great quantities. He was a fine marksman and used to hunt with the friendly indians, who were numerous. The howl of the wolves at night was very common and they would often steal away the fattening hogs and eat them.

SECOND CHILD OF A. B. AND H. C. ROSS.

SARAH CONGER ROSS bore the name of her aunt Sarah Conger, her mother's sister. She was reared and married in South Carolina. After her marriage to John O'Quin, whom she had doubtless known from childhood, she lived near her parents and spent a great deal of her time with them. Nearly every Saturday the O'Quin family went to spend the week end at the home of A. B. Ross. Reference to the diary will give these weekly visits. It was the custom of the parents to ride part of the way home with their children on their return home on Sunday afternoon or Monday morning.

When the family of Sarah C. Ross O'Quin moved to Mississippi, they remained in South Carolina until after the death of John O'Quin and Daniel O'Quin, in 1824. In 1825 Sarah C. R. O'Quin with her mother-in-law, Mrs. Daniel O'Quin, and a number of others came to Mississippi where she lived the rest of her life. Sarah Conger Ross O'Quin was a devoted wife and fond mother. She bore the trials of life with fortitude and reared her children in a home of refinement and fully equipped them for the stern realities of life. (See A. B. Ross diary. Also Ross O, Quin diary.)

John O'Quin was the son of Daniel O'Quin and Elizabeth Singleton. Daniel O'Quin was b 1746 and d Sept. 10, 1824. Elizabeth Singleton was b 1749 and d July 14, 1827. They were married Aug. 19, 1766. Their son Daniel was b 1772 and d Feb. 1797. This Daniel had a son Daniel b Feb. 20, 1791. He went west and was never heard of again. John O'Quin was b June 7, 1768 and died in South Carolina April 13, 1824. He married Sarah C. Ross Dec. 3, 1789.

After the death of Daniel and John O'Quin, which occurred in 1824, the family removed to Mississippi. The following account taken from the diary of Ross O'Quin describes the journey west and the difficulties which were encountered during the first years of residence in Mississippi.

DIARY OF ROSS O'QUIN.

South Carolina, Richland District, the place of my nativity and Oh, how it grieves my heart to leave it and all of my friends and acquaintances, but that solemn moment, that serious day has made its appearance and I must leave native state to try to make and add to what was left me by an affectionate father and beloved grandfather whose remains I must leave mouldering in their graves. When I think that mine will be in the southern states, I know not where, I am brought to consider and think seriously of the example they set before me. They lived the lives of christians and died the same. I am lead to believe while I am writing this, that they are adoring around the throne of God.

March 10,, 1825, was the day I bid farewell to all and started to Jefferson county, Mississippi state, sobbing heart, weeping eyes, lamenting all around me. But O, 'tis too late, the wagon is off, and all that is to be said now is, that we trust that it is right.

Our company is fifty negroes and eight whites, which were an aged grandmother and mother, brother, sister, child and husband, a young man—myself. I will give here their names. Elizabeth O'Quin, Sarah O'Quin, Briant O'Quin, Abagail Harrison, Wade Harrison, Battle Harrison, Stephen Richey, Ross O'Quin. Harrison and wife and child lived in Mississippi, went to South Carolina on a visit. I have made a mistake, there were nine whites, sister Jane O'Quin is the ninth. I am sorry for this mistake but I have gone through so much since that time that I am very forgetful and did not keep an account of the travels as I should have done and I expect for there were none of the company that attended to that but myself.

I will try to give a small account of the travels and of the crop of 1825. March 10, 1825, I, Ross O'Quin, in my 17th year left South Carolina with the company of servants and relatives that is named above and came to the state of Mississippi, Jefferson county. I cannot give satisfactory account of the difficulties we had in moving to this state, but I can say we had a great many to encounter, for we were two months, lacking five days. We landed at Cherry Grove May 5, in the year of our Lord one thousand eight hundred and twenty-five. When we got to Pearl river, 110 miles from Cherry Grove, we had to swap our horses for oxen, which was a bad piece of business for us for it was late in the season and we had to make a crop. 8th of May 1825 we were ready to work corn. Uncle John I. W. Ross had planted our crop for us and helped us work it and it took within $300 of all we made by the cotton to pay him for what he did for the crop. We made lots of corn but only made 25 bales of cotton, got $15 a hundred for it.

I went to school six months that year and stayed with a loving old mother, an affectionate brother and sister Jane. We all farmed together this year. I was in debt at this time about $350 and going in debt every day and I had but three negroes and one of them is the oldest of the sixty and one a boy six years old and one first rate fellow. I will give their names here for the satisfaction of all who know them. Old Aunt Tinder is the oldest of the sixty, Andrew, just grown, and Sam, a boy six years old. These are all the negroes I had at this time. This is all I can say about this year 1825.

Jan. 1, 1826, Brother, Mother, Jane and myself moved from Cherry Grove to land which Brother bought, which goes by the name of Ely Mer Rouge on the Herrin plantation. In 1825 we made a very bad crop of cotton which left us in debt about $340, for my father owed a good deal when he died and the debt was divided among the rest of us. If it had not been for a good brother I do not know what I should have done, but he acted as a father with me all the time and if it had not been for him I should have been cut out of one family of negroes. These things I will never forget while life lasts and I hope, my sons, that you will never forget you uncle. I have given out ever going to school any more and now start to farming with Brother and Mother.

Marrying is all that I am thinking about at this time. I don't think it will be long before I will have Madam at brother's house, to double the joys and divide the sorrows of a poor farmer's life. I am going on very well with my farm for a beginner. Sure enough, this day the 9th of March, 1826, I married Miss Hannah Ross Sims, took her home, worked hard, mane a bad crop which left me more in debt, as I now had a family to provide for, and but those three negroes named above, so this appears to be a bad beginning for a young married couple. This is about all that I can say about 1826 except that I had a fine son the 28 of December, 1826.

Jan. 1, 1827 I set out with mother and brother for another crop and made a very good crop this year and got out of debt Jan. 1, 1828. This year, 1827, was the last year that we ever lived together for grandmother died this year, the 14th of July, 1827. When we divided the property, increased my stock of negroes from three to twelve and I think I will make more by myself.

On the 1st day of Jan. 1828, brother and mother moved off down on Cole's creek on a plantation that brother bought from Bolls and left me on his land to do the best I could. I had twelve negroes and one horse was all I had clear of debt. With everything to buy for the house and farm would put me very much in debt for I had not one dollar to begin with.

In 1834, he mentions that he has not kept a strict account of his work as he has been staying with Aunt Elizabeth Sims, "she departed this life the 16th of April and I and family came home on the 18th.

May 12, 1834, this day myself and wife, A. B. Sims and wife and daughter start to Copiah county and I have to stop one of my best plows, it may be for the best but I cant think so as the grass is growing very fast at this time. We returned home on the 15th and found all well. Had a very pleasant trip aud all straight when we got home.

May 17, 1834, my boy, Martin, got married to Mrs. Isaac Scott's Mariah and my overseer and his wife went to her father's visiting, so we lost this day with all hands.

Monday the 26th of May 1834 my dear brother sent for me to go and stay with him and nurse him for he is more severely attacked than any person I ever saw to recover and has suf-fered more pain. Hope at this time he will recover. I stayed with him ten nights. Dr. Walton and Dr. Duncan attended him. There has been no pains spared with them and with me for his recovery. (Briant O'Quin died soon after.)

1836, I shall work this year, if I have good luck, twelve hands. I hope that the Good One will bless my labors and give all my family good health as I am much behind, say at least $3,000. I have a bad start but I hope to catch up. I wish to recollect that I am a bad hand to trade, for I have sunk at least $300 this winter by trading and buying horses. I also wish to recollect all of this year that I am miserably behind with my own business and must not go security for any one, as I am on as much paper as I am at this time worth. Now if I will recollect this and do my best and have no security debts to pay, I shall come out clear in two years.

It has been more than two months since I wrote in my book and I don't know what to write about at this time for I am in great trouble. On the 8th day of April, 1837, I lost my dear wife, Hannah Ross O'Quin, we lived together eleven years and one month, lacking one day. The loss of her never can be made up to me, this I am well aware of. She lived the life of a christian and died the same. Her last moments were her happiest, and while I am writing this her happy soul is praising God in glory, I know or I should sink with any other thought.

Saturday the 27th of May, the most miserable day of all my life. My dear wife who I lost on the 8th of April is constantly on my mind but it appears more today than ever that I have no one to console me in my troubles and they are certainly more now than they were ever before. I know that she is at rest while I and my three little boys are here in trouble without many friends. Lord help us in our time of need.

In June 1837 he writes: God alone can tell what I felt on that drear day when the Lord gave the signal for separation and I was compelled to return the last parting kiss, it appeared to me that for some time I could only breath. Oh, my God, may my end be like hers. Oh, come quick-ly, quickly and prepare me to follow her. (This prayer was answered in less than two years. Ross O'Quin died Feb. 8, 1839.) The journal from the time of the death of his wife till the close of the book in 1839, was filled with endearment for his wife and grief at his great loss. His crops were not good and his debts did not decrease much. He lived an active, honest life of only 30 years and yet the philosophy expressed in his journal would do credit to a man of twice his age. This journal is prized above all else by the owner of it, Charles O'Quin, (a grandson of Ross O'Quin's) who lives at Red Lick, Miss.

SECOND CHILD OF A. B. AND H. C. ROSS.

SARAH CONGER ROSS, second child of Arthur Brown Ross and his wife Hannah Conger, was b in South Carolina Sept. 23, 1771 and d in Mississippi Aug. 11, 1831, m John O'Quin, Dec. 3, 1789. Issue:—

    BRIAN O'QUIN, b in South Carolina Aug. 1791, d in Mississippi in 1834, unmarried.

    HANNAH O'QUIN, b March 4, 1794, d Oct. 1, 1799.

    ELIZABETH O'QUIN, b Feb. 14, 1796, d Sept. 23, 1796.

    JANE O'QUIN, b June 28, 1801, m her first cousin Brown Sims. (See page 23.)

(6.)   ABAGAIL O'QUIN, b April 5, 1798, d Nov. 1831, m Battaille Harrison. Issue:—

        (1.)   Wade Harrison, b 1841 m to Mary Nicolls. (See letter.) No issue.

        Mabella Harrison, m Dr. T. H. Smith. Issue:—

            *Thos Wade Smith, b 1855, m Julia Hall, she died several years ago. Issue:—

                Susie Belle Smith, b 1883, m B. G. Umstead.

                Jennie Lee Smith, b 1886, m Mr. Hollady. Issue:

                    Wade Dumond Hollady, b 1911.

                Robert Battaile Smith, b 1889, m. Issue:—

                    Ida May Smith, b 1910.

            Two sons dead.

---

*T. W. Smith and daughters live at Leola, Miss.

*Battaile Harrison Smith, m Viola Shields. Issue:—
   Laura Bell Smith, b Aug. 26, 1896.
   Louise Bisland Smith, b Sept. 25, 1899.
†Robert Moore Smith, m Etta Cully, both d without issue.

ROSS O'QUIN, b Feb. 23, 1808, m March 9, 1826 to Hannah Ross Sims, daughter of Thomas and Elizabeth Sims. They were first cousins. (See Thomas Sims line page 23.) Issue:—
   ‡John O'Quin, b Dec. 28, 1826, m Margaret A. Shaw, she was b Dec. 2, 1831, d May 24, 1867. He d Dec. 12, 1866, age 48 years, 11 months, 15 days. Issue:—
      ¶Nancy Gertrude O'Quin, b March 5, 1853, d July 15, 1903, m Cornelius Walter Kelly Oct. 20, 1875, he d Oct. 11, 1904, Issue:—
         Maude Ethel Kelley, b Aug. 7, 1876, m March 29, 1903 to Reason Elexandra Owen. Issue:—
            Maud Leslie Owen, b Feb. 1, 1904.
            Walter Elexandra Owen, b March 27, 1905.
            Roena Gertrude Owen, b July 11, 1906.
            Vardaman Lee Owen, b Dec. 32, 1908.
            Stanley Shaw Owen, b Feb. 15, 1910.
         John O'Quin Kelly, b March 3, 1878, m Mary Lou Olive Adair Nov. 7, 1901. Issue:—
            DeWitt Miller Kelly, b Nov. 19, 1902, d Dec. 15, 1902.
            Olive Gertrude Kelley, b Oct. 8, 1903.
            Alma Annie Kelley, b July 12, 1904.
            Benjamine Huntly Kelley, b July 30, 1906.
            John O'Quin Kelley, b Jan. 11, 1910, d Feb. 4, 1910.
         Ida Lee Kelley, b March 11, 1882.
         Clarence Cornelius Kelley, b May 3, 1884.
         Blanch Estelle Kelley, b Nov. 16, 1886, m Harmon William Adams, March 3, 1911.
         Nannie Gertrude Kelley, b Aug. 18, 1888.
         Charles Sidney Kelley. b Dec 12, 1889.
         Rosa Mae Kelley, b Aug. 26, 1893.
      Mary Hannah O'Quin, b Feb. 12, 1855, d Aug. 4, 1866.
      Charles Shaw O'Quin, b Dec. 29, 1854, unmarried.
      Sidney Walter O'Quin, b Sept. 15, 1857, unmarried.
      Ida Catharine O'Quin, b Aug. 24, 1859, m Louis M. Tills Sept. 24, 1885. Issue:—
         Hugh Stanley Tills, b Aug. 19, 1886, m Laura Lee McDonald, Sept. 24, 1910.
         Claud Shaw Tills, b Jan. 10, 1888.
         Evan Gardner Tills, b Sept. 13, 1889.
         Ruby Leona Tills, b July 21, 1891.
         John Albert Tills, b Nov. 17, 1893.
         Myrtle Elizabeth Tills, b Oct. 23, 1895.

---

*Mrs. Viola Shields Smith and her children make their home at Church Hill, which was near the old home of the Harrisons.

†R. M. Smith was a prosperous planter and stock raiser. He died a few years ago.

‡John O'Quin served as a private throughout the war. One of his captains was Captain Burch.

¶"My parents lived at 'Smithland Hall,' the old O'Quin home near Red Lick. Jefferson county, Miss., where all the children were born. The old home was burned on the night of Aug. 25, 1866."

Clarence O'Quin Kelley.

Ada Leona O'Quin, m Frank Baker. Issue:—
Frank Baker.
Robert Baity O'Quin, b Feb. 11, 1829, d March 1, 1876, m Feb. 9, 1859 to
Elizabeth Grant Short, daughter of Andrew and Charlesly Short.
Issue:—
Hannah Ross O'Quin. b Dec. 15, 1860, d June 21, 1861.
(2) Robert William O'Quin, b May 18, 1862, d March 5, 1911, m
April 17, 1885 to Belle Hester, daughter of Ephram and
Mary Hester. Issue:—
(2) Mary Elizabeth, b March 18, 1886, d June 11, 1904.
Robert Ephram, b Nov. 19, 1887, m George Stur-
ges Dodds, son of William Dodds and Tem-
perance Corley. Issue:—
Willie Belle, b Nov. 19, 1887.
Isaac Cornelius, b July 28, 1891.
Mattie Quitman, b Feb. 20. 1896.
(3) Isaac Calvin O'Quin, b Aug. 23, 1865, d Dec 25, 1910.
Marie Mittielon O'Quin, b June 24, 1876, m Dec. 22, 1897 to
Hugh Craft, son of Heber Craft and Mary Bowman.
Issue:—
Anabel Craft, b Nov. 16, 1899.
Heber Hugh Craft, b Jan. 6, 1904.
(4) Thomas Jefferson O'Quin, b Oct. 11, 1830, d April 18, 1899, m Minerva L.
Vauss, Jan 12, 1852. Issue:—
Josephine O'Quin,
Medora O'Quin.
William Ross O'Quin.
(5) Edgar Byron, b April 3, 1870, d Sept. 7, 1892.
Thomas Jefferson, b Dec. 17, 1861, m Jan. 12, 1881 to Mary
Ellen Stephens, she was b Dec. 17, 1861. Issue:—
Mary Ruth O'Quin, b Oct, 3, 1881, m Nov 20,1907
to Louis L. Posey. Issue:—
|Louis L. Posey, b Nov. 1, 1908.
Olive Aline O'Quin, b April 28, 1883, m Dumont
Freeman, May 13, 1906. (See Sims line.)
Bessie O'Quin, b June 20, 1884, d July 26, 1884.
Francis Minerva O'Quin, b Nov. 11, 1885.
Edith Pearl O'Quin, b Aug. 22, 1887, d Oct. 15,
1888.
Thomas Jefferson O'Quin, b Jan 15, 1889.
Medora Eva O'Quin, b Sept. 26, 1890.
Kate Holmes O'Quin, b Nov. 10, 1892.
Edgar Byron O'Quin, b Nov. 4, 1893.
Elizabeth O'Quin, b Jan. 26, 1906.
Alice Eugenia O'Quin, b Feb. 8, 1898.
William Daniel O'Quin, b Aug. 23, 1899.
Ruby Inez O'Quin, b March 11, 1901.
Marcus Stanhope O'Quin, b Sept. 10, 1864, m Jan 12, 1888 to
Amelia Victoria Furr, daughter of M. L. and J. H.
Furr. Issue:—
Malonie Louisa, b Oct. 12, 1888, m Wiley Beasley
Dec 29, 1908.
Robert Earl Lee O'Quin, b April 20, 1889.
Lilla Belle O'Quin, b Sept. 10, 1891.
Nettie Alberta O'Quin, b June 16, 1893.
Marcus Daniel O'Quin, b Dec. 24, 1894.
Johnnie Modena O'Quin, b Nov. 4, 1896.

Hannah May O'Quin, b Jan. 20, 1898.
Jewel Victoria O'Quin, b April 25, 1900,
Garland Deloit O'Quin, b Oct, 19, 1904.
Maggie Lee O'Quin, b Sept. 11, 1907.
Louis B. O'Quin, m Feb. 5, 1869 to Alma Stephens, he d Dec. 18, 1906. Issue:—
Essie Lee, b Nov. 24, 1889, d April 17, 1891.
(4) Hannah Ross O'Quin, b July 31, 1873, d April 14, 1904., m May 21, 1902, to J. R. Burks. Issue:—
Hannah J. Burks, b April 14, 1904.
John S. O'Quin, b 1896, is unmarried.

NOTES

St. Joseph, La., Aug. 11, 1892.

My Dear Cousin:—

(1) Your letter of the 7th came duly to hand, contents noted. From your knowledge of my dear husband's ancestry, knowing him as I did, I am glad to acknowledge and address you as a cousin. Your statement of the ancestry of the O'Quins, as well as I can remember, is correct. Mr. Battle Harrison, my husband's father. was married to Abagail O'Quin at Mr. Brown Ross's, near Red Lick, Jefferson county, and they, and my husband too, always called old Mrs. Ross, who had been a Miss Wade, aunt Jane. In 1841 I married Mr. Wade Harrison and went to Mr. Battaille Harrison's for a while, who lived on the beautiful old homestead of the Harristons, which now belongs to Mr. R. M. Smith, my husband's sister's child, which has been in the family for four generations of Harristons and now belongs to a Smith, whose mother was a Harriston. She left three sons, two only living. Wade Harriston Smith who lives, I think, on the river in Bolivar county. R. M. Smith lives at my husband's lovely old home "Everton," near Church Hill, owning three places that belonged to his grandfather, Uncle Wade Harriston and the other to Mr. Richard Harriston.

We were not blessed by God with any children but never felt the want of them, having raised and educated several adopted children, first a girl cousin of his then a boy cousin of mine, Emmet Newton, then two orphan girls, then Mr. Newton lost his wife and left two children, one a boy baby, and having neither mother or sister had to bring his two babies to us at Everton. Then when God took my good husband to himself I came with Emmett and his children to live here in Louisiana, near his plantation, leaving my home where we had lived thirty years, a perfectly happy home. Yes I consider it was a benediction to have lived with so good and noble a man as Mr. Wade Harrison. Our adopted ones are as good and devoted as own children could possibly be. My husband was respected and honored by all who knew him. Since his death I have devoted my life to Mr. Newton's children, who are now 14 and 15 years old. I am 77 years of age and cannot expect to be here very long, tho in good health, will try to be prepared to go whenever called away. Would be glad to know how you are related to Mr. Harrison. Hope you will succeed in completing your tree.

Sincerely,
Mary Nicolls Harrison.

(2) Brief mention is made of some prominent traits in his character that those who knew him as father, friend and fellow citizan may emulate his worthy example. His occupation was that of a farmer which he followed with marked success. In his home, presided over by his amiable wife, the friend and stranger had a welcome. His generous nature went out in helpfulness to the needy and distressed. He was a pillar of strength in his church. In his young manhood he gave himself to the Lord and was baptized into the fellowship of the Beech Grove Baptist Church, Claiborn county. While in this membership he was set apart to the office of Deacon. Removing to Jefferson county he aided in the organization of Unity Church where his membership remained until the little band became self-supporting, Though modest and unassuming he found a place for work in the Lord's vineyard wherever his lot was cast. He was successively Superintendent of the Sunday Schools in Brushy Fork, Antioch and Smyrna churches. Near this last

REV. EDGAR BYRON O'QUIN
See Pages 35 and 38.

church he built a splendid home and served as deacon, superintendent and faithful friend to his pastor until fell disease forbade his longer service in a cause so dear to his heart. "He loved God and little children." What higher praise can human tongue bestow upon fellow mortal? He was the friend of education; the earnest advocate of good schools. He gave his influence and his means to this end. His eldest daughter, Mary Elizabeth, was pursuing her collegegiate course in Hillman College. the school in which her mother was educated, when death, like an untimely frost, took from our view this lovely flower. Her college president, Dr. J. L. Johnson, together with her pastor—the present writer—paid the last tribute to this young and beautiful life in June, 1904. God honored the Christian faith of the parents in giving them great grace for this trying ordeal. Not only was our friend and brother the friend of general education, but was also the firm advocate and liberal supporter of Ministerial Education. He was giving $100 a year to this worthy cause with the intention of making it $1,000 in ten years when prostrated by disease.

His devotion to his friends was beautiful. Wearing always a cheerful countenance, and having a pleasant word brought sunshine to old friends and helped to make new ones from the large list of his acquaintances.

---

(3) "The 25th of December, 1910, the day set apart in our calendar as a memorial of God's greatest gift to man, and designed to make glad the soul with its sunlight of hope and good cheer, was darkened by clouds of sorrow which broke in a storm of grief upon the hearts of the loved ones and friends of I. C. O'Quin. His life, so sweet to himself, and so sacred to loved ones, was suddenly snuffed out by a ruthless hand. We would draw a veil over the assassin and look for the best in the character of his victim. It is not claimed that his was a perfect life. Like all men, he had his imperfections, faults that called for the forbearance of our fellow man, and remind us, that ere we become too severe or violeut in our accusations we should give heed to the admonition of the Great Teacher, 'let him that is without sin be the first to cast a stone.' It is the good in man's character for which we should look, and finding the best virtues, to emulate them.

"Mr. O'Quin was esteemed by those who knew him best for his nobleness of soul. They saw in him the adorning traits of honesty aud truth, fidelity and charity. His friendships were true. His spirit of forgiveness as a charming grace and his affection for Mother, Sister and Brother was a crowning excellence of his soul."

I. H. Anding, Summit, Miss.

---

(4) Thomas J. O'Quin was born in Jefferson county, Miss., Oct. I1, 1830 and died at his residence April 18, 1899, near where he was born and raised.

On Jan. 12, 1852 he was married to Miss Minerva Vause, also of said county, who received a liberal education at Fayette Female Academy, now the Jefferson County High School, where a granddaughter has been an honor student during the session recently closed. Mr. O'Quin appreciated the importance of a good education and gave his children the best opportunities and advantages that his means would afford, and thereby left a posterity of children and grandchildren not surpassed in their vacinity, for good citizenship and religion.

Two of his sons went to Centenary College, La., one of whom graduated at an eminent college in the state of Georgia and became a minister in the M. E. Church. His daughter, Miss Hannah, has been a highly respected and useful teacher in the public schools of this eounty for several years.

If nothing more could be said of Mr. O'Quin these alone would show him to have been a kind and affectionate father and useful citizen and will stand as a living monument to his memory.

But when we consider that the war between the states had reduced him from affluence to straightened circumstance, and that it was a hard and continuous struggle to do what he accomplished for the support and education of his family, his character shines forth clearer and brighter to the close of his life.

The writer knew him from his youth up. He was quite considerate and gentle in his early life and in manhood and old age, these admirable traits never forsook him. While in the Con. federate Army, the place to try men's souls, he was the same quiet, brave man amid the storm of shot and shell from the ememy's guns that he had been and was before and after the war. Duty was his watch word in peace and in war and he was ever at his post. So lived and died Mr. O'Quin, without an enemy, beloved and honored by family and neighbors. Some years ago he became a candidate for county assessor and was elected over several honorable competitors, but he loved home and family too well to remain in public life and at the close of his term of office, retired thereto. He leavs an aged and afficted wife and numerous children and grand-children and other relatives to mourn their irreparable loss. May God bless and preserve them through life and in the end save them in heaven, is the praver of a friend.

J. D. S. Davenport.

He was a member of Company H, 1st Mississippi Regiment, Abby's Battery. Was at the battle of Port Hudson, he was sent to Ship Island and served throughout the war as a faithful soldier.

---

(5) Rev. E. B. O'Quin, of the class of 1892, was born April 3, 1870, and died at Red Lick, Miss., Sept. 7, 1892. He was converted and joined the church August 1883. He was licensed to preach January 1884, at the early age of fourteen. He was subsequently a student in Centenary College and from there came to Emory College in the autumn of 1889. In the year 1890-91 he was forced, by providential causes, to withdraw from college life but returned the following year and was graduated with distinction in the class of 1892. Immediately after his graduation he was elected to a professorship in the Piedmont Institute at Rockmart, Ga. With eagerness he looked to his work there and with sadness resigned his position when informed by his physician that he would not be able to undertake its responsibilities.

His life-work he had carefully planned, and to its accomplishments he had been working with patience and heroism since childhood. In a letter which he sent to me a day or two before his death he said: "I will be glad if I can get well, pay my debts and enter the conference as I have always intended." The God and Father of us all can only know what high hopes and noble plans the young soldier had when he fell dead upon the field.

He was not a man of showy gifts, but of solid worth and great perseverance. He was not a brilliant genius but a man of talent who was faithful to his duty. During eight long yeare he struggled through adverse circumstances and over well nigh insuperable obstacles to educate himself for the ministry. I have confidential knowledge of the details of that manly struggle, it was a contest of a dauntless spirit, who in the age of martyrs could have died for couscience sake, without a fear. The struggle brought him hardships and humiliations, but he never whined nor retreated nor magnified his troubles by superfluous discussion of them. He was a self-respecting Christian man who glorified trials by conquering them. What untold heroisms are held in the history of christian students in the south since the war, who in the fear of God and the love of man have toiled and suffered to make themselves able to serve their generation well.

His modesty was such that many overlooked his merits. When, therefore, duty called him to the front he surprised, by the excellence of his work, even those who knew him best. His graduating speech on "Sidney Lanier" was a gem. How skillfully he sustained criticism by quotations his hearers will well remember.

In the greatness and goodness of God he walked and worked from day to day, and now the young pilgrim has passed before us out of sight, and still finds rest in his Father's love and strength. His was a noble, victorious warfare, albeit to our dull sense his end seems so untimely.—W. A. Chandler in issue of Wesleyan Christian Advocate, Oct. 26, 1892.

(6) Hay Battaile Harrison and his two brothers came from South Carolina to Mississippi and settled in Jefferson county near Church Hill. In the old family burying ground near the old home, lie four generations of Harrisons. Of the grandsons of Abagail O'Quin and H. B. Harrison only one is now living, Thomas Wade Smith, who resides at Isola, Miss.

THIRD CHILD OF A. B. AND. H. C. ROSS.

ELY KERSHAW ROSS was named for Col. Ely Kershaw who was a close friend of his father's. It is now believed that Arthur Brown Ross was a soldier of the Revolution under Col. Kershaw but the records, which are not complete, give no record of service by A. B. Ross. Ely K. Ross' boyhood was spent in South Carolina and it was there that he married Elizabeth Hill. In James Kershaw's diary, under date of Aug. 22. 1793, is found this mention of Ely K. Ross: "Ely Ross began to beat indigo." Inference is made that he was a planter and from his letter, I note he continued planting indigo after his removal to Louisiana. Sometime about 1800 he moved to Tennessee, near Newport, and there his father visited him and the account of that visit is given in the diary of Arthur Brown Ross. (See diary.)

The removal to Mississippi occurred about 1805 and he first settled in Jefferson county as the census for 1805 contains his name. The census for 1808 gives the following:

"Ely K. Ross—3 white males under 21; 1 white male over 21; 3 white females under 21; 1 white female over 21 and 6 slaves." Thos. Hinds and Ely K. Ross were superintendants of that census. Census for 1810 gives his total whites as 7, other free persons 5 and slaves 12

Ely K. Ross and Thos. Hinds were intimate friends and this friendship was further strengthened by their association during the war of 1812. At that time we find Ely K. Ross was major under Col. Thos. Hinds. He served with distinction at the battle of New Orleans.

After the death of his first wife Maj. Ross removed to Louisiana, having sold his place in Mississippi to his O'Quin nephews. His life in Louisiana is described in the foilowing letter, which is a more intimate description than I could give. Also see letter from John B. Conger. (See Conger chapter.)

LETTER FROM ELY K. ROSS TO JOHN I. W. ROSS

Mer Rouge, May 15, 1827.

DEAR BROTHER:—

Yesterday was one of the greatest political days we have ever seen in Mer Rouge. We have elected police members. Twenty votes in quietude, yesterday 56 votes were given in wrath and loud declamation and personal enmity. Our side were tranquil and successful. Persuant to what I wrote you in my last, the girl was offered on the 5th inst. Not one bid; my friend observed, "let her go home to make cotton." On the 7th one of similar value and sex was offered and sold for less than $40 00. A tract of land not long since sold for $5,000 was sold for the taxes for less than $10.00, one negro man for less than $60.00. 25 head of black cattle sold for $37.50, all the property of the same person, and from the present appearance of money matters there will be other and others' property have to stand the same or similar test.

Colonel Morgan said, to my son Ely, that he would accommodate me, if such I could think it, by letting me have the use of $350.00 if I would leave the girl with him, which Ely complied with, subject to redemption at any time in my power. Five of my last cotton bales sold for 4 cents, one Brazil sold for 9, net something like $20.00 per bale. Wretched reward for labor. I am still growing in favor of an indigo crop. I have sown near half an acre for seed, should it fail to succeed well I wish you to reserve for me one and one-half or two bushels from the growth of this year. The cotton seed received from you does not raise one seed in ten, consequently my cotton crop will be late and not of the quality I could wish. The time is drawing near and still rolling on, that you proposed to visit our section of the country, at which time I shall be glad to see you and should you have a flattering prospect of indigo weed and not any person to aid or instruct you, if compatible with my worldly arrangements I may return with you, give you. or those you intend to do the beating, some information. A person of attention and discernment can, by a few times seeing the process of steeping and beating, form a sufficient idea to proceed to advantage.

16th. Went to Monroe intending to have finished and mailed this, but leaving my artificial eyes at home I could not.

17th. Confirmed etc. with Colonel Morgan. After night Judge Morgan came from the post office with your friendly letter and one from Mr. Haile, of Woodville, Mississippi, which letters I could not read.

18th. Arrived at home 1 o'clock, P. M., found all well and now hasten to finish (and answer yours,) this letter. In answer to the article of indigo, when young it may appear to be entirely too scarce, be the more careful to prevent stock from it, cultivate it well and you may save very considerable of seed from apparently few stalks. It bears similar comparison to the mustard stalk. You have above my ideas concerning indigo, etc. ere I expected your letter. What corn I have planted took   -:-   -:-   . We are over run with rain and still raining, our farming interests not much different from last year. Dear Brother, I know not how to answer your description of the extent of your wealth, extended farms, etc., than to refer your attention to Luke XII Chapter, from verse 17 to 21 inclusive. I know of no shipment I have made for some time that I have had equal anxiety in, to that of your goats having a safe arrival, not doubting the Caps but being fearful of the L shipment. They were not on board at a late hour of the night and received as singular freight etc. My Pumphrey got gored by a large scrub not long since. It is yet doubtful if he may recover, consequently, I may be under additional obligations to get his place re-instated, which in the event of his death I shall have two young calves not larger than those of one year old, such is difference in the blood.

With regard to Madam Ross' stock you will have to indulge me until my next letter as the season has been so cold and wet that the stock has not been annoyed by insects as usual, therefore not herded. This I can say, they could not be sold for much here. Good beef can be had for 2 1-2 cents per pound on foot. Prime milch cows offered for $12.00. I received a letter from herself on the subject of her cattle a few mails past. I will answer it shortly. I would like to know if you intend moving or enlarging the stock where they are, do not purchase. On the subject of my son, I have reflected when I should have slept. The sons of many remain at home with quietude, until married or arrived at considerable years not so with mine; avarice, a thirst for freedom or some other cause induces them to withdraw from praternal care and home. Ely remained longer with me than any. I am glad to hear Brown is well and doing well. I should be glad to see him. He writes me seldom. At whatever time you all may come if apprised I will meet you at Monroe or Lake Providence. Though as yet there appears to be a degree of uncertainty which dampens my own flattered hopes. We have five children in school, our two sons increase in learning not to be surpassed by any of their age, the best proof of their mental excellency; the physical of the younger proportionate to his mental. J. O. R. and L. Q. R. are at home, the latter dimutive, pretty and smart as you can possibly flatter yourself that yours are. Should not this, when we look around and see a   children the offspring of our fellow creatures born in deformity (as it were) and with limited intellects make us unfeignedly thankful to our Great Father of the universe? I can more sensibly feel for Hannah O'Quin, than express and for the family.

Rankin sends Howdy to Little Jane and Uncle John. Remember me to my brothers and sisters, yourselves. The girls join us in respects to you and their relations. Reserve for yourself and Jane our every good wish etc.

ELY K. ROSS

Postscript—The girls say they wish Adelaide to accompany you to Mer Rouge.

E. K. R.

ELY KERSHAW ROSS, third child and oldest son of Arthur Brown Ross and Hannah Conger Ross was b Oct. 6, 1773, in South Carolina. He d in Louisiana, Jan., 1843. He m Elizabeth Hilll daughter of Robert Hill and Margarite Allison, in South Carolina, July 26, 1791. She was b Sept. 30, 1774 and d Jan. 20 1812. Issue:—

    HANNAH CONGER ROSS, b in S. C. Aug. 31, 1793, m John Kemp.

    MARGARET ALLISON ROSS, b in S. C. Feb. 29, 1796, m Montague.

    MARY A. ROSS, b Sept. 7, 1799, nothing further is known.

    (1) ARTHUR BROWN ROSS, (called Brown) b April 4, 1801, in Tennessee near Newport. Name of wife unknown. Issue:—

        Isaac A. Ross, b 1830, d 1873.

        Mary E. Ross, b 1832, d 1854 at Belle Grove (Remains were removed to

Gibson by Ely R. Jones.)

*ISAAC JOHN ROSS, b Jan. 9, 1804, d June 1834.

ELY KERSHAW WILES ROSS, b Aug. 26, 1806, m Ann L, Wiles in Prairie Mer Rouge, La., May 12, 1836, daughter of Joseph Wiles and Lucy Ann Henderson. He died in 1880. She was born Feb. 19, 1823. Issue:—

Henry P. Ross, b March 14, 1840, d Oct. 8, 1841.

Robert Lemuel Ross, b June 15, 1843, d Nov 12, 1844.

Ely Kershaw Wilds Ross, b Jan. 8, 1845, m in 1869 to Callie Taylor, of Bastrop, La. Issue:—

Ernest Ross,
Edwin Ross,
Aubrey Ross.

Mary Elizabeth Ross, b May 8, 1840, and died unmarried in Oct. 1867.

‡Sallie Malinda Ross, b Aug. 6, 1850, m †Rev. Thomas S. Randall Aug. 6, 1687. Issue:—

†Rev. Thos. Randall is a member of the Conference of the M. E. Church, South, and has two sons who are also Methodist ministers.

*"Uncle Isaac was a merchant, first at Red Lick and afterwards at Vicksburg, where he died childless.

"Uncle Arthur Brown left two children, Isaac Alexander and Mary, their parents willing them to my parents, and they were raised with us. Cousin Mary was a beautiful woman, highly educated, and engaged to a wealthy young man of Claiborne County, Mississippi, when she died with typhoid fever at Belle Grove, our old home, August 19, 1863.

"Isaac A. Ross was as true and brave a Confederate soldier as ever shouldered a gun, from start to finish, in the Tensas Cavalry. He died a few years after the war, of cancer. Peace to his ashes. He was my mess-mate for three and a half years,   Ely R. Jones."

‡My mother was left an orphan when quite young. She and her sister, Mary Wilde, were put in Jackson, La., in a boarding school, where they stayed until my mother was 15; she then came to Morehouse Parish, near Bastrop, to live with her grandmother. There she met my father, who was in business at Bastrop, Miss., and took charge of Bastrop. When they met and fell in love they had a hard time, as grandma wanted her to marry a wealthy lawyer of Mobile; but love conquered, and on a bright Sabbath, the 10th of May, they rode horseback to church in Bastrop and were married and a happier couple never lived.

He came immediately and took charge of my mother's plantation. She had a few negroes, and they economised and worked together.

We were all born on this place except I. A. Ross, of Bastrop, La., who was born in Waverly, Texas, during the war. We had a delightful home, and, oh, in memory I go back and see the old house with its beautiful flowers and such orchards of luscious peaches and mellow apples! I can almost taste them yet, and how I loved to climb up in the trees and drop them in my mother's apron!

My father was born in Mississippi, in August, 1805. He lived to be 75 years old. They lie side by side in Bastrop. My father had a large lot enclosed so all the family could sleep together, but we are scattered here and there. We will meet where there is no good-bye, for my parents were Christians. My father was a steward in the M. E. Church, South, for 42 years, and our home was a preachers' home.

I remember my father was a fine business man, and the soul of honor. I remember so well when he sold the old home. He then owned 100 slaves, and they loved him so much. When he told them he was going to sell out, they cried and begged him not to sell them.

I was a delicate child, and it was during one of my hard spells that he got on his knees by my bedside, with his dear hands on my head he promised God that if He would spare my life he would sell out and move to a healthier place. He was true to his promise, as he always was, and when Mr. Waddill came and looked at the place, having seen the advertisement in the paper, the negroes gathered around the house and my father told them that he thought this man would be their new master, they set up such a cry it almost broke our hearts for we loved our negroes and they loved us and how could we let our old mammy go, the one who had always stayed with us when we were sick and let Pa and Ma go to their meals, and went with us to church with her white apron and white handkerchief tied on her dear old head, but she had a son, our carriage driver, who had a wife and 10 children and we would not need so many in town, for we moved to Homer La., so they were sold, after many tears and sad good byes.

I was 9 years old and remember well how I hugged all the old negroes and how they plead with us not to forget them, and I never have. About six months after the sale we had a letter from Mr. Waddill saying: "Major, send after Phil. He will not eat, is a shadow grieving for you and your children." Pa sent for him and had him a house built and he was with us until he was freed, and never would have left but for his large family. If I remember right he was the father of 22 children, all by Caroline, his only wife. He was killed by lightning while getting ready to go with our oldest brother hunting. He always called him "Mars Wilds," and strange to say, when I was called to my brother's death bed whom did I find but one of Phil's sons as my brother's nurse.

I went back to Bastrop after my father had been asleep in Jesus 20 years and a man shook hands with me and said: "Mrs. Randle you look so much like the Major and I want to shake hands with you again for his sake; we miss him so much yet." My father was a successful business man, he sold our old home and negroes for $175,000 but the war came on and he lost a great deal. I remember he has often said: "I did not have much chance. I only went to school 6 months but I am going to educate my children." My mother had a finished education for her day, she loved music and had such a sweet voice and all of us have been able to sing. My sister Mary and my sister Mrs. Hart and her children all love music and sing. My brother R. R. Ross, had a musical family, his oldest daughter, Annie Lelia, has been much sought after to sing for church and social meetings. Our oldest sons, Ross and Robert, our preacher boys, helped their sisters Nannie, Mary and Pauline with church music. Nannie has been her father's organist for years.

                                                                              Mrs. Sallie Randall.

—41—

Richmond Ross Randall, b Oct. 4, 1860, m Edna Anderson, of Pleasant Hill, La. Issue:—
Lillian Randall.
Maud Randall.
Robert Randall.
Nannie May Randall, Jan 23, 1873.
Rev. Robert W. Randall, b Oct. 20, 1875, m Rosella Wilcox, Jan., 1895. He d Feb. 1900. His wife died in 1904. Issue:
Thomas Wilcox Randall, b 1899.
Thomas Scott Randall, b Jan. 24, 1882, m Mrs. M. E. Gilbert, of Gilbert, La., March 1911.
Hattie Pauline Randall, b Feb. 2, 1891, m J. Clyde Tharpe, of Sibley, La., July, 1908. Issue:
Thomas Clyde Tharpe, b July 19, 1910.
Caroline Amanda Ross, b April, 1852, m *Rev. Wm. Hart in 1872 at Bastrop, La. Issue:—
William West Hart, b Jan. 13, 1876.
Arthur Wilds Hart, b Sept. 24, 1878.
Mary Lyde Hart, b Jan. 20, 1882, m June 17, 1903, to Joseph Hielscher.
William Hielscher, b April 10, 1905.
Charles Newton Hielscher, b April 29, 1911
James Newton Hart, b Sept. 20, 1884, m Lucy Kline, June 17, 1910.
Silome Hart, b Oct 5, 1886.
Lilly Eugeneia Hart, b Dec. 8, 1889, in Bastrop, La.
Lucy Ann Ross, b in Bastrop La., May 3, 1855, m Dr. Isaac James Newton, of Hamburg, Ark., April 13, 1881. He was born in Hamburg, Jan. 3, 1855. Issue:
Isaac Jasper Newton, b in Hamburg Jan. 8, 1882, m Irma Hosmer, of Ft. Worth, Tex. Jan. 12, 1908.
Lucile Newton, b and d in 1883.
Annie Lavinnia Newton, b and d in 1884.
Erle Jackson Newton, b in Bastrop, La., Dec. 2, 1887, m Julia Cone, of Ark., June 26, 1909.
Iris Ross Newton, b in Bastrop Aug 10,, 1890.
Richmond Randall Ross, b in Bastrop, La., in 1857, m Ida Hope, of Bastrop, in 1881. She d Sept. 18, 1900. Issue:—
Annie Lelia Ross, b Jan. 1882, m Alex. May, Dec. 23, 1903. Issue:
Phillip May.
Hope May.
Ida May.
Eli Hope Ross, b July 27, 1883, m Margaret Green, of Monroe, La., Dec. 24, 1903.
Wiles Harry Ross, m Maud Fenton, Aug 1810.
Ralph Richmond Ross, b Oct 24, 1888.
Bernard Ross, b March 10, 1890.
Eula Louise Ross, b Oct. 3, 1896.
In 1902 he married Maud Flint, of Chicago. Issue:—
Ruth Richmond Ross, b 1903.
Isaac Arthur Ross, b in Texas in 1862, m Nora Pope. Issue:—
Isaac Arthur Ross.
Nora Ross.

gyman in the Episcopal Church, in the Diocese of Texas, residing at Houston, Texas.

He m 2nd the sister of his 1st wife, Jessie Pope.

He m 3rd to Ora Hall, of Bastrop, La.

JANE OLIPHANT ROSS, was born in Jefferson county, Miss., Feb 15, 1803. She d during 1880, and was m in Mer Rouge, La., Aug. 31, 1828 to Rev. John G. Jones, son of William and Phoebe Jones, who were m in South Carolina in 1744. Rev. John G. Jones was one of the most prominent ministers of the M. E. Church in Mississippi and a writer of note. Issue:

Daughter, b and d July 31, 1829, in Jefferson county, Miss.

*John Alexander Barnes Jones, b in Warren county, Miss., Dec 9, 1830, m Lucy Cotton.

Sarah Jane Jones, b in Warren county, Miss., June 7, 1833.

William Foster Jones, b at Jefferson College, Adams County, Miss. Sept. 21, 1834.

†Frank A. Jones, b in Sharon, Madison Co., Miss., Nov., 1837, m Jan. 1, 1861, to Olivia Wailes, dau of Col. E. Lloyd Wailes. Issue:

Olivia Lloyda Jones, b June, 1862, m April 30, 1892, to Capt. Scuyler Marvin. Issue:

Scuyler Marvin, b August, 1895.

Frank A. Jones, b 1864, m April, 1892, to Ella Waller, of Missouri. She d 1902. Issue:

Lloyd Wailes Jones, b 1896.

Ruth Jones, b 1900.

Adopted by her aunt, Mrs. Marvin, and her name changed to Marvin.

Mattie Eugenia Jones, b April 5, 1866, m 1891 to W. H. Brown, who was b at Riskmore, La., d July 24, 1895, age 40 years. Issue:

Eleanor Wailes Brown, b 1892.

Henry Frank Brown, b 1895 (daughter.)

John Howard Jones, died in infancy.

Minnie Milton Jones, died in infancy.

Baby, died in infancy.

Baby, died in infancy.

Leonard Wailes Jones, b 1878, m 1906 to Lillian Keller. Issue:

Lillian Artis Jones, b Feb. 14, 1909.

Wimer Lloyd Jones, b August, 1910.

Bennie Rebecca Jones, b 1881, m 1899 to T. N. Nicolls. Issue:

Louis Nicolls, died in infancy.

Eleanor Frank Nicolls, b 1904.

Hattie Nicolls, b 1907.

(2) Ely Ross Jones, b 1840, m Mary West, dau of B. F. West and granddaughter of Gov. Cato West, of Mississippi. Issue:

John G. Jones, b 1869, m Eugenia Melchoir. Issue:

John M. Jones.

Evelyn Jones.

B. W. Jones, b 1872, m Marie Ott. Issue:

Bennie Ross Jones.

Grace Jones.

M. C. Keith Jones.

Laurabell Jones, m C. M. Yard. Issue:

---

*Is a Methodist minister of the Mississippi Conference.

†Graduated from Centenary College in 1858. Entered the Confederate army, Tensas, La. Cavalry, in 1862. Was Superintendent of Education for many years.

Beatrice Yard, b 1904.
Marcell Yard, b 1906.
Katherine Louise Yard, b 1911.
Ely Ross Jones, b 1879, m Alice Bright.
Mary Louise Jones.
Eugenia Jones, b 1843, m R. W. Millsaps. Issue:
R. W. Millsaps.
Janie Ross Millsaps, m Robert Burnley. Issue:
Ruby Millsaps, m James Peeler. Issue:
Matilda Jane Jones, b March 13, 1847, m Rev. T. B. Holloman. No issue.
(She has been a mother to the sons and daughters of her
husband, and has reared them all to be useful citizens.)
SARAH M. ROSS, b Jan. 12, 1812.

ELY KERSHAW ROSS, was first married to Elizabeth Hill, second married to S. Collier (widow), Dec. 17, 1816. She died Dec. 25, 1817. Married third to Elizabeth Henderson (widow), Nov. 1, 1818.

John R. Ross, b Jan. 1, 1826, Morgan C. Ross, b Oct. 4, 1821, Lavinia Quincey Ross, b Oct. 31, 1825, were probably the children of E. K. Ross by the third marriage. They may now have descendants in Louisiana and Texas.

NOTES.

WILL OF ARTHUR BROWN ROSS, Jr.

(1) Having been bereaved of my companion and having but two little children, Isaac Alexander and Mary Elizabeth Ross, I first give and bequeath unto my son Isaac (now between five and six years old) all the tract or parcel of land on which I reside, containing between 900 and 1,000 acres and bounded by T. H. Wade, D. G. Torrey, and J. Rail and R. Hardy, to have and to hold same, etc., also the following slaves: Mose, Lucinda, and their two children, William and Amily, Tom and Kitty, Sam and Amy, Agnes and Henry B., Gilly and Shelby.

2nd. I give and bequeath to my daughter Mary, now three years old, lauds lying in county and state aforesaid, containing 280 acres, and slaves, Bill and Hulda, and her two children, Easter, Sarah Ann, Aaron and Nina, Ephriam and Phoebe and child Malinda, Lucinda Torrey, and Gilly, Hettie and child Maria, thirteen in all.

Rev. John G. Jones and Geo. Hill, executors, and Rev. John Jones, sole guardian.

Signed Nov. 30, 1829.

---

(2) Cousin Ely has inspired me in my work for many years. I have never asked him for help and been denied. On the other hand, he has promptly given me assistance whenever called upon. The following came in answer to my request for something about his own life, and, like the true soldier that he was, he seems to have forgotten most of his past except that which related to his war experience.

"I was born in Jefferson county, Sept. 18, 1840, and as Grandpa Ely Kershaw Ross was there at the time on a visit to my mother and his army friend, Col. Thomas Hinds, who owned the adjoining place, I was named for him Ely Ross. I was educated in the country schools, sent to Centenary College, La., in 1855, and graduated with honor in 1859. I taught school and studied law with Col. H. L. Ellet, of Port Gibson, in 1860-61.

On the 4th of May, 1862, I was enlisted in the war in the Tensas Calvary by Col. Stanhope Posey, at Fayette. I went to Jackson overland armed with a bird-gun, but was splendidly mounted, and the State of Mississippi had given me eight yards of Confederate gray cloth and the brass buttons, which mother had made into a uniform, and you must know that the jacket had a very short tail—in fact, it had no tail at all—was only a round-about. After two days' waiting in Jackson I got a train for Meridian, and after staying three days there I went to Corinth and at once in to the firing line. My bird-gun caught the fancy of Col. Frank Moreton, of the Third Louisiana Infantry, who was officer of the day, and he wanted to try it on the squirrels that were so numerous in the beech trees along our picket line. He killed five that morning, gave me two, and asked the exchange of his breech-loading sharp-shooting rifle that carried an ounce ball, as

MAJOR ELY KERSHAW WILES ROSS

See Page 41.

MRS. ELY KERSHAW WILES ROSS
See Page 41.

he wished it for his boy in St. Mary's parish, Louisiana. We made the exchange. That gun I carried throughout the war as high private. I received my parole on July 1, 1865, at Monroe, La., in company with Ely K. W. Ross.

In March, 1864, as we had been ordered to Alexandria, La., and were on the way, I was run down with chills, so Col. Harrison told me to get out of camp whenever I could and stay in the house at night. We bivouaced one night in the woods eight miles west of Columbia, La., on Spring Creek. I went, as usual, to the nearest house to stay all night. It was just over the creek on the high ground, and on the main road to Alexandria. The stable was on the south side of the road while the house was on the north side, and as I rode up the old man was just closing the lot gate ready to go to the house over the road. On my asking if I could stay all night, "Why yes, but you will have to see to your own horse. Ride in." I did so, and after attending to the horse we went over to the house. It was a cold evening, and a bright fire was blazing in the fire-place. "Ma, here's a sick soldier who wants to stay all night," to a very old lady in the corner by the fire. The old lady, to my surprise, grabbed me in her arms. "You need not tell me who you are. You are Jane Ross's son, and the living image of your father, Cousin John Jones, and I heard his voice when you and Abe were talking." And this was my step-grand-mother and her son Overton. I stayed there that night and the next day and night, as our command did not move sooner.

Grandma had much to say about Grandpa (Ely K. Ross), whom she spoke of as Major, but as I now remember, what impressed me most was her account of his invariable cheerfulness at all times. "The Major used to say, 'Don't take more trouble on your heart than you can kick off at your heels, and this terrible trouble will be gotten over if we go to Him right, wife.'" That was the only time I ever saw Grandma (Elizabeth Henderson Ross), for when we came back after the Red River campaign Grandma had crossed over."

Ely Ross Jones.

Harriston, Miss., March 21, 1911.

FOURTH CHILD OF A. B. AND H. C. ROSS.

ABIGAIL GIBSON ROSS was the first person interred in the Beech Hill cemetery. One of the most pathetic incidents related in her father's diary is the description of the farewell between father, mother and the daughter and her family when they began the long journey to this far western country. The pathos of the incident is deepened for us, because there was never another earthly meeting of parents and children. Abigail Ross died soon after coming to this new country. Her grave and that of her husband are shown in the picture of old cemetery. (See diary,.)

ABIGAIL GIBSON ROSS, daughter of Arthur Brown Ross and Hannah Conger, was b in South Carolina Dec. 6, 1775 and d in Mississippi in 1864. She was m in South Carolina to David Sims, who was a brother to Thomas and James Sims. Issue:—
   HANNAH BROWN SIMS, m Richard Harrison. Issue:
      Louisiana Harrison, m first to Frank McCaleb had several children, all died without issue. She m second Randal Gibson. Issue:
      Olean Gibson m Mr. Hoggett. No issue.
      Lep Gibson, d young.
   ARTHUR BROWN SIMS, m Phœbe Conger, daughter of Johnathan Conger. (See Conger line.) Issue:—
      Wayne Sims, d infant.
      Fannie Sims, d infant.
      Allison Wade Sims, lived to be grown, died unmarried.
      Phœbe Conger Sims, m second Mr. Kenley.
   *ELIZA HILL SIMS, was b Oct. 22, 1803 d Oct. 3, 1865. She first m Joseph Harmon, son of Hezekiah Harmon and Mercy Leonard. Issue:—
      Elizabeth Ann Harmon, d age 15 years.

---

*See note pages 46-47.

Rebecca Jane Harmon, was b June 9, 1826. She d Jan. 14. 1960. She m
first on Aug. 1, 1803, to Joseph Reed Neal of Pittsburg, Pa., who
was b Feb. 27, 1816 and d Sept. 14, 1863. Issue:—

Francis Elizabeth Neal, b Mar. 5, 1846, d Aug. 21, 1900.

¶Ida Agnes Neal, b Nov. 20, 1848.

Martha Letitia Neal, b Nov. 20, 1848, she m Isaac Dunbar
Magruder, son of Thomas B. Magruder and Sarah Olivia
Dunbar West, on Dec. 22, 1868. Issue:—

Ida Neal Magruder, b July 4, 1870.

William Sims Magruder, b June 17, 1872.

Sarah Oliva Magruder, b Oct. 30, 1874, d Oct. 6,
1876.

Rebecca Harmon Magauder, b Sept. 17, 1877, m
Apr. 25, 1906, to Walter Scarborough.
Issue:—

Walter Magruder Scarborough, b
Aug. 10,1907, d Nov. 24, 1908.

Lawrence Dunbar Scarborough, b
Dec. 22, 1908.

Robert Harmon Scarborough, b
July 6,1911.

Thomas Baldwin Magruder, b Sept. 14, 1879, m
Feb. 22, 1909 to Laura Turpin.

Joseph Moore Magruder, b Sept. 9, 1881, m
Fleta Kimber Jan. 21, 1907.

Isaac Dunbar Magruder, b Apr. 11, 1884.

Robert Walter Magruder, b Dec. 5, 1886.

*Rebecca Jane Harmon Neal, m second on Dec. 3, 1856, to ‡William
McDonald Sims, son of James Sims and Elizabeth Conger. He was
b May 9, 1810, and d Feb. 27, 1882. Issue:—

Louisiana Emily Sims, b Sept. 25, 1857, d Oct. 24, 1865.

Carrie Jane Sims, b July 7, 1860, d Dec. 10, 1880, m Jan. 22,
1880 to Robert Walter Magruder, son of Dr. Thomas B.
Magruder and Sarah Oliva Dunbar, who was the Widow
West at the time of this marriage. Issue:—

John Martin Magruder, b Nov. 18, 1880, m Nov.
15, 1905 to Katherine Crane Daniell,
daughter of Thomas F. Daniell and Katherine M. Crane. Issue:—

Katherine Daniel Magruder, b Sept.
27, 1905.

John Martin Magruder, b March 8,
1908.

Phoebe Francis Newland Harmon was b Sept. 6, 1828, m March 22, 1850
to John Fletcher Venable, son of John Venable and Elizabeth Conger Sims Venable. (See Sims line.) She d June 2, 1852. He was
b Dec. 25, 1824, d Feb. 10, 1860. Had several children who died
young.

---

†When a little girl my mother used to visit Aunt Eliza Hoel at her lovely home in Port Gibson. The house surrounded with sweet olive, cape jesamines, magnolias and live oaks is standing and is one of the most attractive places in
that quaint city.

‡William McDonald Sims was a prominent merchant and man of affairs in his day. He amassed great wealth and lived
to enjoy the benefits thereof. (See pictures)

¶Ida Agnes Neal though afflicted with blindness since childhood, is highly educated, a very entertaining talker and is
dearly loved by a large circle of friends and relatives. She supplied the place of mother for John Marlin Magruder and
now that he is married she has taken into her affection his wife and little ones. Cousin Ida lives at the old Sims place
near Port Gibson where it was the writers pleasure to visit recently.

*See pictures.

†ELIZA HILL SIMS HARMON, m second Amos Hoel of Ohio. No issue.
*DAVID SIMS, m second to Sophie White. Issue:—
    Thompson Sims, m and had several children.
    Aurian Sims, m Mr. Walker and moved to Texas.

FIFTH CHILD OF A. B. AND. H. C. ROSS.

JOHN ISAAC GATES ROSS was born in South Carolina, April 19th, 1778. He married and had one son, who died witnout a name. I have no record of his marriage nor name of his wife. He is not mentioned in his father's diary, which was written in 1800 to 1803. This leads me to believe that he died soon after his marriage.

SIXTH CHILD OF A. B. AND H. C. ROSS.

ISAAC ARTHUR BROWN ROSS, sixth child of Arthur Brown and Hannah Conger Ross, was born in South Carolina, April 30th, 1772, and died in Texas in 1842. He married Jane Hill, daughter of Robert Hill and Margaret Allison. (See Hill line.) I. A. B. Ross and his brother, John I. W. Ross, were the last to leave the paternal roof. During their young manhood they shared the responsibilities of the farm with their father, and turned their hands to any work that needed attention. We know more about these two younger sons than any of the other children, because they lived with their parents during the time that the diary was being written and were mentioned in it by their father every day.

"Brown" was the finest shot in the community. He therefore liked hunting, and enjoyed all of the sports of the times. Neither he nor his brother were addicted to strong drink; they were manly boys, and were a source of great pleasure to their parents

"Brown" married late in life, for those times. He was about 32 at the time of his marriage to the younger sister of his brother Ely's wife. His second marriage was to Patsy Thomas. All that is known of his married life and mature manhood is given in the following sketch, taken from the manuscript written by his nephew, John I. W. Ross 2nd.

In the same part of Texas in which I. A. B. Ross lived there are now a family that bear the name of Ross, but it has not been the writer's pleasure to communicate with them; but they are probably descendants of I. A. B. Ross. Any information concerning any of his descendants will be gratefully received. While it is a regrettable fact that we can not trace his descendants to the present time, we will derive much pleasure from the many incidents related in the diary of the fat bucks, turkeys, etc., that were laid low by "Brown," and sigh for the days that made such sport possible. His many errands for his father and his exemplary life related of by his father, make us believe that his children will yet rise up and call him blessed.

---

†Eliza Hill Sims was 6 months old at the death of her mother. Afterward she lived with her grandmother and Ross relatives until her father married again to Miss Sophie White.

*David Sims' body lies beside that of his first wife, Abigail Gibson Ross.

—47—

CHILDREN OF I. A. B. AND JANE ROSS.

ALEXANDER ROSS, m Agnes Scott. He died without issue.

FRANKLIN ROSS, m Mary Scott, a sister of Abe Scott. Issue:

> Alexander Ross, m Rebecca Trimble, dau of Mike Trimble, of war of 1812 fame. (See his diary in Claiborne's History of Mississippi.) Issue:
>
>> Margaret Ross, m Lawrence Wade. (See Wade line.)
>> Frank Ross.
>> Mary Ross.
>> Robert Ross.
>> Willie Ross.
>> Isaac Ross.

FRANKLIN ROSS, m second to a Miss Hodge in Texas, and it is not known which of the above children were by the second wife. He married twice after this the last time after he was 60 years old.

DAUGHTER, who died single.

Isaac Arthur Browu Ross, m 2nd to Patsy Thomas, a sister of Louisiana Thomas, who m John Burch. Issue:

> THADDEUS ROSS, m in Texas. "He was one of the best of the name I ever knew. His first wife died, leaving two or three children. He went to Kentucky to study medicine in 1844, and there married a young lady whose name I do not know, and on his way home stopped in Red Lick to visit his relatives, was taken sick and died, and is buried at the graveyard of Lawrence Ross by the side of his mother."—From MS. of J. I. W. Ross 2nd.
>
> ELIZABETH ROSS, m David Darden. Issue:
>
>> Son, who died in the army without issue. "She was one of the handsomest of the Ross ladies."—J. I. W. Ross MS.
>
> OSCAR ROSS, went to Texas in 1841, there m, his wife died leaving Sam Ross, who lost his life in the Confederate Army.
>
> O. ROSS, m again, but his wife died soon after. "He remained single for nearly forty years, and died partially blind."
>
> WINIFRED ROSS, died the first summer in Texas, on the Brazos river.
>
> MARTHA ROSS, died the first summer in Texas, on the Brazos river.
>
> BROWN ROSS, died the first summer in Texas, on the Brazos river.

SEVENTH CHILD OF A. B. AND H. C. ROSS.

JOHN ISAAC WAYNE ROSS was the youngest child of Arthur Brown and Hannah C. Ross and as such received the affections due the last born in a family. During the old days, his boyhood days in South Carolina, he enjoyed hunting and fishing and was considered a fine shot in the community in which he lived. As early as 1802 he was a member of a military company and attended "muster" in Camden.

He was the companion of his father and shared in the burdens and pleasures of farm life. He was called "Jacky' by his father, but as he grew to manhond he was dignified by the name "John Isaac Wayne" by that parent.

He removed with his father to Mississippi in 1805. In 1810 the census of Jefferson county gives the following:

John I. W. Ross—1 male over 21; no males under 21; 1 female over 21; 3 females under 21; 18 slaves. His mother was included in the number of females. Another list from Jefferson county, without date, gives the number of slaves 21; other free people 19 and 4 in family.

—48—

WM. McDONALD SIMS

See Page 46.

MRS. REBECCA JANE HANNA NEAL
SIMS

THE OLD SIMS GRAVEYARD.
The peculiar slab tombstone marks the grave of ELIZA K. SIMS. (See page 23)

THE "BRICK" PRESBYTERIAN CHURCH.

. JANE BROWN ROSS YOUNG, wife of DR. BENJ. FARRAR YOUN
who died in Paris, France while on her wedding tour.

See Page 50.

MRS. JOHN I. W. ROSS, 2nd
See Page 50.

JOHN I. W. ROSS, 2nd
See Page 50.

COLE'S CREEK
On the banks of this stream our early ancestors made their homes.

"OAK HILL"
Home of JOHN I. W. ROSS, in Jefferson County.

PARLOR AT "OAK HILL"
The wall paper was hung in 1830 and is in a perfect condition now. The paper and
furnuture was bought in Philadelphia in 1830

JOHN I. W. ROSS, 3rd

JOHN I. W. ROSS, 4th
See Page 50.

In the tax list of Jefferson county, under date of 1807 is given: 200 acres of land on Cole's creek assessed to John I. W. Ross. Cole's creek, a beautiful stream running through Jefferson county, was a favorite stream which lured these early settlers. It was on the banks of this stream that many of these kinsmen made their homes. (See picture.)

John I. W. Ross was a prosperous planter and was obviously identified with all enterprises in his new home. He layed the foundation for the beautiful old "Oak Hill" home, still standing, but before it was entirely completed he died, and his plans were carried out by his step son, Judge Isaac Ross Wade. This home is a monument to the ambitions of its founder. (See picture of home.)

John I. W. Ross was a member of the Presbyterian church and his descendents today are staunch adherents of that faith. He was successful in business and gave his children the advantages that only wealth can afford. His home was the center of refined society and the influence of that home lives in the homes of his children today.

His body lies buried in the old Beech Hill cemetery near his parents' children and grandchildren. He erected the monuments over those who went before him and he selected the verse which is inscribed on his mother's tombstone which is so descriptive of that dear mother.

JOHN ISAAC WAYNE ROSS, eighth child of Arthur B. and Hannah C. Ross, was born in Kershaw County, South Carolina, March 4, 1785. He died in Jefferson County, Mississippi, November 5, 1832. He married first Jane Patterson Bisland daughter of John Bisland. She was born September 23, 1790, died July 31, 1816. Married second Mrs. Jane Brown Ross Wade, widow of Daniel Wade, February 13, 1823, his first cousin. (See Chap. 2.) Issue:

JANE BROWN ROSS b February 1, 1824, m February 26, 1851 to Dr. Benjamin Farrar Young. She died in Paris, France the next year. (See Picture.)

FRANCES TOLEDO SEABORN ROSS, b July 29, 1828, d October 15, 1837.

JOHN ISAAC WAYNE ROSS, b Tuesday, November 8, 1825 d July 22, 1898 at Oak Hill in Jefferson County, where he was married to Hellen Perine Green, who was born May 23, 1830 and died April 7, 1900. She was the daughter of Charles Beatty Green and Mrs. Helen Perine Andrews, nee Girault. Issue;—

(1) Charles Beatty Green Ross born April 12, 1852 married Betty Corley daughter of James and Elizabeth Corley. Issue:—

John L. W. Ross 2nd occupied many prominent positions in his county. He built up the estate left him by his father and left to his children an immense tract of land, surrounding the "Oak Hill" home. He kept up the records of the family until his death and was considered an authority on family genealogy, and his efforts made possible this family history. His home was furnished with the handsomest furniture money could buy in Philadelphia and not only the luxury of the home but its cordial welcome attracted many guests there.

He was an ardent Presbyterian, a member of the Brick Church (See picture) at Red Lick. He was generous in his nature and well beloved by all who knew him.

His wife was an ornament to his home and a mother, in the highest sense, to her children. Both lived long and useful lives and their memory still lives in the hearts of all who knew them.

John L. W. Ross first married a daughter of John Bisland, who lived only a few months after marriage. The old Ross Bible was presented to her by her father, John Bisland. Her husband transferred the early Ross records to that book and it is today in the possession of Mrs. Anon Killingsworth, at Red Lick, Miss.

In the old Ross Bible are found the following entries: "James Bisland and Abigail Ross were married 13th day of March, 1817. James Bisland was born 23rd Sept. 1780. His father, John Bisland, was born the 26th of March 1742; his mother, Susannah Rucker, was born 2nd Feb. 1767."

The third Presbyterian church established in the South West was erected by John Bisland and John Henderson two sturdy Scotchmen who were brought up under the instructions of the Presbyterian Church in their native land and who carefully preserved the religious faith of their fathers. This church was at Washington, Adams county, and was organised by Rev. James Smylie, Feb. 25, 1807.

Charles Wayne Ross b August 18, 1880 m Alma Calhoon.
Bessie Pauline Ross b April 12, 1883.
James Maurice Ross b July 25, 1885 m Lura Donaldson.
Hellen Perine Ross b August 22, 1888 d September 15, 1888.
William Stanley Ross b July 22, 1889.
Kennith Gordon Ross b November 26, 1891.
Infant daughter b November 1896 d December 24, 1896.
Daughter b July 26, 1898 d same day.

Seaborn Frances Toledo Ross, Jr., b July 22, 1853 m Jane Killingsworth, daughter of Anapias and Martha Trimble Killingsworth. (See Killingsworth line.) Issue:—

Frances Alexander Ross b April 10, 1889.

John Isaac Wayne Ross, 3rd., b December 4, 1854, m January 2, 1889 Florence Chamberlain. Issue:—

John Henry Ross b November 9, 1889 d July 13, 1891.
Samuel Thaddeus Ross b September 17, 1891.
William Bingham Ross b October 3, 1892.
Proctor Wayne Ross b May 9, 1894.
Cordelia Ellen Ross b October 6, 1895.
Daughter b and d November 1896.
John Isaac Wayne Ross, 4th., b May 7th, 1898.   (See picture.)
Patrick Henry Ross b September 27, 1899.
Louis Spence Ross b September 10, 1900.

William E. Ross b June 12, 1856 d October 4, 1887 m February 16, 1879 to Josephine Wade daughter of Col. W. W. Wade. Issue;—

John Burch Ross b June 8, 1881 m Emma Allen. (See pictures.)

W. Wilson Ross b June 21, 1883 m Catherine Wade.

*Percy J. Ross b April 19, 1889 m Freda Fraas. Issue:—

Elvin Anon Ross, b July 12, 1909.

Hellen Ross.

Eugene Allison Ross b June 16, 1860 m Margaret Idella Wade. Issue:—
Eugene Allison Ross, Jr., b November 6, 1891.
Robert Winfield Ross b January 24, 1893
Daughter b February 9, 1894 d same day.
Arthur Bernard Ross b March 24, 1895.
Nellie Laura Ross b June 25, 1897.
Mary Agnes Ross b September 25, 1897.
Daughter b December 19, 1898 d January 14, 1899.
Girault Beatty Ross b November 15, 1899.
Lucy Guy Ross b July 19, 1901.
Della Wade Ross, d December 10, 1903.
Daughter b and d February 24, 1904.
Minnie Jane Ross b November 15, 1905.
Son b and d January 23, 1909.
Virgie Irene Ross b August 15, 1910.

Charles Beatty Green was born in Deerfield in 1776. After the death of his father his mother moved to the vicinity of Trenton, where he went to school. In 1798 he received a lieutenant's commission in the war with France. He resumed his studies in 1802 and began the practice of law in his native state, but being discouraged he started on horseback in June 1808 for the Mississippi Territory. On Dec. 13, having come by way of Pittsburg, Louisville and St. Louis, thence by river, he arrived at Natchez. He succeeded in the practice of law in Natchez and acquired some property in that vicinity. In 1817 he was elected to represent Adams county in the first State Legislature. He was also a member of the State Senate until 1828, when he removed to Madison county. He was elected Speaker of the House in 1827. He occupied many prominent positions in the state and at one time owned 12,000 acres of land in Madison county. In June 1814, he married Mrs. Hellen Perrine Andrews, daughter of Col. Girault. They raised a large family of children whose descendants are among the first citizens of Mississippi today. Their daughter, Helen Perine Green, married John I. W. Ross.

JOHN B. ROSS
Page 50

MRS. JOHN B. ROSS
Page 50

MRS. WILLIAM E. ROSS
Page 50

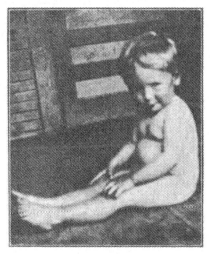

ELVIN ANON ROSS
Page 50

†Hellen Perine Ross, born April 25, 1862 married December 3, 1890, to Anon R. Killingsworth (See Killingsworth line.)

Clara Green Ross born January 25, 1864 died September 11, 1864.

*Janie Brown Ross born June 20, 1865.

Elvin Bernard Ross born August 20, 1867.

‡Cordelia A. Ross born December 3, 1869 died August 9, 1896.

Abagail A. Ross born October 8, 1877 died September 4, 1877.

Jackson, 31, May, 1857.

(1) MY DEAR SIR:—

Yours of the 26th inst has just reached me.

When in Jefferson, a few days ago, my daughter mentioned the subject to me. My reply was, that, *she must consult her own feelings and wishes on the subject.*

If it be her wish, it is my pleasure to consent.

With yourself I have no personal acquaintance, but from information received from friends in whom I have great confidence I have received very favorable accounts of your intelligence, industry and good habits.

With your Aunt Reed, Uncles Isaac and Allison, I was well acquainted, and had great respect and esteem for them. With your grandfather and Captain Ross and father I was slightly acquainted, not intimately so, but of all formed the most favorable opinion.

Under all circumstances, I cannot, do not, hesitate to give my cordial approbation to your union. Remember me kindly to Helen and believe me to be with great regard your obedient servant

CH. B. GREEN.

---

*Miss Janie Ross lives at the old homestead. Oak Hill, and has with her several nieces and nephews who are fortunate in having her as a companion and counselor.

†At the death of Mrs. John I. W. Ross, wife of John I. W. Ross, 3rd., Helen Perine Ross (Mrs. Anon Killingsworth) took to her home and heart the manly little boy who is to carry down the Ross name—John L. W. Ross the 4th. While she has no children of her own, her mother heart has gone out to many, and the light of her attractive home is now thin son she has in her charge.

‡She lived to womanhood and was beloved by all who knew her.

DIARY OF ARTHUR BROWN ROSS.

This diary was written by A. B. Ross while he was a resident of South Carolina. His home was near Camden and also near the Wateree River. He operated a ferry on the Wateree, and his various plantations are shown on the map.

There was also a diary written after he came to the Mississippi Territory, but its owner is not known. The volume containing the writings, from which the following are taken, is the property of Miss Jane Ross, of Red Lick, Miss., who very kindly allowed the writer to make typewritten copies from it. To those who are interested in reading the entire diary, arrangements will be made to allow them the use of the typewritten copies.

The task of selecting portions of the diary for this volume was a hard one. The whole book is interesting, and would add to the value of this history; but, on account of the space it would take, I have selected the parts which in my opinion are of most interest to the most of the descendants.

RELATING TO HIS HOME LIFE.

January 1, 1800—WEDNESDAY.

I was qualified as a Justice of the Quorum. Gave Mr. Lang a due bill for the ferry, he and his to pay the ferry and twenty trips of a wagon. Bought sundries of Clark 1-19-9. (This was in side note.) Loaded the wagon. Stephen drove it to Camden, but it was too wet. I bought of Mr. Clark six lbs of sugar; cheese at 1-6, 3 coffee—spent in all 1.19.9. Gave Mr. Lang and signed agreement for the side of the ferry near Camden for 42. 10.0 I was qualified as a Justice of the Quorum by Dr. J. or I. Alexander. Divided the subscription for ferry with Thos. Dinkins for the year 99.

THURSDAY, 2nd.

Rose early, went to Camden, got agreement signed by Thos. Dinkins and myself of Dr. Alexander. Gave Lavick Rochel a state's warrant against David Minton. Went to Capt. John Kershaws, agreed with him for west side of the ferry near Camden for one hundred and fifty dollars or 35 pounds sterling. Mrs. Rebecca Brown and her wagon people to pay I. Ross the 3.15.0 for use of flats. Bought of Smith & Carpenter two yards cloth at...........for a coat. Came home, had Dick c— at ———. I and the old lady rode up to Maj. Whitaker's and the boys came home from Mr. John Hill's.

(The rest of page is so dim and torn it cannot be read.)—A. M. W.

WEDNESDAY, 8th.

Rose early. Four plows at work. Went to Brown's. Ate in Camden. Saw the judgment against Ned Rutledge for me. Mr. Brown said I need not come about it. I told Mr. Brown he must give 30 dols. a year for the ferry. Ned gave me 1 dol. and a half at the ferry. I came home. S. Ross making back bands. Dr. Nath. Alexander and lady are at Mr. D. Brown's. Samuel Ross went to Mr. David Sims to keep tally tomorrow Ned came and brought me $3.00 from the ferry. I went to Dan's shop and to Burn's and by Roberts and to Dan's and got two— saw three deer.

THURSDAY, 9th January.

Rose early. Sent three hands to help D. Simms to thrash out corn. Bought one barrel for whisky. Left. I saw a boat pass at the ferry. David Simms there. I went for hogs. Saw a bed of hogs, or rather where they lay. Saw nine deer. Saw Holliday. He says the mare John Cantery rode from Georgia is a stolen one. Mr. Jas. Morgan and Thos. Holland Davis came late last night.

FRIDAY, 10th.

Rose early. Holland, Brown, Samuel Ross and I and Bill went to the hog-bed. I shot one and catched four more and brought them home. It snows fast, and the snow is now two inches deep. We went up to Comfort Hill, catched a large sow, killed her, took her to the house, then a hunting more. Found a black listed sow and four pigs, marked 5. Catched four more pigs and brought them home and put them with their mother. Bill took twenty gallons of whisky to the ferry and left it with Ned for Messrs. Smith and Carpenter. Bill to mill, no meal. In evening two Morgans came. Ned sent $3.00.

SATURDAY, 11th.

Rose early. Two Morgans here. Wrote T. H. Davis and Cousin Morgan went away. Brown gone to ——for leather. Now fixing the still-house. William Walton here, and I paid him 1-7 one to 3 1-2, and he had three quarts of whiskey, which pays for three 14-gallon kegs. I and Jackey went to find a sow and pigs, but could not find her. I shot at a turkey running. Jacky shot at a deer. I saw six deer. Ned sent $2 by S. Ross.

SUNDAY, 12th.

I did not rise early. Foddered the cattle for the first time this winter. David Simms and family here. I and the old lady rode in the cart to the ferry. Ned gave me 5 dollars. Saw Dinkin's Tobe take eleven sheep over the river. Came home. My brother came. Mr. A. Kelly came and an Ivey. Ned came and brought me one dollar. Mr. D. Carpenter came and borrowed Fane and the cart.

MONDAY, 13th.

Rose early. My brother and Mr. Kelly here. David Simms came day before and got cart and Fane. Sent Brown with $2 and one bushel wheat. He sent the wheat by Tobe. Brown got a paper of ink powder. My brother and Brown went to David Martin's. I and the old lady rode to the ferry. Received $1.50 of Ned.

TUESDAY, 14th.

Rose early. Had breakfast. My brother wrote Crimm and sent Brown with it to him My brother, Holland, I and Tobe all set off for Holliday's. Met Mr. Gus Hill. Told my brother his boat hands were gone home, and he went home and we went to Holliday's, and he went with us a cow hunting. Found four heads and came home. Miriam   of dolls. Ned brought $2 from the ferry late.

WEDNESDAY, 15th.

Rose early. Now for hog-killing. All hands—Jacky, Brown, Cousin Davis. Killed forty-three hogs. The negroes and Cousin Samuel shoe-making. I sent my brother's negro, Tobe, home. I went to the ferry. D. Burns paid me one dollar towards last year's ferriage. Ned gave me 3 1-2 dollars. Got Dan killing hogs about midnight.

THURSDAY, 16th.

Rose early and went to Camden. Bought of Adamson 1 lb black pepper, 7 lbs saltpeter; no pay. Put a letter in the post-office. Took Dr. I. Alexander's spectacles home, at Mr. Fisher's. Bought of L. Sipel's four pen-knives at_____. Came home, sent to Mr. Adamson eleven hogs, netted 1,413. Cutting and salting up hogs. Sent old Cameron two hogs. One net 104 and the other 56 lbs., he to pay $5. Mr. Gardner Ford here all night to stay. Holland Davis got one pen-knife at_____.

FRIDAY, 17th.

Rose early, before light. Got ready, with Cousins —— and Brown, Mr. G. Ford, went to D. Martin's. We went on——, Mr. Jas. Terry and D. Holliday with us, all went cow hunting. S. Ross shot twice at a deer. I saw no deer today. Cold rain with high wind. We went to Killingsworth's; many there. Came back to Mr. Holliday's and dined there. Then home. Ned brought 2 dollars.

SATURDAY, 18th.

I did not rise till light, then hollowed to hands to cutting wood. Hunted sheep, but found none. Was at the ferry. Killed some partridges. Samuel Ross went to Camden, bought papers in which he inserted the death of our dear Washington, who is now no more. He was ill twenty-three hours, and then no more. He died the 14th, at night, between 10 and 11 o'clock, of December last, 1799, being 68 years of age. O, cruel death! None freed of it. Polly Hill had a son born.

SUNDAY, 19th.

I read news till breakfast, then arose. Dan Williams came and brought $2.50 from Ned, being yesterday's pay. Ate breakfast then I and the old lady rode up to Comfort Hill. The boys went up there, too. The old lady and I called at the ferry. A. F. Brisban's Pete there. They had a fight last night with——. They went down the river. Dr. J. Alexander came over, had a little chat, and he went down to Mr. Mackey's, for Mackey had whipped Bracey's negro Stephen for being sassy (saucey.) Fine weather for my pork.

MONDAY, 20th.

Rose early. Tobe went away without the letter. Peter Crim here and went to the ferry with me, he to Camden, I with John Kershaw, Esq., to the boat. Had brandy, then he came and looked at my sheep, I to have his negro Sarah for twenty-four head of sheep and two........for one year. I came home and dined, then went to my brother's boat. His man out of his element. Came home with David Simms and wife, as they are from the PeeDee. All well. Ned gave me $3. My brother came up late. All here.

TUESDAY, 28.

Rose early. My brother went away before breakfast. Thrashing flax seed out and drawing rails. David Simms came and I went to the ferry with him, and I weighed three hogs; weight 872 pounds. Sent Stephen with Simms and cart to Dr. Isaac Alexander's. Saw my brother. Says Col. Cantey asked him to the wedding of Mr. W. L. Whitaker and Miss Betsey Brown, and of course W. L. will be Col. Cantey's uncle by marriage. Took Doctor Logewood to Camden by Simms' cart. The sun shines warm.

WEDNESDAY, 29th.

Rose early. Had breakfast, then I and my brother went to Camden, he to I. (or J.) Dinkins and I to X. Brown's; he a-bed. I then went to John Alexander's; says he can buy sheep at a dollar and a quarter a head. I said, "Well." Then we went to his boat; was there a while, a (aranee) there. He bottled a bottle of wine. There was of corn 200 bushels. Came to Camden. Bought of Coleman one pair of woman's shoes at $6. Came to Mr. J. Adamson's; bought 8 lbs twine at 6.3 and a chair whip at 9.4; no pay. Bought of Clark two whip-stocks; paid $2. Came home, had dinner, finished the flax, made a cow-rack. My brother and Cousin Holland walked down to the boat; came back.

THURSDAY, 30th.

My brother went away before I was up. Cold and cloudy. Cleaning the flax seed with Stephen, Tom and Sue. Bill drawing straw and putting it in the cow-rack. A cold northeast wind. I went to the ferry. Ned gave me $3. Mr. Hoskins there, groggy. Lost a pair of cotton cards. Ned found them. Ned came up and gave me one dollar and a half more. Hoskins came up with him.

FRIDAY, 31st.

Snow in the night. Hoskins rose early and went away. Repairing fence and fixing trough to feed cows. Mr. Johnson Elkins came and brought seven belts that he took to mend. I paid him $7 for them. He paid three dollars in part what he owed me for whiskey he had some time ago, and left seventeen belts to sell for 3.0.6, and he got 35 gallons whiskey 3-6 if paid by the 20th of next month, or 4-8. I and the old lady rode up to D. Simms; got a pair of shoes for Stephen. Called at Mr. Thomas Whitaker's; read and chatted. Sally and two granddaughters rode in the chair. I called at the ferry and got of Ned five dollars. Negroes plenty at the ferry. Cold and clear.

SATURDAY, February 1, 1800.

Had the wagon yoked. Bill drove it to John Burns', took iron and a brass kettle, to get a new wagon or old one repaired. Took the old irons, two sides of leather and a little piece of skin to Dan's shop; left the wagon at Dan's shop to be repaired. He drew a load of lightwood home. Mr. John Burns sent George Martin for a horse to go and get his land through the office. I sent his horse and five and a half dollars by G. M. Saw B.

SUNDAY, 2nd.

Cold, snow and rain. David Simms and wife and child came. He went to the plantation of D. Brown, and Holland with him. Snow a-plenty. He says Wm. Mackey a-moving. Ned came; said that a dollar and a quarter is belonging to this side this month of the five dollars he left. Simms and wife went home.

MONDAY, 3rd.

Rose early. Bad weather, but has appearance of better. I went to the ferry to see Mackey, but he has gone over the ferry and moved. Two hands thrashing oats. Bill and Tom getting fire-wood. David Simms called by; has been in Camden. Got a note of Mackey for 36 1-4 dollars. Received $2 at ferry.

TUESDAY, 4th.

Rose early. Had the wagon yoked and drew the flax in the cotton field to lay on and rot. Sue and Stephen threshing oats. Tom cutting wood, Bill and Charley drawing flax and wood. I worked with Tom. I went to the ferry; received $3. Simms and Cook there. My brother wrote me by Caleb; all poorly; and wants to know how the river is. Thomas Simms came from Peedee and took supper and went to David Simms'.

WEDNESDAY, 5th.

Rose early. Jackey and Bryant to school. I fixed the whiskey reime(?), went to the river; it's falling. Mr. Bracey came yesterday and paid me 40 shillings for his wagon crossing the river eight times back and forth. This should have been written in yesterday's register. Bill and Tom cutting stalks, Stephen and Sue thrashing oats. Wrote my brother a letter by Buck. Cold rain; southeast rain. I was in the field, tasked Bill and Tom in cutting down stalks. Mr. Crimm came; says the 25-mile creek is high and rising. He wants whiskey for rye and a still. David Simms and Thomas Simms came and dined. David got two quarts of whiskey. I went to the ferry. Received of Ned $5 for last and $6 for this. Came home; Thomas Simms here. Rain and good weather; 15 lambs.

THURSDAY, 6th.

Rose after day; got ready for my brothers. The old lady and I in the chair went by Mr. O'Quinn's. Sally has been down to the raft to see Johnny yesterday; came home. Then up to my brother's; all got colds. Had a good dinner and tea in the evening. Good weather. My brother has a good house half finished, and all live together.

FRIDAY, 7th.

I am now at my brother's. Had breakfast, then the old lady and Mrs. Belton (she was Polly Allison, sister of Jane Allison, who married Isaac Ross) in the chair, Miss Jean Brown and Margaret on horseback. I rode with them to Collo Creek, saw them safely over, then I rode back and found my brother and Drew Harris at Terry's Branch. Now to kill a deer. I saw two and shot at one, but no kill. Went to Wade's Mill. Phelps at work there. Then to John Hill's. The above women ready to go away. Dined there on plenty, but I begrudged myself to eat their provisions, for they have a great charge of children. Dr. Knox came with us to my brother's. Dined.

SATURDAY, Feb. 8, 1800.

Cloudy, cold morning. Dr. Knox with us. Had a good breakfast, then asked sister her child's name. The name was Arthur Allison. Bid good-bye and came away in the rain. Cold. Got to Mr. O'Quinn's. Sarah and her child and Ben came with us. Rain and cold. Got home wet. Thomas Simms here. David Simms came after dark. Brown had $9 and Ned had $2 for me. David Simms and family with Thomas.

SUNDAY, Feb. 9, 1800.

David Simms and family, with Thomas Simms, came. I lent D. Simms $18. Had breakfast then Ned sent for us. David Simms and I went to the ferry. Mr. Thomas Simms gone to Pee-Dee. There were three men at the ferry did not appear willing to pay for their ferriages, as a good many travelers. I got $5 at the ferry. Came home; dined on good dinner—turkey, etc. River rising. Brown went to my brother's to let him know, Holland with him. They came late, my brother with them. Cold and cloudy.

MONDAY, Feb. 10, 1800.

Rose early. My brother here. He and I went over the river, he to his boat, I to Brown's; he away, I to Michael Ganter's. Received $6 for the past crossing the river on the east side for the year 1799. Went to John Fisher's; got receipts for my............. Went to borrow a compass to survey, but in vain. Went to Clark, and agreed for a barrel to put whiskey in and a barrel of flour. Called at Sipel's; bought one-half lb of tea and a canister; paid 8-2. Came home. Mr. A. Belton came and left at 3:30. I went to Wm. Watts'. He at home, and a Wm. Miller wants a summons for Watts. I was there a-while. Came home and Watts and Richardson came and got a pint of whiskey each; no pay. Cold and cloudy. R. R. here all night; about the ferry last year.

TUESDAY, Feb. 11, also WEDNESDAY, Feb. 12, 1800.

Rose early. Cold and cloudy; snow but little. Mr. Abraham Belton and son John came and left three notes on William Watts to be collected. Charlie came and says Mr. David Martin departed life last night. I and the old lady rode there in the chair and found the news true. Mr. J. Burns and son are making the coffin. I assisted, but my big thumb is very sore. A dry burial, for there were neither tears nor drink. He lies low in the earth. Came home late. R. R. here. I had a bad night, for the tooth-ache and thumb-ache was very bad. David Simms and John Hill came, breakfasted, had the wagon yoked and sent to D. Brown's plantation for D. Simms' barley. In the afternoon I went to Mr. Thomas Whitaker's, he to send for oats. Carpenter there, getting hog bristles. He came home with us and got a few bristles, and I rode to the ferry with him. Ned gave me two dollars and I came home. Stephen working for Brasey. Mr. Whitaker's wagon came by and got in his wagon thirty-five bushels of oats. I am very unwell indeed. Can't sit up nor lay down in ease.

THURSDAY, February 13, 1800.

Mr. John Burns came. Major Whitaker and old Mr. O'Quin all here. Mr. O'Quin says his son has come up in the boat. I can't rest. Cleaning barley and thrashing it out is a bad bargain for me.

FRIDAY, February 14, 1800.

I am unwell. Rain and cold yesterday, and not much better today. Two hands laying flax out to rot. Mr. William Miller came and took my hand-saw to whet and handle. Mr. O'Quin came and dined. I and the old lady rode up with him to D. Simms'. Came home by the ferry. Ned gave me four dollars. Cleaned out D. Simms' barley, and there is 20 1-2 bushels. John O'Quin came.

SATURDAY, February 15, 1800.

I was very unwell all night and all the morning. John O'Quin went away early. David Simms and family came. Brown and Jackey out all night, and killed a coon. The ladies, Sarah and Abigail, went to Camden. D. Simms with theirs are hanging out bacon. I gave Brown six dollars to buy cards or otherwise, that may best suit. Sent for ginger cake and a little baker's bread. Brown bought cards, and he went back and got one gallon rum of Clark.

SUNDAY, February 16, 1800.

I a-bed sick. Simms and family here. They all went to the boat to see John O'Quin. They came back later. Sarah and Bryant went to meet John O'Quin, but he did not come. Sarah sorry and I not pleased, for a man has not any business with a wife_____.

MONDAY, February 17, 1800.

I sick a-bed and sore. Sarah O'Quin went early to the boat and took O'Quin's clothes and went away. The old lady and Abigail went to Camden, bought six yards calico at 4-8, and 1-4 yards muslin. Sent Stephen with the flaxseed to Mr. Broom's mill. Got receipt of Mr. F. Lee. Stephen called at Mr. Clark's store, got a barrel of flour and an empty barrel to put whiskey in for Mr. Clark. Stephen drew a load of fodder from Simms'.

TUESDAY, February 18, 1800.

I never had a worse night in all my life. I think I slept little, but rested none. I neither could rest in bed or out of bed. My wife sent Croaker for two yards of calico of Mr. D. White at 4-8. Allen Perry called, got pint whiskey, paid 7d. Dr. I. Alexander came, lanced my jaw. It ran plenty, and used the_____and went home. David Simms and I settled and he paid me and bought side leather and belt; paid. Now we are even. Green Martin here, and bought Simms' mare. Sold one belt at 3-8.

THURSDAY, February 20, 1800.

Cold, hard, frosty weather; nothing doing, and I fear won't be much better till the weather alters. This day David Simms is to move for the western country. I and the old lady rode up in the chair. They all seemed to be busy. Came home; plenty of travelers on the road. Had rye sown on the west side of the ditch and river. Had the wagon yoked, Stephen driver, and I and lady and he went to David Simms', they loading cart and the wagon. Came home by the ferry. Ned up at home. David Simms and all here, for the last night, I expect. Received $7 from the ferry.

FRIDAY, February 21, 1800.

I sick a-bed till day and after. D. Simms went to Thomas Whitaker's for a _____. I had the chair yoked and Pernasus broke it into shatters and came back home. Now D. Sims is getting ready to set off for the western territory. I wrote Ely a long letter; tears plenty. Now we all set off—David Simms and family, Sarah O'Quin and daughter, I, old lady, Brown and Jackey We went to Horsepen Branch, then I and the old lady parted with the rest. I heard my daughter cry a quarter of a mile, I think. Came home. Holland went to ferry, and Ned sent five dollars. Richard Richardson here. Cold weather. David Simms gone to Mississippi.

SATURDAY, February 22, 1800.

A cold night indeed, and a hard frost in the morning. The children are still away. Hands at very little. Dutch here caulking a boat. The two Misses Lanters want a horse to go to see Miss B. B. Martin, and they got one and went. Brown came first, then Jackey and Sarah—all well—with D. Simms. They say Brown went to Camden. Got two pounds of twine for Mr. Addison; no pay. Got of Mr. Clark a loaf of sugar, seven pounds four ounces; no pay. Got of A. Smith and Carpenter six pounds lead; no pay. Ned sent two dollars by Brown.

SUNDAY, February 23, 1800.

I a-bed late. Green Martin came early; he went away. I am poorly. A fine day. I and the old lady rode in the field and to the ferry, noon, then out D. Brown's, Esq., wagon with hay. Ned came and brought four dollars.

MONDAY, February 24, 1800.

Rose early. Set three plows to work. Went to the ferry. All well. Mr. Lang's two wagons met at the ferry. Making rum. Mr. Abraham Belton here; says I must push William Watts to trial on Wednesday next. A fine south wind. I making ready for fishing. Messrs. Russell and Jenkins here.

TUESDAY, February 25, 1800.

The Messrs. Russell and Jenkins here; they went away. I to see my seine flat. The chain is gone. Mr. Thomas Whitaker at the flat with me. Called at the ferry; three carts there. Received two dollars; came home. Hanging seine. Brown took a summons to Jameson against William Watts. I granted the summons yesterday evening. The boys quit going to school; they brought their books home. Two Russell and Jenkins came in the evening. Covered goards late.

WEDNESDAY, February 26, 1800.

Rose early. Russell and Jenkins went to Mr. Whitaker's for a plat of this plantation and got it. Granted a summons for William Miller against William Watts for a sum under three pounds. Mr. Jameson here and took the summons. Got my seine hung. Luke White got one gallon whiskey, 4-8. Henry Braswell wanted to sue_____to a settlement. Jameson called, with Jake Killingsworth. He wanted to see oats. Jameson says William Watts is in custody of the sheriff. I sent Mr. Belton word. He came, got a sheriff's warrant and 11 pounds. Davis carried it on two horses, I heard them say. Mr. Belton left the horses in my care, one a gray, one a bay. Major Whitaker and family here. Mrs. Mary Whitaker and son, John Whitaker, all dead. Messrs. Russell and Jenkins here. Dr. Knox came late. Ned brought $3 from the ferry.

THURSDAY, February 27, 1800.

Rose after light. Dr. Knox paid me $15 for a Reffield gun I sold him a year ago. I paid Mr. —— $60, $15 in part of last year's land rent. He receipted on the back of the obligation. He and Jenkins went for home. Dr. Knox and Brown went to Camden. Brown bought of Mrs. White a gown pattern or six yards calico at 4-8 per yard. Russell directed me to tell Mr. Samuel Mathis to proceed against Major Whitaker and take a receipt for whatever cash I paid him, but wished Mr. Mathis to wait, or that I would pay him out of next year's rent. Sarah received a letter from John O'Quin, and she and Mrs. Fortenberry went to Major Whitaker's again.

FRIDAY, February 28, 1800.

Rose early. Dr. Knox came late last night pretty happy, for I don't think I ever saw him so groggy. I pity him. I gave him a receipt for $14 he gave me to give Dr. J. Alexander, and an order on William Watts for $2, and an order on David Jameson for a proved account on Samuel Duke for _____, and if I get the two accounts I am to pay Dr. Alexander for Dr. Knox four pounds. I had the wagon yoked and drew forage for the cattle. Dr. Knox bid good-bye. The river down at Isaac Ross' place. Very cold, sleet, and snow and rain. I. Ross, S. Martin and R. Richardson all went to fish, but had no seine. Got the flat in the river, Bill and Stephen bringing it up to the landing. Brown and I came home cold indeed. Now ends the month of February, 1800.

SATURDAY, March 1, 1800.

Rose early. Let George Watts have one quart of whiskey and gave him six shillings for six pounds of deer skins. He went to Camden, I went to William Watts'. I shot a crow there. Watts said he would pay Dr. Knox's account if he said it was that sum before Mr. Aaron Taylor. I went to Dan's shop. Beach was there. Says some —— has tried to defame his character, and says he has as good a character as any man whatever. Says he bought twenty head of good horses when he left the State of Kentucky. I came home. Saw three deer. Ned came and brought $6. River rising, he says. Good weather.

SUNDAY, March 2, 1800.

Fine, warm morning. A wild goose set with our geese. I and the old lady rode to the ferry. Brasey there. I and the old lady came home. I went back to the ferry. Nixon there. Says William Owens died last night; says if D. Brown, Esq., don't pay, he will, for the use of the ferry. A man there says the Spradlings owe $72 of him. I bought one pair of stockings at a dollar. I did not want to buy the stockings. Came home. I am tending the ferry; Ned gone after a flat. Dined on plenty and good. Put the rye in the barn.

MONDAY, March 3, 1800.

Rose early. Rainy. Jackey went to Mr. John Burn's for a plow. He took the cart and brought it. Brown, Jude and Bill plowing. Stephen and Charley thrashing corn and drawing wood for the stills. Brown made two plow bridles. Ishemeal and Bryant went to mill; got meal. Ned brought $4 from the ferry.

TUESDAY, March 4, 1800.

Drawing light wood and wood. Two plows at work. Bill cutting wood. Mr. Willie M. Long came and I paid him $40, L. 9.6. He said he would give an agreement credit for that sum, and I sent with him for 100 pounds thin bar iron. Now for my brother's. Sarah and children, with Meriam Laseter with ours, called at Jameson's, got out against S. Duke's for 28 of Dr. Knox'. Met Sarah O'Quin and overtook Mariam Laseter. Went to D. Holladay's. He won't take the cattle, but offered to throw up for them. Had a chat with Hill, came home and I went to my brother's. They all a-bed. Had supper. He came from Charleston today to bed.

SATURDAY, March 8, 1800.

I never saw such a day, for the ground is covered with sleet and the trees and fences all hung with icicles. All idle. William Wilson came on Dan's horse. Got two shad for himself and four for Dan Williams; no pay. Dr. I. Alexander sent order by Mr. Bracey's negro Stephen, and got eight shads at 7d; no pay. Mr. Solomon Roberts brought Brown a saddle and got one quart of whiskey for 1-2 and borrowed a bottle and got four shads and borrowed a wallet, the shad at 7d each. I heard the cannon firing in Camden—general muster.

SATURDAY, March 15, 1800.

Rose early. Now for fishing. T. H. Davis, three negroes, Jackey and I catched six and a good trout. Dr. I. A. came, got four soft shad, paid 2-4. Ned gave me $3. Now for to kill a deer. T. H. Davis, Brown, Jackey and myself. I saw fifteen or sixteen deer. Killed a fine doe. Brown one, Holland two. Came home late. Mr. George Watts got one gallon whiskey. He drank a pint here.

SATURDAY, March 29, 1800.

Rained hard this night past. Rose; took five hands to fish. Made two hauls; did not catch one. Ned gave me $2 and I and all came home. West wind. Now for planting corn and cotton, with four hands. Stephen threshing rye and Bill helping him. Rain and rainbow. Brown, Holland and I to kill a deer. I saw two, Brown saw six, Holland saw none, as they say. I called by Mrs. Whitaker's.

SUNDAY, March 30, 1800.

I a-bed late. Rainy night and wet morning. Jacky came from Mr. Holliday's; says the cattle are all up but two yearlings. Holland and Brown went to Daniel Williams' for a hound, but she was over the creek. River rising. Old Berry came in the evening; says a great many things, and lies, I expect. Ned gave me one dollar.

TUESDAY, April 1, 1800.

Did not rise early. My brother, sister and three children here. My brother to Camden before breakfast; Brown to Mr. Crimm's, for him to meet at Camden tomorrow to bargain. Two plows at work. Making fence for pasture. I and my brother went to Esq. Whitaker's. saw his Bell Grade stud. Then to Major Whitaker's. Tead with his wife, brother and wife Came home after dark. I am in poor hope of getting money of Rutledge.

SUNDAY, April 6, 1800.

Rose early; had breakfast. Sarah, Bryant, Ben and the old lady went to see John O'Quin. I took a nap. Mrs. Doty came; wants a cow and calf. She went away. I went to the ferry. Berry whipped Whitaker's black. Wadkins and Bathney there. Mrs. Perkins and Mrs. Brown came over in a chair, and S. Kershaw with them. The old lady and Sarah came back. Ate dinner. Sarah, Ben and Bryant went down to Mr. O'Quin's place.

SATURDAY, April 12, 1800.

Rose after day. Richard Richardson here. Made T. Whitaker title for his land, he says. I wrote Ely, D. Sims and S. Ross. R. Richardson paid what he owed me and bought a shirt of S. C. O'Quin. Paid 11 1-2, and Sarah gave me the money and a $20 bill of R. Richardson, and David Jameson came, and it rained. They dined, bid good-bye and went. Daniel Harkins came and got summons for William Watt's undertwo. Jameson showed me a summons for trial next Friday for four or five. Rain. John O'Quin came, and Brown and he went to kill a deer, but in vain. Sent Bill with the cart for the seine to the ferry, and he brought it and Ned sent $2 by Bill. Richard Richardson set off for the Mississippi today. Has $500 with him.

SUNDAY, April 13, 1800.

This is Easter Sunday. Is a cold, blasty southwest wind. Sarah and daughter, Ben, Joney and George all set off for home. I and the old lady went up to my old Avenue, bid good-bye and came home. Saw Mr. Coleman and T. Dinkins going to Columbia. Brown, Jackey and Holland gone to Mr. Cook's. He is going to Mississippi. Old Berry came and dined. The boys came and got old Richardson's gun. Ned came and brought $4 from the ferry. Cold southwest wind and rainbow.

MONDAY, April 21, 1800.

I arose early and went to Thomas Whitaker, Esq. He in the field. I then went to Camden, bought one red, blue and white Bafalone handkerchief. paid 7c. Got of Fisher 40c. Agreed to give B. Perkins $10 to go to Columbia out of Daniel Brown's money. Came over the river with Champeson, Dickens, Brevard, Black and Mr. Lang. I went again to Mr. K. W. and got a dollar to get B. Didgeon's plat for land secured before 1770, and got $25 and 12 pounds in three bills. Came away. Gave a receipt to Mr. T. Whitaker. Ned gave me $6 and I sent him 3.6. Now getting ready for Columbia. I and the old lady rode to the ferry. Met the post rider, and I went to D. Holliday's. It rained, and I tarried there.

TUESDAY, April 22, 1800.

Now early. I am at Holliday's and set off for Columbia and got to L. Dinkins'; all at breakfast. Went in the office; got account of plats for Mr. Thomas Whitaker of Ben Pideon— 100 acres. Paid 5. Gave me account of what was to be registered by him from Hamison. Got Charles Goodman to plead to my case, and I gave him three pounds, and I gave the beloved Ben Perkins, Esq., two pounds, and I had better have thrown it in the river. Bought a paper; paid 7 pence. Got the account of what was to be entered in the office. Dined, and got one pint brandy at 1-2 and punch 3-6.

WEDNESDAY, April 23, 1800.

Rose early. At Columbia. They drank wine plenty last night, and now drinking. Sling Goodwin advised me to sell Rutledge negroes and so did Perkins; but my advice to all friends, and particular to my children, is to have little to do with liars, as they are all for getting money at any rate whatever. Called at J. Smith's; drank cold water. Called at D. Holliday's; drank ditto. Got home. Mrs. Mary Whitaker there. I have given her the plat. She gave me three pence in full. Planting corn. Two Martin boys called. Ned came; gave me $2 from the ferry.

THURSDAY, April 24, 1800.

I a-bed till late. Hands planting corn. I wrote Simms at Peedee and went to the ferry. Left the letter with Ned and he gave me $2, and I came home. The bees have swarmed and the old lady gave them to Brown. Jameson came and got two quarts of whisky, and says if D. Burns brings a dollar here on Saturday next to pay myself out of the dollar for the whiskey. Clear weather.

SUNDAY, April 27, 1800.

Now for a day's rest. The old lady has gone a piece with my grandson, Brown, as he has gone home. I walked to the ferry. John Burns came over the river and Messrs. D. Brown and C. Polk came in a chair. Had a little chat, then went to Camden. D. Burns walked on to West-erkania house; chatted. He went for home. I came home, dined, and then I and the old lady walked in the field, saw the wheat, rye and oats. Want rain. Brown and Holland Davis went up to my old place. They say they saw eight or ten deer. Major Whitaker and lady came, as little Willie was stung by ants, and he was so ill did not know what to do, but is better; and so ended the day. Rain in the evening.

MONDAY, April 28, 1800.

Rose early. Plowed up the lot and had it sowed with hemp. Had a fine rain last night, cool for the season. I went to Camden. Was at D. Brown's; then he and I to Fisher's. Had cherry bounce. Then to Mr. Champeson's. There was an order of four judges at Columbia. Brown swears he be d— if ever my judgment will be shaken, and tells Mr. Bynehan to hold the negroes until full and ample security be given or sell them on Monday next. I called at Mr. P— and paid L. 10.10.0 on Mr. Brisban's account. Came home. Ned gave me $2.

WEDNESDAY, April 30, 1800.

Rose early. Cloudy. Planting highland corn. This is my son Brown's birthday, and the

18th year of his age. Now for a good dinner. Had plenty. Bees swarming, and gave them to John I. W. Ross. Fine south breezes. This is the last day of April, 1800.

SATURDAY, May 10, 1800.

The coldest morning I ever saw so late in May, for I had a good fire made. Cold northwest wind, with heavy black clouds. I am for Camden. Went to Daniel Brown's, Esq.; he at breakfast. Then to Benj. Carter's for three pair shoes. He owes for unloading three boat-loads of tan bark at my landing. He told me to go to the house and ask any of the negroes for the shoes, but the shoes for Ned were too little and good for nothing. Mr. John Chestnut, I am told, has set off northward to spend the sickly season. I to Daniel Brown's again, then I went with him to Clark's office; was there a good while. Carpenter came and went with him. Bought one pound of tea, paid 14. Bought twelve yards of Orzenburg at 1; no pay. Got a five-dollar bill and gave $4.50 to Messrs. Smith and Carpenter. Went to D. Brown's again, had cherry bounce and came to the ferry. Ned gave me $1.50. Came home. This is Thomas Holland Davis' birthday. Had a good dinner—roast shoat, pie, etc. Conrad Keller came; got one gallon whiskey. Paid Mr. James Berry's account for his making Brown's bootlegs smaller. Mare Fannie is about to die. Sent by Martin to Mr. D. Brown a quarter of pork, lettuce and three shads. Sarah O'Quin and children came; all well. Received a letter from Elizabeth at Peedee.

THURSDAY, May 15, 1800.

Rose early. Stephen took the sheep to D. Brown's, and bought four leather collars. I sent leather to North Carolina with David Roundsavall last winter. I and Brown a-cow hunting. Came home. Mr. Samuel Kelly here. Captain John Kershaw came and I gave him $14.00, he to give credit on agreement between his sister, Mrs. Rebecca Brown, about the ferry. Had a little whiskey. George Harbeson came, to know if his judgment was good on any property the defendant owned at the time obtained. I said yes. Kelly had breakfast and dinner with us. Warm weather. Major Whitaker and family came and took tea.

WEDNESDAY, May 21, 1800.

Rose early. Wrote Mr. Cudworth and J. I. Pringle, Esq. Gave Brown directions and wrote Mr. D. Brown a line. Gave Brown $30 to be handed Mr. Pringle as a fee to give his opinion on the case pending between me and Evert Rutledge, he to be back on Sunday next if nothing happens. I and the old lady walked down to the small grain, soon ready to harvest. Mr. John Burns came. Wants paper money. I had none of paper money and very little of any whatever. Brown, my son, set off for Charleston. I wish I had never begun this law at all. Perkins was the cause of it from first to last, and he wants a case and fees. I had better never have seen him.

FRIDAY, May 23, 1800

I rose early. William Martin came, got 2 1-2 bushels of corn for Mr. J. Burns. Stephen went to John Burns' to work today and tomorrow. I think of my son, Isaac Arthur Brown Ross, often, and wish I had him at home; the law might go to Guinea. I and the old lady went a-cow hunting. I shot a fine buck and the dog catched him, all bloody. I and lady went to see if we could find him; no. Called by the ferry; $2 cash. Came home. Bryant and Ben came.

SUNDAY, May 25, 1800.

Did not rest well, for I thought of Brown many times. I at home all day. Ikey and Holland went to my old sand hill place and came home and dined, and then they went to meet Brown. I and the old lady walked in the field, came home and Mr. Samuel Rutledge came, and a little after dark Brown, Ikey and Holland came, and he brought me a letter from Mr. D. Brown he had of Mr. J. R. Pringle, in Charleston. Ned sent me $1.50 from the ferry.

SATURDAY, June 7, 1800.

I went to Dan's shop, but settled with Mr. Geo. Watts first. He was here all night. I gave him 15.2, and he gave me a receipt. I paid Bryant and Ben's schooling. I went to the shop; worked hard at the chair. Abram Beach worked a little. Burns did not come in, as he promised. Quit about 1 o'clock, and Dan came home with me. I and the boys went a-driving. I saw three deer and killed one. Came home. My brother had been here, and his daughter, Jane Brown and Margaret Allison were here. Dined on plenty. Sent Croker yesterday to Camden, and got of D. Brown, Esq., fifteen pounds of coffee and thirty-nine pounds of sugar, and of Dr. Isaac Alexander I got forty-five pounds of flour. Dan Williams called late and dined and got one bottle of whiskey. He don't like Burns to get quite all his notes I have. Very warm weather.

WEDNESDAY, June 18, 1800.

Rose early. Sent Croker to Camden with 1-4 mutton to be exchanged for beef. This is my harvest day, if any. Appears for a rain. Croker got no beef and Dr. Isaac Alexander got the

1-2 mutton. Robert Kelly, Major Grant, D. Martin, D. Williams and Mr. A. Belton's two sons all came to reap, but rain in the morning and rain in the afternoon came. Major Whitaker and family came and dined on plenty. Major Whitaker says he saw Dick Berry yesterday, and he said he saw Ely, Knox and others at French Broad river when going with the Moores.

SUNDAY, June 22, 1800.

Dan rose early, and went away before we all were up. I wrote my daughter Sarah a long letter, and wish her to come and see us. Miss Mariam Lassiter is now off for home; I expect she is getting ready. She is to carry the letter to Sally and the two grandsons to come up directly. I and the old lady rode a piece in the chair with her. The old lady got sick and we came home. Two sons, Holland and John Belton, all to the old sand hill. A very hard gust of wind, rain and thunder. Mr. Richard Kirkland came with a letter to S. C. O'Quin, from Daughter Simms, I expect, and says he was with Ely all night and half a day. They are all well. Am sorry they did not write me.

SUNDAY, June 29, 1800.

Had breakfast, then the three boys went with Sarah O'Quin to Mr. Daniel O'Quin's. They dined there. They say old Berry was here all day and went away. My brother's Tobey came with a packet of letters, two for S. C. O'Quin, one for A. H. Davis, one for Brown, one for John I. Ross, three for me, one from Ely, one from Simms and one from my brother.

MONDAY, October 27, 1800.

Rose early. Fixed the outside gate and Brasey's tents. Stephen drawing rails to fence in my own ground to sow rye. Martin's boys came late to deliver me corn. Mr. Thomas Whitaker came and borrowed $100. Amy Grant here. Mr. Whitaker returned the $100. He did not get his bargain. Wm. Martin delivered thirty-five barrels, each lacking nine pints of two bushels. Ned came with a letter from Mathew Harris and $3 from the ferry.

FRIDAY, October 31, 1800.

I had a bad night's rest. Rain in the night. Ray is making a board fence. Martin's boys came. Want me to take the wet corn, that has paid higher since last week. I believe I said, if they had no other corn I would take it, as there was plenty in the fields besides. I would not take it. They said Green was going away with the wagon on Saturday. I said they had better fulfill our bargain before they engaged another, but that to be neighborly I will hire them my wagon to draw the corn. But he went away. Very cloudy weather. Stephen and Bill sitting a tan kiln. I went to Camden to Mr. Daniel Brown's Stark's and Rembert's. Brown told me to come over next week and then perhaps he could tell me something better. I went to Carpenter's store, bought half a pound of tea and two pounds of coffee, and paid. Got three pair women's shoes; no pay. Got two papers. Called at Messrs. McRae & Canty's store, chatted a-while, then to Belton's store. Bought one bottle of British oil, five pounds sugar; paid. Went to Mr. Cipel's store; bought 8 1-2 yards duckcloth at 7d 1-2 for all; 3 1-2 for tacks; paid. Bought 20 yards Ozernburg; no pay. Came to the ferry, received $2, and then home.

WEDNESDAY, November 5, 1800.

In the night late past Major Whitaker's Argile came for Bateman's Drops and got them. Jones here by light. Jacob came with a message that Tildy was dying. I and the old lady walked up to the Major. Thomas Whitaker, Esq., there and put blisters on the child. I came home. Jones got a quart of whisky. I, Jones, Brown and Ikey a-cattle hunting; found Jones' cattle near Albert's. Went to Widow Turner's; bought her heifer, $4.50, Jones' $3.50. Drove them home. Late saw a deer. Mrs. Dotey sent me $3.50, Ned $4.

THURSDAY, November 13, 1800.

John Belton, two boys and I went early to Mr. Samuel Kelley's, then we all in the swamp. John Belton killed a doe, I killed a turkey, Brown two turkeys and Kelley one. Found the cow, drove her home, and I paid Samuel Kelley $13 for the cow. Dined on beef and pork. Paid or lent Samuel Russell $15, John O'Quin and family went home. I went to the ferry. Ned paid me $5; the best day for many.

WEDNESDAY, December 3, 1800.

I heard a great noise at the ferry in the night. I and the old lady rode in the chair to Thos. Whitaker's child sick. Came home. Louis Grant and wife came; Gideon Lowry, James Grant, Arnold Grimes, Bineer Jones and Mrs. Dunbar. They made up, Grant to pay his cost and Ben. Majors his cost. All went away. Jennie Grant mad. Old Mr. Harbeson here. Mrs. Turner bought a total of $7.50, half cash, a bedstead 4.8, wool at 7c; to bring in chickens, ducks and geese. Vinein Jones here, and I gave him two quarts brandy.

THURSDAY, December 25, 1800.

Now at my brother's. Five or six Mathas came last night. They were groggy, and shot several shots. Drue and Gum Harris came, and we went a-bear hunting. I shot a turkey, Brown killed a buck. Had a hard hunt in the cane. Drue Harris dined and we all went fox hunting and to Widow Jacobs'. There were about twenty mulattos dancing, and all very lively. Then my brother, Brown, John and I all for a fox. Had a long hunt, killed one opossum and got back by 3 o'clock.

WEDNESDAY, May 20, 1801.

Rose early. Hayes here yet. He is to have thirty or forty sheep next Monday. He breakfasted and went away. Mr. John Kershaw came. Brown, I and George Crimm went to near Dan's shop and began a survey on a pine corner for me and run to a black gum station mark and a chain cross Twenty-five Mile Creek to a pine station and then to a holly station, etc. Came back to pine corner and then ran to Twenty-five Mile Creek to an oak station, then across to willow station one chain, then home. Dined on plenty. John Kershaw, Esq., went home. Ned gave mn $4 from the ferry.

THURSDAY, May 21, 1801.

I hear the sound of cannons, which was abolished from our land. Cold weather. I hope it won't be injurious to the crop of wheat. This is general muster day, I hear, but no captain, as my son was never warned nor I. Am of opinion there is not a man warned in this company. I went to Dan's shop; no man there. Put the chair wheels on the drag and brought them home and had them well painted with pitch. Joah Lawrence here for a cow, but got none. Dry weather.

AT GREEN SPRINGS PLANTATION FOR THE SUMMER MONTHS.

TUESDAY, June 16, 1801.

Rose early. Now for moving. Loaded the wagon and was on the seat when old Tommy mare fell against me and had almost killed me. The old lady and the wagon and three hands to Green Springs. John went for doctor. I knew nothing of his coming till in the house. Dr. Debour bled me a-bed. Rain plenty somewhere. No ploughing today.

WEDNESDAY, June 17, 1801.

They rose early. Brown got $1.50 of Dennis Burns; says he will pay the balance tomorrow. I rode in the chair, but it hurt me much. Brown brought from the ferry $5. Now at Green Spring place. Can't get up or down without help.

THURSDAY, June 18, 1801.

Moving to Green Springs. Now at Green Springs. I was worse last night than ever. The old lady went to the plantation early; had a load of pots, etc., brought up. O'Quin's George came with a letter to Sarah and for peas. Brown went to the plantation and gave O'Quin's George about three pecks of peas, and then he went to Camden for cash of Dennis Burns, but got none He brought an ounce of camphor; came home late.

FRIDAY, June 19, 1801.

The old lady and Brown set off, I asleep, to the plantation for geese, and Slephen to bring a load of plank and sundries. They came with the geese and the wagon. Fixing a chair shade and gate. John a-ploughing, three hands hoeing cotton. John O'Quin came and brought his grandmother and granny. John Burns called; says my wagon body is done. I am now sending Stephen in a wagon for it to take it to Dan's shop. Rain. Stephen came from taking my little wagon from Brown's shop and has singletrees, and Stephen took the wagon home.

SATURDAY, June 20, 1801.

I had a bad night, and am but poorly today. Jude went to mill, got a bag of corn at Mr. Carpenter's. I expect John, Brown and Johnny O'Quin have all gone a-hunting, and they expect to meet John Belton. They had a long hunt, but came with a fine, large buck. John Isaac Ross killed him, and Mr. John Belton says he shot a large rattlesnake. They all dined. John Belten took a hindquarter and went home. Dan Williams got a piece of venison.

TUESDAY, June 23, 1801.

I did not rise today, for I can't sleep with my broken ribs. Brown took two shovel plows to the shop to be sharpened and get them done before breakfast. Two boys gone to plowing. The old lady rode in the chair with little Abigail to the plantation. Dan Williams called. Wants me to give him corn of Carpenter. I said no. He went away. Jean Arnold brought some spun cotton and wants 1 1-2 pounds of cotton to spin. I could not tell her and she went home. The old lady came from the plantation. A little rain. Major Whitaker and family came to see us. Gave his children some raisins. Brown to Camden and bought one gallon of rum from Clark; paid $2 for it. Hot and dry.

WEDNESDAY, June 24, 1801.

I did not sleep for my broken rib; awake all night, and is bad today. Stephen fixing a shad for the cook at the door of the smoke-house and fixing a shade for the chair. Appearance of rain, but none. Jean Arnold, Harbeson came; had one-half a pound of picked cotton. Sent her and Daniel for ploughs to plantation. Came up with ploughs before dark. Bill sick.

SATURDAY, June 27, 1801.

Boys rose early and set off to meet John O'Quin and to kill a deer. Bryant came soon with a yearling doe that he says his uncle Brown killed near Gum Swamp. Had the chair yoked, I and the old lady and little Abby in the chair. Daniel driving geese to plantation. I turned and came back. Andrew Sdradling brought me a newspaper from Camden. I received a line from Rudolph and Murray, an order from Jonas Arrne for $18 and credit by Ma. White for $7.50. The latter I know nothing about, the former due the last of August. A man by the name of William Congers left a note for Mr. James Stewart, 18 3-4 dollars, to be used for———. Charley gone with two plows for shop. Warm, dry weather. I granted a summons for Congers against James Stewart. John O'Quin, Brown and Jackey came with two more deer, one the fattest deer I ever saw for the season. Had venison a-plenty. Sent Major Whitaker some venison and plenty for the negroes at the plantation. Sarah sick. I wrote Ely, Simms and my brother two letters and sent Daniel to the post-office.

FRIDAY, August 14, 1801.

Brown, poor fellow, came home at nearly day. Says Emerson's flat is on the hard ground, and getting there he lost one finger and had two more ruined, and a negro served as bad. Rose early, although I was very weary. Set off for the river. Old Mr. Lott and many others, with nine wagons, waiting for the flat. I put nine spikes in three planks of the flat that was off at one end and the middle. Gave a dollar for a man to go to Camden for whiskey, but he never came back with the whiskey. They all wanted to cross the ferry free. I told Ned to let three wagons pass for 3.6, but I said afterwards that they didn't come with the whiskey I would not pay them only 2.4 each. Ned gave me $8.50. Boys and I hunted home. Brown sick and I tired. Got breakfast about 2 o'clock. Brown could not eat in the night. A. Sanpher came for fire and water. Said a man in the wagon was very ill. Gave four Hooper's pills. He got better and called late. His brother said he was near dead.

MONDAY, August 24, and TUESDAY, August 25, 1801.

Rose after sunrise. Mr. Samuel Perry came. Says he saw my steer some time ago. We had a very long hunt. Found the steer on the head of Bridge Creek. He ran away with my mare. We went to Spring's and dined on plenty. Went home, and I was very near worn out. But we are to go in the morning, by light. Fixing my tent, and the full moon and the weather fine. Rose very early; breakfasted by light. A big man named Brown borrowed my inkstand to number the people. I and Perry went a-steer hunting. I saw a fine big buck and a small deer. Had a long hunt. Found the steer. I shot at him and blooded him. Followed him about a mile, he running at Rice Creek. Lost him. We went to Mrs. Daugherty's, got Jack and dog, and had a long hunt, but no steer. Went to camp. Stephen came with two horses for I and the old lady, as Cousin Enoch Morgan and wife and three children are to ride. We left Stephen and Hayes to keep camp. I, the old lady and Daniel for home. Left word with Stephen for Mr. Perry to get the steer and pay himself out of the cash. Major Benson came today with many others. We got home at dark.

TUESDAY, August 27, 1801.

We all rose early and had a dram of good rum. Old G. Lott called at the gate. Wanted to sell wheat, but I had bought. We all set off for to kill a deer, but none to be seen. Ned sent $2 from the ferry. I and old lady, Mrs. John Morgan, daughter and son all rode in chair, I behind on chair. The old lady mad. All went to Major Whitaker's. I walked to plantation, had the cattle turned out. Saw two steers I had of John Burns. Crop and under sloap dark brindle, one heifer, and one white heifer, crop and slit in each ear and a heart in face. Walked back to Major Whitaker's, dined on a good dinner, and we all came away. The Major sent a quarter of pork.

Came home. John went to Camden with Enoch Morgan and son Ross. John bought one gallon rum, paid $2. Bought one and a half yards girth webb, paid. Bought one pound of 20 nails at Carpenter's, no pay. John left a tea kettle at Mr. Langley's and brought an iron kettle, $3.00 in all. Brown brought $1.50 more from the ferry.

FRIDAY, August 28, 1801.

This morning the old lady rose before day and got breakfast. Cousin Enoch Morgan and all bid good-bye and left for home. Boys went to the ferry with them and brought $1 from the ferry. I and the old lady for the Springs; got there before night. The boys killed a fox. I hear my brother and all came from the Warm Springs, all glad and all well. We all supped together on plenty. Sent Stephen and Daniel home for provisions for my horse and to come back to-morrow.

SATURDAY, August 29, 1891.

Rose before day. Went to my brother's. They set off for home. I took the numbers, and there were 123 whites and blacks. Duke came with beef, and I got 2.4. Mr. Jesse Perry came, and I paid him 7 for copper-ware. Mrs. Lassiter and Woodward breakfasted and Mrs. Woodward dined with us. Mr. Charles Meeks brought six head of collards. Daniel came from home; all well. Brought food for horses. I bathed, and am sure it is good.

TUESDAY, September 1, 1801.

I am not well, and a-bed till late. Colonel Hutchison came and went for home. I am resting all day. Many coming and going to and from the springs. Mrs. Braswell came. I bought four lbs cheese, paid 1.2. Solomon Niper came and brought me 100 pounds of flour. I paid him $6.50, and 1.9 for bran. I bathed twice today.

WEDNESDAY, September 2, 1801.

Rose early. Colonel Hutchison and Major Watts came and drank plenty. My two sons, Brown and John, came and we went driving. I saw a faun. Anton Perry and son John all had a shot at a deer. They say no meat to be had. Jesse Perry says the beef was 75 pounds. The boy went off for home. I had a little look for deer, but saw none. I gave Mrs. Jones a dollar for four little cheeses. A hard thunder, wind and rain. Jack Perry's son came with a tub and three pounds of powder to pay for beef.

THURSDAY, September 3, 1801.

I arose by light. Had a look for deer, but saw none. The Colonel took the census of the people. Says 87 is all that are here. Now for Norris's. Saw deers going to camp. I told Norris I wanted him to go with me to Esquire Jones', but he is to pay today or tomorrow. I hunted to camp, but saw no deer. Samuel Dukes brought a buck to camp; sold it soon. I got 1.9 worth.

FRIDAY, September 4, 1801.

I was sick all night and am poorly. Jesse Perry came with the butter, and I paid him for a tub. He had a sick child with him. I a-bed nearly all day. Norris and wife came to camp. He paid me $16, in full. He owed it a long time. Goodman Hughes and five daughters in camp. A round-about today. The Kelleys here. I bathed today. Late came my son John and Isaac Conger—came, supped and went home.

SATURDAY, September 5, 1801.

Now we are for home today, as my brother, John Conger, is at our house. Stephen came. I went, and Mr. High paid 3.6 and a feed of corn for my horse. Now breaking up my house and loading my wagon. Set off for home. Called by Andrew Spradlings'. Got watermelons and brought four home. Got there before dark. Brother John and sons there and all well. Good-bye to the springs this year.

SUNDAY, September 6, 1801.

We are all silent till breakfast. Had a hot dram. Brother John gave me an account of his land being under execution. Had watermelons plenty, and I find they hurt me. I find there was $4 received from the ferry since I went to the springs. A very warm day indeed. Now for rest.

THURSDAY, September 10, 1801.

Now at home resting till after breakfast, then we got ready and all walked to the planta-tion—my Brother Conger and son, Isaac Conger, Brown, John and myself. Got horses and went driving. Brown saw two bucks rise and run. Brother Conger shot, but no venison. Had a long hunt. John shot at a turkey, but no meat yet, and so home. Big Jude took horses to the plantation. I wrote letters to my friends in the North and Northwest till late, then there was singing done by I. C., S. C. O'Q. and others.

FRIDAY, September 11, 1801.

Rose early. Signed a title to 177 acres in South Carolina to John Conger, only warranting it from me and my heirs. Bought a grey horse of John Conger for $60; paid $45 down. Brown with his uncle to Major Whitaker and borrowed $15 more, and I gave them to him at the ferry. I gave a due bill for $15, to be paid in ....days. John and Brown went to Camden, or set off to go there. I and the old lady went with them to the ferry, and called by the plantation for Daniel, as he has been away three days. Ned gave $5 from the ferry. Brown gave his Cousin Conger a coat in Carpenter's store. John bought a little history, 1.2—no pay. Had a watermelon from the plantation. Major Whitaker and lady here.

VISIT TO TENNESSEE AND NORTH CAROLINA.

WEDNESDAY, October 1, 1800.

At home. Sue had a daughter born, I find when I came home. Now at D. Simms' and E. K. Ross'. Settled up all accounts, and it cost me $12 coming. Ely and mine, etc.

THURSDAY, October 2, 1800.

I am now a-resting at Simms'. Dr. Knox and I chatted. D. Simms went to the mill; no meal. I am poorly, so far from home.

FRIDAY, October 3, 1800.

I slept with Dr. Knox. We had a great deal of chat. Didn't rise early, being sick. Had breakfast. All of us went to John Hill's to dine. I had a good dinner. I talked to Mrs. Hill till she was almost willing to go down the river French Broad. She will give her answer tomorrow. Bought eight pounds bar iron at Newport. Came back to the children's.

SATURDAY, October 4, 1800.

Now for getting my horses and to drive with Dr. Knox. The boys and the horses to the smith's shop; no smith at work. Dined on a good dinner. Rain. I wanted Mrs. Sarah Hill to give a final answer. She said she would see me tomorrow. Dr. Knox wrote to his father. We called at Major Fines' store house. Got apples and brandy. Mrs. Killingsworth with me.

MONDAY, October 6, 1800.

Rose early. Frost plenty. D. Simms divided band leather with Colonel Gray's brother-in-law. Ely and Brown took the horses to Mr. Forrey, a blacksmith, and got them shod, all but Clovis. I walked to Newport; bought six yards of flannel for my grand-children. Paid 7d for Jackey's jew's harp at Herald's store. Gave $2 for shoeing horses. Now I am out $20 since I left home. We are asked to a husking bee. Snow in the mountains. I hear the boys say they saw it.

TUESDAY, October 7, 1800.

We all rose early. I breakfasted with Samuel Ross. The boys ran too free. Mr. Jonathan Fine here; brought a cutter of brandy. D. Simms is making shoes for my old lady. I say they are too small. Boys gone for a beef; brought and killed it. Blunt Gray came to get shoes made. Dr. Knox and John Hill's family came. Dined on a very good dinner. Went to the bowling ball alley. Bid good-bye.

WEDNESDAY, October 8, 1800.

I gave my grandson, A. B. Ross Simms, a dollar to buy him a sow, gave Abigail a dollar to pay for the whiskey, and gave Mary Abigail a dollar. Now for Camden. All came to Dr. Knox's. Ely and Brown went to get a shoe on Clevis at Mr. Forbey's. We parted with wet eyes. Gave Brown $3 to buy a dog. Ikey and I came on to Colonel Croox's. Fed; paid 11d Ely and Brown came with the dog Stormer;· gave $5. They say a man by the name of Hendricks and Garrett, one with only one foot, came on over the Point Rocks mountains. It exceeds everything for badness. Oh, how I pity my daughter Betsy passing over it—came though the shut-in up to Nelson's. He is a hoggish kind of a man. Bad lodging.

THURSDAY, October 9, 1800.

Rose early. Paid $2 for express. Ely with us up to Long Ferry. I drank at the Warm Springs. Paid ferriage, 1.9. Bid Ely good-bye with wet eyes. Now on to Barnell's station. Paid for feed 10 1-2. Sol. Berry and Killingsworth with us. Fed at Clack; paid 10 1-2. On to Oster's, on Swannoa, 35 miles.

FRIDAY, October 10, 1800.

Rose early. Paid 2.4. Overtook Mr. Coleman, a clover man from Petersburg, Ga. Came on to Murry's; got horses fed two quarts chestnuts, and I breakfasted. One-half pint whiskey; paid 3.6. On to Widow Meems'; fed. Coleman paid to Simons, drunken rascal. Rain, hail and very hard thunder near Merritt's mill. Now I got to Capt. Joseph Terry's.

SATURDAY, October 11, 1800.

Paid at Mr. Terry's 3.6. Parted with Mr. Coleman at Lunsford's store. On to J. Wilson's; fed; paid 7d. Then on to Fowler's; fed; paid 3 1-3d Then on to Isaac Crood. This day fifty-six miles. This day many people at Mr. Crood's. Had supper for Brown and myself; our own tea.

SUNDAY, October 12, 1800.

Rose long before day. Six or seven men played cards and swore all night. Paid 2.4. On to Bodo's, got horses fed and pint of whiskey; paid 1.9. On to Mr. Phillips'; got fodder and breakfast; paid 2.11. This is twenty-eight miles today. Called on Mr. Coggs for a spear. Away on to Reese Evans'; got corn; paid 7d. On to Broad river to Ben's.

MONDAY, October 13, 1800.

Lodged at the Widow Beems', or stayed all night. Set off early. Paid 1.9. Now it is twenty-four miles to Waynesboro. Met on the way Thomas Gladney. He fed the dogs. Got cider and apples, paid 1.9. Ikey and dog in the borrough behaved very bad indeed. Then on to Coleman's; fed; paid 1-2—the dearest of any place yet. Then on till we were glad at home. Dan Williams met us in the field; came back and supped.

SECOND VISIT TO NORTH CAROLINA.

WEDNESDAY, September 30, 1801.

Set off for North Carolina. I arose before day. My brother and two sons, wife and Stephen all on to Camden. I bought of Carpenter a hat for Stephen, 4.8; bought four pounds cheese, 4.8. We parted above Logtown. On to Craton's—on to Usher's. Gave Brown a $500 note, to go to Mr. Thomas Whitaker and get a receipt. Fine weather.

THURSDAY, October 1, 1901.

Now at Usher's. Paid 2.4. On to Drake's. Breakfasted, paid 7d, fed. On to Stewart's for corn; paid 7d. On to Powers', Anderson's Creek.

FRIDAY, October 2, 1801.

At Powell's, paid 2.4. On to Paul Surrs'. On to Sasaman's, fed and tead, paid 1.9. On to Cabel's. Susana patrolled as to mill. I gave Susana Cabel 1-2. Cloudy and rainy.

SATURDAY, October 3, 1801.

At Fralack's mill. Rain in the night. Lay a-bed late. Had fodder and corn. Paid 1.2. Then to Chambers' ferry. Paid 1.9. Then I heard Brother Wm. Moore was to Cumberland. I went to Brother John Conger's. Hardy was there. I and Brother John went to Mr. Henry Braney's. I took a gun to be stopped. It is to be done next Friday.

SUNDAY, October 4, 1801.

After breakfast William Moores, Isaac Conger and Phoebe Hendly with us, all set off for Brother Ben Davis'. Oh, the distress! And nothing to eat!

MONDAY, October 5, 1801.

Rose and got horses shod. I sent and got cider. They drank freely. They went hunting. Children sick with the whooping cough. Horses fared well.

TUESDAY, October 6, 1801.

Got breakfast, then all to Mr. Cox's. Paid $2 for yesterday's work. Brother Ben and Holland with us. Bid good-bye to Brother John Conger. Had a good hunt; no meat.

WEDNESDAY, October 7, 1801.

Now at Brother John Conger's. I went hunting, but no deer for me. I and Brother John Conger to Mr. Henry Druner's. My gun was done; the cost is $6.50. Coming home, set in with Mr. Sandy Froohook. He lent me his gun. Mr. Douen there hound hunting. The hounds ran very long and late.

THURSDAY, October 8, 1801.

I a-bed late. Had a morning dram of rum. Had rockfish for breakfast. They are getting corn in. Brother John gone for a gun and hand to hunt. They sent for cider to Cox's; got plenty. Went hunting. I killed a doe; saw five more. Shot two times. Mr. Frohock with us. Had a good dinner and plenty.

FRIDAY, October 9, 1801.

I rose early. I and Brother John Conger went to Mr. Bruner's. I bought a horn, paid $1.25; got my gun, paid $6.50 Then a-hunting. I shot at a deer, but did not kill it. Shot at another, and blooded it much. Brother Ben, son and daughter came late.

SATURDAY, October 10, 1801.

Rose early. A bad time crying. I gave Cousin Joshua Conger's two sons a dollar each. All on to Leonard Smith's—good-bye. Isaac Conger with us to Ned Chambers'. Had breakfast and brandy. Chambers filled a bottle with brandy. My sister, Elizabeth Moores, departed this life on the last of April. Paid ferriage, 2.4. On to Salsbury. Got horses fed at Brin's, paid 2.9. Bought of Mr. Richard Trotter two sifters, paid 16.4. Bought loaf sugar, paid 12; a tumbler and two nutmegs and silk mits, paid 9.4. Then on with Wm. Moores and Isaac Conger to David Roundsval's.

SUNDAY, October 11, 1801.

Now at B. Roundsval's a-bed. Isaac Conger and Wm. Moores came from D. Anton's. They bid good-bye and went back after breakfast. Went to D. Anton's. There was Granny Sally. Aunt Sally named Sally White, ditto Black. David Roundsval and wife came late. They bid good-bye.

MONDAY, October 12, 1801.

Rose early. Had to kiss plenty. Came away. D. Anton went with us a piece. Bid good-bye. On to Phifer's. Had horses fed, paid 1.10. On to E. Morgan's.

TUESDAY, October 13, 1801.

Had a good breakfast. Before day bid good-bye. On to Drake's. Fed; paid 9 1-2d. Then on to Usher's. Had our tea and bought one bushel of corn.

WEDNESDAY, October 14, 1801.

At Usher's had an early set-off. Paid 3.6. On to near Fork's road. Had a good breakfast. On to Thomas Creighton's. There Lenear horse very sick. Had dinner and good water. On to Captain Wm. Nettle's. There our Lenear horse died at dark, and we jogged on till late and got home. Ned gave me $3. Brown said he had received $20.25 of Ned, that $23.25 from ferry.

THURSDAY, October 15, 1801.

I a-bed till late. Luke White here with interrogatories, and I gave him 4.8 for a side of leather I had some time ago. Cloudy and rainy weather. I and the boys went to the plantation. Hands picking out cotton. I found a bee tree. John shot at a buck, he says. Hunted home.

FRIDAY, Octocer 16, 1801.

I a-bed till late, then I and the old lady rode in the chair to the plantation. Brown went to Mr. Rudolph's store. Bought one gallon rum, 9.4, one pound gunpowder, four pounds of cork at 1.8, one ounce thread at 1.9. I took Stephen and Charley and cut trees pretty good. Sent some to Mrs. Thomas Whitaker. I and the old lady took some to Mrs. Whitaker. Dined there on plenty. Miss Nancy Brown there. Pretty clever. I brought the rum, coffee and honey home. Brown got $5 of Ned at the ferry. The boys killed three squirrel, they said. Brown said Mr. Rudolph sent the wagon and horse home with twenty-five bushels of wheat bran. He wrote me I could have 100 bushels.

MAP OF CAMDEN AND ADJACENT COUNTRY.

A close study of the map shown on the opposite page, will acquaint the reader with the various points of interest associated with our early ancestors. The old roads which they traveled, the names of the streams, etc., were closely related to them in their every-day life.

The following letter from the Surveyor of Kershaw County describes the map, which was drawn by him from records found in the Camden Court House:

Camden, S. C., Sept. 28, 1911.

Mrs. W. R. Wright, Jackson, Miss.:

Dear Madam—I am sending herewith a map of Camden and the Wateree section. The dates on the map indicate location and the date of original grants. Some grants to A. B. Ross are recorded in the office of the Secretary of State as follows:

Book R R R,   page 256—190 acres, in 1774.
Book R R R R, page 203—300 acres, in 1786.
Book R No. 5, page 212— 63 acres, in 1797.
Book S No. 5, page 457—420 acres, in 1799.

The Daniel Brown tract was under a grant of 1780, containing 640 acres, situated on the Great Road at the Flat Rock, and was sold by Daniel Brown to Thomas Creighton in 1793.

The Isaac Ross place, on Twenty-five Mile Creek, was granted to him in 1765, and was sold by Isaac Ross, Jr., in 1812, to Joseph Breward, book D, page 77, Kershaw County records. Isaac Ross also owned a plantation near this, joining the land of Major Whitaker and John Rutledge, book B, page 281. I have a plat of the Ross plantation, that is, the Sand Hill place, as it was known in 1844.

The place owned by Isaac Ross, the younger, on the old road west of Isaac Ross, senior, was in the sand hills and contained 250 acres. He also owned a place on the west side of the Wateree river, bounded on the east by the river, and was about three and one-half miles west of Camden. This place contained 310 acres, and the original grant was made to Isaac Ross, the younger, in 1790. In the year 1793 he sold 90 acres out of this river tract to Roger Cibson.

The three grants that were made to A. B. Ross north of Jumping Gully, dated 1774, 1797, 1799, respectively, were sold about the year 1800 to Major Whitaker.

You will note there were two roads from Camden to Rocky Mount, but the road on the west side of the river was the one known as the Rocky Mount road.

The ferry I have put down as Peay's ferry may not have been known by that name prior to 1800, but from the oldest information I can get it was called Peay's ferry.

I found on record several plats of these old plantations.

John O'Quinn, in 1806, sold 1,400 acres to Daniel Horton. John O'Quinn also owned other lands on Lynch's Creek.

Mary Brown, widow of Daniel Brown, also owned property and was a resident of Camden as late as 1810.

I trust this map will be satisfactory. Any further information wanted will be cheerfully given.   Yours very respectfully,

R. W. MITCHAM.

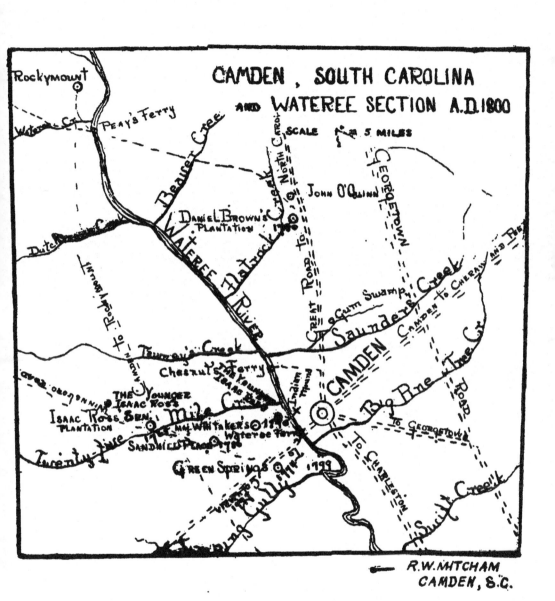

CAMDEN , SOUTH CAROLINA
AND WATEREE SECTION A.D.1800
SCALE 5 MILES

R.W. MITCHAM
CAMDEN, S.C.

CHAPTER II.

CAPTAIN ISAAC ROSS, SECOND SON AND YOUNGEST CHILD OF ISAAC ROSS AND JEAN BROWN.

Capt. Isaac Ross was born January 5, 1700. He was the youngest child of Isaac Ross and Jean Brown Ross. When he was a small child his father died and his mother, after remaining a widow only a few years, married Aaron Alexander. John Brown Alexander, the child of this last union, being near the age of his half brother Isaac, was his companion during the years of childhood. Soon the death of their mother occurred, followed by the second marriage of Aaron Alexander. It was possibly about this time that Isaac Ross, as a young man, went to seek his fortune further down the Wateree river in what was then Orangeburg County, S. C.

In Orangeburg County there had already settled "Stony Hill" Isaac Ross, who in 1765 was "Collector" for Saxa-Gotha township and the fork between the Congaree and Wateree rivers and adjacent places. (Statistics of S. C., Vol. IV., page 217.) This part of Orangeburg County afterward became Richland and Kershaw Counties. During the years 1864-65 the position of Assessor for this same district was held by Andrew Allison. It was possibly here that Capt. Isaac Ross first met Jane Allison, the daughter of Andrew and Margaret Allison, whom he afterward married. *The Allisons were from the north of Ireland, and were wealthy land owners there, but were forced to flee to America in pursuit of religious freedom.

By reference to the map showing the lands owned by the Ross family in South Carolina, we see that the lands of Isaac Ross and his brothers were near enough for frequent visits. The diary of A. R. Ross mentions these visits.

Issac Ross was captain of a company under Sumpter during the Revolution. He was a member of the Continental Association in 1770, and was a staunch supporter of the Whig party and one of the party leaders.

Capt. Ross did not come to Mississippi with the large company of relatives who came in 1805, but remained in South Carolina till 1808, which was two years after the death of the brother, A. B. Ross. He settled at Prospect Hill, in Jef-

---

That Andrew Allison left Ireland with his family on account of religious persecution is proved by the fact that there now hangs in the old Prospect Hill house a portrait of Mary (Polly) Allison Belton with an open Bible in her hand to show the religious freedom she enjoyed in this new country. This Mary Allison was a sister of Jane Allison, who married Captain Isaac Ross. Mary Allison married John Belton, who came from Queens County, Ireland. His sister married Samuel Kelly and lived in West Wateree, north of Camden, S. C. The Beltons were Quakers. (Historic Camden) ferson County, Mississippi, where he built the first Prospect Hill house, which was burned by his slaves after his death. (See account of burning.) He patented a large tract of land, as shown by the records in Claiborne County. The following is taken from the book of original entries: 97 acres, 626 acres, 138, 158, 158, 159, 159, 626, 553, 535, 158 acres were patented between the time that he came to Mississippi and 1832. Captain Ross owned hundreds of slaves and amassed a large fortune. The view from the Prospect Hill house is one of grandeur. The house is built on a high hill surrounded by sloping meadows and hills of great size. It was over this expanse that Captain Ross could survey his abundant harvests, for as far as the eye could reach his possessions lay.

In the Prospect Hill house there now hang portraits of Captain Ross and his wife, Jane Allison Ross. The portrait of Captain Ross has suffered the loss of one eye; the expression of the face, however, is not much changed thereby, and shows a man of middle age, with blue eyes, dark hair and florid complexion, a man one would judge possessed a strong will and steadfastness of purpose. He was of a deeply religious nature. †This and other causes led to the liberation of his slaves.

After the death of his daughter, Captain Ross was so overcome with grief, he left the familiar scenes and went with his nephew, John B. Conger, through the then wild Indian country to Mobile, where he took a boat for the North. He visited Princeton, where his son was at school, but not wishing to burden him with grief, he did not even call on him. On his return, by way of the West, he was taken ill in the Indian country and was found by some hunters, who took care of him and sent word to his family. His son-in-law, John I. W. Ross, and nephew, John B. Conger, went to his assistance and brought him home, where he died Jan. 19th, 1836. His grave at Prospect Hill is marked by one of the finest private monuments in Mississippi. His desire was that a simple box tomb should be put over his grave; however, the American Colonization Society did not accede to his wish, and bought the monument with money from the estate of Captain Ross.

The will of Captain Isaac Ross (see Claiborne's History of Mississippi) was a very unusual one, but for the great length of the document, it would have been given here. He provided that his slaves be given freedom, sent to Liberia and an institution of learning established there. There were special bequests of slaves, etc., but the heirs were not pleased because the wealth that was theirs by inheritance should be disposed of in this way.

The American Colonization Society was given charge of the slaves, but while awaiting the decision of the courts they were held by *Judge Isaac Ross Wade, executor of the will and a grandson of Captain Ross. The courts decided, after a long litigation conducted by the ablest lawyers in the State, that a man can dispose of his slaves while living or by will, and can manumit them after transporting them to another country. (Freeman's Chancery Report, 587.) Claiborne states (History of Mississippi, page 391): "Thus we have an authoritative

---

†His great-granddaughter, Mrs. Roger Killingsworth, writes: "Captain Ross was a religious enthusiast, and his wife had very kindly views about freeing his slaves. She died in 1829 and Captain Ross lived till 1836, under the influence of the powerful churchman and minister: Zebulon Butler, of Port Gibson."

*The correspondence between Judge Wade and the American Colonization Society relative to the litigation is contained in the publications of the Mississippi Historical Society, Vol. IX. There will also be found letters from the slaves after they reached Africa.

exposition of the laws of Mississippi on the subject of slaves and the power of enfranchisement, and but for the mischievous interference and menace of Northern politicians and clergymen in pursuit of pelf and power, many slaves, after this decision, would have been transported to Africa from the South."

The estate of Captain Ross was valued at about $100,000.00, besides about 200 negroes. Very little of this wealth was left to his descendants. The lawyers' fees consumed a large amount and the American Colonization Society was entrusted with the balance. Judge Wade, who was the executor and a grandson, received only his per cent for managing and settling the estate. He bought the Prospect Hill house and some lands with the amount he received, and in that way the old home has remained in the family. Prospect Hill is now the property of Mr. Battaille Wade, a great grandson of Captain Ross. He keeps the old cemetery in perfect condition, and is ever ready with a hearty welcome to show the points of interest to visitors to the home.

CAPTAIN ISAAC ROSS, son of Isaac Ross and Jean Brown Ross, was b in North Carolina, Jan. 5, 1765, and d in Mississippi in 1836. He m Jane Allison, dau. of Andrew and Margaret Allison. She was b in 1765 and d in 1829. Issue:

*MARTHA B. ROSS, b in South Carolina in 1793, d in Miss. at Franklin Springs on July 30, 1818.

MARGARET ALLISON ROSS, b in South Carolina in 1787, d at Prospect Hill, Miss., Sept. 14, 1836. M first to Dr. Archer. No issue.

M second to Senator Thos. B. Reed. He d in Ky. en route to Washington to take his seat in the U. S. Senate.

†ARTHUR ALLISON ROSS, b in Kershaw County, S. C., in 1800 (see diary), d in Mississippi, July 22, 1834. M Octavia Van Dorn in 1832. She afterwards m Dr. Vance M. Sullivan. No issue.

ISAAC ROSS, b in Kershaw County, S. C., in 1796, d in Mississippi Nov. 5, 1832. M Sarah Elliot. Issue:

Isaac Allison Ross, m Eugenia Calhoun. No issue.

JANE BROWN ROSS, b in South Carolina in 1786, d at Oak Hill, Jefferson County, Miss., May 19, 1851. M first Daniel Wade, son of George Wade. (For issue, see Wade line.) M second her first cousin, John I. W. Ross 2nd. (For issue, see John I. W. Ross line.)

From the above we see that Capt. Isaac Ross has no descendants that bear his name, while through his daughter, Jane Brown, his descendants are numerous; but the Ross name today is extinct except through his brother, Arthur Brown Ross.

I believe Dr. Ker was one of the selected executors of Capt. Ross' will, and I think he selected the monument and Mr. Coulter wrote the inscription. I have often heard my father say his grandfather had told him repeatedly he wanted a plain box tomb, like others he had erected in the graveyard. I can't imagine why his wishes were not carried out, as some of the slaves had to be sold to help pay for the splendid monument, that being one of the unexpected drains on the estate along with the lawyers' fees.

*She was engaged to be married to a Mr. Fry, a young lawyer, who was killed in a duel with Mr. Beasley, who was afterwards killed in the massacre of Fort Mimms, he being in command of the fort, but being without caution, let the Indians surprise him, and was killed at the gate in a vain effort to shut it. Martha Ross afterwards became engaged to a Mr. Rankin, a lawyer, but he died of yellow fever at Wild Woods Springs, in Franklin County, while waiting on my mother, whose health was very poor at that time and who also had yellow fever. (Manuscript of John I. W. Ross, Jr. written Oct. 22, 1888.)

†My uncle, Mr. Allison Ross, married Miss Octavia Van Dorn, daughter of Peter A. Van Dorn, of Port Gibson, and sister of General Earl Van Dorn, of the Confederate States of America, in 1832. He died at White Hall, near Brandywine Springs. Octavia Van Dorn afterwards married Dr. Vance M. Sullivan, I think in 1839. Dr. Sullivan was killed in 1849 by Dr. Moorehead, of Grand Gulf. Judge Peter Aaron Van Dorn, father of Mrs. Ross, was a lawyer by profession, and held the office of Probate Judge in Claiborne County for many years. His wife was a Miss Caffery, blood kin to Donaldson Caffery, of Louisiana, also to General Andrew Jackson's wife and to Gov. John Sevier's wife, of Tennessee. Judge Van Dorn always claimed to be descended from the Prince of Orange. (Judge Isaac R. Wade's account of his uncle, Allison Ross.)

CAPTAIN ISAAC ROSS' COMPANY, REVOLUTIONARY WAR.

Roll of Capt. Isaac Ross' Troop in the Second Regiment, State Dragoons, commanded by Colonel Charles Myddelton, April 18th, 1782. (Taken from Documents relating to the History of South Carolina during the Revolutionary War, by Salley.)

Isaac Ross, Captain; Wm. Akins, First Lieutenant; Thos. Jackson, Second Lieutenant; John Whitaker, Second Lieutenant; James Bell, Sergeant; George Campbell, Sergeant; James Hayes, Sergeant; Lodwk. Hill, Sergeant; Samuel Hatfield, Sergeant; Wm. Pullan, Sergeant; Jesse Bisto, Sergeant.

Privates—Britton Jones, John White, Wm. Wilkinson, John Wilkinson, Thomas Wilkinson, James Miss. Kelly, Thomas Watts, Shadr. Jenkins, John Hardgrove, John Flint, John Tapley, Thomas Gregory, Wm. Boyce, John Boyders, Kinchin Pennington, John Ezell, Samuel McWaters, Daniel Brannan, Aorm Miller, Stephen Sweatman, Burrel Cooke, John Carter, Martin Martin, John Jackson, Leo. Duggin, John Griffin, Mason Harris, Griffin Harris, Edward Harris, David Pone, Jonathon Outson, William Ware, Matt Laws, Andrew Howser, Adam Carick, John Dash, Martin Kitts, John Gapam, William Pawling, William McGrew, Hance Kerr, Alex. Grehan, Thos. Yates, Henry James, Henry Smith, Jesse Henson, William Murchey, James Winingham, Martin Irish, James Sellers, Richard Boyd.

(Signed)   ISAAC ROSS, Captain.

Sworn before me this 18th April, 1682.   RICHARD BROWN,
                                     J. P., Camden District.

BURNING OF THE WADE RESIDENCE.

Newellton, La., Aug. 31, 1902.

Editor Revielle:

In your issue of the 28th inst. there appears a letter headed, "Burning of Judge Wade's Residence," and signed "Reader." This brings to the memory scenes, incidents and events of the past, connected with the old home, Prospect Hill, around which sacred spot many million memories cling, so often related to us by my father, Isaac Ross Wade.

This great tragedy in his life was a favorite theme, when we were gathered around the fireside, especially in the declining years of his life.

It would require many columns of your valuable space to write a complete history of all the circumstances and events leading up to the burning of the Prospect Hill house and subsequent events connected therewith, so I will content myself by giving "Reader" a few facts related to the burning of the house and the cause thereof.

At 1 a. m. April 15, 1825, this house was set on fire by some of the Prospect Hill slaves, and completely destroyed in a very short time. My father, mother, and three small children, Isaac, Dunbar and Catherine, now Mrs. Newell, of this place, my mother's niece, Miss Mary Girault, of Grenada, my father's sister, Mrs. Adelaide Wade Richardson, and three small children, Martha, about 6 years old, Cabell and Addie, now of our town, his brother, Dr. Walter Wade, and his business partner, Mr. Bailey (his given name I do not remember) were asleep in the house at the time. The coffee for supper on the night of the fire had been drugged by the cook, and the older members of the family drank of it except Dr. Wade and Miss Girault. The house was a large, two-story house, and Dr. Wade, Mr. Bailey, Mrs. Richardson and children and Miss Girault occupied the rooms in the second story. Dr. Wade was the first occupant to discover the fire, and immediately set to work to arouse the family. This he found a difficult task, and probably would not have succeeded, owing to the size of the house, had it not been for the assistance of one of my father's own slaves and body servant Major, who was faithful, and rendered every assistance in his power.

They all succeeoed in escaping save Martha Richardson. Miss Girault, who occupied the room with Mrs. Richardson, did not drink the drugged coffee, so was active and alert, and discovered that Mrs. Richardson was dazed and stupefied. She took charge of the two youngest children, Cabell and Addie, and requested Mrs. Richardson to bring down Martha, the oldest. She did not discover that Mrs. Richardson, in her dazed condition, had left the child in bed until they all met in the yard. When this was discovered, Mrs. Richardson, terror stricken, frantically appealed for assistance and volunteers to go with her to the second floor to save her child. To this appeal a brave and faithful slave, Thomas, responded, and started with her up the steps to

The Second "PROSPECT HILL" House
Page 70

Residence of CABEL RICHARDSON, Page 168

This ancient pile of brick and morter is to persons who delight in research into the past, quite a notable house having been built during the Spanish occupation of this section of Mississippi and is nearly, in fact, quite a century and a quarter old.

MRS. JANE BROWN ROSS WADE ROSS
Page 71

the second story, but before ascending very far the steps sank under them into the fire. They were both rescued from the flames, but badly burnt. Mrs. Richardson was pulled out by her hair. The next morning the child's heart was found and buried in the family grave-yard, only a few paces from the spot where she met her tragic death.

When the family were aroused, my father went to the outer doors to open them that all might escape. The front door was hard to open, but after some efforts he succeeded in throwing it open, but did not go out. Mrs. Ross immediately ran through the door, and to her horror there stood Esau, one of the estate's slaves, with a drawn ax, evidently with the purpose of killing my father, whom he expected to pass out that door, as it was nearest his room. Miss Girault bounded out unexpectedly, and seeing Esau with a drawn ax, quickly remarked, "Uncle Esau, are you here to help us by cutting away the door?" He replied, "Yes sum, Mistus," and walked off. My father afterwards learned that Esau had been standing at the front door some time, and did not make any effort to arouse them or knock the door in, and that he had gone there for the purpose of killing my father should he escape from the flames. Esau, with six or seven other leaders, were burnt or hung. This was all done by the neighbors, without my father's knowledge, as he was then with his mother, Mrs. Ross, at Oak Hill, two miles away. He did not know of the vengeance taken upon these guilty slaves until it was reported to him by his overseer, Peter Stampley, a man well known to many of our older citizens, and who probably has descendants in your county now. It would not be amiss for me to state that my father held Mr. Stampley in the highest esteem, as he proved himself loyal, brave and efficient in this hour of trouble and sorrow.

If any of these slaves were ever sent to Louisiana and sold, then brought back and executed, as related by "Reader," my father never knew of it, for he never spoke of the circumstance. I do not think it could have happened without his knowledge. He related that two young negro men ran off when the leaders were executed, but were caught in the woods just north of the spot where the Glen shanty house now stands, and were hung on the spot and left there. He found their bodies afterwards by the buzzards hovering over them.

Will give, as briefly as possible, the causes that led up to these tragedies. Captain Isaac Ross, my father's maternal grandfather, was a gallant Revolutionary soldier, who commanded a company under the gallant Sumpter in many a hard campaign against the British Regulars and Tories until he fell, sorely wounded, at the battle of the Cowpens. He came to Mississippi from South Carolina in the early years of the last century (I cannot recall the exact date.) He settled at Prospect Hill, Jefferson County, where he accumulated a large fortune for the times, and died in January, 1836, leaving an estate valued at about a quarter of a million dollars. Captain Ross gave his slaves, about 250 in number, their freedom, and his entire estate for their benefit; some $10,000 he gave his granddaughter, Mrs. Adelaide Richardson. Judge John B. Coleman, Mr. Daniel Vertner, my father and two others I cannot recall, were executors. Under the provisions of the will my father, his grandson and namesake, was to have active control of his estate, at a fixed salary per annum, and, of course, he was allowed under the law a commission on the gross receipts of the estate.

It was not expected that the heirs of Captain Ross would quietly permit this valuable estate to pass out of their possession. So the will was contested to the bitter end, and after twelve years of litigation the highest court of the State sustained the validity of the will. During this long litigation and strife the slaves became restless, as they knew their old master had given them their freedom and his estate. They could not understand the delays of the law, and became insanely imbued that my father, the acting executor, was responsible for the delay, and if they could get rid of him their longing to be delivered from bondage and transported to their native shores would be quickly consummated. This alone was the cause of the burning of the house and the attempted murder of my father and family. Some time after these tragedies some of the more intelligent slaves admitted this fact to my father, and told him that they had been told by some white people that if they could get rid of my father the provisions of the will would be carried out; that they would be sent to Liberia at an early date. My father was charitable enough to believe that, if any white person had told these things, they did not mean it in the literal sense, but to get rid of him by the process of law as acting executor.

At the conclusion of this celebrated case, which I believe is reported in the sixth Howard report, these slaves were sent to Liberia in 1849—I think 210 in all. My father received letters from them as late as 1861, on the eve of the great civil war, but we have never heard of them since. The last letters received discussed their pitiable condition; they applied for help, and begged to have him send them some farming and mechanical instruments and clothing, especially calico dresses. Their colonization in Liberia, judging from their letters, was an absolute failure.

On closing the succession of Captain Ross's estate several hundred thousand dollars passed through his hands, during these twelve years of litigation, on which he received a commission. For this claim he was given the Prospect Hill plantation, then consisting of about 500 acres.

On the very spot where the old house was burned he completed the present house in May, 1854, and continued to live there until his death, January 10, 1891. This old home is now owned and occupied by my brother, B. H. Wade.

Respectfully,

THOMAS MAGRUDER WADE.

JURAVI ET ADJURAVI

Moores

CHAPTER III

MOORES FAMILY.

The Moores family are found on both sides of the Tweed, but that they are of Scottish origin is shown by the St. Andrews cross on the coat of arms. A the present time members of the family are found holding honored positions in England, Scotland, Canada and the United States.

Not having absolute proof of the beginning of the family in this country, two views are held by different branches of the family. One legend is that the Moores, together with the McDonalds, Alexanders and other Scotch-Irish Presbyterians, found a refuge in North Carolina in 1745. The three named families intermarried and lived in the same part of the State, which would naturally give rise to the belief that they came to this country about the same time.

In 1638 one Edward Moores settled in Newbury, Mass., and his descendants are scattered through New England and New Jersey. In Hanna's Scotch-Irish in America, mention is made of certain Presbyterians who, on account of Puritan intolerance, were driven out of Massachusetts and into New Hampshire, Pennsylvania, Maryland, Virginia, New Jersey and finally into North Carolina, where they established colonies. As no names are given of the families, we may suppose that the Moores were among the number. Certain it is that one Moores family, of which *J. H. Moores, of Lansing, Mich., is a member, settled in New Jersey.

We know that our Conger family went to North Carolina from New Jersey, as many others did, and found congenial surroundings in what is now Rowan, Mecklenberg and Davidson Counties. This gives rise to the belief that the parents of Henry and William Moores were of the New Jersey family, and through the New Jersey family possibly of the Massachusetts family, of which Edward Moores was the progenitor.

---

*"My great-grandfather's name was Robert Moores, and he lived at Hanover Neck, Morris County, N. J. He had one brother, Phineas, and his wife's name was Kesiah Pierson. In a talk I once had with Mr. Chas. Moores, who lives in New Orleans, he told me that his great-grandfather also went from New Jersey to South Carolina." (From J. H. Moores.)

WILLIAM MOORES AND ELIZABETH ROSS MOORES.

ELIZABETH ROSS MOORES, oldest child of Isaac Ross and Jean Brown Ross, was born in North Carolina, April 15, 1844. In the list of her father's children, after her name you will notice "no records" follows it, which may be misleading, as we have records of the descendants of one of her children, Josiah.

Arthur Brown Ross was two years the junior of his sister Elizabeth, and must have been her playmate, but in after years, his removal to South Carolina and her marriage to William Moores in North Carolina necessarily caused a separation, which was a grief to both.

Arthur Brown.Ross mentions the death of his sister, Elizabeth Moores, in his diary, and this simple statement, together with the record of her birth, is all that we have to chronicle of her.

William Moores, who was a brother of Henry Moores, lived near Salisbury, N. C., in the same neighborhood with the Congers, Morgans and Rounsavals. The date of birth, marriage and death of William Moores has not been found in the various family records. but he is mentioned in A. B. Ross's diary, and was living in 1800.

It is a regrettable fact that complete records of the descendants of William Moores and his wife, Elizabeth Ross Moores, have not been furnished by their descendants, but enough has been given to form a nucleus for further research, and will therefore be of interest to the families connected with them.

Record of only one child of this union is here given. Further information will be appreciated.

WILLIAM MOORES married ELIZABETH ROSS, dau of Isaac and Jean Brown Ross. She was b Ap. 15, 1844, d April, 1800. Issue:
- JOSIAH MOORES, m Eliza Givens. He d Aug. 18, 1858. Issue:
    - Rev. William Moores, b in South Carolina, Jan. 26, 1806, d Jan. 31, 1891, m Juliet Susan Hardwick. No issue. M 2nd on Jan. 21, 1844, to Eldridge Maria Greening. Issue:
        - Twelve children, eleven of whom lived to maturity. Of the number—
        - Fanny G. Moores, m Mr. Kerns, address 916 Gratton St., Los, Angeles, Cal.
        - Mrs. J. O. Butler, address 1314 Orange St., same city.
        - *Charles William Moores, b in Nevada County, Ark., Dec. 9, 1847, m 1st to Susan Kansas Steel, on Sept. 25, 1872? She d Jan. 19, 1879. Issue:
            - Henry Moore, b Jan. 26, 1874, d Jan. 24, 1875.
            - †Eldredge Morton Moores, b May 3, 1876, m Oct. 15, 1902, to Annie Caroline McKusick. Issue:
                - E. M. Moores, Jr., b July 6, 1904.
                - Sophronia Steel Moores, b June 6, 1908.
                - Julia Ann Moores, b Nov. 3, 1909.

---

*C. W. Moores joined Company E, Bird's Battalion, Nov. 20th, 1863, Trans. Miss. Dept. Served as a courier until parolled at Camden, Ark., May 20 or 22, 1865. Served with Generals Holmes Price and Kirby Smith. He delivered a dispatch to General Price telling him of Banks' defeat at Pleasant Hill, La. The dispatch had come by relays; the last was fourteen miles.

†Eldredge Morton Moores served in the Spanish-American war, going to the Philippines in the First Cal. Regiment of Volunteers. He enlisted May 8, 1898, as a private, returning in August, 1899, as first corporal.

Wade Greening Moores, b Jan. 19, 1878.
‡Charles William Moores, m 2nd to Mary Brue, on Dec. 30, 1880. Issue:

    Son, b and d Feb. 20, 1882.

    Elizabeth Marie Moores, b Nov. 23, 1883, m Sept. 3, 1907, to Emile John Brizzolara. Issue:

        Mary Angela Brizzolara, b July 8, 1909.

        Emile John Brizzolara, Jr., b May 5, 1911.

    Louise Trumbull Moores, b Oct. 12, 1886, d Aug. 29, 1890.

    Charles Bruce Moores, b Nov. 6, 1889.

‡Mrs. Charles W. Moores is deeply interested in the history of her husband's family, and to her, credit is due for the above records.

CHAPTER IV.

HENRY MOORES AND JEAN ROSS MOORES.

JEAN ROSS was born in North Carolina, Jan. 28, 1757. She was the seventh child of Isaac Ross and Jean Brown Ross. Of her personality we know nothing, but from the noble characteristics and high mental attainments of her posterity, we would judge that she and her husband were possessed of brilliant minds and sterling qualities.

HENRY MOORES was a brother of William Moores, who married the eldest sister of Jean Ross, and must have been his junior. This is the first marriage of two of the descendants of Isaac Ross and Jean Brown Ross, into one family, but as our history proceeds, this custom will be found very frequently followed.

Henry Moores and Jean Ross Moores lived in North Carolina and South Carolina, and later we find them in Kentucky and their descendants in Tennessee.

Henry Moores' service in the Revolutionary War is recorded in the War Department at Washington. The following will establish eligibility in the D. A. R. and S. A. R. for their descendants:

WAR DEPARTMENT,
The Adjuant General's Office,
Washington, D. C., October 4, 1911.

Mrs. William R. Wright, 406 North State Street, Jackson, Mississippi:

The records show that one Henry Moore served in the Revolutionary War as a lieutenant in Captain William Mitchell's Company of the South Carolina Continental Regiment of Artillery, commanded by Barnard Beekman, Esq. His name appears on a company pay roll of that organization covering the period from November 1, 1779, to January 1, 1780, with remark showing that he served during that period and that he was allowed $266 2-3 for pay and subsistence for the time stated. His name also appears as that of a lieutenant of artillery in a receipt book for certificates of South Carolina Line with remark showing that he received a certificate March 1, 1785, for $1,889 29-30, in balance of pay and commutation due him. Heitman's Historical Register of Officers of the Continental Army, an unofficial publication entitled to credit, shows that Henry Moore, of South Carolina, was appointed a lieutenant of South Carolina Artillery 25th October, 1778, and was taken prisoner at Charleston, May 12, 1780.

F. C. AINSWORTH,
Attorney General.

Hon. Merrill Moores, who holds a high position in the Society of Colonial Wars, in Indiana, has made a study of the early history of the Moores family. Therefore the following letter from him will be of interest to the members of the Moores-Ross family:

Mrs. William R. Wright, 406 North State Street, Jackson, Mississippi:

DEAR MRS. WRIGHT—Some time ago I wrote to my first cousin, Charles Bruce Moores, of Portland, Oregon, asking for certain data which you required for your book, and heard from him that the Revolutionary grant which I had discovered in Frankfort, Kentucky, of lands in Madison County, Kentucky, near Richmond, was undoubtedly made to our great-grandfather, Henry Moores. The date of the grant is 1788, and it covered 1,000 acres in Madison County, where my grandfather, Isaac R. Moores, was born.

This grant is recorded as to Henry Moore, and I suppose it was made out in that way because his name appeared as Henry Moore on some Revolutionary muster roll. The grant is by Governor Richard Henry Lee, and was undoubtedly for services rendered to the State of Virginia. It could easily be so, for I searched the rosters of New York Colonial troops in vain for another great-grandfather who served as a captain on General Philip Schuyler's staff, to discover at last the fact that this ancestor, whose name was Robert Anderson, held a captain's commission from New Jersey, and had been transferred for service to the New York troops.

I thank you very greatly for the report of the Adjutant General in relation to Henry Moore, which I have copied and which I return herewith.

Wishing you success, I am,
Very truly yours,
MERRILL MOORES.

HENRY MOORES, b Oct. 7, 1744 (old style), m JEAN ROSS, dau of Isaac and Jean Brown Ross. She was b Jan. 28, 1757. Issue, twelve children, as follows:

CHARLES MOORES,	Born April 4, 1776
JOHN MOORES,	Born October 9, 1777.
ELIZABETH MOORES,	Born July 9, 1779
MARY MOORES,	Born November 15, 1782
PHOEBE MOORES,	Born January 11, 1785
ISABELLE MOORES,	Born February 4, 1787
SARAH MOORES,	Born September 22, 1788
MARGARET MOORES,	Born December 25, 1790
HENRY MOORES,	Born Thursday, August 13, 1793
ISAAC MOORES,	Born Monday, March 21, 1796
JANE BROWN MOORES,	Born February 25, 1800
WILSON ALEXANDER MOORES,	Born September 28, 1802

FIRST CHILD OF HENRY AND JEAN MOORES.

May 4th, 1841 or 49, Texas.

My Dear Son:

Yours of the 16th of March came duly to hand. It was truly gratifying to me to hear that you were enjoying the blessings of health and as comfortably situated as you say you are, considering you are from home. I received your letter when in South Carolina, but, having a good deal of business to attend to, I neglected to answer it. When I arrived home I found my business had been sorely neglected and very much behind, therefore I had not time to write—it was not because I have forgotten you or intended to do so. Before I proceed further with your affairs, I will tell you some of my own doings. I found my domestic affairs were not going on as I wished without a woman about the house (there was always a rowdy about me), and last but not least in consideration, I was so lonely I could not stand it any longer, so when I was in South Carolina I took unto myself a wife. I married your mother's cousin, Mrs. Rabb, one whom she dearly loved. I have had no cause, nor do I fear any, to repent taking such a step. She is so kind to me and treats me with so much affection. I hope you will be satisfied, too, as it adds to my comfort and happiness in my declining days. I did not think there was so much pleasure for me as I have realized in the last three months. There is a change in aspect of house, kitchen, garden and in my own appearance. My health is fine and my spirits are remarkably so. Taking all these things in consideration, I know you cannot blame or censure me for marrying.

. To add to our own satisfaction, we had to come along with us J. W. Moores' family. He is a brother to James and married a cousin of yours, granddaughter of my present wife. They are going to settle over in Cass, about one and a half miles from Reuben's. After we had been home about a week, David and some of the others that came with us took measles and were pretty sick. It has been a great hindrance to me about my crop. Nearly all on my place, from old Dan down to the youngest, had to have it. I lost two or my best negroes, Zilp and Mary. They died down at my Sulphur place. The rest are getting well, though, now. My crop looks pretty well, considering the chance we have had.

You wished me to tell you all about my affairs; I think I have done so minutely. You are getting anxious to hear my advice concerning your arrangements. I am now, as I have ever been, dear son, willing to advise and assist yon in any way I am able or capable of doing. You can learn from those who are capable of judging which of the two colleges is best for you, and you have my hearty consent to go to the one you choose, and I wish to have you improve every moment of your time, as you are advancing rapidly to manhood. You are old enough now to appreciate a good education, and as far as I am concerned I don't intend you shall have it in your power to reflect on me in after life for any deficiency on your part. But I want, you as a compensation, to study hard and make a smart man. You are capable, I am sure, and you shall nqt lack for the best opportunities. I think it a good plan to keep an account of your expenses. In looking them over monthly you may afterward find a dime or more spent that might have been laid out to more advantage. I will be pleased to see you study economy, too, as it will be essential for your future interests, at least. I will like, also, to see an account of your expenses every two months, as you propose.

Your cousin, Betsy—as all my children call my wife—and Elizabeth Moores send their love to you. I shall be glad to hear from you often.

In conclusion, my dear boy, keep out of bad company; be as much afraid of the gaming table and wine bottle as you would of the most loathsome pestilence. Receive this advice kindly, my absent son, from your affected father,   CHARLES MOORES.

(Written to William H. H. Moores by his father, Charles Moores, just before the former left for Princeton.)

CHARLES MOORES, b in Fairfield District, South Carolina, April 4, 1776, d March 6, 1850. He married 1st Mary Harrison, dau of Reuben Harrison and Sarah Burge or Burgess. Mary H. Moores was b April 4, 1792, d July 18, 1844. Issue:
Nancy Moores was b June 23, 1809, m James Rochelle about 1825. She d Feb. 28, 1843. Issue:
John Ross Rochelle, b Oct. 17, 1827, m Julia L. Fort Dec. 12, 1849. He died March 13, 1881. She d Aug. 14, 1857.
J. R. Rochelle m 2nd Sarah Ann McCutcheon, Oct., 1860.
Charles Moores Rochelle, b May 7, 1829, m Elizabeth Janes in June, 1855. He d Jan. 26, 1884. She d Oct., 1904.
Anderson Franklin Rochelle, b Feb. 9, 1831, d Sept. 18, 1831.
Henry Pinkney Rochelle, b Dec. 28, 1832, m Sarah Cordelia Fort, July 26, 1855, d Jan. 19, 1884. She was b in Carroll Co., Miss., July 16, 1837, and m at Myrtle Springs, Texas. Issue (ten children):
Jethro Battle Rochelle, b May 24, 1856, d Feb. 16, 1860.
Henry Pinkney Rochelle, b Aug 13, 1852, unmarried.
Mary Florence Rochelle, b April 3, 1861, m David Harrison, Feb. 28, 1883. He d Oct., 1893. Issue:
Cordelia Harrison, b June 14, 1885, m Harry Witterstaedter, Sept., 1902. Issue:
David Harrison Witterstaedter, b May 25, 1904.
Marvin Ross Witterstaeder, b Aug, 1905.
Harry Witterstaedter, b Aug., 1907.

RALPH D. MOORES
Page 99

KENNETH MOORES
Page 99

ALTHEA MOORES
Page 99

LUCILE ROSS CULLOM
Page 87.

FRANCIS HUNTER WHITAKER
Page 85.

HOME OF CHARLES BRUCE MOORES.
PORTLAND OREGON.

WILLIAM HENRY HARRISON MOORES 3RD.
Page 87.

WILLIAM HENRY HARRISON MONRES 1ST.
Page 87.

MARIE LOUISE ROSS MOORES.
Page 87.

WILLIAM HENRY HARRISON MOORES 2ND.
Page 87.

JOHN, WALLACE AND EDNA FONTAINE.
Page 87.

MRS ALBERT S. WELLS.
Page 98

MERRILL B. MOORES
Page 98

GORDON C. MOORES
Page 98

CHESTER A. MOORES
Page 98

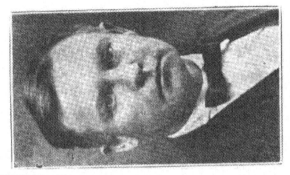

J. F. ROCHELLE
Page 81

JOHN HILL
See Page 192

Elizabeth Ross Harrison, b Feb. 28,
1887, m Thomas Fisher, April,
1907. Issue:
Lillian Fisher, b June,
1909.
Jimmie Harrison, b Anr. 3, 1890, d
March, 1903.
Silvester Douglas Harrison, b July
9, 1892.
(a) James Fort Rochelle, b Feb. 15, 1864, m Ella J.
McMickle, Dec. 20, 1893. Issue:
Artie Stuart Rochelle, b Oct. 4, 1894.
Murill Rochelle, b Feb. 15, 1896.
James Fort Rochelle, Jr., b Jan. 30,
1898.
Fay Rochelle, b May 29, 1902, d
March 26, 1903.
Edmund S. Rochelle, b Jan. 15, 1904.
Ruth Rochelle, b July 9, 1908.
Rollin R. Rochelle, b Oct. 16, 1910.
Temperance Runnels Rochelle, b Feb. 28, 1866,
d Oct. 16, 1874.
Edmund Shackleford Rochelle, b Sept. 4, 1868, d
Jan. 1, 1896.
Jethro Battle Rochelle, b Aug. 21, 1871, m Eliza-
beth Moore, Dec. 22, 1897. Issue:
Maggie Belle Rochelle, b Sept. 24,
1899.
Henry Moore Rochelle, b 1901.
Norman Rochelle, b Dec., 1903.
Jethro Battle Rochelle, Jr., b May
13, 1906.
Sarah Elizabeth Rochelle, b May 13, 1874, m
Milton H. Chance, Feb. 27, 1907.
Nancy Jane Rochelle, b May 26, 1876, m Julian
M. Edwards, Jan. 2, 1901. Issue:
Elizabeth Edwards, b July 10, 1902.
Meredith Rochelle Edwards, b July
9, 1904.
Julian McKinley Edwards, b Jan. 4,
1906.
Milton E. Edwards. b Oct. 11, 1911.
Eli Moores Rochelle, b Jan. 22, 1882, unmarried.
(b) Eugene B. Rochelle, b about 1833, m Catherine Anderson,
July 31, d Feb. 16, 1885. Issue:
Eugene Rochelle, Jr., b May 24, 1856, d young.
John Ross Rochelle, b Aug. 9, 1858, m Nov. 28,
1888, to Mattie Rochelle.
Jefferson Davis Rochelle, b Feb. 19, 1851, d
young.
Margaret Rochelle, b Oct. 10, 1865, d young.
Edward Tisdall Rochelle, b July 18, 1867, m to
Mollie Rochelle, Jan. 16, 1891.
Mattie J. Rochelle, b April 27, 1869, m her first
cousin, J. R. Rochelle. He d March 9,
1904. Issue:
Chester A. Rochelle, b Sept. 11, 1889.
Jack Tisdall Rochelle and

Eugene Rochelle were b June 8, 1891.

Nellie J. Rochelle, b Nov. 15, 1893.

Catherine S. Rochelle, b Aug. 10, 1896.

Gordon Rochelle, b June 24, 1899.

Julia May Rochelle, b June 27, 1900.

John Ross Rochelle, b Sept. 23, 1903.

(c) Mattie J. Rochelle m 2nd to Sam Watlington, July 29, 1909. Issue:

Sam Fred Watlington, b Fed. 11, 1911.

David Moore Rochelle, b May 24, 1871, m Jan. 20, 1902, to Cora Cuthbertson.

Nannie Rochelle and

Hessie Rochelle were b Mch. 12, 1874, d young·

George Gordon Rochelle, b Oct. 1, 1875, m Nov. 15, 1899.

Mary M. Rochelle, b Sept., 1836, d Feb. 5, 1848.

Reuben Moores, m Jane Godbold. Issue:

Mrs. J. E. Morris, 1103 Wood St., Texarkana, Tex.

Thomas B. Moores, m Sarah Norvel, his first cousin, she being the dau of Margaret Moores Norvel. (See her line.) Issue:

Margaret Moores, m James T. McDonald. Issue:

William H. McDonald m Edna Turner. Issue:

Twins, d in infancy.

Charles Moores McDonald, m Lelia Wardell. Issue:

James S. McDonald.

William McDonald.

Charles Moores, m Annie McClane. No issue.

Charles Moores, d in infancy.

Anderson Ross Moores, m Pauline Garrett. Issue:

Mrs. Robert Dunn, of Spokane, Wash.

Francis Moores, m Dr. Allen.

Jane Ross Moores, b Jan. 18, 1818, in Columbia, S. C., m James Moore, of Charleston, S. C. Issue:

Charles Moores Moore, d in infancy.

*Mary Elizabeth Harrison Moore, m †Dr. John F. Hooks, of Selma, Ala. Issue:

James Moore Hooks, d in infancy.

Jane Ross Moore, m Samuel Johnston, of Arkansas. Issue:

James Moore Johnston, m Eva Pickard. Issue:

Lucille Johnston.

Margaret Johnston.

James Hooks Johnston.

Chas. Pickard Johnston.

Samuel Moore Johnston.

---

*Cousins, for fear you will think I have done very little for my country, I will tell you. not egotistically, for I wish I could have accomplished more, my sister who married my husband's brother had a large family, and I loved children and insisted on her giving me her second boy, James Moore Hooks, who we took at eight years, educated, and gave him many advantages. He is an M. D. and a great light as a surgeon, and my brother, David, dying very soon after the birth of his only child, Dasye, requested I should have her half of the time, so finally her mother gave her to me, who has developed into a grand character, surpassingly beautiful, who has a little boy. The three constitute my life, making sunshine and radiance where gloom would exist to a widow. If I can in my humble way assist you farther, it will give my great pleasure.   Devotedly,   MARY E. HOOKS.

308 South Main, Paris, Texas, Oct. 31.

†Dr. John F. Hooks was a surgeon general in the Civil War, on the Southern side.

Mrs. Eva Pickard Johnston, m 2d to J. A. Stone-
ham, of Canada. Issue:
Jack Johnston Stoneham.
Infant, d unnamed.
Percy Godbold Johnston, m Anne Malhern
No issue.
Samuel Moore Johnston, d in youth.
Lucile Harrison Johnston, d in youth.
Francis Harrison Moore, m Charles A. Hooks, a bro of Dr.
John F. Hooks. Issue:
John F. Hooks, m Mable Dick. No issue.
*James Moore Hooks, m Maude Hancock. No
issue.
Payne Thomas Hooks, m Minnie Moore.
Issue:
Lillie Hooks.
James Moore Hooks.
Katheryn Hooks.
James C. Moore, m Sarah Stell. He d soon after his mar-
riage. Issue:
James William Moore, m Marjorie McCreiston.
Issue:
Mary Elizabeth Moore.
Eleanor Myrtle Moore.
Richard Harrison Moore, m Mary Godbold. Issue:
Infant, d unnamed.
David Harrison Moore, m Marvin Ownsby. Issue:
Dasye Moore, m Alfred Haejele. Issue:
Alfred Haejele.
Richard H. Moores, d unmarried.
Sarah Harrison Ross Moores, b Nov. 10, 1810, d Sept. 19, 1893, m July 31,
1833, to Willis Whitaker. (See note.) Issue:
*Willis Whitaker, b in Fairfield District, S. C., July 25, 1834,
m Feb., 1865, Charlotte June. He d at Texarkana,
Tex., Sept. 6, 1886. Issue:
Willis Whitaker, the 5th, unmarried.
Mary Jane Whitaker, m Philip D. Vincent, of
Texarkana, Texas.
Bessie Peay Whitaker, d age 16.
Carrie Allison Whitaker, d infant.
John Seldon Whitaker, d infant.
Henry Moores Whitaker, d infant.
Sally Williams Whitaker, d infant.
Mary Harrison Whitaker, d infant.
Charles Moores Whitaker, d infant.

*"My father, Willis Whitaker, was a graduate of Princeton University in 1857—a man of beautiful address, a most
fluent talker, which, together with his education and travels, made him a man of affairs in his early manhood. He was
possessed of that happy faculty of winning friends and retaining their friendship throughout life. He enlisted as a
private at Jefferson, Texas, in May, 1861, in Company A, First Texas Regiment, Hood's Brigade. He served with this
company in the Virginia campaign, where, shortly before the battle of Gettysburg, he was transferred to a North Carolina regiment, with the rank of lieutenant. In the battle of Gettysburg he sustained very severe injuries, having his
right arm shot away. He lay on that battle field, unable to move, faint and sick from loss of blood, was captured by the
Federals, taken prisoner, and remained in prison, in Baltimore, from July 8, 1863, until the close of the war. During those
two years his friends held no direct communication with him. From prison he went to North Carolina, where he and my
mother were married. While Sherman was burning Columbia, they could hear the explosions and see the red glare in the
sky at night. They went to Florida on a wedding journey, and from there they set out for Texas, his home. This trip
was made in a covered wagon—a very eventful one, fraught with danger and great difficulties. They were compelled to
travel this mode, however, since the railroads had been destroyed by Sherman in his march to the sea. They traveled
this way until they reached the Mississippi river, where they took a boat for Jefferson, Texas. My parents were among
of Texarkana, Texas, my father being its first postmaster, and my mother being the only postmistress the place has ever
had. It was while filling this appointment he died, in September, 1886. My mother was appointed to serve out his
term." (By his daughter, Mary Whitaker Vincent.)

—83—

Elizabeth Harrison Moores, b Sept. 3, 1814, d May 30, 1877. M 1st to Dr. James T. Rosborough, in Fairfield District, S. C., Nov. 22, 1838. He d Aug. 15, 1842. Issue:

Mary Ann Rosborough, b Sept. 10, 1839, d Aug. 15, 1899, m Oct. 9, 1861, to James B. Hooks, in Marion Co., Texas. Issue:

Elizabeth Hooks, b Jan. 28, 1863.

Mary Rosborough Hooks, b July 19, 1868 m Hugh Grafton, in Texarkana, Tex., April 23, 1890. Issue:

Ruth Grafton, b March 6, 1892.
James Grafton, b Aug. 4, 1894.

Nancy Jane Hooks, b Aug. 1, 1874.

Pearla Hooks, b Jan. 9, 1877.

*Capt. James Thomas Rosborough, b in Fairfield District, S. C., July 31, 1842, m Aug. 16, 1865, near Jefferson, Marion Co., Tex.. to Martha Farish, of Vermont. Issue:

Mary Converse Rosborough, b Aug. 31, 1866, m April 24, 1889, to F. C. Dumbeck. Issue:

Mattie Fletcher Dumbeck, b Feb. 14, 1890.

Thomas Whitaker Rosborough, b Sept. 7, 1868, m June 28, 1906, to Winifred Melville. Issue:

Thomas Whitaker Rosborough, b Aug. 25, 1907.

Ellen Parish Rosborough, b Oct. 28, 1870, m Dec. 4, 1894, to Lawrence P. Beidelman. Issue:

Elizabeth Beidelman, b Dec. 15, 1896.

Mary Beidelman.

Martha Beidelman, b June 7, 1901.

Elizabeth Rosborough, b March 18, 1873, m May 29, 1895, to Wm. N. Bemis. Issue:

Hannah Bemis, b Mch. 14, 1896.

James Rosborough Bemis, b Oct. 25, 1898.

Elizabeth Bemis, b Sept. 30, 1905.

Dorothy Bemis, b July 4, 1907.

Martha Parish Rosborough, b July 24, 1876, m Nov. 26, 1903, to Orlando S. Holliday.

Jennie Parish Rosborough, b Nov. 26, 1878, m Oct. 12, 1904, to Benj. G. Cox. Issue:

*James T. Rosborough was attending a military school in North Carolina at the breaking out of the civil war, and volunteered in one of the first companies formed in that State. The Governor placed this company (G) in the Sixth North Carolina State Troops, and commissioned him lieutenant. His initiation in battle was at Bull Run, July 21, 1861, and he was in all the principal battles of the Army of Northern Virginia from that time on. He was first wounded at Malvern Hill, and again severely wounded at Sharpsburg. During the progress of the war, his Colonel, W. D. Pender, was advanced to Major General, and he then selected him to serve upon his staff. At Gettysburg, Captain Rosborough was carrying orders upon the battlefield when his General fell, mortally wounded. He remained in the Confederate army until May 20, 1865, making four full years of constant and hard service, gladly given, and he would willingly have extended it.

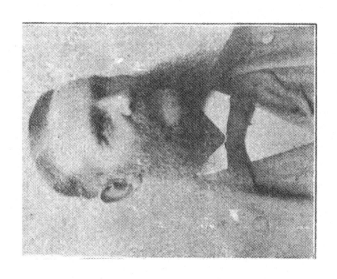

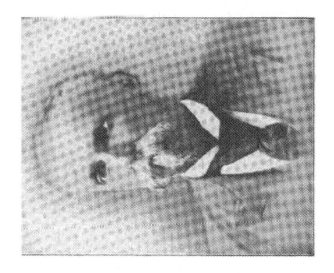

Jennie Rosborough Cox,
b Apr. 11, 1906.
Benj. G. Cox, b Sept. 18,
1908.
James Thomas Rosborough, b Oct.
24, 1881, d Jan. 10, 1888.
Rachel Collison Rosborough, b Dec.
6, 1883.
Annie Thomas Rosborough, b April
19, 1887, m Nov. 18, 1908, to
Geo. W. Jacks.
Elizabeth Harrison Moores Rosborough, m 2nd to Willis Whitaker after
the death of his first wife, who was her sister, Sarah Harrison
Ross Moores. (See her line.) They were m July 27, 1844. Issue:
Benjamin Whitaker, b Dec. 20, 1844, in Bowie Co., Texas.
He m Adine Patton. Issue:
Waverly Whitaker, m and living in Louisiana.
George Wheatly Whitaker, d without issue.
James Rosborough Whitaker, d young.
Benjamin Whitaker m 2nd to Anna Fowles. Issue:
Benjamin Whitaker, d young.
Elizabeth Moores Whitaker, b Dec. 10, 1847, m Robert J.
Haywood, Dec. 12, 1866. Issue:
Nancy Haywood, m Frank Hiller.
Elise Haywood, m Weyman B. Dunlap.
Abbie Haywood, m Henry D. Keith.
William H. Haywood.
Robert J. Haywood.
Benjamin Whitaker Haywood.
Nancy Martha Whitaker, b March 10, 1849, m George A.
Wheatly, and d Feb. 9, 1874, without issue.
(d) William Lowndes Whitaker, b Sept. 15, 1850, m Dora Dunn,
dau of Hon. Poindexter Dunn, M. C. He d Oct. 14, 1905.
Issue:
William Lowndes Whitaker.
Hubert Whitaker.
Norman Whitaker.
(e) Harrison Moores Whitaker, b in Cass Co., Texas, Feb. 9,
1852, m 1st Martha Matilda Bonner, dau of Judge M.
H. Bonner and his wife, Elizabeth Taylor. Issue:
William Whitaker, b July 21, 1875, m Alice
Simmons.
Harrison Moores Whitaker, b Feb. 18, 1877, m
Alice McKowen.
Elizabeth Whitaker, b Nov. 17, 1878.
Hubbard Bonner Whitaker, b June 19, 1881, d
infant.
Annie Whitaker, b 1885.
Judge Whitaker's first wife d May 22, 1892. He m 2nd Mary
Eleanor O'Rouke, on Feb. 25, 1897. Issue:
*Francis Hunter Whitaker, b Oct. 30, 1898.
David Harrison Moores, m Rachel Godbold. No issue.
Eli Harrison Moores, b at Thorn Creek, Fairfield District, S. C., April 20,
1815, d March 10, 1885. He m Minerva A. Janes, who was b on
Fisher's Prairie, Ark., Jan, 13, 1826, d June 8, 1868. Issue:
Charles Harrison Moores, b Dec. 17, 1848, d June 12, 1906, m
†Tamar Hargrove. Issue:

‹ Moores was born at Williamsburg, Miss., near Brandon. Her father, J. L. Hargrove, was a
he seventies. She has freely assisted the writer with this branch of the Moores family, and
rds would not have been as complete as they are.

Eli Hargrove Moores, b Mch. 22, 1882.

Charles Gaither Moores, b Sept. 22, 1883.

Mary Minerva Moores, b April 20, 1885, m Mr. Dixon. Issue:

    Lena Tamar Dixon, b Feb. 11, 1909.

John Hargrove Moores, b March 22, 1887.

Tamar Hargrove Moores, b Nov. 8, 1888, m Mr. Clay. Issue:

    Pauline Clay, b Jan. 1, 1909.

    Mary Louise Clay, b May 27, 1911.

Mary Harrison Moores, b Mch. 4, 1851, d Aug. 4, 1857.

William M. Moores, b Dec. 30, 1852, m Rilla Bonham. Issue:

Minnie Minerva Moores, b June 28, 1875, at Texarkana, Tex., m W. A. Boon, of Simms, Tex. Issue:

    Mattie Elizabeth Boon, b Jan. 14, 1897.

    Charlie Massack Boon, b Oct. 6, 1899.

*Minnie M. M. Boon, m 2nd Crawford L. Cox.

Mattie Moores, b Nov. 23, 1878, m J. M. LaSalle.

Willie B. Moores, b Dec. 4, 1896.

Eli Harrison Moores, b Jan. 1, 1856, d Feb. 22, 1882.

Thomas B. Moores, b Nov. 29, 1857, d Feb. 3, 1920 m, 1st Mary Ann Bonham. Issue:

Miner A. Moores, b Dec., 1882, m Charlton Winfield.

Thomas B. Moores, m 2nd Stella Jenks. She m 2nd Louie Rillings.

Mary Moores, b March 15, 1898.

Nancy Harrison Moores, b Oct. 28, 1859, m John C. Watts. He was b in Lownes Co., Ala., July 22, 1846. Issue:

Dr. Eli Moores Watts, b Jan. 2, 1885.

Lizzie E. Watts, g Aug. 12, 1886.

John C. Watts, b Aug. 28, 1888.

Thomas Jefferson Watts, b July 18, 1890.

David Moores Watts, b June 15, 1892.

Minerva Janes Watts, b Jan. 21, 1895.

Monroe P. Watts, b Dec. 19, 1897.

Mamie Harrison Watts, b Nov. 4, 1899.

Sarah B. Moores, b Dec. 24, 1861, d Jan. 22, 1896, m Jackson Clements. Issue:

Jennie Moores Clements, b Sept. 22, 1882, m William Carroll Timberlake.

Peter Clements, b Nov. 3, 1888.

Minerva A. Moores, b Feb. 7, 1864, d July 23, 1883, m W. H. Cullom. She died. He m Maria L. Moores.

lliam Henry Harrison Moores, youngest child of Charles and Mary Harrison Moores, was b July 23, 1830, and d April 25, 1898. He m 1st Matilda Cooper, Dec. 25, 1852. Issue:

Southern Moores, d at about 10 years of age.

Dickie Moores, d at about 14 years of age.

Matilda Moores, d at about 3 years of age.

Jane Ross Moores, b Sept. 2, 1858, m Dec. 11, 1877, to John M. McGill. Issue:

Lillian Douglass McGill, b Oct. 19, 1878, d Sept. 13, 1885.

Son, b Jan. 1, 1879, d Jan. 7, 1879.

Boon with her two children moved to Montana in 1906, where she married Crawford
Busteed, Montana, where they still reside, in the sheep business,

Mary McElwee McGill, b April 16, 1881, m R. H. Burgess, June 6, 1900. Issue:

    Matilda Cooper Burgess, b Oct. 2, 1904.

Matilda Cooper McGill, b Nov. 14, 1883, m John S. Burgess, Apr. 10, 1903. Issue:

    John S. Burgess, b Jan. 1, 1904.

    Richard Cooper Burgess, b Aug. 23, 1906.

Willie Moores McGill, b Dec. 17, 1887, m W. H. Vaughan, July 1, 1910.

Margaret Jane McGill, b July 13, 1889.

Latona Bruce McGill, b Jan. 1, 1891.

John McElwee McGill, b Nov. 24, 1893, d Oct. 4, 1895.

W. H. H. Moores, m 2nd to Marie Louise Ross, who at the time of her marriage to W. H. H. Moores was the Widow Adams. She d Mch. 19, 1875. This marriage was on Sept. 24, 1863. Issue:

*William Henry Harrison Moores 2nd, b May 22, 1865, m Mary Lunsford Thorne, June 19, 1888. (For her lineage, see Wade line. Issue:

    ‡William Henry Harrison Moores 3rd, b Feb. 10, 1890.

    Lunsford Thorne Moores, b Oct. 14, 1892.

    Francis Maryon Moores, b Oct. 24, 1900.

    "Baby Moores," son, b July 28, 1902, d July 31, 1902.

    Martha Moores, b Feb. 25, 1906, d March 6, 1906.

    "Our Little Boy," b Sept 21, 1907, d Sept. 26. 1907.

Maria Ross Moores, b Aug. 14, 1867, m William Heber Cullom, Nov. 18, 1885. Issue:

    William Heber Cullom, b Jan. 13, 1890, d Feb. 22, 1891.

    Douglass Moores Cullom, b Jan. 13, 1890, d Mch. 6, 1891.

    Lucile Ross Cullom, b Feb. 9, 1892.

    Robert Bruce Cullom, b Aug. 5, 1900.

Latona Moores, b Nov. 30, 1869, m 1st to Robert Carey Bruce, May 15, 1889. No issue.

L. M. B. m 2nd to Bruce Christopher, June 3, 1908.

Nora Lee Moores, b Dec. 10, 1872, m John Clelland Fontaine, Nov. 28, 1895. Issue:

    Edna Fontaine, b Nov. 1, 1896.

    John Clelland Fontaine, b Feb. 28, 1897.

    Wallace Moores Fontaine, b Feb. 12, 1899.

W. H. H. Moores m 3rd on April 20, 1876, to Mary Letherd Douglass. No issue. (For her lineage see Wade line.) Mrs. Mary Moores died Oct. 12, 1900.

---

†Col. W. H. H. Moores, Sr., was born near Longtown, Fairfield County, S. C., on July 23, 1830. He was the youngest son of Charles Moores. When about 10 years of age his father moved from South Carolina to Bowie County, Texas. The remainder of his life was spent in this county, and until a few years before his death, on the farm settled by his parents in the early days. He was generous to a fault. In his lovely country home hospitality reigned supreme. He was a typical Southern gentleman. His motto must have been, "Whatsoever thy hand findeth to do, do with thy might," for his flowers, gardens, orchards and farms were kept in perfect order. It was told that on one occasion he had bought quite a number of fruit trees from an old friend, but he was disappointed in them, and had this friend to come over and inspect the orchard. After looking for some time he remarked, "Why, Mr. Moores, you have assassinated them with kindness." In all of his undertakings his work was thorough. He was sent to Lexington, Ky., to school, and afterward attended Princeton. He was a great reader, and kept up with current events, etc. A few years before his death he left

(Notes continued next page.)

NOTES.

(a) "The story of the material and progressive development of Bowie County and Texarkana would not be complete without the name of James F. Rochelle.

Just as the old-time spinning-wheel and loom was a fixture way back in the halcyon days of Possum Trot, so the name of Rochelle is known to every man, woman and child in all this section of country. Jim Rochelle was born and raised here. All his life has been spent right here, and every interest he has this side of the great beyond is right here in Bowie County. In fact, he is identified, and has been identified since he was a child, with everything that makes for the development in the very best way of Bowie County and the section in which he has lived.

Among the pioneers and settlers of the great East Texas Wilderness, the name of Rochelle stands out prominent and significant.

Jim Rochelle in his capable and honest way has served the people in the capacity of Constable and Sheriff. The records of the office show that his administration has been one of impartiality. His every act has been without fear or favor, keeping at all times in view the fact that the laws were paramount and must be observed regardless of those whose toes were pinched or stepped upon. It has made not a particle of difference to him whether the enforcement of the laws has met with the approval of certain friends. As long as the law remains on the statute book, he states that he is going to see that people obey the laws, whether they like it or not. Whether in office or out of office, it is his plain intention to treat everybody alike, enforcing the law as he finds it on the statutes.

He is now filling the office of Sheriff for the third term, is an active member of the Texas Sheriffs' Association, and is retiring voluntarily from politics for the present at the expiration of his term."—Clipping.

(b) Eugene H. Rochelle, Sr., was born in North Carolina and very early emigrated to Texas. He was a successful physician and surgeon, and began the practice in 1855 and continued until a year before his death. In 1862 he was called into the service of the Confederacy in the capacity of Surgeon, in which position he continued, and gave relief to many suffering and wounded soldiers throughout the war. In 1855 he married Catherine S. Anderson, in Clarkesville, Red River County, Texas, but moved to Bowie County, where he died in 1885. He was a devoted father, husband and friend, and counted his friends by the score. His talents were unusual, and his nobleness of heart caused all to love him. His wife and five children survived him.

Mrs. Catherine Rochelle was born in Richmond, Va., December 6, 1836. She received a liberal education in literature and music, and was a fine pianist, being sought after to play in all the large gatherings in her vicinity. She was the mother of eleven children, only five of whom lived to maturity, and at the present time only two are living. The shock of her husband's death completely changed her from the sunny, happy woman she had always been to one of sadness. She survived till 1896. Though depressed by the grief that had been hers, she did her utmost to make the lives of those around her happy and bright.

---

his country home and moved to Texarkana, Texas. Here the last few years of his life were spent. He was a member of the M. E. Church, South. The ministers of the Gospel always found a hearty welcome in his home. (See picture.)

*William Henry Harrison Moores, Jr., was born at the "old Moores home," in Bowie County, Texas, May 22, 1865. At 19 years of age he had the management of his father's saw-mill. He followed this avocation for some years. When about 25 years old he was elected Treasurer of Bowie County, holding this office three terms (six years.) He assisted in organizing the City National Bank of Texarkana, Texas, and was Vice-President and Cashier of this institution until failing health forced him to resign and seek out-door employment. He therefore began again in the lumber business, and since has been General Manager for companies in Louisiana and Texas—is at this time General Manager for the National Lumber and Creosoting Mills, at Saltillo, Texas. He is a member of the Southern Presbyterian Church, and has served as an Elder for a number of years. His kind and sympathetic nature has made him many true friends. (See picture.)

‡W⁺ H. H. Moores 3rd, "William the Third," was born in Bowie County, Feb. 10, 1890. He attended the public and private school of Texarkana, Texas. Was a student in the Peacock Military School, in San Antonio, for one term. Has been in Austin College, Sherman, Texas, the past three years, where, in connection with his literary course, he has taken civil engineering, which he hopes to finish at the University of Texas or Boston School of Technology. He has been a member of the Southern Presbyterian Church since 16 years of age. (See picture.)

Most of the descendants of Charles W. Moores live in and around Texarkana, Texas, and hold positions of honor and respect in the social and business world of that section. They have followed the example of their worthy ancestor, in giving their children the best opportunities for education, and therefore have equipped them for their rightful spheres in life.

(c) Mrs. Sam Watlington lives at Hooks, Texas. She and her family are devoted Christians. She has a great pride in her ancestry, and is rearing her children to be a credit to their ancestors.

(d) "The passing away of Mr. W. L. Whitaker takes from active life a man of fine executive ability, the best years and efforts of his life having been given to Texarkana.

He and his family of brothers and sisters were among the pioneer citizens of the West Side. The most beautiful modern homes in the Texas city have been built and occupied by his people. Every church on the Texas side of town stands on ground donated by a member of his family—his mother's brother.

His executive ability, aided by the co-operation of his brother, Ben Whitaker, and James Rosborough, gave to our city the K. C. S. Railway, one of the greatest commercial arteries of business that brings its load of important financial wealth to our coffers. This family of brother finally lost heavily, in a financial sense, in the disposition of this road in its embryo, but Texarkana lost nothing. Texarkana has today, in full force of wealth and influence, this mill train, now grown to a mighty trunk line, and for this W. L. Whitaker and his brothers gave their years of vigor and their best financial force. They came to Texarkana with an ample bank account, and the best they had has been given to the city.

W. L. Whitaker belonged to a family of social and intellectual culture. He was educated in the University of Virginia, and took a finishing course at the University of Berlin, Germany. He spoke the modern languages fluently, and was equally conversant with the ancient. He was a linguist of wide scope of culture and a scholar of deep thought and untiring energy.

W. L. Whitaker's father, Capt. Willis Whitaker, came from South Carolina to Texas in its Republic days, and settled six miles west of Texarkana, and this son, W. L., was born Sept. 15, 1850, on this home, the head-right survey of Capt. Willis Whitaker. South Bowie County can claim with pride this noble son. His father was the best farmer in all the country around. Thus we see this executive ability is an inheritance in this family.

His surviving sons, William L., Jr., Hubert and Norman, are left to take up his worth, and right well will they receive the mantle of their noble sire. His mother was a Miss Moores. From this maternal ancestry this family are immediate descendants of same family of Harrisons as President W. H. H. Harrison. The name W. H. H. Harrison runs through every branch of the family. His ancestors on both sides are South Carolinians, and among the prominent leaders, socially, commercially and politically.

Mr. Whitaker had three sisters and four brothers. Of these the survivors are James T. Rosborough, Ben Whitaker, of Alexandria, La., and Judge Harrison Moores-Whitaker, of Beaumont, Texas, and Mrs. Sallie Moores-Haywood, of Beaumont, Texas.

Mr. Whitaker was a brainy man, in thought and enterprise twenty years ahead of his times. This advanced enterprise often caused people not to understand him. But he was admired and respected, deeply loved by all who knew him intimately. Texarkana of today owes him a debt of appreciation for the useful enterprises inaugurated by him twenty years ago.

W. L. Whitaker's present home was in Alexandria, La., and he leaves there to mourn his absence the widow and three sons. Mr. Whitaker married Miss Dora Dunn, daughter of ex-Congressman Poindexter Dunn, in June, 1876, and to this marriage six children have been born.

He was a communicant in the Episcopal church."—Clipping

(e) It is interesting to note that the Willis Whitaker mentioned on page 85, belonged to the same Whitaker family, who lived near A. B. Ross, and was mentioned by him in his diary almost daily. Willis Whitaker who married Elizabeth Harrison Moores was the son of "Major Whitaker," and at the time the old diary was written he was a small child. The lands owned by "Major Whitaker" were purchased by him from A. B. Ross, and were near his home. The following in regard to the Whitaker family was furnished by Judge Harrison Moores Whitaker:

"The Willis Whitaker mentioned in the diary of your grandfather, Arthur Brown Ross, was my grandfather. The Mrs. Mary Whitaker mentioned was probably the wife of Thomas Whitaker, a cousin of my grandfather. She was a sister of my grandmother. My grandmother died about 1801, when my father was only 3 years old. I have my grandfather's walking stick now, and prize it very highly."

"Willis Whitaker, son of James Whitaker, was born about 1750. Served first as a captain in Joseph Kershaw's regiment in the Revolutionary army. After release from his imprisonment by the British at Charleston, he served under Sumpter, and afterwards in some other command, holding, as I understand, the rank of major. He served twice as a member of the South Carolina Legislature in the early formation of the government.

He married Sarah Williams, about 1794, and to them were born four children, James Wiggins, Matilda, who died young and without issue, Mary, who married Dr John Milling, and Willis Whitaker, my father.

"Historic Camden," on page 396, gives something of the Whitaker family, but is in error in saying that we are descended from the Rev. Alexander Whitaker, the Apostle to Virginia. He remained a bachelor, and was drowned in the James River. We are the descendants of his half-bother, as I understand.

My father, Willis Whitaker, was born on the 23rd of September, 1798, in Kershaw District, South Carolina. Came to Texas in 1840. Lived for a time in Bowie County, Texas, afterwards removed to Cass County, Texas, where he died on the 19th day of March, 1867. He was a man of gentle manners, superb dignity, great executive ability, and born to command. Taking into consideration the natural bias of a son, I believe I can truthfully say that, in these respects, he was the most remarkable man I ever knew. You will notice by reference to pages 84 and 85 that he was first married to Sarah Harrison Ross Moores and then her sister, Elizabeth Harrison Moores Rosborough.

I am a descendant of Henry Moores and his wife, Jane Ross, through their oldest child, Charles Moores, who was my grandfather. Charles Moores married Mary Harrison, who was the daughter of Reuben Henry Harrison and his wife, Sarah Burge or Burgess. This Harrison family is the same as that which furnished the signer of the Declaration of Independence and two Presidents. They came originally from Virginia and settled on the Wateree River, in Fairfield District, South Carolina, where my grandfather, Charles Moores, and grandmother, Mary Harrison, were married. There were born to this couple fourteen children, twelve of whom lived to mature years and nine of whom left descendants. My mother was Elizabeth Harrison Moores, daughter of Charles Moores and Mary Harrison. She was born Sept. 3, 1814, and was married to my father, Capt. Willis Whitaker, here in Texas in July, 1844 (second marriage), and I, who am their youngest child, was born in Cass County, Texas, on the 9th of February, 1852, and, as you will note, was named for my mother, leaving off the Elizabeth. In his day and generation my father was well to do, as riches were then measured—was a large slave owner. He died on the 19th of March, 1867, and my mother died on May 30, 1877.

The children of this couple had the advantages of a liberal education. I received my training in preparatory schools in North Carolina and Virginia and finished at the University of Virginia. I prepared myself for the law, to which I have given the years of my manhood without intermission. I was appointed by the Governor of Texas, Judge of one of our District Courts, when I was 25 years of age, and have the distinction of having been the youngest man who ever held that office in Texas. I have never been a politician, and my time has been too much taken up with my profession to give it to anything else."

SECOND CHILD OF HENRY AND JEAN MOORES.

*JOHN MOORES was b Oct. 9, 1777, and d Oct. 29, 1844, in Tennessee. He m Jean Conger, a dau of John Conger and Mary Ross. (See Conger line for her lineage.) She was b Oct. 12, 1777, and d July 25, 1840. Issue:

†Eli Moore, b Mch. 29, 1798, d Aug. 17, 1855, m 1st to Finnetta Hines, who was b July 12, 1807, d Dec. 19, 1834. Issue:

Alexander Moores, m Minerva Burgess. Issue:

John E. Moores, m and lives in Huntsville, Ala.

Henry Moores, unmarried.

---

*John Moores dropped the "s" from his name and was known as Moore, as are some of his descendants today. He was a well educated man. He studied medicine, but his tombstone gives him the title of Major instead of Doctor. His wife was a sister of Isaac Conger's. The two swapped sisters. Both John and Jane or Jean Conger Moore are buried in the old Conger graveyard in Tennessee, near Fayetteville. His tombstone bears this inscription, "Let this commemorate the birth and death of Major John Moore, the Friend of the Orphan, Widow and Suffering Humanity."

†Both Eli Moore and his wife, Finnetta Hines Moore, are buried in the old Conger graveyard near Fayetteville, Tenn. Mrs. Thos. J. Moore, with her son Thomas and daughter Nannie, live in Italy, Texas, where Thomas E. Moore is a prominent business man. Just one-half a mile east of Italy is their old home, where all the family were born and reared to be grown.

Eli Moore lived near Fayetteville, Tenn., until his second marriage, when he moved to Connersville, Tenn., where the sons of his son James now reside.

Shelby Moores, unmarried.
Daughter, who m Mr. VeHamlin. Issue:
One child.
Mrs. Maittre Clayton. Issue:
Minerva Clayton.
Joseph Clayton.
Thomas Moore, b Apr. 3, 1832, m Nannie P. Nichols, Jan. 26,
1859. He d Feb. 6, 1898. Issue:
Alexander D. Moore, b March 26, 1860, d Nov.
22, 1899, m Alice Collier, Dec. 21, 1882.
Issue:
Lillian May Moore, m Dick Moberly,
of Albany, Texas, Feb. 25,
1904. Issue:
Sam Tom Moberly, b
June 7, 1909.
Wilna V. Moore.
Beatrice Moore, m E. L. Stone, June
14, 1911.
Johnnie Lee Moore.
Nannie Laura Moore.
Thomas C. Moore.
Ammie Moore.
Nannie D. Moore, b April 8, 1862.
Thomas E. Moore, b Nov. 22, 1864.
Joseph N. Moore, b March 1, 1867, m Sammie
Davis, Oct. 18, 1898. Issue:
Bonnie Belle Moore.
Joe Davis Moore.
Lynette Moore.
Jack Hamilton Moore.
Emily R. Moore.
Helen D. Moore.
John H. Moore, b Dec. 9, 1871, m Dec. 30, 1894,
to Bettie Price, of Italy, Texas. Issue:
Pearl Moore, d March, 1898.
Ruby Moore.
Thomas B. Moore.
Otto Moore.
Leonard Moore.
Alexander Moore.
Alton Moore.
Mary Moore, b Feb. 26, 1834, d Oct. 28, 1844.
*John D. Moores, b March 27, 1830, m Lucy Caldwell in 1859.
She was b April 1, 1837. Issue:
Finnetta Moores, b May 21, 1862, d young.
Mary Pearl Moores, b July 20, 1878, d young.
James Horton Moores, b Oct. 4, 1880, d young.
Lizzie Matt Moores, b May 21, 1862, m John Tim-
mins. Issue:
Iliff Timmins,
John William Timmins.
Robert Timmins.
William Hester Moores, b Dec. 7, 1868, m Miss
McKibbon. at Mooresville, Tenn. Issue:

rent out with Forest's Cavalry; was only in a few skirmishes before I fell sick.
 ractice just at the beginning of the war, which made me a farmer.

Mary Pearl Moores.
Marvalin Moores.
John D. Moores, unmarried.
Eli Moore m 2nd to Agnes Broadway. Issue:
James B. Moores m Emma Davis. Issue:
Mary Moores, age about 17.
William Moores, age about 14.
Garrett Moores, age about 12.
Thomas Moores, m May London. Issue:
Sadie D. Moores.
Willie Emma Moores.
London Moores.
*Elizabeth Damo Moores, b Jan. 8, 1842, m Mr. Davis.
No issue.
*Martha Conger Moores, b Jan. 8, 1844, m Mr. Clayton. No
issue.
Eli Moore m 3rd Rachel Hunter. No issue.

THIRD CHILD OF HENRY AND JEAN MOORES.

ELIZABETH MOORES, dau of Henry Moores and Jean Ross, was born in South
Carolina, July 9, 1779, m Joel Payne. Issue:
Hiram Payne, b 1803, m Maraldon Hamilton, in Shelby County, Tenn.,
March 1, 1831. Issue:
Aramintha Payne, b Sept. 22, 1834, m †Earl C. Bronaugh at
Jacksonport, Ark, July 11, 1854. He was b March 4,
1831. Issue:
Anna Hamilton Bronaugh, b at Little Rock, Ark.,
Aug. 1, 1855, d Jan. 6, 1869.
Jerrie Watkins Bronaugh, b in Brownsville, Ark.,
March 16, 1857, d May 6, 1858.
Earl Williams Bronaugh, b in Helena, Ark., Feb.
27, 1859, d Nov. 15, 1861.
Mary Belle Bronaugh, b in Helena, Ark., May 29,
1861, d Oct. 14, 1862.
Elizabeth Craig Bronaugh, b in San Francisco,
Cal., March 8, 1864, d Dec. 31, 1868.
‡Earl Clapp Bronaugh, b in Cleburne, Ark., Feb.
26, 1866, m Grace L. Huggins, who was b
Sept., 1869. Issue:
Elizabeth Bronaugh, b May 31, 1889,
m Nov. 20, 1910, to J. E. Hall.
Lewis Judson, Bronaugh, b Feb. 28,
1892.
Earl Clapp Bronaugh, b May 19, 1894.
Polly Bronaugh, b July 20, 1898.
Joel Bronaugh, m Oct. 21, 1891, to Ella Jeffrey.
She was b in 1871. Issue:
Lucile Bronaugh, b Oct. 1, 1892.
Margaret Bronaugh, b Jan. 27, 1894.
Anna May Bronaugh, b July 20, 1898.
Joel W. Payne, b in Portland, Ore., Jan. 23, 1869, m Anna
Bigbee. Issue:

---

*Mrs. E. D. Davis, Mrs. M. C. Clayton and John D. Moores are the only surviving members of their generation. They furnished the above records.

†Earl C. Bronaugh, Sr., Circuit Judge, State of Arkansas.

‡Earl C. Bronaugh, Jr., Circuit Judge, State of Oregon.

Augusta Payne.
Julia Payne, m Earl Cleland.
Frank Payne.
George Flanders Payne.
*Robert Payne.
Marilla Payne, m John Manning.
Harriet Payne, m Humphey Cobb.
Culberson Payne, m Miss Scott.
†William Payne, m Jemima Holloway.
Henry Payne, m Harriet Judson.
Margaret Payne, m Alex. Stephens.
Mary Ann Payne, m Dr. Lewis.

FOURTH CHILD OF HENRY AND JEAN MOORES.

MARY MOORES, b Nov. 15, 1782, m her cousin, Isaac Conger, son of John and Mary Ross Conger. She d March 4, 1857, in Tennessee, and is interred in the Conger graveyard near Fayetteville, Tenn. (See Conger line for her descendants.)

FIFTH CHILD OF HENRY AND JEAN MOORES.

PHOEBE MOORES, b Jan. 11, 1785. She married Mr. Stillwell and lived in Tennessee. Nothing further is known of her.

SIXTH CHILD OF HENRY AND JEAN MOORES.

ISABELLA MOORES, b Feb. 4, 1787. No records.

SEVENTH CHILD OF HENRY AND JEAN MOORES.

SARAH W. MOORES, dau of Henry Moores and Jean Ross, was b Sept. 22, 1788, d June 22, 1857. She m James Higgins, who was b Oct. 11, 1772 and d April 18, 1858. (See picture.) Issue:
  Anne Jane Higgins, b Nov. 23, 1829, d Dec. 11, 1865, m Sept. 2, 1847, to George Whitaker, who was b June 13, d June 17, 1900. Issue:
    **John J. Whitaker, b Nov. 15, 1850, d Nov. 25, 1901, m Sept. 1, 1885, to May Etta Prosser. Issue:
      Ross Landers Whitaker, b June 24, 1890.
      Anne Jane Whitaker, b July 1, 1892.
      Gladys Whitaker, b April 12, 1899.
    Sallie Hammond Whitaker, b Sept. 9, 1852, m Jessie Childers. Issue:
      James Robert Childers, b Nov., 1875, m Sept. 1, 1897, to Beatrice Prosser. Issue:
        Ethel Childers, b Nov. 2, 1898.
        Roberta Childers, b July 6, 1906.
    Sallie H. Whitaker, m 2nd to †Dr. Francisco Rice. Issue:
      George Whitaker Rice, b Oct. 10, 1889.
      Holden Moores Rice, b Dec. 1, 1892.
      Florence Ellen Rice, b April 27, 1905.

A fruitless effort has been made to locate the descendants of the other children of Elizabeth and Joel Payne. Please send information, if possible.

I know but little in regard to the Payne descendants. When I was small I remember two girls named Amelia and Lizzie Payne They went to school in my home town. This is all I know.   CORDIE M. JONES.

*Died in the Philippines from exposure in the army.

†He was many years a steamboat captain on the Mississippi River, between New Orleans and St. Louis.

**His widow married M. D. Mansfield, and lives in Fayetteville, Tenn.

‡Francisco Rice was a veteran of the Mexican war, an officer in the Confederate Army and a prominent physician. He also served in the Alabama State Senate for twenty years.

William Rufus Whitaker, b Aug. 12, 1859, d about 1891, m
    Lucy Taylor. Issue:
        William Ross Whitaker.
Henry Ross Whitaker, b Sept. 25, 1857, d July 24, 1901, m
    Pink Rhea. No issue:
Mary Washington Whitaker, b July 23, 1860, m Feb. 14, 1884,
    to Douglas Sugg, who was b Oct. 29, 1856, d July 3,
    1897. Issue:
        Mag Ellen Sugg, d age 14 years.
        ‡Anne Sugg, b Sept. 11, 1888.
Mary W. Whitaker, m 2nd to N. A. Sorrels, and resides at
    Fayetteville, Tenn.

EIGHTH CHILD OF HENRY AND JEAN MOORES.

†MARGARET MOORES, b Dec. 25, 1790, m Mr. Norvel. Her dau, Margaret Norvel, m her first cousin, Thos. B. Moores. (See page 82.)

NINTH CHILD OF HENRY AND JEAN MOORES.

HENRY MOORES, son of Henry Moores and Jean Ross, was born Aug. 13, 1793, and died Sept. 21, 1840. His wife, Fannie Reese, was b Feb. 6, 1797, and d Jan. 28, 1829. (See her picture.) Issue:
    *William Hopkins Moores, b Aug. 6, 1818, d May 7, 1884, m Margaret Mertilla Bell, March 30, 1841, who was b June 1, 1818, d April, 1874. Issue:
        Fannie Reese Moores, b Jan. 31, 1842, m 1st to Hildreth Wells, Jan. 1, 1868. She d April 29, 1900. Issue:
            William Hildreth Wells, b Nov. 26, 1868, d March 28, 1909, unmarried.
        Fannie Reese Moores, m 2nd to Wesley Light, Feb. 18, 1883.
        John Bell Moores, b July 29, 1844, d March 6, 1845.
        Mary McCord Moores, b Oct. 6, 1846, m Charlie Jones, Nov. 3, 1876. Issue:
            Horace Moores Jones, b Nov. 26, 1878, m Margaret Lucile Franklin, Mar. 23, 1905. Issue:
                Mary Erline Jones, b Nov. 24, 1906.
                Howard Moores Jones, b Oct. 11, 1909.
            Earl Hopkins Jones, b Jan. 5, 1882, m Oct. 14, to Mary Jane Huffman. Issue:
                Louise Jones, b Oct. 19, 1910.
        Martha Jordan Moores, b Nov. 4, 1850, d Dec. 13, 1854.
        William Henry Moores, b Dec. 19, 1853, m Mary Margaret Taylor. She d July 23, 1883. Issue:
            Mary Mertilla Moores, b Nov. 21, 1878.
            Fannie Bell Moores, b April 6, 1881.
        William H. Moores, m 2nd Mrs. Hattie Park, Jan. 8, 1902.
        Oscar Moores, b Nov. 30, 1859, d May 2, 1862.

---

*Inlisted in war in 1862 as Captain and was promoted to Major and served until close of war.

*My father, Wm H. Moores, was a farmer. I wrote you his war record. My husband is a farmer. Our oldest son (Horace Moores), is telegraph operator and Depot Agent at Huntland, Franklin County, Tenn. Our youngest (Earl Hopkins), is manager of a flouring mill at Fayetteville, Tenn. I suppose brother (William Henry Moores) has written you that he is manager of a mercantile establishment in his town (Bevier, Ky.) I will anxiously await the tidings of the destination of the picture.   Lovingly, your unknown cousin,   MRS. CHARLIE JONES.

†She was also called Peggy. John D. Moores, of Connersville, Tenn., writes: "Aunt Peggy had three children, Jane, Brown and Henry. Since the war I have lost sight of them. When I was a boy, I used to visit my aunts with my father. They lived at Bell Buckle, Tenn. Since the civil war I have lost sight of them."

‡Anne Sugg is the genealogist of this branch, and, for one of her age, is unusually interested in family history.

Mary Leftwich Moores, b July 29, 1820, m Aug. 30, 1838, to E. G. G. Beanland. Issue:

    Francis Mary Beanland, b Aug. 15, 1839, d Nov. 1, 1843.

    Margaret M. Beanland, b Feb. 28, 1841, d Dec. 27, 1845.

    *Henry E. Beanland, b Sept. 10, 1842, died in prison in the service of the C. S. A., at Alton, Ill.

    †James H. Beanland, b March 25, 1844, m Sept. 27, 1870, to Sallie A. Pitts. Issue:

        Charlie E. Beanland, b Oct. 18, 1871.

        May B. Beanland, b Jan. 24, 1875, m W. P. Holmes. Issue:

            Alice Holmes.

            Finnie Holmes.

            James Holmes.

            Anna Holmes.

            Mack Holmes.

            Ed Holmes.

            Leonard Holmes.

            Oliver Holmes.

            Riley Holmes.

        Ray H. Beanland, b July, 1877, d infant.

    J. H. Beanland m 2nd to Mary F. Sherrill, Feb. 6, 1879. Issue:

        Jessie M. Beanland, b Jan. 22, 1882, m H. L. Thomason: Issue:

            Charles Thomason.

            Ed Thomason.

            Dewey Thomason.

            Ray Thomason.

            Thomas Thomason.

            Jewel Thomason.

            Eber Thomason.

            Helen Thomason.

        W. H. Beanland, d 1900.

        Luther W. Beanland.

        Curtis M. Beanland, b Sept. 1, 1887.

        Hugh S. Beanland, b Nov. 14, 1892.

        Charles Ed Beanland, m Anna Keene. Issue:

            Thelma Beanland.

            Kenneth Beanland.

    ‡William F. Beanland, b April 2, 1846.

    Martha R. Beanland, b Sept. 27, 1847, m Jan. 20, 1870, to G. W. D. Porter. Issue:

        Zuella Porter.

        Frank Porter.

        Wesley Porter.

        Carl Porter.

        Terry Porter.

    Jane Brown Beanland, b Dec. 6, 1849, m Edwin B. Forbes, Dec. 6, 1870. Issue:

        Mary Lou Forbes, b Feb. 6, 1872, m Geo. L. Murray, Apr. 28, 1911.

---

*Henry E. Beanland joined the Confederate Army and fought in the battle of Perryville, and afterwards joined the Cavalry and was captured and taken to Alton, Illinois, where he died in prison.

†James H. Beanland joined the Confederate army, 32nd Mississippi regiment, and was wounded at the battle of Perryville, Ky., and came out of battle with seven bullet holes in his body, and also received a severe wound at the bottle of Atlanta, Ga.

‡William F. Beanland was a soldier in General Forest's body guard. He fought in the battle of Franklin, Tennessee, and split his life's blood there.

J. Berton Forbes, b Feb. 4, 1874, m
Eddie Carter, Sept. 27, 1903.
Issue:
Carter B. Forbes, b June
29, 1904.
Bert Forbes.
Nellie Brown Forbes, b April 1, 1876, m W. M.
Reid, Sept. 6, 1898, d Mch. 10, 1910. Issue:
Whitney Beall Reid, b June 6, 1900.
Velma Francis Reid, b Oct. 16, 1901.
Wayne Edwin Reid, b Jan. 20, 1907.
Joseph L. Beanland, b Jan. 18, 1852, d 1854.
Jordan M. Beanland, b Nov. 27, 1857, m Alice Weldman.
Issue:
Charles Beanland.
James Beanland.
Crocket Beanland.
Charles Ross Wilson Beanland, b Oct. 18, 1861, d Aug. 25,
1869.
Jane Ross Moores.
Jordan Moores, was killed at the battle of Gettysburg.
HENRY MOORES, m 2nd to Fannie Cole. Issue:
*Henry R. Moores, b May 7, 1835, in Lincoln Co., Tenn., d Sept. 1, 1903,
in Prentiss Co., Miss. M Sinie Crocket Wileman (widow), b
Mch. 7, 1835, in Coffee Co., Tenn., d Mch. 2, 1881, in Miss. Issue:
Fannie Moores, b Feb. 19, 1874, m A. A. Tays, Dec. 12, 1894,
in Prentiss Co., Miss. He was b Oct. 8, 1868. Issue:
Virgie M. Tays, b Sept. 22, 1895.
Wesley A. Tays, b Nov. 13, 1897.
A. Rodney Tays, b May 28, 1899.
F. Sybil Tays, b Feb. 3, 1901.
Leland C. Tays, b May 2, 1902.
Henry Clyde Tays, b Oct. 18, 1903.
Edith C. Tays, b Nov. 24, 1905.
Mildred K. Tays, b Oct. 6, 1907.
Lila M. Tays, b Oct. 7, 1909.
Fannie Ross Moores and Charles Bryce Martin were married about 1880.
Issue:
Charles Bryce Martin, m ——. Issue:
Happer Williams Martin, m ——. Issue:
Three children.
Charles Bryce Martin, married, and is living in
Milwaukee, Wis.
Fannie R. M. Martin m 2nd to Charles Wesley Williams, in 1860. Issue:
James Henry Williams, m Fannie Taylor Lawrence. Issue
Coday Wesley Williams, b June, 1895.
Mary Fannie Williams, d in 1882.
Robert Alfred Williams, d in infancy.
Julia Ada Williams, m George Calvin Taylor, in 1892. Issue:
Wesley Williams Taylor, b Sept., 1893.
George Calvin Taylor, b Jan., 1896.
Mildred Haight Taylor, b May, 1898.
Hattie Moores Williams, m J. W. Price, in 1898. No issue.

---

*Henry R. Moores served 3 years, part the time in Forest's command, Capt. H. George Company, Col. Nixon's Regiment, 20th Tennessee Cavalry Bell's Brigade, Bufort's Division. He was a brave and faithful soldier, always ready for duty under all and every circumstance.

H. C. WRIGHT former Captain.

ISAAC AND JANE ALEXANDER MOORES.
Page 98.

MRS. MARY LEFTWICH MOORES
Page 95

JOEL AND SARAH MOORES PAYNE.
Page 93.

(1) Charles Moores, b Jan. 12, 1829, d Jan. 8, 1866.
(2) John C. Moores, b March 6, 1831, d March 5, 1848.
James W. Moores, b at Fayetteville, Tenn., July 25, 1837, m Virginia Molley, in 1870. He died May 13, 1905. (See picture.)

NOTES.

(1) Charles Moores was burned to death in his store building in Memphis. He was engaged to be married to a young lady of Edgefield. He was well and favorably known in the social and business world; was a man of excellent habits and of urbane and genial disposition.

(2) J. W. Moores was reared in the Fayetteville, Tenn., neighborhood, but moved to Memphis a few years before the war between the States. He entered the Confederate service in 1861 as a member of Shelby's Grays, and left a sick bed at Memphis for Corinth just before the advent of the Federal troops, where he received an indefinite furlough to await convalescence from inflammatory rheumatism. He remained with the army, rendering the best service he could as Assistant Quartermaster with Hood and most of the time with Gen. Pat Cleburne, with whose command he was at the battle of Franklin. He surrendered at Greensboro, N. C. After the war he engaged in business in Memphis as commission merchant and cotton factor until 1880, since when his life was spent in Kentucky, where he operated a coal mine until his health failed. A devoted Christian gentleman, he bore without reproach the "grand old name of gentleman."— From a sketch in the "Confederate Veteran."

TENTH CHILD OF HENRY AND JEAN MOORES.

Isaac Ross Moores bore the name of his grandfather, Isaac Ross. He married his cousin, Jean Alexander, who at the time lived in Illinois. About 1852 they started on the long journey to Oregon, accomplishing it in about five months, after passing through many dangers. He and two cousins, Alexander and McDonald, together with a friend, Fithian, purchased the town site of Milwaukee from Adam Juneau, the French owner, and repudiated the purchase when they learned that Fithian, who conducted the negotiations with Juneau, had paid $9,000, collecting $3 000 each from the three cousins on the statement that he had paid $12,000. They forced him to take all the land and to return the money, and Fithian's forced purchase made him a very rich man. Isaac Ross Moores was a Colonel in the Black Hawk war, a member of the Oregon Territorial Legislative Assembly and member of the first and only Oregon State Constitutional Convention. He was defeated by a narrow margin, just before his death, for the Oregon State Senate. He was a man of firm purpose and noble attributes.

Placerville, California, Sept. 7, 1851.

Cousin Sarah:
According to promise in Newt's letter, I now commence writing to you for the first time in my life. I will have to give the same excuse to you I gave to Emma for not writing to you long ago, viz: what time I have had for writing, when I felt in the mood, was occupied principally in answering letters I had received, and, as I had not incurred such debt at your hands, this was laid over for the first convenient season, which time having "arriv," I am now ready to fulfil my promise. Whether or not you have been standing back and not writing to me for fear of infringing on some of the rules of etiquette concerning epistolary correspondence, I am unable to determine, as my "edication" is most lamentably deficient in that respect; but something of awful importance must have been in imminent danger of violation by writing, or you would certainly have written to me before this. Or perhaps domestic cares have occupied your attention. This latter apology I might urge with some show of propriety, as you are doubtless aware I have to do my own cooking, mending and washing, which occupies no inconsiderable portion of my time. I flatter myself that, with a little more experience, I will be a good cook. I can now boil potatoes, wash dishes (query, are tin cups and plates dishes?), and turn slap-jacks in the most approved style. It might interest you to know of some of our numerous dishes, for they are new. A favorite dish with us is flamgurgeon, but for delicacy of flavor it will not compare with

grizzlespling. I would tell you what a good cook I am, but you might let it get out and I would be tormented beyond measure when I got back, for I can't marry all of them, much as I would like to accommodate them—but enough of this nonsense.

The Fourth—the glorious Fourth—went off about as usual in the States, with the exception of a public procession, oration and dinner by the "Independent Order of Grizzels," a secret organization somewhat similar to the Masons and Odd Fellows. Their object is unknown to me, but I rather suspect that there is a snipe at the bottom, although their appearance was most exemplary. They gave a splendid dinner at the Empire, the price of which was five dollars where everything could be had in the eating line; yet, notwithstanding the immense attraction, we decided to take dinner at home, and thus parted with the "Grizzels." The Masons had a public celebration here June 24th, and quite a number were from a distance. They gave a ball in the evening, but not soon enough for all to participate, as a few were overcome by the heat and were past dancing long before night. A few emigrants have already arrived from the States and a great many from Salt Lake.

Our summer so far has been most delightful. When there is no breeze stirring, which is not very common, it is very warm in the middle of the day, but the nights are universally pleasant, which you know is not the case in Illinois. The snowy Sierra on one side and the ocean on the other renders the temperature much more uniform than it is at home. I wish you could enjoy one of our moonlight evenings—you would then know something of a delightful climate.

As my sheet is nearly full, I must "rein in." Attribute all defects to lameness in my head, pen, feelings, etc., as I feel but little like writing. But don't forget to write a long letter—longer than this, as this is not as long as I usually write. But I don't like to bore you with any more such stuff as this, and I couldn't write sense now if I tried.

Remember me to all of our folks, grandma and all the rest of the connection, and don't forget to speak a word for me to the girls.

I remain, as ever, your affectionate cousin,
ISAAC R. MOORES.

To Sarah McDonald, Georgetown, Ill.

ISAAC ROSS MOORES, son of Henry Moores and Jane or Jean Ross, was b in Madison Co., Ky., March 12, 1796, and died in Lane Co., Oregon, April 15, 1861. He m Jane Alexander, who was b in Georgia, Dec. 27, 1793, and died in Salem, Oregon, Jan. 20, 1868. (See Alexander line.) Issue:

*John H. Moores, b near Huntsville, Ala., June 26, 1821. Died in Salem, Oregon, Dec. 16, 1880. He m Virginia L. Lamon, May 11, 1847. She was b in Bunker Hill, Va., in June, 1825, and d in Portland, Oregon, in June, 1897. Issue:

Infant dau, b and d in Benton, Mo., in 1848.

†Charles B. Moores, b in Benton, Mo., Aug. 6, 1849. He m Nov. 1, 1881, to Sarah E. Chamberlain, who was b in Michigan, Oct. 20, 1853. Issue.

‡Gertrude E. Moores, b in Salem, Ore., Dec. 15, 1882, m Dec. 4, 1907, to Albert S. Wells. Issue:

Virginia Wells, b in Portland, Ore., Nov. 16, 1908.

Bruce Arrington Wells, b in Portland, Ore., March 4, 1911.

‡Merrill B. Moores, b in Salem, Ore., Feb. 8, 1884.

‡Gordon C. Moores, b in Salem, Ore., Feb. 7, 1885, m Feb. 23, 1911, to Jessie Hurley.

‡Chester A. Moores, b in Salem, Ore., Feb. 10, 1889.

---

*Three times Mayor of Salem, Oregon, and member Oregon State Senate, 1870-1874.

†Charles B. Moores, Chief Clerk Oregon House of Representatives, 1880; Private Secretary to Governor of Oregon, 1882-87; Speaker Oregon House of Representatives, 1895; Register U. S. Land Office at Oregon City, 1897-1905; Commissioner of Public Docks, city of Portland, 1911.

‡See pictures of the home of Charles B. Moores and his four children.

Gertrude B. Moores, b in Danville, Ill., Sept. 26, 1851, and d in Salem, Ore., Oct. 12, 1877, was m July 1, 1874, to Miles M. Miller, who was born in Michigan, July, 1849. Issue:

> Bruce Albert Miller, b and d in Salem, Ore., 1876.
> Guy Chester Miller, b in Salem, Ore., in March, 1877. He m Blanche Meyer. Issue:
>> Max Miller, b in Palo Alto, Cal.
>> Kenneth Miller, b in Palo Alto, Cal.

Albert N. Moores, b in Salem, Ore., May, 1855, m May, 1886, to Cora C. Dickinson, who was b in Salem, 1857. Issue:

> **Ralph D. Moores, b in Salem, January, 1888.
> **Althea Moores, b in Selem, Ore.
> **Kenneth Moores, b in Salem, Ore.

Althea Moores, b in Salem, Ore., Nov. 6, 1856, d Apr. 29, 1883.

Bertha Moores, b in Salem, Ore., Nov. 6, 1856.

Carrie V. Moores, b in Salem, Ore., April 15, 1863.

Martha A. Moores, b in Danville, Ill., in 1824, d in Danville, Ill., in 1847. She was m Oct. 22, 1845, to Judge Josiah McRoberts, who was b in Monroe Co., Ill., June 12, 1820, d in Joliet, O., June 4, 1885. Issue:

> Samuel McRoberts, b in Danville, Ill., Dec. 13, 1845, d in Salem, Ore., March 21, 1864.

Mary Matilda Moores, b in Danville, Ill., in 1827, and d in Salem, Ore., April 21, 1864, unmarried.

†Charles W. Moores, b in Georgetown, Ill., Nov. 2, 1828, and d in Stevenson, Ala., June 10, 1864. M Julia Merrill, of Indianapolis, Ind., dau of Samuel and Lydia Jane Merrill. Issue:

> *Merrill Moores, b April 21, 1856, in Indianapolis, Ind.
> Janet Douglass Moores, b March 20, 1858, in Indianapolis, Ind., d March 1, 1905, unmarried.
> ‡Charles W. Moores, b Feb. 15, 1862, in Indianapolis, Ind., m Oct. 5, 1896, to Elizabeth Nichols. Issue:
>> Elizabeth Bishop Moores, b Dec. 25, 1897.
>> Charles W. Moores, b June 24, 1903.

‡Isaac Ross Moores, b in Danville, Ill., Feb. 14, 1831, d in Portland, Ore., July 24, 1834, m in 1856 to Ellen R. Lamon, who was b in Bunker Hill., Va., Jan., 1831, and d in St. Louis, Mo., Sept., 1896. Issue:

> Infant dau, b and d in Salem, in 1857.
> Ross E. Moores, b in Salem, in 1857.
> William E. Moores.
> Wylie A. Moores, m Florence Elgin, now deceased, leaving no children.
> Charles H. Moores.
> Carroll L. Moores, b in Salem, July, 1870.

ELEVENTH CHILD OF HENRY AND JEAN MOORES.

JANE BROWN MOORES, b Feb. 25, 1800, d Dec. 25, 1858, unmarried.

TWELFTH CHILD OF HENRY AND JEAN MOORES.

WILSON ALEXANDER MOORES, b Sept. 28. 1802.

---

*Merrill Moores. B. A. Yale, 1878; LL. B. Central Law School of Indiana, 1880; lawyer. (For biography, see "Who's Who in America," 1910-1911.) He was a member of President Taft's class at Yale University; was Deputy Attorney General of Indiana, and made a close run for the Attorney Generalship. Was once President of the Indianapolis Bar Association and also of the State Bar Association. He recently refused tender of the U. S. Marshalship of Indiana, tendered by President Taft.

‡Charles Washington Moores. B. A. Wabash 1882, M. A. 1885, LL. B. Central Law School of Indiana 1908, married in Philadelphia, October 5, 1896, Elizabeth Nichols, daughter of Aurin B. and Mary (Thompson) Nichols, of Philadelphia, Pa., lawyer. For biography, see "Who's Who in America," 1910-1911. Author of Lives of Abraham Lincoln and Christopher Columbus, published by Houghton, Mifflin & Co., Boston. Charles W. Moores is a capable lawyer, and was defeated a year ago by a narrow margin for a nomination to the Supreme Bench of Indiana.

†Charles W. Moores died in the Union army, member 132d Indiana Volunteer Infantry.

‡Colonel Oregon National Guard, Speaker Oregon House of Representatives, 1864.

**See Pictures.

CHAPTER V.

CONGER FAMILY.

The town of Woodville, N. J., was settled by a company from Newby, Mass. To this settlement, came John Conger, in the early part of 1667, and with him his wife, Mary Conger. John Conger was not of the original colony, but was present at the first distribution of town lots, as will appear later, and was one of the commissioners for the second distribution of lots to freeholders. From whence he came, there is no record, but a probable tradition is that this family came from Alsace, then a French province, from whence they were driven on account of religious persecution, first to Holland and later to England. The name being originally *Koeniger adds to the probability of the correctness of this belief.

All of the Congers living in America up to the middle of the last century, are believed to be descended from John Conger of Woodbridge. It is not the purpose of this sketch to include them all, but the present aim is to give more than the bare †genealogy of John C. Conger of Rowan County, North Carolina, a grandson of John Conger of Woodbridge, and leading up to the North Carolina branch it will be interesting to acquaint ourselves with our first ancestor and the kindred of John of North Carolina.

The first mention of John Conger in America is under date of January, 1668, the record of birth of his daughter, Sarah, is given in the town record of births. In the Woodbridge Town Land Records, in the possession of the New Jersey Historical Society, on page 17, is found the following entry:

"October ye 18th, 1669. Laid out for John Conger, by virtue of the Governor's warrant dated August the 17th, 1669, one house lot and addition containing fifteen acres bounded north by the meadow of Papiack; in length fifteen chains to a great white oak marked on all four sides, from thence extending s : : ten chains to a tree and a steak, by it marked on all four sides; from thence running s : w : fifteen chains to a walnut tree marked on all four sides standing nex (sic) the highway; from thence ten chains n : w to the meadow side, where we first began.

Item three acres and a half of meadow next adjoyning to his house lot and addition, bounded north upon Papiack Creek, s : w : by the meadow Matthew Moore, n : e : by the meadow of Daniel Robins.

---

*It was related by the late C. B. G. Conger, of Washington, editor of the Conger Union, that one George Koeniger, an Alsacian, came to Kenockee, St. Clair County, Michigan, about the middle of the last century. He was universally known by his neighbors as Conger, and his descendants bear that name.

†Charles L. Conger, of Mackintosh, Minn., is preparing a genealogy of the Congers.

Item one hundred and twenty acres of upland butting upon Rahawack River beginning at a red oak near a cove called George Little his cove, from thence running east along the river thirty chains to a stake marked with three notches; from thence extending south forty chains to a walnut marked on all four sides and four notches; from thence running west through a great swamp to a beach tree marked on all four sides and four notches, and from thence running north, crossing a small fresh brook forty chains to the red oak where we first began, allowance being given for highway to fetch hay; two small bits of meadow joyning to the front of said land at each corner.

Item thirty acres of meadow at Rahawack or elsewhere not yet laid out, in all containing one hundred and seventy acres, English measure. This record attested on the certificate."

This John Conger, our first ancestor, is frequently mentioned in the records of this part of New Jersey. He is referred to as John Conger, planter, and the number of deeds recorded show that he was constantly exchanging and buying and selling land. Some of the deeds, in their description of this land, are very interesting. They are found in the archives of New Jersey, and the following are taken from those records.

On June 24, 1672, he sold to Richard Smith, of Newton, L. I., for 16 pounds, 60 acres of upland on the Rahway River and 6 acres of meadow. Nov. 5, 1674, he exchanged 39 acres of his land with Obediah Winter for an equal amount at "Chestnut Plaine." Dec. 3, 1683, he sold to Micael White his ten-acre house lot and six-acre addition that had originally been granted to Jonathan Haines. On April 1, 1691, was recorded the survey of five acres of meadow and sixteen acres of upland by a grant of the Town Committee, dated April 1, 1684. Oct. 9, 1691, he purchased from Josiah Winter the 30 acres of land which he had traded off to Obediah Winter (the father of Joseph.) On March 24, 1692, he sold to Ebenezer Foord, of Woodbridge, 16 acres at the west "of my Accommodation," not yet laid out.

John Conger witnessed will of Obediah Winter, alias Graham, of Woodbridge, Feb. 1, 1674-5.

March 26, 1692-3, deed, John Conger, of Woodbridge, to Ebenezer Ford, for sixteen acres E. grantor, N. a common or sunken meadow.

April 14, 1691, deed, John Conger to John Coddington, both of Woodbridge, for two acres of Rahawack meadows, part of five acres laid out for grantor April, 1684. S. upland, E. grantor, W. Thos. Thorp.

Deed, John Conger, of Woodbridge, to Daniel Robbins, Jr., of the same place, for three acres of Rahawack meadows, E. and W. John Coddington, S. Daniel Stillwell, N. F. First Creek.

John Conger was active in the management of the affairs of the town of Woodbridge. He was Town Clerk, and late in the year 1688 eight men were chosen by the town of Woodbridge to protect the common land from depredations of cattle thieves. John Conger and Noah Bishop were chosen for Rahway and parts adjacent. In 1687 these two men were sued by Thomas Thorp for removing from the commons the latter's dressed trees. The case was decided in favor of Thorp, and the cost of the litigation was borne by the two.

On Feb. 15, 1687-8 John Conger was one of a committee of ten appointed to lay out the second division of common lands, sixty acres of this land being given to each freeholder. In 1691 the town Constables were John Conger and Gawen Lockhart (Dally, p. 138. Feb. 27, 1694, John Conger registered a protest against the vote of the town that John Brown, of Amboy, be schoolmaster for the following year at a salary of 54 pounds. September. 1684, John Conger served on a jury in Middlesex County to try Philip Gunter on a charge of petit larceny. A list of the members of Christ's Church at Woodbridge shows that Sarah

Conger became a communicant Dec. 26, 1708, and that John and Mary Conger joined May 12, 1709. This John was evidently the son John and his wife Mary.

A memo. in S. H. Conger's note book, p. 167, probably taken from the Proprietor's Record at Amboy, states that on April 27, 1670, John Conger sold to Samuel Moore, of Woodbridge, 3 1-2 acres of meadow land for "10 pound and 10 shillings in corn and cattle," "and also he did deliver a turf and twig of the same meadow to Sam Moore, at the same time declaring that he delivered that part in relation to the whole."

WILL OF JOHN CONGER, SR., OF WOODBRIDGE, N. J.

In the name of God, amen, the eleventh day of January, 1710-1711, John Conger, of Woodbridge, in the County of Middlesex and Province of East New Jersey, planter, being in bodily health and in perfect mind and memory, thanks be given to God therefor, calling in mind the mortality of this body and knowing it is appointed for all men once to die, do make and ordaine this my last will and testament, that is to say, principally. And, first of all, I give and recommend my soul into the hands of God that gave it, and for my body I recommend it to the earth, to be buried in Christian-like and decent manner, at the discretion of my executors, nothing doubting but at the general resurrection I shall receive the same againe by the mighty power of God, and as touching such worldly estate wherewith it hath pleased God to bless me in this life, I give, devise and dispose of the same in this following manner and form:

Imp. my will is that my farme or plantation on which I now dwell be equally divided into two parts, beginning at the river and running with a direct line through the whole length of my said farme or plantation, the eastern division whereof I will and bequeath to my son, Benjamine Conger, to be by him quietly and peaceably possessed and enjoyed as soon as he shall arrive at the age of twenty-one years, and if my son Joseph please he shall have liberty to live upon it twenty years after my decease, paying the charge arising thereon.

Item—The use of and improvement of the westerne division of my said farme or plantation and my dwelling house standing thereon I give to my wife during her state of widowhood, and when her condition shall change either by marriage or death I will and bequeath the said western division of my farme, together with my now dwelling house and all other buildings standing thereon, to my son, Job Conger.

Item—I will and bequeath to my son, Joseph Conger, all my freehold right in the towne of Woodbridge.

Item—My will is that if either of my three sons above mentioned, viz: Joseph, Job or Benjamine, shall die without issue, then what land I have willed to them doe descend to the survivor or survivors and be equally divided between them.

Item—I give to my son my carts and plows, with all the taceling belonging to them, my son Joseph to have liberty to use them when they can be spared, soe longe as he lives upon the place, he being at equal charge in repair with them.

I give to my son John 10 shillings, to my son Jonathan 5 shillings, to my son Gershom 5 shillings, and to each of my daughters 5 shillings, all to be paid by my son Job if demanded.

Lastly, I give all my cattle, horses, sheep and household stuff to my faithful and well beloved wife, Sarah Conger, whom I do nominate and appoint my sole executrix, to see that this my last will be punctually filled, and I doe declare to be my last will and testament hereby revoking and renouncing and making void all other wills by me formerly made. Witness hereof, I have hereunto set my hand and seale the daye and yeare first above written.

JOHN CONGER.

Signed, sealed, published and declared by the said John Conger as his last will and testament, in the presence of us the subscribers, viz: James Connet, James Connet, Jr., Richard Bangburne, John Bishop.

June 14 I, the above named John Conger, being very sick and not expecting to live many houers in this life, and my son *Gershom being borne since the making of this will above written, doe declare that my will and desire is that my three sons, Joseph, Job and Benjamine, as they come to age, give unto my son Gershom 10 shillings each of them, and that seven pounds out of

*This was evidently his grandson, Gershom.

GLADYS WALKER
Page 189

HELLEN LIPSCOMB
Page 198

FRANCES M. O'QUIN
Page 35

ELEANOR FRANK AND
HATTIE S. NICHOLS
Page 43

LUCY ELIZABETH AND
ROBERT S. LAMON
Page 151

VIRGINIA AND
DANIEL SHELBY MACKEY
Page 222

ROSEMARY BUTLER
Page 222

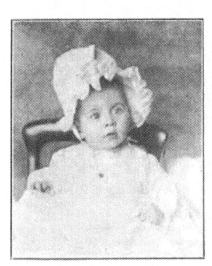

ROSE FULGHAM WELLS
Page 221

ROSABELL AND JAMES McKEY
Page 222

ELIZABETH WOOD
(See Appendix.)

RUTH EVELYN BEESON
Page 192

LOUIS LORENZO POSEY
Page 35

MARY THECKLA HOLLINGSWORTH
Page 191

JOSIAH CONGER
Page 121

LETITIA GRACE WYATT
Page 113

MYRTLE REID CONGER
Grand Daughter of Josiah Conger
Page 122

my movable estate be put out for his use when he comes of age. This I declare to be my desire before these witnesses: John Sille, John Moore, John Bishop.

Proved before Thos Gordon, the 27th of August, and approved and sealed by his Excellency, Col. Hunter, etc., the 17th day of October, 1712.   J. BASS.

Liber. I. Folio 382.   N. J. WILLS, Secretary of State's Office.

JOHN CONGER, was married twice, although not much is known of his wives; but it is certain that the first wife was Mary, and her children were:

SARAH CONGER, b in January, 1668-9. Either she or an older sister married the father of Edward and John Wilkinson.

JOANNA CONGER, b Aug., 1670, m in 1667-8 Joseph Fitz Randolph, of Piscataway. In some records she is called Joanna and some Hannah.

JOHN CONGER, b May 24, 1674.

ELIZABETH CONGER, b Jan. 1, 1678-9. No records further.

LYDIA CONGER, b Jan. 1, 1679-80, apparently died young, as another child was given that name.

*JONATHAN CONGER, b Mch. 29, 1683. He removed to Newark some time before his death. In 1726 he witnessed the will of Joseph Wheeler, of Newark. He died May 8, 1733, and is buried at Newark. His children as given were:

Samuel Conger, b Feb., 1715.

Mary Conger, m Nehemiah Baldwin, of Newark, b 1722, d 1765.

The children of JOHN CONGER by his marriage with Sarah were:

ENOS CONGER, d Nov. 21, 1689.

JOSEPH CONGER, b May 17, 1692. In 1715 he and his brother, Job, were privates in Col. Parker's Company of Col. Thos. Farmer's Militia Regiment, New York. He m Mary Marsh.

JOB CONGER, b June 9, 1694, m Keziah, and according to his will his children were:

Job Conger, b about 172—, 173—, m Lydia Coddington.

Enoch Conger, m Zillah Coddington, a sister of Mary.

Moses Conger.

Ruth Conger, m Nathaniel Price.

Sarah Conger, m Nathaniel Coddington.

Elizabeth Conger, m Reuben Heard.

Esther Conger.

Bathia or Bethia Conger.

Jonathan Conger, born May 29, 1664, at Woodbridge, New Jersey, and died at Newark, N. J., May 8, 1733. Married and known to have had a son Samuel, and daughter Mary. The son Samuel was born in 1715, and died in Newark, N. J., December 14, 1852. The last genealogist whom I have employed thinks that John Conger of Rowan County, N. C., and Jonathan of Woodbridge were also his sons and were older than Samuel. Jonathan, Sr., seems to have removed from Woodbridge to Newark and his son Samuel went with him, but both John of Rowan County and Jonathan, Jr. of Woodbridge remained in that vicinity, Jonathan, Jr. dying there in 1779, and John Conger, supposed to be John Conger of Rowan County, was there as late as 1745, and owned land there and at Paypack, N. J.

My reason for connecting John Conger of Rowan County, N. C., and Jonathan, Jr. of Woodbridge, N. J., is as follows: Jonathan Conger of Woodbridge had three sons named in his will, David (dead at the making of the will, as it mentions Mary Conger, widow of his son David), Jonathan and John. I have nearly complete records of the sons David and John.

The son David married Mrs. Mary Green, nee Mary Darby, and had two sons, David, Jr. and Elias Darby. Both of these sons removed to Washington County, Penn., and David Conger died there. His grandson, Henry Conger, now of Hackney, Penn., tells me that he remembers hearing when he was a small boy that there were three brothers, and one went to North Carolina, one to New York and one to Pennsylvania. Now if it is true that Jonathan, Jr. of Woodbridge and John of North Carolina were brothers, then it was the nephews of John of Rowan County, one of whom went to New York (Washington County) and the descendants of the other nephews who went to Pennsylvania.

Furthermore, the wills of John Conger of Rowan County and Jonathan Conger of Woodbridge read nearly the same and the children's names are about the same. This, together with this North Carolina story from the Pennsylvania Conger, have given me this idea. It may be flimsy, but until something more positive shows up I shall group them this way. Furthermore, there are only three Congers whose parentage are unaccounted for of anywhere near that date, and they are John of Rowan County, Jonathan, Jr. of Woodbridge and Nathaniie, all of whom were about the same age or a few years apart.   CHARLES L. CONGER.

*Mr. William Conger, now 84 years old, relates that his father, Josiah Conger, met some of his New Jersey Conger cousins when on a visit to Ohio. This is only one of the many proofs that the North Carolina branch is of the New Jersey stock.

—103—

RACHEL CONGER, b May 12, 1696.
LYDIA CONGER, b April 28, 1696.
GERSHOM CONGER, b about 1685, m Anna (DeSignye.)
BENJAMINE CONGER, b about 1700. It is very probable that his mother was Sarah, 2nd wife of John. He was m twice. The name of the first wife is not known. In 1743 he was living in Morristown, N. J., with his second wife, Experience, several years younger than he and 17 years older than her step-son, Daniel. There is a probability that she was his only wife and that he married her as a young girl. She d Sept. 30, 1784, aged 84. His children were:

Daniel Conger, b about 1728.
Elizabeth Conger, m at Morristown, March 3, 1757, to Benj. Gobel.
Benjamine Conger, m Elizabeth Gobel. Had a daughter, Lydia.
Simeon Conger, m Abigail Gobel. Had daughters, Sarah and Martha.
Abigail Conger, b 1730, m 1st to Simeon Gobel, Feb. 23, 1749, and 2nd to Ebenezer Stiles.
Enoch Conger, b about 1742, m Nov. 14, 1762, Susannah Whitehead. He had several children.
Noah Conger, baptized March 5, 1743.
David Conger, baptized Aug. 12, 1744.
Lydia Conger, baptized Aug. 17, 1746.

NEWSPAPER EXTRACTS.

Broke into the pasture of the subscriber, in Morristown. on the 24th day of June last, a bay mare, with an old saddle and part of a bridle on her. In about 14 1-2 hands high, trots and paces, but mostly inclines to a pace; a large white streak on her face, branded with an H on her near thigh, but not easily perceived; shod before; supposed to be about 6 or 7 years old. The owner is desired to prove his property, pay the charges and take her away, otherwise she will be sold, as she has been advertised for astray.   ENOCH CONGER.
Aug. 24, 1778.

Joseph Conger signed Articles of Association of Freeholders and Inhabitants of Pequanock, in the County of Morris, pledging themselves to sustain the action of the Continental and Provincial Congresses in defending the Constitution. Signed by 180 persons. May, 1776.

Notice is hereby given that the plantation of Moses Conger is to be sold, by public sale, to the highest bidder at vendue, on the 25th day of next March, afternoon, if not sold at private sale before. It is well situated for a gentleman, tradesman or farmer, allowed good land lying in Woodbridge, Rahway Neck, adjoining that pleasant river, which affords fish in plenty in season and is navigable for boats, sloops, etc. There is on it a tolerably good house and barn; it is exceedingly well watered, some wood, a fine young orchard, and another considerably older. It contains by estimation between 70 and 80 acres of upland, nearly 15 acres of salt marsh, as handy and as good as any in that part. Any person wanting such a place may apply to the subscriber before the day of sale, who will give a good title and sell on reasonable terms.
                                                                MOSES CONGER.
N. B. Said place lies convenient for a ferry to be erected across Rahway river to Elizabethtown.—From the N. Y. Gazette or Weekly Post Boy, No. 1498, Feb. 18, 1771.

THE NORTH CAROLINA BRANCH.

Jonathan Conger, b 1683, son of John 1st, was known to have children, Mary and Samuel. The latter was born about 1715. These were supposed to be his younger children, and they removed with their father to Newark. John Conger of Rowan County, Jonathan, Jr., of Woodbridge, and Nathaniel are believed to have been older children. John of Rowan County remained in New Jersey until about 1745, as the public records give no mention of him after that time.

Jonathan, Jr., had three sons, David, John and Jonathan. John of Rowan County also had sons John and Jonathan, and John, Jr., of Rowan County repeated these names with his children. Such a repetition of names is confusing, and it is very difficult to ascertain which John or Jonathan is referred to.

About 1750 John Conger, grandson of John of Woodbridge and believed to be a son of Jonathan Conger, moved to Rowan County, North Carolina, in that portion which is now embraced in Davidson County. The lands owned by John Conger and his sons lay on both sides of Abbott's Creek, in Healing Springs and Cotton Grove Townships, and at what is now Hannersville, North Carolina, in Conrad Hill Township.

There are three old Conger graveyards on these lands. Two are on Abbott's Creek. The one which is on the original lands owned by John Conger, Sr., is on the right side of Abbott's Creek, one mile north of the Yadkin River. In it is buried Zipporah Conger, beside what is supposed to be the grave of John Conger, Sr. Her grave bears the following inscription:

Deceast March the 14d in ye year of our Lord 1783, and in ye 73 year of hir age. Hear lays the body of Zipporah Conger.

Her death occurred one year previous to that of John Conger, Sr., and as his will makes no mention of his wife, we infer that she was his wife.

The body of Jonathan Conger, son of John Conger, Sr., lies in this graveyard. The following refers to this Jonathan Conger:

RAILROAD BUILDERS OPEN AN ANCIENT GRAVE.

While excavating the right of way of the south-bound railroad on the farm of Mr. H. L. Holmes, in Healing Springs Township, this county, Mr. A. K. Lookabill, who has employment on the new road, unearthed an ancient grave wherein reposed the remains of one Jonathan Conger, so the inscription on the stone ran, who was among the early settlers in this section. The railroad will run directly through this graveyard, and it may be that other graves will be forced to give up their dead by the call of progress. This particular grave was six feet deep, with a vault of 3 1-2 feet. The bones were intact and properly arranged, with the arms, according to the old custom, parallel with the body, instead of crossed, as is the present day custom. The hair was well preserved, although the date on the stone stated the man died May 7, 1793, more than 116 years ago. The date of his birth was given as Januvry 22, 1732, his age being 61 years, three monts and sixteen days. On the stone also was his message from the 18th century to the 20th century railroad builders, whose surveyors had led them into the old-time burying ground:

"Remember, man, as you pass by,
As you are now so once was I.
As I am now so must you be;
Prepare for death and follow me."
—Clipping from the Lexington Dispatch.

Across Abbott's Creek about one-half mile, in another graveyard, we find the only tombstone whose inscription is legible, bearing the following:

Mary Conge, deceast Jan. the 4d, 1795. Was born Jan. the 28d, 1751.

*Remember, man, as you pass by,
As you are now so once was I.
As I am now so must you be;
Prepare for death and follow me.

This Mary Conger was Mary Ross, the daughter of Isaac and Jean Brown Ross, who married John Conger, Jr., son of John Conger of Rowan County. In another grave next to hers, and with a tombstone exactly like that which marks the grave of Mary, probably reposes the remains of her husband, John Conger, though the inscription has pelled off.

The third graveyard is near Hannersville, on the land now owned by Mr. Plummer, but originally bought by Jonathan Conger (son of John Conger of Rowan), in 1763, from Henry McCullob. The graves on this place bear tombstones that are illegible.

DEEDS.

A deed from Jonathan Conger to Leonard Smith, Feb. 4, 1796. Registered April 12, 1796, book No. 14, page 251. It states that this tract of land was obtained from John Conger, Sr., and has Jonathan and Margaret Conger's names signed to it.

A deed from John and Judith Conger to Leonard Smith, made October, 1801. In this deed is mentioned the line of Jonathan Conger, Sr., and says this land is a part of the original tract granted in 1778, May 6, to John Conger. Registered in book No. 18, page 173.

Deed from John Conger to John Ward, made in 1801. No mention of it being registered.

Deed from Daniel Riles, attorney for Isaac Conger to Reuben Holmes, made February, 1805. Registered in book 19, page 80.

These deeds show that the Congers once owned near or over 1,000 acres of land in this vicinity (now Davidson County), on both sides of Abbott's Creek.

There was another Conger place, about twelve miles distant, at what is now Hannersville, N. C. Of this place Jonathan Conger bought about 200 acres of land from Henry McCullob about 1763. The State grants of land made to the Morgan family in 1785-86 called for corner on Jonathan Conger line (now the Plummer place, near Hannersville, N. C.) There is an old graveyard on this place. The graves are not all marked.

FROM CENSUS REPORT 1790.

In Franklin County, North Carolina, were Ephriah Conger, with one son, two daughters and two slaves; Richard Conger, unmarried, six slaves; Joel, unmarried, one slave; William, married, six slaves; Ross, married, no children.

In Rockingham County was Benjamine Conger, married, with two sons and one daughter.

In Wade County was John Conger or Congress, married, no children.

The Congers of Franklin County were evidently of the line of John Conger of Rowan County.

WILL OF JOHN CONGER, OF ROWAN COUNTY, NORTH CAROLINA.

In the name of God, amen, know all men that I, John Conger, Sr., of the County and State aforesaid, being of perfect mind and memory, yet knowing that it is appointed for men once to die, and knowing not the time when it shall please God to call me hence, that I be no more, do find it necessary, for divers good causes, to me agreeing to constitute this my last will and testament.

And, first of all, at my decease I bequeath my soul to God who gave it, as the receiver of spirits, which through faith I hope to be united with my body at the general resurrection and received into glory in the heavens. Furthermore, at my decease I commit my body to the earth with all the charges of a decent burial, and my funeral charges to be paid out of my estate; and next my desire is that all my debts be paid, and as to the disposal of my worldly goods I do appoint it in the following manner, to-wit: At the time of my death, or as soon after as may be, that my executors take an inventory of all my goods and chattels, real and personal, and at the

*It is interesting to note that this same verse is found on Conger graves in the Conger graveyard near Fayetteville, Tenn.

proper time expose them to public sale to the highest bidder, at the time of the receiving of the money to dispose of in the following manner:

First of all I bequeath to my oldest son, Jonathan Conger, ten pounds and no more. Next I give and bequeath to my youngest son, John Conger, ten pounds and no more, and lastly all the right of my estate to be equally divided between Sarah Rounsaval, Phoebe Randal and Hannah Ross, my daughters, and Jane Ross, daughter of Nicholas Ross, my granddaughter, which four persons above named are to hold the same, them and their heirs forever. In consideration whereof and for which as touching the premises I do constitute and appoint Richard McGuire and Thomas Smith my executors in all cases as touching the premises. In witness whereof I have hereunto set my hand and have fixed my seal this seventh day of February, seventeen and eighty-four. (Seal.) JOHN CONGER, Sr.

Signed, sealed, ratified and pronounced in the presence of Benjamin Rounsaval, Jr.

JOSEPH WARFORD.

FIRST CHILD OF JOHN AND ZIPPORAH CONGER.

*JONATHAN CONGER, son of John and Zipporah Conger, of Rowan County, North Carolina, was born probably in New Jersey, Jan. 22, 1732, died in Rowan County, N. C., May 8, 1793. Name of wife unknown. Issue:

BENJAMINE CONGER.

ISAAC CONGER, d in McLean County, Ill., in 1842. He married Susannah Barrett. Issue:

Jonathan Conger.

Robert Barrett Conger, was born in Bowling Green, Ky., March 5, 1804. He died in McLean. County, Illinois, Aug. 21, 1860. He married Nancy Howell, in McLean County, Ill., Oct. 27, 1836. She was born June 14, 1817, and died June 14, 1866. Issue:

†Samuel Oscar Conger, b Oct. 30, 1837.

Susan Conger, b Oct. 30, 1839, d Mch. 29, 1905.

Emma C. Conger. b Dec. 24, 1841.

Mary A. Conger, b Dec. 24, 1843, d Aug. 16, 1865.

Sarah E. Conger, b Mch. 26, 1846.

Benjamine F. Conger, b in McLean Co., Ill., Sept. 8, 1848, m Mary Snedeker, at Cedar Rapids, Iowa, March 6, 1876. She was b in Knox Co., Ohio, Aug. 11, 1854. Issue:

Robert Guy Conger, b Dec. 12, 1876, d Oct. 16, 1881.

Claud Merritt Conger, b in Dallas Co., Iowa, Oct. 28, 1881, m Ethel Siglin, at Woodward, Iowa, June 14, 1904. Issue:

Daughter, b and d Oct. 14, 1910.

Emma Mable Conger, b Aug. 13, 1883, d June 10, 1884.

Cleo Clare Conger, b Nov. 6, 1897 or 1887.

Amanda A. Conger, b Nov. 22, 1852.

Robert Lee Conger, b Jan. 12, 1860, d Feb. 7, 1887.

‡Benjamine Conger, b near Bowling Green, Ky., June 5, 1809, d in Coffey Co., Kan., May 9, 1881, m Nancy Warwick, in McLean Co., Ill., 1836. She was b near Lexington, Ky., Nov. 1, 1810, and d in McLean Co., Ill., 1863. Issue:

---

*Served as Quartermaster Sergeant, 4th N. C. Reg., in the Revolution. (See mention of deeds and grave on pp. 105-106.

†Samuel Oscar Conger, enrolled at Danver's, Ill., in the 94th Illinois. Transferred to Company F, 37th Ill., Feb. 7, 1875. Mustered out Feb. 6, 1866. (Page 57, Adg. Report.)

‡Benjamine Conger, enrolled at Bloomington, Ill., April 23, 1832, in Captain M. L. Covell's Company, in Col. James Johnson's Regiment, Mounted Militia, General Samuel Whiteside's Brigade. The command was mustered out May 27, 1832, at the mouth of Fox River, now Ottawa, Ill., 135 miles from place of enrollment, he being absent with leave. (Vol. 9, page 102, Adj. Report Black Hawk war.)

—107—

Isaac Conger, b 1838, d June 2, 1862.

Elizabeth Conger, b in McLean Co., in 1839. She m Jesse
Bensen, in McLean Co., Ill., Sept. 24, 1864. Issue:

Infant, d age 15 months.

Nannie Bensen, b Nov. 12, 1865, d 1899.

John F. Bensen, b 1868.

Bruce Bensen, b Aug. 15, 1872.

Frank Bensen, b Aug. 23, 1875.

‡Robert M. Conger, b in McLean Co., Ill., May 14, 1843, m
Melissa A. Bensen, in McLean Co., Ill., Dec. 5, 1866.
She was b Nov. 24, 1840. Issue:

Isaac D. Conger, b Nov. 27, 1867, m Miss Hitch-
ens, at Burlington, Kan., April 15, 1895.

Nannie B. Conger, b in McLean Co., Ill., April
23, 1869, m Cassius M. Chrisman, at Burlington, Kan., Feb. 19, 1893.

Lorain B. Conger, b in McLean Co., Ill., Aug. 12,
1872, m Pearl Watkins, at Burlington,
Kan., Mch. 7, 1899.

Ollie Conger, b in McLean Co., Ill., July 6, 1874,
m Joseph F. Grennan, at Burlington, Kan.,
Feb. 21, 1900.

Louella Conger, b Sept. 24, 1876.

Robert W. Conger, b July 25, 1880.

Nicholson Conger, b Dec. 3, 1843.

SECOND CHILD OF JOHN AND ZIPPORAH CONGER.

SARAH CONGER. No record of her birth, death or family, except the mention of her name, Sarah Rounsaval, in the will of her father, and her
brother, Arthur Brown Ross, mentions a visit to David Rounsaval, when
he visited the Conger settlement in Rowan County in 1801. (See diary,
page 67.)

THIRD CHILD OF JOHN AND ZIPPORAH CONGER.

PHOEBE CONGER. No records except her name in her father's will as
Phoebe Randle. Arthur Brown Ross mentions Phoebe Henly in his
diary, and it is barely probable that she is identical with Phoebe Randle.

FOURTH CHILD OF JOHN AND ZIPPORAH CONGER.

HANNAH CONGER, b Feb. 5, 1747, d Apr. 15, 1820, m Arthur Brown Ross.
(See A. B. Ross' records for descendants.)

ANOTHER DAUGHTER WHO WAS POSSIBLY THE OLDEST CHILD.

*LIZZIE CONGER, m NICHOLAS ROSS, who was the youngest brother of
ISAAC ROSS.

The following is reproduced from Dr. Graham's History of the Mecklenberg
Declaration of Independence:

---

*In the Harris records the name of Lizzie Conger is given as Jane.

‡Robert M. Conger, enlisted in the 94th Infantry, Feb. 15, 1864. Was transferred to Company F, 37th Ill. Infantry,
and discharged June 16, 1866.

"On the Yadkin River, in Rowan County, one Nicholas Ross early settled, marrying Lizzie Conger, daughter of John Conger There were many wild horses then running in the woods. Having a fine animal of his own and needing another, Ross went in the spring of the year to the range and selected one that he thought would suit his purpose, and started to run him down and halter him. But in the race the horse plunged in a hole, turning a complete somersault, and fell back and crushed his pursuer. He left a widow and two little daughters."

Issue of Lizzie or Jane and Nicholas Ross:

*JANE ROSS, b in North Carolina, m Enoch Morgan, who was b in Wales and d in South Carolina. Issue:

Rev. Nicholas Ross Morgan, m Mary Wilson Alexander, granddaughter of Robert Harris (son of Charles) and Mary Wilson and daughter of Jane Wilson Harris and Nathaniel Alexander (son of Abraham Alexander.)

HANNAH ROSS, b in North Carolina, m Mathew Harris. He was the son of Samuel Harris and Martha Laird, and was born in North Carolina. She died in Georgia in 1845, aged 102 years. Issue:

Ross Harris, b in Georgia, unmarried. Killed by Indians in the Seminole war.

John Nicholson Harris, b in Georgia, d unmarried.

James Harris, b in Georgia, m Lucretia Jones. Issue:

Mathew Harris.
McCamey Harris.
Margaret Harris.
Sarah Harris.
Jane Harris.
Priscilla Harris.
Jessie Harris.
Martha Harris.

Charles Harris, m Tabitha Gibbs. Issue:

Lucy Harris.
Ann Harris.
Elizabeth Harris.
Mathew Harris.
James Harris.
John Wesley Harris, killed in the Mexican war.

†LIZZIE CONGER, m 2nd ZACCHEUS WILSON. She died in 1796. Zaccheus Wilson was a surveyor, and was an elder in the Steele Creek Church in 1767, a member of the Mecklenberg Convention in May, 1775, a member of the Provincial Congress in 1776, was a captain at King's Mountain, where, among the plunder which was assigned to the different officers was a surveyor's compass and instruments, which were presented to him and are among the relics of his descendants now. He was a member of the North Carolina Convention of 1788, for the reconsideration of the Federal Constitution. When Caburrus county was set off from Mucklenberg, in 1792, he was chosen county surveyor. After the loss of his wife, in 1796, he moved to Sumpter County, Tenn., where his brother, Major David Wilson, already resided. Just prior to his departure he visited his step-daughter, Mrs. Morgan, and the following is related by Rev. N. H. Morgan in regard to that visit:

"The last night he spent with us, I slept with him, and about midnight the wolves raised a furious howling around the cow-pen. The old gentleman went out and chased them away, and I as a mere lad remember how I trembled lest he should be devoured."

Capt. Wilson settled at Gallatin, Tenn., where he died in 1824.

*It is probable that there are numerous descendants of Jane Ross Morgan, and further information will be appreciated.
†The descendants of this couple are asked to furnish records.

CHAPTER VI.

YOUNGEST SON OF JOHN AND ZIPPORAH CONGER.

JOHN CONGER was probably born in New Jersey or North Carolina. He is mentioned in his father's will as "my youngest son, John Conger." He married Mary Ross, daughter of Isaac and Jean Brown Ross and a sister to the husband of his sister, Hannah Conger Ross' husband, Arthur Brown Ross. The marriage bond of John Conger, Jr., and Mary Ross, dated Jan. 5, 1769, is signed by John Conger, Jr., and his brother, Jonathan Conger, they being bound in the sum of fifty pounds. Under the bond is the following: "This is to satisfy you that I give our consent that John Conger and Mary Ross should marry. Given under my hand this 5th of January.   JOHN CONGER."

Mention has already been made of the burial place of Mary Ross in North Carolina and also of the deeds to lands owned by John Conger. It is related, that after the death of his first wife and his marriage to Judith Runyon, that his children scattered from the parental roof and sought homes for themselves in Ohio, Tennessee, Mississippi and Kentucky.

John Conger was commissioned as Ensign by the Committee of Safety of Rowan County, North Carolina, Nov. 11, 1775. This service entitles his descendants to membership in the D. A. R. and S. A. R. Issue:

JOHATHAN CONGER, m Margaret.

ELIZABETH CONGER, m Cole.

JOSHUA CONGER, m Lucinda Rounsaval.   .

ELI CONGER, m Mary.

†JEAN CONGER, m —— Moores. (No records.)

ISAAC CONGER, m Mary Moores, dau of Henry and Jean Moores.

JOSIAH CONGER, m Katherine Runyon.

MARY MOORES CONGER, m Elston. (No records.)

JOHN B. CONGER, m Elizabeth Archer.

HANNAH CONGER, m John Railsback.

FIRST CHILD OF JOHN AND MARY ROSS CONGER.

JONATHAN CONGER, son of John and Mary Ross Conger, was born in Rowan County, N. C. He married Margaret —— and removed to Mississippi and settled in Claiborne or Warren County, about 1810. Issue:

ELIZABETH CONGER, m 1st James Sims, 2nd John Venable.

WILLIAM or WILSON CONGER.

PHOEBE CONGER, m Simon Lane.

MARY CONGER, m John Lobdell.

JANE CONGER, m Wilson Cummings.

SALLY CONGER, m Felix Thompson.

MARTIN CONGER, m Susan Garner.

JONATHAN LEE CONGER, m Sara Faulkner and 2nd to Susan Neal.

ELIZABETH CONGER, was born Aug. 6, 1789, died April 26, 1827, and married to James Sims, a brother of Thos. and David Sims, of South Carolina, who came to Mississippi about 1802. James Sims was born Nov. 30, 1783, and died March 7, 1821. Issue:

> David Griffin Sims, b March 10, 1809, d Sept. 10, 1831, m *Jane Eleanor Briscoe, Jan. 7, 1830. Issue:

>> Emily Jane Sims, b Jan. 21, 1831, m William Lee Roberts, of Hinds Co., Miss., Nov. 28, 1861, son of Jeptha W. and Mary Taylor Roberts, of Kentucky Issue:

>>> ‡Mary Jane Roberts, b Nov. 28, 1864, in Warren County, Miss., m April 21, 1885, to Charles Rutledge McQueen, son of Rev Henry Holcomb and Mary Elizabeth Rutledge McQueen. Issue:

>>>> Henry Holcomb McQueen, b Sept. 3, 1886.

>>>> Mary Rutledge McQueen, b Jan. 1, 1890.

>>>> Emily Mable Briscoe McQueen, b Nov. 15, 1891.

>>>> Charles Roberts McQueen, b Nov. 2, 1893.

>>> Maggie Grace Roberts, b Nov. 14, 1866, m Isaac Ransom McElroy, Feb. 2, 1886, at Meridian, Miss., where they now reside. He is the son of John McElroy and Grace Cameron. Issue:

>>>> Mary Hebron McElroy, m Paul D. McRoy, Oct. 31, 1907. Issue:

>>>>> Bessie Louise McRoy.

>>>>> Pauline McRoy.

>>>>> Infant son.

>>>> Bessie Emily McElroy, m Feb. 12, 1910, William France Bonifay. Issue:

>>>>> Isaac McElroy Bonifay.

>>>> Louise McElroy.

**William McDonald Sims, b May 19, 1810; m his cousin, Rebecca Jane Harmon Neal. (See page 46.) 1810

---

*She was the daughter of Philip Briscoe and Margaret Elliot. Philip Briscoe was the son of Capt. William Briscoe, of the Revolutionary and French and Indian wars, also a signer of the Albemarle Declaration of Independence.

†It is probable that she married William Moores, Jr., son of William and Elizabeth Ross Moores.

‡Mrs. C. R. McQueen has been active in church work for a number of years. She now holds the position of Rec. Sec. of the Woman's Home and Foreign Mission Society of the M. E. Church in Miss. She has reared her children to be good citizens and ornaments to society, and her home is one of culture and refinement.

**Those records were given, by mistake of the compiler, to the wife's branch.

Martha Conger Sims, b Feb 11, 1812, m David Snodgrass Burch, son of
Rev. John Burch, of Virginia, and Louisiana Thomas. Issue:
*Cordelia Burch, b Nov. 14, 1828, m Dec. 15, 1842, James Mon-
roe Brown. Issue:
Amelia Josephine Brown, b April 25, 1844, m
David M. Herring, Feb. 14, 1860. He died
in a Federal prison during the civil war,
on Nov. 14, 1863. Their child was born
two months after his father's death. Issue:
David Monroe Herring, b Jan., 1864,
m Lillian Burk, of Amite Co.,
Miss. Issue:
Jack Raiford Herring, b
about 1891.
Amelia J. Brown, m 2nd Prosper Pearcefield,
May 29, 1867. Issue:
Jennie Pearcefield, m S. L. Davis,
who died in 1896. Issue:
Louise Davis.
†Sidney L. Davis.
Jennie Pearcefield, m 2nd to L. D.
Pearce, of Bolivar Co., Miss.
No issue.
Ida Pearcefield, m Wm. H. Groome.
Issue:
Thomas P. Groome.
David Herring Groome.
Hilda Groome.
David Sims Brown, b Oct. 5, 1846, m Marie F.
Herring, dau of Alex. Herring, brother of
David M. Herring, Oct. 8, 1873. Issue:
Francis Brown.
Myra Brown, m to Jap Jones.
Nettie Brown.
Jessie Brown, m Tom Bell. Issue:
One child.
Alexander H. Brown.
George Brown.
Lamar Brown.
Vera Brown.
Marshall Eugene Brown, b May 27, 1849, m 1878
Ida Clark, of Mer Rogue, La. He d March
31, 1899. Issue:
Louie Clark Brown, b April 10, 1879.
m Rosa Hall, of Liberty, Miss.
Issue:
Rosa Lee Brown.
Maurine Brown.
Ella Brown, b April 25, 1882.
Lilly Brown, b Sept. 22, 1883, m Geo.
D. Andrews. Issue:
Daughter, d aged 1 year.
Alfred Penn Andrews.
Jessie S. Brown, b Feb. 14, 1885.

*Cousin Cordelia has had a wonderfully useful, active life. Her picture shows the radiance of the love she sheds
upon all with whom she comes in contact. Though now at an advanced age, she is not content to sit idly all day long, but
fills every moment with work for those she loves. She has given valuable assistance in the preparation of these records.
(See picture.)
†Now 19 years old. Is in the University of Virginia at school.

Robert Cotton Brown, b Feb. 22, 1886.

Marshall Brown.

Vertner N. Brown, b Dec. 24, 1888.

Ida Clark Brown, b Oct. 6, 1894.

Mamey Frances Brown, b Nov. 18, 1895.

Allen Eugene Brown, b Dec. 31, 1896.

Charlie Stanton Brown, b Sept. 5, 1351, d Aug. 16, 1867.

James Monroe Brown, Jr., b Feb. 19, 1854, d Oct. 7, 1858.

Louie Washburn Brown, b Feb. 3, 1858, d April 27, 1878.

Louisiana Burch, b 1830.

Henrietta Burch, b 1833.

Mabella Burch, b 1835.

*Capt. David Stanton Burch, b Aug. 7, 1838, in Jefferson Co., near Fayette, Miss. Died Jan. 24, 1905, at Fayette. He married 3 times, 1st to Fannie S. Jones, in 1858. Issue:

Lula Sims Burch.

William Cameron Burch, b Feb. 25, 1859, m 1st Mary Clark. No issue.

William C. Burch m 2nd Ruth Hedrick Issue:

Cameron William Burch, b July 20, 1909.

Stanton Chaffin Burch, b 1911.

Cora Hill Burch, b Dec. 21, 1865, d Dec. 29, 1894, at Caseyville, Miss.

Lelia Cleburn Burch, b April 21, 1868, m Prof. L. A. Wyatt. Issue:

John Cameron Wyatt, b March, 1888.

Stanton Wyatt.

Wiley Wyatt, d April, 1907.

Letitia Grace Wyatt. (See picture.)

Lamar Wyatt.

Capt. David Stanton Burch m 2nd Theodocia Eleanor Green, near Utica, Miss. She d at Caseyville, Miss. Issue:

Fannie Eleanor Burch, b June 21, 1875, m Nov. 17, 1896, to Duncan Bennette Easterling. Issue:

Annie Eleanor Easterling, b Feb. 10, 1897.

Duncan Bennette Easterling, Jr., b Aug. 14, 1909.

Eugenia May Burch, b April 20, 1875, m E. W. Fairley. No issue:

Wade Hampton Burch, b May 26, 1877, was killed by a falling tree at Union Church, Miss., June 16, 1891.

Grace Amelia Burch, b June 8, 1879, m Wallace Cornforth. Issue:

---

*David S. Burch, in 1861, was made sergeant of a company that organized in Franklin County, at Meadville. This company was called the Franklin Beauregards, Co. E, Capt. D. H. Parker, 7th Miss. Reg. At Corinth this company was reorganized, and Sergeant Burch was made captain. He was in many of the prominent battles—Shiloh, Atlanta, Chickamauga, Missionary Ridge, Mumfordsville, Ky., Perryville, Ky., Murfreesboro, Tenn. He fought throughout the war as a brave soldier.

Lelia Grace Cornforth.
Willard Stanton Burch, b March 14, 1881, m
Myrtle Edwards. Issue:
Willard Burch.
Luther Sims Burch, b Aug. 24, 1884.
†Frank Harmon Burch, b Sept. 24, 1886, un-m.
Mary Rebecca Burch, b Dec. 31, 1887, m Horace
Truly Myers.
‡Emmett Preston Burch, b July 12, 1889.
Capt. David Stanton Burch m 3rd Tenia Guilminott, of Fay-
ette, Miss. No issue.
§Martha Conger Sims Burch m 2nd, March 2nd, 1852, Valentine W. Brock,
of Tensas Parish, La. Issue:
Son, d age 2 years.
Mattie Valentine Brock, b Sept. 26, 1858, m in Clinton, Miss.,
to Jack Brown.
ELIZABETH SIMS, m 2nd to John Venable, in 1822. Issue:
John Fletcher Venable, b Dec. 25, 1824, m March 22, 1850, to Francis
Harmon, dau of Joseph Harmon. She d June 2, 1852. Issue:
Two children, d young.
Letitia Ann Venable, b Dec. 25, 1826, m William Clark, of Claiborne Co.,
Miss. Issue:
Mary Elizabeth Clark; b Jan. 23, 1850, m Charlie Brock, son
of Valentine Brock. Issue:
Theodore Brock.
Lilly May Brock, d young.
Charlie Brock.
Mary E. Brock m 2nd to her cousin, Cammie W. Burch. She
d Dec. 22, 1907. No issue.
Letitia A. Clark m 2nd John W. Andrews. She d Jan. 16, 1908.

WILL OF JAMES SIMS.

I deem it expedient, while in good senses of mind, to make my last will and testament. I do, therefore, leave my wife, Elizabeth Sims, sole executrix of my estate, and I do moreover leave to her my whole estate during her lifetime, and at her death do revert to my bodily heirs, David C. Sims, William Sims and Martha Sims, to be equally divided between them, and so it is my wish. I acknowledge, in the presence of those witnessing, this is my last will and testament.
(Signed)   JAMES SIMS.
Witnesses: Josiah Flowers, Benj. Newton.

WILLIAM or WILSON CONGER, was born in Rowan Co., N.C. He died in Warren or Hinds Co., Miss. He and his wife died when his children were young, and they were raised by his brother, Martin Conger. Issue:
Viola Conger.
Sidney. Conger, b in Mississippi. He m Mary Boles, in Warren Co., Miss.
He died in 1857. She died in 1859. Issue:
John Jeptha Conger, d Nov. 12, 1878.
Nancy Conger, b Sept. 27, 1853, m C. W. Stout, at Black-
monton, Miss., May 17, 1870. He was b Sept. 24, 1843.
Issue:
Sidney Stout, b Aug. 9, 1872, d May 23, 1910.
Daisy Stout, b Nov. 9, 1874.
Ida Stout, b Feb. 10, 1878.

---

†Joined the U. S. Navy, and is at present on the U. S. battleship Franklin.
‡Joined the U. S. Army, and is now at Fort Sheridan, Ill., company L, 27th Infantry.
§Martha Sims Burch, after the death of her mother, changed her name to Elizabeth Martha.

RICHARD NUGUENT LOBDELL
Page 116

JOHN VENABLE LOBDELL
Page 116

EDNA L. CONGER
Page 129

MRS. JOHN V. LOBDELL
AND SON
Page 116

MRS. MARTHA SIMS BURCH
Page 112

Burch Descendants of Isaac Ross

Burch Descendants of Isaac Ross and Jean Brown

Isaac Ross (1710-1762) and Jean Brown (married 1743, both Scottish)

Mary Ross (born 1751) and John Conger (married 1769 in North Carolina)

Jonathan Conger (went to Mississippi in 1810) and Margaret ?

Elizabeth Conger (born 1789) and James Sims (1783-1821)

Martha Conger Sims (born 1812) and David Snodgrass Burch (1813-1844)

David Stanton Burch (1838-1905) and Frances S. Jones (1840-1871)

Cameron William Burch (1859-1917) and Ruth Hedrick (1876-1945)

Stanton Chaffin Burch (1911-1972) and Mary Irene Slay (born 1919-1998)

Stanton Wesley Burch (born 1953) and Susan Deifenderfer (born 1958)
Beverly Denise Burch (born 1979)
Stanton Thomas Burch (born 1982)

MRS. CORDELIA BURCH BROWN
Page 112

JULIETTE AND CALEB L. LOBDELL
Page 115

JOHN VENABLE LOBDELL
Page 115

CAPTAIN DAVID S. BURCH AND HIS FIRST WIFE
Page 113

MRS. EMILY JANE SIMS ROBERTS
Page 111

REUNION AT OLD CONGER HOUSE NEAR FAYETTEVILLE, TENN.
Page 126

CONGER GIRLS, DESCENDANTS OF
SION MOORES CONGER
Page 126

Jeptha Conger, m Carey Warner, in Hinds Co., Miss. He died in Arkansas, in 1897.

Hed a large family, one of whom is J. E. Conger, of Shreveport.

JANE CONGER, m Wilson Cummings. Issue:

Frank Cummings.

SALLY CONGER, b in Mississippi, m Felix Thompson. Issue:

*Mary Thompson, m about 1858 to a Presbyterian minister—Yeagly.

Frank Thompson.

PHOEBE CONGER, m Simon Lane.

†MARY CONGER, b in Rowan Co., N. C., March 3, 1792. She was the dau of Jonathan Conger, granddaughter of John Conger and great-granddaughter of John Conger, who d in 1784. (See will.) She m Sept. 15, 1808, near Vicksburg, Miss., John Lobdell, who was b at Renselear, N. Y., May 16, 1782, and was the son of James and Mary Venable Lobdell. She d near Vicksburg, Miss., Jan. 6, 1835. Issue:

Thomas Llewellyn Lobdell, b Dec. 3, 1810, m Eliza Ann Grafton. Issue:

Livingston Llewellyn Lobdell, m Tennessee Estelle Watson, at Houston, Texas. Issue:

Robert Livingston Lobdell.

Jonathan Conger Lobdell, b April 16, 1813, m Emily Stowers. Issue:

**Juliette Lobdell, b Nov. 9, 1844, m Louis E. Stowers. Issue:

Margaret M. Stowers.

Benj. F. Stowers.

Louis E. Stowers.

**Caleb S. Lobdell, never married. Died about 12 years ago.

Volney Stamps Lobdell, m Amanda Hale, of Albany, N. Y. He d about 20 years ago. Issue:

Volney H. Lobdell, m Lawrence Bass., of Greenville, Miss. Issue:

Lawrence Bass, Jr., d two years ago.

Volney Bass, aged 2 years.

Joshua Lobdell, b July 3, 1815, d Dec. 15, 1816.

Isaac Elum Lobdell, b April, 1817, d May 23, 1831.

Martha Margaret Lobdell, b Oct. 8, 1820, d Oct. 30, 1838.

Eliza Mary Lobdell, b March 20, 1822, d Sept. 2, 1822.

‡John Venable Lobdell, b Jan. 12, 1824, d Aug. 13, 1859, m Sept. 5, 1848, to Minerva Lee Coffee, dau of Thos. J. Coffee and his wife, Malinda Graves W. Haley, of Brandon, Miss. Issue:

Henry Lee Lobdell, b Sept. 5, 1850, d Aug. 23, 1852.

Elizabeth B. Lobdell, b Oct. 4, 1853, m Holland T. Coffee, Sept, 1868, d April 26, 1870.

Florence Coffee Lobdell, b July 27, 1857, m Thos. McLemore, d in Bolivar Co., Miss., leaving an infant son, who followed his mother a few months later.

*John B. Conger, of Grand Gulf, Miss , in a letter written about 1840, tells of taking a grandchild of Brother Jonathan Conger as a companion to his daughter, she being a daughter of Sally Conger, who married Felix Thompson. This grandchild was Mary Thompson, who lived with her cousin, Martha Archer Conger, even after her marriage to Gov. Teighman M. Tucker. Before her marriage to Gov. Tucker, Martha A. Conger made a will, which provided very handsomely for Mary Thompson. After her marriage she made a second will, but it could not be found after her death. Mary Thompson therefore received the bulk of the large estate amassed by John B. Conger.

†"I have heard my mother say that my grandmother, Mary Conger, was a very noble woman, and that my father told her that she lost her life doing a kindly act of charity. During a severe storm she left her house to visit a sick negro slave, and died from the resulting attack of pneumonia.   JOHN V. LOBDELL."

‡Thomas Llewllyn, Jonathan Conger and John Venable Lobdell, attracted by the fertile lands and fine opportunities for investment in the Yazoo-Mississippi Delta, came to Bolivar County in the early forties, where they purchased lands, and with their slaves opened large cotton plantations. They were among the first pioneers in this rich Delta section, and though all three of the brothers died before reaching middle life, they were highly esteemed in their new homes, and, dying, left honored names behind them.

'*See picture.

John Venable Lobdell, b Oct. 26, 1859, m June 1, 1887, to Maria Coralie
Nugent, b in New Orleans, Jan. 21, 1867, dau of R. J. Nugent and
Marie Coralie Smith. Issue:
  Richard Nugent Lobdell, b May 27, 1888.
  Coralie Guilbert Lobdell, b Dec. 19, 1889, m Dr. Llewellyn
    Coppedge, March 26, 1912.
  John Venable Lobdell, b Jan. 8, 1892.
  Florence E. Lobdell, b Sept. 4, 1894, d Oct. 12, 1894.
  Lillian Hardeman Lobdell, b Sept. 7, 1895.
  Mildred Lee Lobdell, b March 18, 1898.
  Anne Nugent Lobdell, b Jan. 27, 1901.
  Ethel Elizabeth Lobdell, b March 24, 1904.
  Hugh Lewis Lobdell, b May 14, 1908.

MARY CONGER LOBDELL, m 2nd William Estes, Aug. 28, 1829, in Warren Co.,
Miss. Issue:
  Sarah Channing Lucinda Estes, b Dec. 12, 1829.
  Oscar William Estes, b Aug. 21, 1831.

MARTIN CONGER, son of Jonathan Conger, was born in Rowan Co., N. C., July 7,
1797. He died at Clinton, Miss., Dec. 13, 1833. Removed to Mississippi with
his father about 1806, and settled in Claiborne Co., where his father was a
planter. (See Jonathan Conger line.) In 1826 Martin Conger was living in
Warren Co., Miss., and that year he was married to Susan Garner, at Monticello, Miss. Susan Garner was born at Monticello, July 7, 1804, and died at
Clinton, Miss., October 13, 1862. About 1830 Martin Conger and family removed
from near Vicksburg, in Warren Co., to Clinton, Miss., and was one of the
pioneer settlers of this region. The road that he traveled to Clinton, Miss.,
in many places was prepared by him before his wagons could travel. In many
places trees were cut down, in this way clearing the road. Martin Conger died
three miles from Clinton, Miss., Dec. 13, 1833, and is interred in the family
burying ground there. After his death his widow married again, to Mr. Gregg,
and many of their descendants are still living.

Issue of Martin Conger and Susan Garner:
  Asbury Bernard Conger, b in Warren Co., Miss., January, 1828, d at Oak-
    ridge, La., January 5, 1863, m to Leann Jones, in 1838. She was
    b in Tennessee. Issue:
    Asbury Bernard Conger, b in Oakridge. La., Dec. 19, 1857,
      m 1st Harriet Jane Cooper, in 1885, who d in 1887.
      Issue:
      Nellie Lee Conger, d April, 1891.
    Asbury B. Conger m 2nd Estelle Margaret Cooper, sister of
      his first wife, at Oakridge, La., Nov., 1888. She was
      b at Oakridge, La., Dec., 1866. Issue:
        James Bernard Conger, b Nov., 1899, d Jan, 1890.
        Asbury Bernard Conger, b October, 1890.
        William Edwin Conger, b February, 1893.
        John Robert Conger, b August, 1895, d Dec. 13,
          1900.
        May Hope Conger, b Feb. 7, 1901.
    John Robert Conger, b Feb. 23, 1860, d July 2, 1837.
    William Edwin Conger, b in Oakridge, La., Feb. 18, 1862, m
      Belle Eason, at Oakridge, La , February, 1893. She
      was born at Oakridge, 1873. Issue:
        Barham Kelley Conger, b November, 1894.
        Elma Jean Conger, b August, 1886.
        Clara Belle Conger, b August, 1898.
        Joseph Bernard Conger, b Feb., 1900, d March,
          1900.
        William Samuel Conger, b September, 1905.

Mary Athelia Conger, b in Warren Co., Miss., d at Clinton, Miss., m to
Henry McKey, at Clinton, Miss. No issue.

Ann Martin Conger, b at Clinton, Miss., d at Houston, Texas, m Dr. Robert Kelly, at Clinton, Miss. No issue.

Susan Margaret Conger, b at Clinton, Miss., d at Chicago, Ill., May, 1898.
She m E. B. Lamon, at Clinton, Miss., 1857. He d at Clinton, Miss.,
January, 1873. Issue:

> Annie Eulalia Lamon, b 1858, m April, 1875, A. L. Brent,
> near Palestine, Miss. He was the son of Mr. and Mrs.
> J. C Brent. He d February, 1884. Issue:
>
> > Bernard Lauren Brent, b April 25, 1876, m Aug.
> > 12, 1907, to Willie Love. Issue:
> >
> > > Samuel Bernard Brent, b July 5, 1908.
> > > William Love Brent, b July 10, 1910.
> >
> > Mary Lamon Brent, b April 5, 1880, m Jan. 17,
> > 1899, to John William Quinn, son of Mr.
> > and Mrs. A. L. Quinn, of Holly Springs,
> > Miss. Issue:
> >
> > > John William Quinn, b June 13, 1900.
> > > Annie Mayre Quinn, b May 11, 1908.
> >
> > Annie Eulalia Brent, b Sept. 4, 1883, m 1904 to
> > Walter Jones, son of Mr. and Mrs. R. S.
> > Jones, of Terry, Miss. Issue:
> >
> > > Dorris Jones, b June 9, 1906.

Mary Athelia Lamon, d age 2 years.

E. B. Lamon, never married.

Milton Powahatan Lamon.

Lauren G. Lamon, m Mathilde Hoffelt. Issue:

> Susan Methilde Lamon.
> Isabel Lamon, b Dec., 1898, in Chicago, Ill.

Eugene Melton Lamon, b in Clinton, d Dec. 10, 1893.

Martin Conger Lamon, m Lizzie Clark, at Sidon, Miss. He d
in August, 1902.

William Orren Lamon.

Frank L. Lamon, d June 28, 1893, aged 21.

Lutie Lamon, d Oct. 25, 1889, aged 19.

---

*JONATHAN LEE CONGER, son of Jonathan Conger, was born near Port Gibson,
Miss., in 1806. He died at Black Hawk, Miss., in 1848. He married 1st Sarah
Faulkner, in Carroll Co., Miss., in 1825. She died Oct. 7, 1840. Issue:

†Amanda Conger, m A. J. Holmes.

William Wilson Conger, b in Chicot Co., Arkansas, Jan. 4, 1833. He died
at Vaiden, Miss., Nov. 20, 1888. He married Susan Ann Holmes,
in Carroll Co., Miss., Oct. 6, 1853. She was born in Union Co.,
Tenn., in 1832, died at Black Hawk, Miss., Nov. 20, 1905. Issue:

> Mary Elizabeth Conger, b Oct. 10, 1854, d in 1903. She m
> J. P. Cain, Nov. 20, 1874. Issue:
>
> > Elma Cain, b Nov. 12, 1875, m Dec. 20, 1900, to
> > Gay Anderson. Issue:
> >
> > > Gay Nell Anderson, b April 6, 1902.
> > > Elizabeth Anderson, b May 10, 1907.
> > > Mary Cain Anderson, b Jan 4, 1911.

*Jonathan Lee Conger was called Lee by his friends. After his first marriage he moved to Carroll County, where
he was a farmer and large slave owner.

†Mr. and Mrs. A. J. Holmes reared a family of seven children, who have married and have families.

Floy Cain, b April 4, 1877, m June, 1906, to Clarence Maynard. Issue:

    Mary Zilpha Maynard, b Mar. 6, 1908.

    Jim Cain Maynard, b Jan. 14, 1911.

Maud Cain, b June 4, 1883, m April, 1904, to Champ Taylor. Issue:

    William Taylor, b June 8, 1906.

Willie Lou Cain, b May 6, 1884, m in 1907 to Dr. C.·A. Moore. Issue:

    Meta Martha Moore, b June 19, 1910.

Hubbard Cain, b April 7, 1886.

Zilpha Cain, b July 7, 1888.

*Lucy Florence Conger, b Feb. 7, 1856, m Ike Jones, of Black Hawk, Miss., Dec. 13, 1876. Issue:

    Mary Myrtle Jones, b Aug. 31, 1870, m Oct. 4, 1901, to A. D. McFarlane. Issue:

        Margaret Ragland McFarlane, b Oct. 1, 1908.

    Isaac Lambuth Jones, b March 14, 1881, m Nannie Montgomery, Jan. 1, 1907. Issue:

        Thad Montgomery Jones, b March 26, 1909.

    Hulda Jones, b Feb. 28, 1889, m H. M. Streator, Jan. 19, 1910.

    Wilson Conger Jones, b April 1, 1884.

    †Sue Holmes Jones, b Dec. 27, 1885, d Feb. 26, 1912.

    Bessie Page Jones, b June 25, 1891.

    John Russell Jones, b April 26, 1893.

Martha Hill Conger, b Oct. 5, 1858, d April 3, 1966.

Lucius Lee Conger, b in Carroll Co., Miss., Sept. 3, 1860, m Alice Heron, in 1882. Issue:

    James William Conger, b Sept. 29, 1883.

    Joseph Clyde Conger, b Nov. 30, 1885.

    Effie Susan Conger, b Jan. 23, 1888.

    Lucius Hal Conger, b Dec. 14, 1889.

    Annie Lee Conger, b Nov. 24, 1891.

    Ben Clower Conger, b Dec. 24, 1893.

    Tom Wilson Conger, b Aug. 13, 1896.

    Alice Maie Conger, b July 9, 1899.

    Goldye Catherine Conger, b May 6, 1902.

Sarah William Conger, b in Carroll Co., Miss., Oct. 16, 1863. She m J. E. Page, Nov., 1888. Issue:

    Lucius Eddie Page, b Nov. 12, 1895, d Nov. 12, 1900.

Susan Elnora Conger, b Nov. 12, m T. Durham, in 1884. Issue:

    Tom Jones Durham, b 1885.

Edna Earl Conger, b April 6, 1867, d 1885.

Benjamine Luke Conger, b Dec. 20, 1869, d 1898.

Bessie Athalia Conger, b April 6, 1872, d 1885.

John Lane Conger, b at Black Hawk, Miss., July 21, 1835, d at Rison, Ark., 1894. He married Frances Cummings, in 1858. She was b in DeSoto Co., Miss., in 1839, and d in Ark. in 1904. She was the

---

*Mrs. Ike Jones is the genealogist of this branch of the family. She has rendered great assistance, not only to the compiler of these records, but also to Charles L. Conger, of Mackintosh, Miss.

†She was a young lady of more than ordinary gifts and acquirements. She was a devoted Christian, and at the time that the fatal malady laid hold upon her, was thinking of offering herself for the mission field. In her, Death had a shining mark, and when she was stricken down, a vacancy was left in many hearts that earth can never fill.

dau of Jane Conger and Wilson Cummings, and was his cousin. Issue:

>William Lee Conger, b in DeSoto Co., Miss., in 1859, m Ella Henry, at Locust Cottage, Ark., in 1877. She was b at Locust Cottage, Ark., in 1858; No issue.
>Florence Conger, b in Grant Co., Ark., in 1861. She m A. J. Sturdivant, in 1878. He was b in Grant Co., Ark., in 1856. Issue:
>>David Sturdivant, b 1881.
>>Bert Sturdivant, b 1885.
>>Austin Sturdivant, b 1887.
>*John Marvin Conger, b in Grant Co., Ark., in 1871. He m Rosa McKenzie, in Carroll C., Miss., in 1902. She was b at Eagle Nest, Miss., in 1880. He d July 26, 1911. Issue:
>>Margaret Conger, b March 7, 1904.
>Benjamine Conger, b 1873.
>Edwin Conger, b 1864, d 1886.
>Cora Conger, b 1881.
>May Conger, b at Rison, Ark., in 1885, m Thomas Golding, in Carroll Co., Miss., in 1902. He was b in South Carolina, in 1880. Issue:
>>Jewel Golding, b 1904.
>>Mabel Golding, b 1906.

Jonathan Conger, b July 21, 1835, d in 1864.
Sarah Lucinda Conger, b in Carroll Co., Miss., Nov. 11, 1838. She m William E. Tyler. Issue:
>††Ella Tyler, m Mr. McChristian. She died.
>William Edwin Tyler, by in 1856, m Jennie Smith. Issue: Four children.
>††Carrie Tyler, b ●66, m Mr. McChristian. She died about 10 years ago.
>Charlie Tyler, m Mr. Olson.

Jonathan Lee Conger m 2nd at Black Hawk, Miss., Oct. 7, 1844, to Susan Neal. She was b in Carroll Co., Miss., April 22, 1813, d 1852. Issue:
>‡Benjamine Neal Conger, b in 1848, d in 1863.
>Edward Lee Conger, b in Carroll Co., Miss., in 1846, m Eliza Cain, in 1846. Issue:
>>Eliza Cain Conger, b April 6, 1876.
>>Mattie Conger, b June 4, 1878.
>>Edwin Conger, b May 12, 1886.
>>†Joe Cain Conger, b March 6, 1884.
>>Mary Elizabeth Conger, b Oct. 14, 1891.
>>Craig Conger, b Dec. 8, 1894.

SECOND CHILD OF JOHN AND MARY ROSS CONGER.

ELIZABETH CONGER, dau of John Conger and Mary Ross, m Mr. Cole. Issue:
>Isaac Cole.
>Felix Cole, lived in Tennessee and Mississippi.

---

*John Marvin Conger was a man of fine character, and beloved by all who knew him.

††These sisters married two brothers.

‡A member of the 22nd Miss. Infantry. Was killed on the railroad while returning to his command.

†Is President of Senior Class, I. I. and C. of Miss., and a young man of brilliant mind and attainments.

THIRD CHILD OF JOHN AND MARY ROSS CONGER.

"JOSHUA CONGER, who was born in Rowan Co., N. C., and who married Lucinda Rounsaval, I am satisfied at one time lived in South Carolina. I have heard Elisha Conger say that his mother came from South Carolina. We also have in our family two hammers that belonged to Joshua Conger and wife, one of them marked N. C. and the other S. C. I think Joshua Conger came to Tennessee, and settled in Smith Co., in the year 1800. He died August 28, 1829, in what was known as the Conger Bottom, on Caney Fork River, near the mouth of Smith Fork Creek, and was buried on the south side of Hickman Creek, about one mile above the bridge. Lucinda, his wife, was born March 15, 1775, and died about 1856, after being insane for several years, and was buried in what is known as the Conger graveyard, in DeKalb Co., on Caney Fork River, about one mile above the mouth of Holmes Creek.   J. E. CONGER."

JOSHUA CONGER, son of John Conger and Mary Ross, was born in Rowan Co., N. C., Oct. 3, 1778. He died in Smith Co., Tenn. Married Lucinda Rounsaval. Issue:

Eli Conger, b Aug. 16, 1795.

John Conger, b June 9, 1798. He d in Smith Co., Tenn., in 1843. He m Jonca Pigg, in Smith Co., Tenn. Issue:

Joshua Conger, b in Smith Co., Tenn., where he also died. He m Hannah Belle. She d in Smith Co., Tenn., July 17, 1853. Issue:

Jane Conger, b May 23, 1838.

John Conger, b Aug. 15, 1840.

Isaac Conger, b in Smith Co., Tenn., Aug. 12, 1842, m Elizabeth Huty, at Marion, Ky., in 1863. He d in Smith Co., Tenn., 1870. She d at Marion, Ky., 1875. Issue:

John F. Conger.

Tishey Conger.

*.   Rebecca Conger, b Jan. 3, 1844.

Paulina Conger, b Dec. 12, 1846.

Isabella Conger, d May 20, 1821.

Elisha Conger, b 1821, d 1885, m Jane ——. Issue:

Manuel Conger.

Lucinda Conger, d Oct. 17, 1826.

Nathaniel Conger, d Sept. 4, 1831.

John Conger.

Lemuel Conger, b April 3, 1827, m Sarah ——, d in 1865. Issue:

F. M. Conger.

Mary Conger, m Mr. Hughs.

Jane Conger, m Mr. Fitts.

Jane Conger, b May 17, 1828.

William D. Conger, b in Smith Co., Tenn., Oct. 7, 1832, d in Crittenden Co., Ky., in 1870, m Martha Paris, at Marion, Ky., in 1852. She was b in Smith Co., Tenn., in 1836, and d in Kentucky, Dec. 24, 1881. Issue:

John B. Conger, b in Crittenden Co., Ky., Dec. 25, 1853, m Dealie Vaughn, in Crittenden Co., Ky., in 1870. She was b in Crittenden Co., in 1852. Issue:

Emma Conger, b May 3, 1878, m William Holt, in Lyon Co., Ky.

Sebbie Conger, b Feb. 18, 1876, m Charles Glasgo, in Lyon Co., Ky., in 1902.

Ada Conger, b Sept. 15, 1885, m William Hammon.

Henry Conger, b Dec. 23, 1891, m
Margaret Glasgo, in Lyon Co.,
Ky., in 1902.
Miles Conger, b March 24, 1835, d in 1852.
Isaac Conger, b Feb. 27, 1837, died in 1865.
†Josiah Conger, b in Smith Co., Tenn., Nov. 27, 1840, m 1st
Arabella W. Young, in Smith.Co., Sept. 23, 1864. She
was b in Putnam Co., Tenn., Jan. 13, 1846, d at Marion,
Ky., July 14, 1885. Issue:
John R. Conger, b Sept. 23, 1865, d Oct. 5, 1865.
Samuel Young Conger, b in Putnam Co., Tenn.,
Nov. 26, 1866, m 1st Josie Fritts, at Marion,
Ky., in 1867, and d at Vale, Tenn., in 1905.
Issue:
Ella Conger, b Sept., 1890.
Elza Conger, b Sept., 1890.
Ray Conger, b 1896.
Samuel Y. Conger m 2nd Lonia Mitchell. She d
in August, 1911.
Minnie Conger, b in Putnam Co., Tenn., Oct. 27,
1869, m. Anthony Griffey, at Marion, Ky.,
July 13, 1889. Issue:
Hammon Griffey, b 1890.
Ruby Griffey, b 1893.
Grace Griffey, b 1896.
Mike Griffey, b 1906.
William F. Conger, b in Allen Co., Tenn., March
3, 1872. He m Clara Roberts, at Benton,
Ky., in 1892. Issue:
Wiley Conger.
Josiah Conger.
Lawrence Conger.
Granville Conger.
Emma Conger, b in Allen Co., Ky., Aug. 29, 1873,
m Charles Morgan, at Marion, Ky., in 1900.
Issue:
Joseph Morgan, b 1901.
James R. Conger, b in Allen Co., Ky., June 15,
1875, m Lona McDaniel, at Hardin, Ky., in
1900. Issue:
Leon Conger, b Dec. 12, 1900.
Hubert Conger, b 1903.
Bernice Conger, b 1905.
Mason Conger, b 1909.
Dede Conger, b in Allen Co., Ky., Aug. 26, 1877,
m Joseph Tucker, at Marion, Ky. Issue:
Lonia Tucker, b Sept. 25, 1901.
Floria Tucker, b 1899.
May Belle Tucker, b Sept. 25, 1904.
Joseph Tucker, b Jan. 13, 1906.
Thelma Tucker, May 8, 1907.
Carrie May Conger, b in Crittenden Co., Ky., Oct.
9, 1879, m Frank Latham, at Lexington,
Tenn., Feb. 6, 1902. He was b at Lexing-

†"My father was in the war of 1812. My brother Elisha was in the Union army four years. I was in the Confederate army against my brother. We were both in the battle of Shiloh two days. He didn't kill me nor I him, so were we
not very lucky?   JOSIAH CONGER."

       ton, Tenn., April 25, 1875. Issue:

                Lindel May Latham, b July 15, 1904.

                Elois Latham, b Nov. 9, 1907.

       Josiah Conger, b March 7, 1851, d Dec. 21, 1896.

Josiah Conger m 2nd to Martha McConnell, at Marion, Ky., Aug. 30, 1885. She was b in Crittenden Co., Ky., April 5, 1852. Issue:

                Cora Conger, b at Marion, Ky., July 25, 1886, m Jackson Roberts, at Benton, Ky., in 1906. He was b at Benton, in 1886. Issue:

                        Lucile Roberts, b Feb. 4, 1909.

                Smith Conger, b at Marion, July 1, 1889, m Myrtle Reed, at Lexington, Tenn., Oct. 24, 1909. She was b at Lexington, Feb. 29, 1890. Issue:

                        Myrtle Conger, b Sept. 22, 1910.

              Elmer Conger, b Oct. 3, 1890.

              Mary Conger, b June 15, 1893.

              Bryan Conger, b Feb. 30, 1896, d Dec. 21, 1894.

Elizabeth Conger, b April 22, 1800.

Isaac Conger, b March 12, 1802.

*Elisha Conger, b Nov. 2, 1805, d at Liberty, Tenn., March 12, 1895, m Nancy Tittsworth, Sept. 27, 1828. She was b Feb. 15, 1810. Issue.

Joshua Conger, b March 6, 1830, d in 1846.

Eli Conger, b Jan. 20, 1832, d August, 1867, m Elizabeth Merritt, July 24, 1856. She d Sept. 24, 1894. Issue:

              William P. Conger, b in DeKalb Co., Tenn., Aug. 18, 1857, m Ellen Foster, Sept. 26, 1878. Issue:

                  Minnie Conger, m Mr. Brown. Issue:

                  Dalton Brown.

                  Homer Brown.

                Napoleon Conger.

              †Lulu Conger.

            W. P. Conger m 2nd to Lillie Gouger. Issue:

              Ruby Conger.

            John E. Conger, b in DeKalb Co., Tenn., Jan. 6, 1859, m March 11, 1880, to M. A. Huddleston. Issue:

              Alvin Conger, b Dec. 30, 1880.

              Ollie Conger, b Feb. 25, 1882, in Smithville, Tenn., m Dec. 20, 1898, to J. H. Christian, at Smithville. Issue:

                  John T. Christian, b Nov. 2, 1899.

                  Violet Christian, b Sept. 23, 1902.

              Solon Conger, b April 30, 1883.

              Ozias Conger, b Feb 5, 1886.

              Elisha Conger, b Jan. 10, 1888.

              William Conger, b May 10, 1890.

---

*Elisha Conger settled in the river, nine miles north of Smithville, DeKalb Co., Tenn., and lived there all of his married life. Both he and his wife are buried on the farm that was their home.

†Lulu Conger is a school teacher in Tennessee, and her brother, Napoleon Conger, is a minister of the Church of Christ. Both are interested in family history.

Fannie Conger, b Feb. 24, 1892.
Jodie Conger, b Feb. 5, 1899.
Ruby Conger, b Aug. 2, 1906.
A. Manson Conger, b in DeKalb Co., Penn., Sept.
26, 1867, m Helen Bond, Jan. 4, 1894. Issue:
Prudie Conger, b May 7, 1896.
Jessie Conger, b Dec. 13, 1897.
John Conger, b Oct. 3, 1890.
Roy Conger, b March 14, 1906.
William Conger, b Sept. 16, 1839, d 1841.
Martha Conger, b in DeKalb Co., Tenn., Aug. 24, 1834, d
Aug. 24, 1885, m in DeKalb Co., in 1852, to A. B. Cheat-
ham. Issue:
Martha J. Cheatham, b in DeKalb Co., Tenn.,
Oct. 30, 1853, m N. Lemuel Corley, Feb. 14,
1887. Issue:
Minnie Corley.
Lilly Corley.
Roy Corley.
Floyd Corley.
William Conger, b Jan. 15, 1808.
Mary Conger, b Nov. 18, 1809.
Nancy Conger, Dec. 18, 1811.
Delilah Conger, b Feb. 2, 1814.
Wiley Conger, b June 3, 1816.
Nancy Conger, the 2nd, b August 22, 1818.

FOURTH CHILD OF JOHN AND MARY ROSS CONGER.

ELI CONGER, son of John Conger and Mary Ross, was b in Rowan Co., N. C., and
after the second marriage of his father removed to Georgia. He m Mary ——.
Issue:
Amos Conger, b in Butts Co., Ga., and emigrated to Mississippi some
time about 1850. He m Rosanna Jenks, of Butts Co., Ga., near
Indian Springs. Issue:
Levi Conger, b in Georgia, about 1828-30.
Elizabeth Conger, b in Georgia, between 1825 and 1830. She
m —— Daniels.
Burrell Conger, b in Georgia, about 1835.
William Conger, b in Georgia, about 1838.
Samuel W. Conger, b in Georgia, about 1840.
Mart Conger, b in Georgia, about 1847. She m —— Kerr.
Simeon Conger, b in Georgia, about 1848.
John B. Conger, b in Mississippi, about 1853.
Marion Conger, b in Mississippi, about 1856.
Eli Amos Conger, b in Georgia, March 16, 1833, m in 1865 to
Sallie Wier Fort, in DeSoto Co., Miss. He d Dec. 17,
1876. She d Aug. 24, 1894. Issue:
Levi Andrew Conger, b Dec. 14, 1865, m Minnie
Wallace, of Coldwater, Miss., in October,
1891. He d Dec. 6, 1902. Issue:
Eutora Conger.
Mary Frances Conger, b April 28, 1868, m John
S. Crasslin, in 1884. Issue:
Nina Crasslin.
Guy Crasslin.
John S. Crasslin.
John Thomas Conger, b July 25, 1870, m Rena

Jones, at Cockrum, Miss., in October, 1893.
Issue:

  Flora Conger.
 ‡Walter Eli Conger, b Sept. 27, 1872, m Lula Rob-
  ertson, at Scooby, Miss. Issue:
   Lucille Conger, b March 6, 1901.
   Infant, b and d July 3 1902.
   Josephine Conger, b Oct. 14, 1903.
   Lorine Conger, b Nov. 24, 1905.
 Addie Conger, b Sept. 4, 1873, d October, 1878.
 Jennie Conger, b Oct., 1876, d Sept., 1881.
*Martin Eli Conger, b June 26, 1815, m Judith Bufford, in Macon, Ga.,
 Feb. 7, 1840. She d Sept. 22, 1872. Issue:
 John Conger, b in Butts Co., Ga., in Nov., 1840, d in 1856.
 †Thomas Eli Conger, b in Butts Co., Ga., Feb., 1843, m Sarah
  E. Jones, of Quitman, Texas, Dec. 21, 1865. He d in
  Mineola, Texas, in 1885. Issue:
  Ada Conger, b in Quitman, Tex., Oct. 5, 1867.
  Stella Conger, b in Quitman, Tex., July 9, 1869,
   d Sept. 12, 1870.
  Eloise Conger, b in Quitman, Tex., May 25, 1872,
   m Sept. 24, 1893, in Greenville, Texas, to
   J. P. Germany. Issue:
    Florence Germany, b Aug. 12, 1894,
     in Greenville, Tex.
    Joseph Alwin Germany, b in Green-
     ville, Tex., Aug. 9, 1897.
    Sybil E. Germany, b April 15, 1900,
     in Greenville, Tex.
    Frank Conger Germany, b Aug. 3,
     in Greenville, Tex.
    Jack Thomas Germany, b June 22,
     1906, in Greenville, Tex.
  T. Elmer Conger, b in Mineola, Tex., Aug. 31,
   1874, m Louise Martin, in 1898.
  W. Alvin Conger, b in Mineola, Tex., Jan. 8,
   1879, d May 9, 1902.
  Vivian Conger, b in Mineola, Tex., Dec. 29, 1881,
   d July 31, 1882.
 ‡‡William Martin Conger, b in Butts Co., Ga., Nov., 1845, d in
  Van Buren, Ark., 1863.
 Mary Ann Conger, b in Butts Co., July 27, 1847, m James A.
  Calaway, in Quitman, Tex., Dec., 1868. Issue:
  Lorenzo Dow Calaway, b Oct., 1870, in Quitman,
   Tex., m Lizzie Williams, of Mineola, Tex.,
   in 1892. Issue:

---

‡Walter Eli Conger has been the genealogist of this branch of the family. On account of his profession, that of traveling salesman, he has not been able to furnish complete records of his branch.

*He emigrated from Georgia to Quitman, Wood Co., Texas, in November 1867. He was a very wealthy planter, and after the war went into the mercantile business and was very prosperous. He was a devout Christian, being a member of the Baptist Church, and at the time of his death was a wealthy retired planter and merchant.

†He enlisted in the Confederate army, in Captain Wilson's Company B, 10th Cavalry of Texas, Ector's Brigade, Tennessee Army, in the summer of 1861, then in November, 1861, he re-enlisted in Jacob Ziegler's. He was in battles on Georgia Campaign, Nashville, Tenn., and other small battles in Georgia. Also in battles in Richmond, Ky., Corinth, Miss., Chattanooga, Tenn., Chickamauga, Tenn., Murfreesboro, Tenn., and many others. After the war he was a merchant, being a partner with his father, but at the time of his death was Wood County Tax Collector.

‡‡He enlisted in the Confederate army in 1863. Served only a short time when he was wounded, and died in Van Buren, Ark., in 1863.

Marie Calaway, b 1892, Minelo, Tex.
Lorenzo Dow Calaway, b 1895, Mineola, Tex.
Sister Calaway, b Nov., 1900, Mineola, Tex.
Estelle Calaway, b in Quitman, Tex., 1872, m Mr. Harpole, in 1898, in Mineola, Tex. Issue:
Jerome Harpole, b 1900.
Sadie Calaway, b in 1873, in Quitman, Tex., m Sidney Bradford, in 1898. Issue:
Sidney Bradford, b 1898, Mineola, Tx.
James Bradford, b 1907, Mineola, Tex.
Twins, b and d in 1875.
Vesta Calaway, b 1879, in Mineola, Tex.
James Calaway, b 1881, in Mineola, Tex.
Andrew Jackson Conger, b in Butts Co., Ga., Dec. 8, 1849, m Louzinka Haynes, Quitman, Tex., Dec., 1876. Issue:
George Conger, b Dec. 21, 1877, d Aug. 22, 1883.
Pearla Conger, b Nov. 24, 1879, d May 21, 1883.
Robert Conger, b in Quitman, Tex., April 1, 1812, m Dollie Stephenson, Feb. 12, 1905. Issue:
Andrew Lloyd Conger, b Dec., 1906, in Quitman, Tex.
Kleber Conger, b Jan. 2, 1885, m Louisa Long, of Greenville, Nov. 1, 1910.
Tom Conger, b in Quitman, Aug. 30, 1888.
Lillie Conger, b in Quitman, March 5, 1890.
Eloise Conger, b Aug. 19, 1892.
Mattie Conger, b March 1, 1897.
Martha Elizabeth Conger, b May 12, 1852, d in 1877.
Rebecca Spear Conger, b in Butts Co., Ga., Jan. 20, 1855, m Lycurgus B. Brown, Quitman, Tex., Feb. 7, 1874. Issue:
Mattie J. Brown, b in Mineola, Tex., Jan. 1, 1876, m Lelias B. Moore, Jan. 31, 1901. Issue:
Nellie Rebecca Moore, b in Clay Co., Tex., Aug. 29, 1903, d June 4, 1904.
M. Loula Brown, b in Mineola, Tex., Dec. 25, 1879, m Edgar Underwood, of Grenada, Miss., Dec. 25, 1901. Issue:
Edgar Buchanan Underwood, b Dec. 19, 1902, d July 6, 1903.
Rosa L. Brown, b in Quitman, Tex., Aug. 10, 1883, m Henry J. Ray, of Grenada, Miss., Oct. 24, 1903.
Lycurgus Bonaparte Brown, b in Mineola, Tex., April 16, 1886, m Jennie Quisenbury, of Bowie, Tex., Jan. 19, 1910.
Eliza Jane Conger, b in Butts Co., Ga., July 3, 1857, m Mr. Bernard, of Kansas City, Mo., in 1887.
Dr. Henry Amos Conger, b in Quitman, Tex., April 8, 1860, m Fannie Anderson, of Mineola, Oct. 25, 1890. Issue:
Four infants, who lived only a few hours.
Essie Conger, b 1887, d 1888.
Dr. Jefferson Davis Conger, b in Quitman, Tex., March 7, 1864, m Jimmie Haynes, of Quitman, Sept. 30, 1886.

Issue:

> Eugene Conger, b in Quitman, March 20, 1887.
> Reber Conger (dau), b in Quitman, Tex., Oct. 13, 1888, m John Critzberg, of Quitman, Dec. 29, 1907. Issue:
>> Franklin Critzberg, b July, 1910.
> Andrew Conger, b in Quitman, Tex., Sept. 10, 1890.

Martin Eli Conger m 2nd, in 1874, to Lizzie Crop, at Winsboro, Tex. He died in 1879. Issue:

> Davis Conger, b in Quitman, Tex., Nov., 1875.
> Beulah Conger, b in Quitman, Tex., in 1877. She m in 1909.

Susannah Conger, m Mr. Walker. Issue:

> John Walker.

FIFTH CHILD OF JOHN AND MARY ROSS CONGER.

JEAN CONGER, m Mr. Moores. No record.

SIXTH CHILD OF JOHN AND MARY ROSS CONGER.

ISAAC CONGER, son of John Conger, Jr., and Mary Ross., was b in Rowan Co., N. C., Nov. 8, 1789, m Mary Moores, dau of Henry Moores and Jane Ross, about 1800. (See Moores, pp. 79 and 93.) She was b Nov. 15, 1782, and d March 4, 1857. Isaac Conger d March 4, 1857. Issue:

Nancy Conger, d in infancy.

Malinda Conger, m Dr. Martin, and d without issue.

Matilda Conger, b April 16, 1807, d Oct. 2, 1812 (burned.)

Delilah Conger, b Aug. 11, 1808, d Oct. 14, 1837, unmarried.

Sion Moores Conger, b March 7, 1810, d Jan. 27, m ‡‡Beall Norton, Nov. 23, 1859. She was b July 16, 1836, d May 26, 1911. Issue:

> Mary Genella Montene Conger, b Oct. 31, 1860, d Sept. 27, 1862.
> †Sion Iliff Conger, b Dec. 22, 1861, m ††Willie Moore Malone, June 14, 1893. Issue:
>> Caroline Beall Conger, b Nov. 18, 1894.
> *Dixie Lamarr Conger, b Feb. 20, 1864, m Louise Shoffner, Jan. 16, 1901. Issue:
>> Glyndon Montene Conger, b March 12, 1902.
>> Iliff Pillet Conger, b Aug. 9, 1903.
>> John Beall Conger, b Nov. 5, 1905.
>> Dixie Lamarr Conger, b Jan. 25, 1910.
> *Charles Henry Conger, b Oct. 7, 1866, unmarried.
> ‡Robert Alonzo Conger, b March 13, 1869, m Ola Ashley Shoffner, Jan. 23, 1893. (She is a cousin of Mary Shoffner.) Issue:

---

*Dixie L. and C. H. Conger live at the old home established by Isaac Conger, about 1800. It is near Fayetteville, Tenn., and is called "Beachlawn."

‡Robert A. Conger lives on an adjoining farm, known as "Eeldon."

†Iliff Conger is manager of the University Supply Store at Sewanee, Tenn., where he lives. He has been a persistent searcher for the early record of the Conger family, and has given the writer very valuable assistance, being the first one to give help, many years ago.

††Willie Moore Malone, daughter of Charles Wesley Malone and Caroline Moore, was born July 7, 1866, and educated in Memphis. Her mother died of yellow fever, in Memphis, in 1878. Her father was a physician, and went through the plague. He died about 1889. She lived with relatives in Louisville for some years, and began teaching in 1891. She was married at Tullahoma, Tenn., in 1893.

‡‡Beall Norton Conger died May 26, 1911, and was the first of her family to die a natural death since her eldest sister died, about 1828. She lost two brothers in the civil war, but all the other brothers and sisters are still living, ranging in age from 66 to 85 years. Her father was 88 at his death, and her mother died at 74.

Bessie Lynne Conger, b Nov. 4, 1898.
Jessie Beall Conger, b Nov. 4, 1898.
*Nettie Norton Conger, b March 15, 1896.
Felix H. Conger, b Dec. 14, 1812, d Dec. 4, 1834, unmarried.
Isaac Conger, b in Smith Co., Tenn., Feb. 28, 1837, d June 20, 1875, m
Dec. 24, 1857, to Nancy M. Swansey, dau of John and Elizabeth
Swansey. She was b Jan. 4, 1842, d April 16, 1873. Issue:
John S. Conger, b July 21, 1859, d June 25, 1877.
Jefferson D. Conger, b and d Sept. 14, 1861.
Henry Miles Conger, b Sept. 3, 1864, d Jan. 7, 1911, m Mar-
garet. Issue:
Harlan Hendrix Conger, b in Johnson Co., Ark.,
Aug. 30, 1889.
Eli Elbert Conger, b in Crawford Co., Ark., Feb.
23, 1892.
Chloe Conger, b in Carroll Co., Ark., June 22,
1894, d May 21, 1895.
Chloe Conger, b in Madison Co., Ark., July 17,
1896, d March 16, 1898.
Oscar Conger, b in Franklin Co , Ark., July 8,
1901.
James Anderson Conger, b Jan. 23, 1868.
Mary Ellen Conger, b April 25, 1870.
Eli Newton Conger, b Oct. 11, 1871, m March 2, 1892, to
Frances Hellen Hampton. Issue:
Carl Henry Conger, b in Franklin Co., Ark.,
Nov. 22, 1893.
Charles Earnest Conger, b in Johnson Co., Ark.,
June 1, 1897.
George W. Conger, b in Madison Co., Ill., Jan.
22, 1900.
Gussie LeRoy Conger, b in Franklin Co., Ark.,
June 17, 1903.
Norman Jefferson Conger, b in Franklin Co.,
Nov. 7, 1906.
Elvis Conger, b in Franklin Co., Ark., Dec. 16,
1909.

SKETCH.

As to a sketch of my grandfather, I am unable to give you very much. My father, Sion
Moores Conger, died when I was 12 years of age, and, being the last of his race—a very modest
man, with quiet manner, seldom speaking except questioned—it happened that I learned very
little from him about his father or antecedents.

Through letters which I found in grandfather's library, from his relatives and from mother,
I learned the following:

Isaac Conger, son of John Conger, Jr., and Mary Ross, left his home in Rowan County. N.
C., and went to Kentucky, after the death of his mother, and was for a time with his uncle and

---

*See picture of Conger girls.

NOTES CONTINUED FROM PAGE 126.

Sion Iliff Conger, educated at the Barnitz school, Tullahoma, Tenn., entered apprenticeship in the drug business
with Dr. S. W. French, in 1877. Later learned watch making. Was for a time with the Spurlock-Neal Co., wholesale
drugs, Nashville, Tenn. Have been since 1894 buyer for the University of the South.

Dixie Lamarr Conger, educated at the Barnitz School, Tullahoma, Tenn. Was in the drug business a short time,
and began farming in 1895.

Robert Alonzo Conger, educated at the Barnitz School, Tullahoma, Tenn. Was in the drug and jewelry business at
Fayetteville, Tenn. Afterwards joined D. L. and Charles in farming. Was married to Ola Ashley Shoffner, Jan. 28,
1898.

aunt (Henry Moores married Jane Ross.) He married Mary Moores, his cousin, and came to Tennessee, settling in Lincoln County, around 1800, which was then a canebrake wilderness.

They were both deeply religious, and members of the Methodist Church. Their home was about seven miles from Fayetteville, and their nearest neighbor was four miles away.

Jane Brown Moores (b 1800—Mary's youngest sister) lived with them (she died a spinster in 1858) about 1809 or 1810. Isaac became convinced that he must preach the Gospel, and so decided. So he made preparation, and was licensed by the Elk Conference in 1811. I have some of his diaries, kept while at this work, that indicate that his wife strenuously opposed his missionary work, which greatly depressed him. Being, however, deeply impressed with responsibility of saving sinners, he persisted in the work while his health would permit, preaching and teaching wherever he went. His usual circuit covered the territory now occupied by eight or more counties, and did not seem to be confined to that especial territory, for he preached at times in almost every settlement in the State.

Sometimes he took horseback trips to Kentucky and Ohio and visited relatives, preaching on the way going and coming. One trip I recall that reached Danville, Ill., where Isaac Ross Moores lived. Several trips were made through West Tennessee and North Mississippi, where Betsy Payne lived, and on down to John B. Conger's home at Grand Gulf, Miss., and to New Orleans. He made one or more trips to South Carolina and through North Georgia, and I recall reading about his being for a time with Lorenzo Dow, and mention of his "powerful preaching." I think I have now a letter to the home folks describing Mammoth Cave, which he visited on one of his trips to Kentucky. One trip to North Carolina is mentioned in a fragment of an old diary about 1812, that refers to having received news, when about half way home on the return, of the death of one of the children Matilda, perhaps.)

Isaac "entered" several bodies of land in what is now Lincoln County, and purchased others, and held at one time some large tracts. Various farms were sold later, and my brothers, D. L., Charles and R. A., live on the old home place, which has not been changed in many years, comprising now about 1,300 acres.

About 1815 he built what has been said to have been the first brick house in the county, sending to North Carolina and Virginia for the artisans. This house still stands and is a part of the old home, has had little repairs except roofing, and the first roof lasted over fifty years. He built a log church near his home about the same time, which still stands, unused, however. He was very energetic, doing much of the work of building himself. Was an untiring preacher, often preaching twelve to fifteen sermons a week, and rarely less than two hours at a time. He died in 1847. He was opposed to slavery, and "turned his members out of society" for "trading in black meat." His wife survived him ten years, dying in 1857. Her maiden sister, who had always lived with them, died in 1858, and my father, Sion M., being the last of his race, decided to get married. He was married in 1859, at the age of nearly 49. He was a planter, and following the custom of the times, was a slave owner, as was also his aunt, Jane Brown Moores. Being possessed of considerable lands in cultivation, and having inherited the slaves belonging to his aunt as well as his own, he had at the outbreak of the civil war perhaps thirty slaves to till his soil.   ILIFF CONGER.

SEVENTH CHILD OF JOHN AND MARY ROSS CONGER.

JOSIAH CONGER and Catherine Runyon eloped on horseback, she being only 14 years old. She had hidden her clothes behind a log; they were tied in a bundle, and these she carried on horseback behind her intended husband. In latter years she often related the incident with pleasure, and said she had never regretted it. They emigrated to Preble County, Ohio, in 1812, and located near Sugar Valley, where he lived and died. He owned some fine real estate and a very large and imposing residence for the times, where a cordial welcome awaited the travelers through that country. The trip from Tennessee to Ohio was made in a wagon, drawn by four horses, and required about six weeks. Josiah Conger was a preacher of the Christian Church. He was a fine marksman. His death was caused by the accidental discharge of a gun, Nov. 8, 1846. While in Kentucky he was a hunting companion of *Daniel Boone, and it is said that he claimed kin with him.

*Daniel Boone was born in Burks County, Pennsylvania, in 1735. His father, Squire Boone, and his mother, Mary Morgan, had eleven children—Israel, Sarah, Samuel, Jonathan, Elisabeth, Daniel, Mary, George, Edward, Squire and Hannah. Daniel Boone's grandparents, Squire and Mary Boone, arrived in Philadelphia from England in 1717. When

JOSIAH CONGER was born in Rowan Co., N. C., near Salisbury, July 28, 1780. He d in Preble Co., Ohio, Nov. 8, 1846. He m Catherine Runyon, in Barron Co., Ky., 1802. She was born in Barron Co., Ky., near Glascow, Jan. 1, 1788, and died in Preble Co., Ohio, March 3, 1890. Issue:

Nancy Conger, b in Tennessee, July 2, 1804, d in Preble Co., Ohio, May 9, 1877, m Thomas Marshall, in Preble Co., Feb. 5, 1827. She d in Preble Co., Jan. 23. 1873. Issue:

**Josiah Conger Marshall, b Aug. 31, 1830, d Jan. 12, 1902, m Oct. 31, 1830, to Sarah Ann Howell. Issue:

Murray Webster Marshall, of Gann Valley, S. D.

Thomas Austin Marshall.

Phoebe Ann Marshall.

Isaac Ross Marshall.

George H. Marshall.

Maggie Marshall, m Mr. Vanbuskirk.

**Jacob Murray Marshall, b Aug. 23, 1832, d March 21, 1866, m Carolina Kenton. Issue:

Sylvania Marshall.

Lula Marshall.

William Marshall.

William Marshall, b Aug. 2, 1838, d Aug. 8, 1838.

Aaron Ross Conger, b in Tennessee, Nov. 7, 1805, d in Preble Co., Ohio, Sept. 22, 1898, m Ruth Marshall, in Preble Co., Ohio, Feb. 22, 1857. She was b July 6, 1807, and d in Preble Co., Oct. 14, 1847. He m 2nd ‡Rhoda Robinson. She was b Nov. 8, 1825. · Issue:

Marshall A. Conger, b July 4, 1828, d Oct 11, 1849.

Thomas Murray Conger, b April 12, 1830.

John Newton Conger, b in Preble Co., Ohio, Oct. 13, 1832, d in Preble Co., Nov. 6, 1904, m Louisa Kennedy, in Preble Co., Feb. 14, 1853. She b Feb. 20, 1836. Issue:

Mary L. Conger, b Feb. 25, 1859, d July 16, 1890.

Albert L. Conger, b in Preble Co., Ohio, Dec. 3, 1860, d April 13, 1901, m Hattie E. Woolman, Feb. 25, 1896.‖

Carrie L. Conger, b in Preble Co., Nov. 5, 1862, m E. G. Harris, in Preble Co., April 6, 1888. Issue:

Zelma Harris, b Aug. 1, 1888, m June 7, 1911, to Frank E. Smith.

Carl Harris, b Oct. 4, 1889.

Grace Harris, b Oct. 18, 1896.

Joseph E. Conger, b in Preble Co., Sept. 29, 1865, m Margaret M. Bussard, March 23, 1900. She was b March 6, 1868. Issue:

†Edna L. Conger, b Dec. 25, 1905.

Herbert A. Conger, b in Preble Co., April 6, 1867, m Lucy Parker, Jan. 9, 1902.

Catherine A. Conger, b in Preble Co., July 5, 1870, m E. M. Shafter March 14, 1888. Issue:

Daniel was 18 his parents moved to North Carolina and settled on the Yadkin river. He met here Rebecca Bryan, whom he married. He was a farmer and hunter, and growing tired of the fast growing civilisation, left his family and went to Kentucky. The history of his adventures in Kentucky are too well known to need repetition. It is probable that the Congers were related to Daniel Boone through the Morgan family.

†See picture.

‡She is still living, and resides with J. E. Conger, near Eaton, Ohio. He has ever been interested in the genealogy of his family.

**An effort has been made to get full records of the descendants of these brothers, but in vain. The descendants ive in the West and also in Ohio.

Myrtle Shafter.

Catherine A. Conger m 2nd to Walter M. Reed, Feb. 24, 1901.

Infant, b Nov. 18, 1873, d Dec. 18, 1873.

Berti A. Conger, b in Preble Co., Jan. 11, 1879, m C. Kennedy, April 8, 1902. Issue:
Russell Kennedy.

Wheeler M. Conger, b in Preble Co., Ohio, Aug. 19, 1834, m Catherine Halderman, Aug. 24, 1857. She was b March 15, 1833. She d in Preble Co., Jan. 15, 1893. Issue:
Lewis Conger.
Myrtle Conger.
Infant.

Rachel Conger, b in Preble Co., Ohio, Oct. 6, 1836, d Dec. 24, 1896, m Nathaniel B. Stephens, in Preble Co., Nov. 6, 1856. No issue.

Anna Conger, b in Preble Co., Ohio, Feb. 4, 1839, m George W. Potter, in Preble Co., Ohio, Aug. 19, 1861. He was b Oct. 29, 1834, d July 18, 1904. Issue:
Elmer Potter, b 1865, m Mary Stubbs, 1895. Issue:
Helen Potter, b 1906.
Ollie Potter, b 1868, m Andrew J. Montgomery, of Newburg, S. C., in 1886. Both are dead.
Infant.

Moses Conger, b in Barron Co., Ky., Aug. 12, 1807, d in Preble Co., Ohio, Aug. 22, 1901, m 1st Proebe Price, in Preble Co., Nov. 13, 1828. She was b in Butler Co., Ohio, Aug. 13, 1807, d in Preble Co., Ohio, June, 1880. Issue:
Isaac Ross Conger, b Oct. 7, 1857, d May 5, 1832.
Sarah Jane Conger, b in Preble Co., Feb. 7, 1832, d March 30, 1887, m Meeker S. Morton, Feb. 26, 1860. He was b Dec. 22, 1832, and d Feb. 3, 1908. Issue:
Stella Morton, b March 29, 1864, d May 1, 1864.
†Charles Morton, b Oct. 30, 1860, d Mch. 13, 1903, m Lena Hubbard, May 16, 1888. Issue:
Winifred Conger Morton, b Jan. 7, 1892.
James Morton, b April 13, 1865, d Feb. 22, 1897, m Annie ——.
Dr. Elmer Morton, b Feb. 9, 1872, m Sarah Boradaier, Dec. 27, 1899. Issue:
Genevieve Morton, b Nov. 23, 1900.
Edward M. Morton, b Mar. 29, 1903.
Arthur J. Morton, b Nov. 3, 1905.
Fred Morton, b Nov. 29, 1873, m Grace Gingling.
Spence Morton, b Aug. 3, 1877, m 2nd to Moranda Gardner.

Elizabeth Ann Conger, b in Preble Co., Ohio, Sept. 1, 1834, d July 20, 1902, m Lemuel Bennett, in Preble Co., Ohio, Dec. 25, 1854. He was b Dec. 24, 1829, and d April 27, 1895. Issue:
Henry Clayton Bennett, b Oct. 11, 1856, d Oct. 4, 1907.
Arthur B. Bennett, b Jan. 8, 1859.
Clara Belle Bennett, b Mar. 14, 1863, m Mr. Wright. Issue:

d in the Indian war of 1891 and the Spanish-American war.

Four children.

Moses Oscar Bennett, b Dec. 5, 1865.

Phoebe Leona Bennett, b Dec. 25, 1867, m Mr. Busher.

Mary Etta Bennett, b Feb. 12, 1873, d Aug. 17, 1907, m Mr. Hendrick.

Mary Katherine Conger, b Dec. 12, 1836, d April 14, 1841.

Eli Moore Conger, b July 16, 1839, d Aug. 16, 1846.

William Wims Conger, b in Preble Co., Ohio, Oct. 18, 1841, d Oct. 9, 1882, m Julia L. Wilkinson, in Preble Co., Ohio, Oct. 1, 1863. She was b June 30, 1843, and d Dec. 27, 1906. Issue:

> Emma Constance Conger, b July 22, 1864, d Mar. 27, 1885, m Charles Cox, Jan. 27, 1885. No issue.
>
> Royal E. Conger, b June 27, 1867, d Jan. 1, 1885.
>
> Edwin Pearl Conger, b Aug. 3, 1870, m Cora Shaw, Aug. 12, 1891. Issue:
>
>> Pearl Conger, b March 29, 1894.
>>
>> Edna Conger.
>>
>> Owen Conger.
>
> Lucy Bertha Conger, b Feb. 27, 1877, d May 24, 1904.
>
> George Wilkinson Conger, b Sept. 27, 1881.

John Armour Conger, b in Preble Co., Ohio, Feb. 3, 1847, m Leah E. Felton, Oct. 6, 1869. She was b March 19, 1848. Issue:

> Perry G. Conger, b June 12, 1871, d Apr. 25, 1892.
>
> Gertrude E. Conger, b Feb. 6, 1883, m George H. Whyte, at Goldfield, Iowa, May 17, 1905. Issue:
>
>> Ruth L. Whyte, b April 4, 1906.
>>
>> Margaret E. Whyte, b July 2, 1908.

Henry Clayton Conger, b in Preble Co., Ohio, Aug. 23, 1849, d in Preble Co., Ohio, Aug. 21, 1908, m Sarah Smith, March 5, 1871. She was b June 15, 1849. Issue:

> Oscar Conger, b Oct. 8, 1873, d Aug. 5, 1885.
>
> Shelby Conger, b July 26, 1875, d Apr. 4, 1883.
>
> Della May Conger, b March 7, 1880.
>
> Ruth Conger, b Nov. 11, 1891.

Anna Conger, b in Barron Co., Ky., Oct. 7, 1809, d in Camden, O., Oct. 3, 1877, m Thomas W. Huffman, in Preble Co., Ohio, Mar. 9, 1831. He was b Jan. 30, 1810, and d in Camden, Nov. 30, 1893. Issue:

> John A. Huffman, b Nov. 13, 1835, m Lizzie McMeacham, Nov. 18, 1858. She was b July 4, 1838. Issue:
>
>> Ada M. Huffman, b June 23, 1860.
>>
>> Sarah Huffman, b Oct. 17, 1869.

Sarah Conger, b in Barron Co., Ky., Nov. 20, 1811, m Alexander Rhea, Feb. 18, 1834, d Sept. 9, 1877. He was b Jan. 14, 1813, d Dec. 16, 1881. Issue:

> James Franklin Rhea, b Feb. 14, 1835.
>
> John Conger Rhea, b Sept. 19, 1836, m Lizzie Pollock. Issue:
>
> Anna Rhea.
>
> Another child, name not given.
>
> Frank Rhea.
>
> Lawrence Rhea.
>
> Daughter, b May 11, 1839, d June 22, 1839.
>
> William Leander Rhea, b Nov. 11, 1840, d July 7, 1854.

Sarah Katherine Rhea, b March 26, 1843; d March 13, 1866, m
Michael Pentecost.

*Robert Milton Rhea, b April 15, 1848, m Sarah Elizabeth
Harvey, dau of Samuel and Safronia Harvey, July 26,
1868. She d Feb. 4, 1811. Issue:

Samantha Leora Rhea, b July 4, 1869, d Dec. 24,
1878.

Rolandus Everheard Rhea, b Feb. 25, 1872, d
Jnly 3, 1888.

Royal Conger Rhea, b Nov. 24, 1874.

Orvie Rhea, b Feb. 29, 1885.

Mary Evaline Rhea, b July 4, 1851, d Aug. 12, 1875, m James
Pottenger.

Samantha Caroline Rhea, b Jan. 14, 1854, d June 27, 1877, m
Julius Lane.

John Newton Conger, b in Preble Co., Ohio, March 13, 1814, d in Preble
Co., Ohio, Oct. 6, 1841, m Rachel Marshall. She was b Jan. 11,
1817, and d Aug. 26, 1840. No issue.

Mary Ross Conger, b in Preble Co., Ohio, Aug. 6, 1816, d June 8, 1875, m
Thomas McWhinney, in Preble Co., Ohio. Issue:

Lee Andrew McWhinney, d unmarried at 24 years of age.

Isaac Newton McWhinney, b June 16, 1845, d Nov. 10, 1904,
m Emma Dutton, Dec. 18, 1866. Issue:

Emma McWhinney, m Mr. Pepper.

Thomas McWhinney.

Sarah Ellen McWhinney, b 1838, m J. C. Aydelotte. He was
b in 1838, d in 1901. Issue.

Halstead Aydelotte, m ———. Issue:

Bessie Aydelotte.

Howard Aydelotte.

Emma Aydelotte, b 1861, d July 26, 1908, m Mart
Kelley. Issue:

Grace Ellen Kelley.

Edgar Lee Kelley, d 1906.

Mary Aydelotte, m Oscar Rowan Baker, July 8,
1878. Issue:

Viletta Ellen Baker, b July 6, 1879.

Frank L. Baker, b Dec. 26, 1880.

Katherine Gladys Baker, b Jan. 21,
1882.

Winona Jenette Baker, b March 24,
1887, m Robt. S. Montgomery,
of Gary, Ind., June 16, 1911.

Paul Theodore Baker, b July 1, 1898.

Omer Ross McWhinney, d age 22, had 2 daughters. Both d.

Eli Conger, b in Preble Co., Ohio, Dec. 20, 1819, d March 12, 1901, m Lucy
McWhinney, Nov. 1, 1853. She was b Oct. 27, 1821, d Oct. 4, 1887.
Issue:

Caroline Conger, b Sept. 13, 1840, m †Andrew Lietner Harris,
Oct. 17, 1865. He was b Nov. 17, 1835. Issue:

*Robert Milton Rhea and family live at Goddard, Kansas. In 1878 he moved from Ohio and settled at Garden Plain,
Kansas. His wife was a devoted Christian, and a writer of many beautiful verses.

†Andrew Lietner Harris was married Oct. 17, 1865; was born Nov. 17, 1835. Was Governor of Ohio, a lawyer by
profession, and has occupied many positions of honor and trust. He was a colonel in the civil war, and at the close was
made brigadier general for bravery. In a Democratic county of over 4,000 majority he was only defeated by about 100
votes for Congress. He was Lieutenant-Governor under McKinley, and a close friend of his. He is an extensive land
owner, and spends most of his leisure time on his farms in Preble County.

Walter A. Harris, b Aug. 17, 1870, m Estherwain
Sherman, in 1898.
John Newton Conger, m Emma Lockwood, Dec. 2, 1875. Issue:
Grace L. Conger, b Feb. 7, 1872, m Wilbert Miller,
Jan. 17, 1900.
Harry E. Conger, b Sept. 10, 1876, d Oct. 6, 1884.
Jessie M. Conger, b Aug. 15, 1884.
Elizabeth Conger, b Sept. 22, 1847, d Aug. 31, 1896, m May
30, to Barney W. Huffman. Issue:
Mary Huffman.
Charles Huffman.
William Huffman.
Frank Huffman.
Harvey Huffman.
Elizabeth M. Conger, b in Preble Co., Ohio, Dec. 5, 1823, d Jan. 16, 1865,
m Henry Overholzer, in Preble Co., Ohio, Feb. 27, 1840. He was
b Jan. 28, 1822, d Jan. 30, 1905. Issue:
*Sarah Jane Overholzer, b June 9, 1842, m †Samuel Fessler, in
Johnson Co., Iowa, 1861. He d Feb. 17, 1906; she d
Feb. 6, 1874. Issue:
Ida M. Fessler, b March 29, 1862, m William C.
Lee, Feb. 17, 1885. He was b April 26,
1855. Issue:
William Howard Lee, b Aug. 13,
1881, m Nora Misner, Feb. 6,
1903. Issue:
Gladys Lee.
Beulah Lee.
Ruby Lee.
Franklin Wilsy Lee, b Sept. 9, 1883,
m Ida Hough, March 8, 1905.
Fredrich Olonso Lee, b Oct. 18, 1885.
Bertha Florence Lee, b Apr. 12, 1889,
m Garvie A. Morse, March 6,
1907. Issue:
William Lane Morse.
Grace Morse.
Chester Lee, b April 12, 1891.
Merle Lee, b March 8, 1893.
Seibert McKinley Lee, b Sep. 21, 1896.
Russell Lee, b June 20, 1902.
Estella Fessler, b Oct. 22, 1865, m Mr. Golds-
berry. Issue:
Kirby Goldsberry.
Charley Goldsberry.
Elmer Fessler, b April 21, 1867.
Addie Fessler, b June 30, 1870, m Mr. Ovis.
Stephen R. Overholser, b Oct. 15, 1859, m Mary E. Scheffer,
April 1, 1882. She was b Nov. 14, 1863. Issue:
Ora Overholser, b July 1, 1883, m M. Maria Peck-
over, June 9, 1909. Issue:
Henry Thomas Overholser, b June
18, 1910.
Arnold Overholser, b Dec. 29, 1885.
Willard Overholser, b Nov. 6, 1902.
Samuel Jaoso Overholser, b Oct. 10, 1863, d Aug. 9, 1865.

‡ County, Mo., where she died. Her husband later moved to Oklahoma.
in the Union army three and a half years, Co. K, 22nd Iowa. He was wounded in the knee.

*William Alexander Conger, son of Josiah Conger and Catherine Runyon,
b in Preble Co., Ohio, Sept. 26, 1826, m Sarah Paddock, Dec. 2,
1847. She was b in Wayne Co., Ind., Dec. 17, 1830. Issue:

Eli Conger, b near Indianapolis, Ind., Oct. 27, 1848, m Lenoa
Lake, Feb. 20, 1872. Issue:

Liene Etta Conger.

Osa Estella Conger.

William Ellis Conger.

Mary Catherine Conger, b Jan. 8, 1850, near Indianapolis, m
Taylor D. Blakely, on Oct. 1, 1867, d March 2, 1885.

Eveline Conger, b near Indianapolis, Oct. 11, 1851, m William
D. Moore, Feb. 2, 1869. Issue:

George Moore.

Frank Moore.

Grace May Moore.

Eveline Moore m 2nd —. —. Baker, June 9, 1889. Issue:

Carrie Ellen Baker.

Elijah Conger, b Sept. 4, 1853, near Knoxville, Ill., d 1854.

Merriam Conger, b near Knoxville, Ill., July 18, 1855, d 1856.

†Samantha J. Conger, b July 6, 1857, near Knoxville, Ill., m
John J. Blakely, Sept. 2, 1874. He d Oct. 9, 1879. Issue:

Zella Blakely, b Dec. 15, 1875.

Erma Blakely, b Dec. 27, 1877.

Anna Blakely, b Sept. 24, 1879.

Samantha J. Blakely m 2nd on March 27, 1881, to J. J. Riddle.
Issue:

Carrie L. Riddle, b Nov. 3, 1882.

Eva M. Riddle, b July 3, 1884.

Sadie F. Riddle, June 29, 1885.

William A. Riddle, b March 6, 1888.

Fred A. Riddle, b March 28, 1890.

Clyde R. Riddle, b June 24, 1892.

Ida M. Riddle, b July 22, 1895.

Guy G. Riddle, b Nov. 7, 1897.

William R. Conger, b near Knoxville, Ill., April 5, 1854, d
in 1859.

Oneta Conger, b near Galesburg, Ill., Nov. 10, 1861, d in 1862.

Sarah Etta Conger, b near Galesburg, Ill., Dec. 3, 1863, m
Frank Keeton, Jan. 29, 1882. Issue:

Sallie D. Keeton, b near Amsterdam, Mo., Nov.
9, 1882, m George Z. Moore, Mch. 3, 1903.
Issue:

Zelma May Moore, b Aug. 12, 1906.

Lillie Beatrice Moore, b June 14, 1908.

William O. Keeton, b May 31, 1885, m Eunice M.
Clinton, Dec. 23, 1909.

Bessie May Keeton, b near Amsterdam, Bates
Co., Mo., April 25, m to Charles Henson,
Aug. 11, 1909.

Emma Frances Conger, b near Galesburg, Ill., Dec. 10, 1865,
d Oct. 4, 1886.

---

*All of the children of Mrs. S. J. Blakely Riddle are married except four. She has twelve grand-children. Names,
dates, etc., have not been received.

†William A. Conger and his wife live at Burdette, Kansas. He is the last survivor of the family of Josiah Conger.
He has been blind for eleven years, but his affliction has only strengthened his character, and, while his eyes are turned
to a happier home, life is still filled with gladness for him. He enjoys playing his own accompaniments on the organ
and singing the hymns he has long loved. His memories of the older members of the family are very clear. He remembers the visit of John B. Conger, of Grand Gulf, Miss., and his daughter, Martha Archer Conger. Martha Archer had
her colored maid with her, and dressed beautifully. He remembers also having seen his aunt, Hannah Railsback. He has
been a member of the Christian Church since 27 years of age.

Oscar Conger, b near Thawville, Ford Co., Ill., Feb. 9, 1869. Unmarried; lives with his parents.

John Harvey Conger, b near Everette, Mo., April 7, 1872, d Feb. 13, 1888.

Evaline Conger, b in Preble Co., Ohio. Aug. 9, 1831, d Dec. 1, 1906, m †Jacob Marshall, in Preble Co., Ohio, Aug. 19, 1851. He was b Dec. 25, 1822, and d July 8, 1889. Issue:

    John Marshall, b Aug. 13, 1832, d Feb. 6, 1892, m Katherine Leslie. Issue:

        Minnie D. Marshall.

        Virgil Marshall.

        Ruby I. Marshall.

    Katherine Alice Marshall, m John W. Lease. Issue:

        DeWitt Lease.

    Mary Anne Marshall, b Oct. 26, 1856, d Oct. 25, 1880, m Nelson Bouta. Issue:

        Homer Bouta.

        Charles Bouta.

        Horton Bouta.

    Martha Rachel Marshall, d 2 1-2 years old.

    Lucinda Clementine Marshall, b Feb. 26, 1865, m Park McGriff, Jr., Oct. 3, 1880. Issue:

        Evaline McGriff, b June 29, 1884.

    Daisy Dean Marshall, m Valentine Tillman. Issue:

        Ina H. Tillman.

        Lela M. Tillman.

        Gale Tillman.

        Paul Tillman.

        DeWitt Tillman.

EIGHTH CHILD OF JOHN AND MARY ROSS CONGER.

MARY CONGER, m Mr. Elston. No records. It is probable that she and her sister, Jane Conger Moores, remained in North Carolina after the second marriage of their father.

NINTH CHILD OF JOHN AND MARY ROSS CONGER.

JOHN B. CONGER moved to Mississippi with the other families of our ancestors, about 1808. His marriage possibly occurred in Mississippi. He patented large tracts of land in Mississippi, where he resided till 1845, when he sold out and moved to Texas. There is today no living descendant of John B. Conger, and his property, by the will of his daughter, has passed out of the family. Mrs. McWillie relates that Mrs. Tucker made a second will after marrying her father, Gov. Tucker, but this will was destroyed, and after the death of Mrs. Tucker, only the first will could be found.

    JOHN B. CONGER, b in Rowan Co., N. Co., d in 1853, m Elizabeth Killingsworth, a sister of Noel and Sarah Killingsworth. (This record is furnished by the Killingsworth family.) Issue:

        Isaac W. Conger, drowned in the Mississippi river.

        Fielding Conger, was cut by a gin. Died young.

        *Martha Archer Conger, m Gov. Tiglman M. Tucker. She d Sept. 8, 1857.

---

†Jacob Marshall was a farmer and lived near Manchester, Ohio.

*Mrs. William McWillie, of Jackson, Miss., is the daughter of Governor Tucker by his first marriage. She has a large and very beautiful portrait of her step-mother, Martha A. Conger Tucker. Her face is expressive of the fine character that Mrs. McWillie says was hers. No real daughter could speak of a mother in more endearing terms than does Mrs. McWillie in telling about this, the only mother that she really remembers, her own having died when she was quite young.

EXTRACT FROM LETTER WRITTEN BY ILIFF CONGER, JUNE 26, 1904.

I have two letters written by John B. Conger, dated in 1839 and 1843. The first is signed John B. and Elizabeth Conger and the second is signed John B. Conger, his wife having probably died in the meantime. I will make a few quotations from them:

In 1839 he mentions that his daughter, Martha Archer Conger, is a very pretty young woman, about 15 years old, and now at school at Donaldsonville, La., near New Orleans, and learning music and French, as well as other studies in literature and politeness.

Isaac W. is a fine-looking young man, about 6 feet tall, weight about 165 pounds. Has been home some time. Has been traveling in the Eastern States. Was in Washington at the sitting of Congress, and had an interview with the President.

Brother Jonathan's children are about all dead. Phoebe, Jane and Jonathan are about all that remain. Uncle Isaac Ross' family are all no more, pretty much, and the Wade children are taking steps to keep all the negroes in slavery. Also the same with Margaret A. Reed's estate (the daughter of Uncle Isaac, formerly Mrs. Archer.) She had about 130 slaves, and willed them to Dr. Stephen Duncan and Zubulan Butler, with a view to having them sent to Liberia.

Eli K. Ross is living in Louisiana, on the Ouchita River, and doing no good.

I am building a fine house on my plantation on the Mississippi River, where I expect to spend the remainder of my days. I have 14,000 acres of rich bottom land and 6,000 acres equally as rich above. More than 300 negroes, as likely as I ever saw. Will make probably 2,000 bales of cotton, which, together with sales of cord-wood to steamboats, should make an income this year of about $130,000. With all this a man is not entirely happy.

In 1843 he mentions a visit just paid by his sister Hannah and brother John Railsback, and their appreciation of his magnificent estate.

I have heard my father speak of the visits of himself and father to John B.'s and of a visit that he and his daughter made to my grandfather's, and my father's overseer says he remembers when they drove from Memphis, he thinks, and Martha caused her father to remain in the carriage while she ran in the house, and, covering grandmother's eyes with her hands, made her guess who her visitor was. This was some time in the 40's—1841 or 1842.

My grandfather was a Methodist minister, and used to make journeys throughout the South and visit his relatives in Mississippi, Georgia and South Carolina. In some of his journals he would make reference to these occasions. I have none of them at hand at this time to refer to.

John B. Conger also mentions, in a letter to my grandfather, Isaac Conger, that he had one of his brother Jonathan's grand-daughters with him for company for Martha Archer, "a daughter of Sally Conger, who married Felix Thompson."

John Conger, who married Mary Ross, wrote a letter to his son Isaac, dated April 9, 1798. Among Isaac Conger's papers was found a cancelled note in favor of "Jushua and Eli Conger, executors of John Conger, dec'd," dated March 30, 1806.

WILL OF MARTHA ARCHER CONGER.

I, Martha Archer Conger, of Claiborne County, State of Mississippi, being of sound and disposing mind and memory, and anxious to dispose of all my property in possession and expectancy, do make and publish this my last will and testament.

It is my wish that all just debts which have been recognized by me, and which are legally provable against the estate of my father and brother Isaac, shall be paid, and also my own debts.

It is my wish that Miss Mary C. Compton shall remain at Eildon, my present residence, if she desires, and that she shall have possession of the slaves Sophia, Phil, Lucinda and Allison, and also to have $250.00 paid to her annually until the debts shall have been paid, and also during the period I wish her to remain in possession of one-third of the stock of cattle and hogs, which I design her to hold. Finally, and when the debts of my father and brother and my own debts have been liquidated, I wish her to have altogether eight negroes of such as will be considered average value, and also the residence and lands known as Eildon as her own property, together with every article upon it and convenience of every kind belonging to the premises except such as shall hereafter remain.

Third—I wish Mr. Franklin F. Thomas, who resides with me, after his salary is paid, to devise to him the tract of land bought from David Lee, guardian of his infant children. I bequeath him also two negroes.

—136—

Fourth—To Rev. Zebulon Butler, I give and bequeath one negro.

Fifth—To Mrs. Mary A. Morehead, I give and bequeath one negro and also a pair of painted china flower vases that ornament the front parlor mantel-piece.

Sixth—To Mrs. Nancy Hughes, I give my mother's gold spectacles.

Seventh—To Julia T. Morehead, I give my elegant center table books.

Eighth—To Benj. H. Morehead, I give the books used in a classical course of study by my brother, Fielding.

Ninth—To Emma McAlpin, I give my watch.

Tenth—For Agnes McAlpin and Mary Sessions, I wish two handsome rings bought, costing at least $50.00 each.

Eleventh—To Mrs. Eliza M. Ingraham, wife of Alfred Ingraham, I give my copy of Humes' History of England, twelve volumes, also forty-five volumes of the writings of the British Essayists and the writings of Josephus, as a token of my recollection of her uncermonious tenderness to me on first acquaintance.

Twelfth—To Dr. Robert W. Harper, of Port Gibson, I give, as a testimonial of my friendly regards, my brother Isaac's gold-headed walking cane.

Thirteenth—To William Sidney Wilson, Esq., of Port Gibson, I give my father's watch and his rocking chair, being a low. hair-covered one, sitting in the front parlor, and also my mother's sofa, it being a very large one standing beneath the mirror in the front parlor, and also the oil painting on the mantel of the same apartment, as a mark of my high esteem, it being a pet ornament with me.

I also give to Mr. W. H. Wilson all the land not already mentioned to which I may have any claim either legal or equitable, and the other third of cattle and hogs, and the other twenty-one slaves, and all the increases of the whole from this time.

(Signed)   MARTHA ARCHER CONGER TUCKER.

Dated June 11, 1853.

TENTH CHILD OF JOHN AND MARY ROSS CONGER.

†HANNAH CONGER, dau of John Conger and Mary Ross, was born in Rowan Co., N. C., April 14, 1787, died at Sugar Valley, Ohio, near Eaton, March 2, 1851. She m John Railsback, in Kentucky,, April 3, 1805. He was b in Kentucky, Dec. 5, 1785, d at Eaton, Ohio, Aug. 7, 1856. Emigrated from Kentucky, 1806. He was a farmer and large land owner. Issue:

    Isaac C. Railsback, b in Kentucky, Sept. 13, 1806, d March 4, 1873, m Elizabeth M. Runyon, Feb. 6, 1834. She was b Dec. 14, 1814, d June 26, 1878. Issue:

        Juliette A. Railsback, b Feb. 6, 1835, d Feb 27, 1886. She m 1st James Everson. June 1, 1857. He d July 4, 1863. Issue:

            Georgia E. Everson, b April 2, 1860.

            Vestella A. Everson, b April 12, 1862.

        Juliette Railsback Everson m 2nd Thomas F. McClannahan, at Eaton, Ohio, May 17, 1869. Issue:

            Thomas Melton McClannahan.

        Sarah J. Railsback, b March 9, 1839, d Sept. 14, 1843.

        William M. Railsback, b April 23, 1845, d Aug. 23, 1868.

        Martha A. Railsback, b at Eaton, Ohio, Feb. 19, 1850, m James M. Davis, at Eaton, Nov. 8, 1870. Issue:

            William M. Davis, b Aug. 15, 1871, d Nov. 12, 1882.

            Edna E. Davis, b Dec. 30, 1874, d Feb. 15, 1875.

        Thomas C. Railsback, b Jan. 25, 1853, d Aug. 11, 1856.

---

†Her remains were re-interred several years afterwards, and it was found that she was petrified. Her features were life-like. The lace about her cap and everything about her was in a perfect state of preservation. The point of a pen-knife was placed under her little finger, to see if it was really petrified, and the finger broke off, showing the inner part to be like the outer, white as chalk.

CHAPTER VII.

THE ALEXANDER FAMILY.

Alexander means "helper of mankind." Alexanders have been noted for patriotism, honesty and devotion to their own family, and up to the present generation many of the descendants of the first who bore this name in America, are exemplifying in their lives the name they bear.

Many records are based on traditions that have been handed from one generation to another. Some are correct in some points, but with the repetition from one tongue to another, additions and deductions have changed them until it is not safe to base our calculations entirely on family tradition. One tradition that has come down in the Alexander family, is that seven brothers landed in America in the pursuit of religious freedom. That they scattered over the country adjacent to the Atlantic Ocean.

A large number of the Alexander family, who trace their ancestry back to William Alexander, who possibly settled at Jamestown about 1640, and had numerous descendants in and around Mecklenberg County, North Carolina, and in other Southern States, bear the same coat of arms that the Lords Sterling of England, and it is a significant fact that the real Lord Sterling of today may be one of the American Alexanders, who does not dream of the distinction that is his.

· The Alexander family under discussion has borne the coat of arms which is different from the Lord Sterling arms, and is identical with that of John Alexander whom, Burk says, settled in Carolina. The following condensed sketch is taken from Burk's Peerage:

The rental book of the Monastery of Paisey, A. D. 1472, gives the name of John Alexander as one of the tenants of the abbot. In 1522, the rental states that the lands of Candren were assessed to John, 'the son of John Alexander,' and in 1552 they are held by him conjointly with his sons, John and Robert. Members of this family continued on this same land for two hundred years. James Alexander, in 1682, and Claud Alexander, in 1733, were designed as 'of Candren.' The second son, Robert, and his wife, Janet Matthie, bought the property of Paisey Tak, in 1759. John Alexander, the brother of Robert, married Elizabeth Carswell, in 1598, and had issue Robert the 2nd; James, who had two sons, James and Claud; Catherine, and Janet.

Alexander

Robert, the 2nd, born 1604, married first in 1633, to Marion Hamilton, second to Janet Orr, by whom he had Rev. James, born 1634, who was one of the few ministers mentioned by the historian, Woodrow, in a reference "he suffered the loss of all things rather than subscribe to the Act of Uniformity." Rev. James Alexander married Mary Maxwell and had issue. Claud Alexander, brother of Rev. James Alexander, had two daughters, Marion and Janet.

Robert Alexander married second to Jean Henderson, and had Robert the 3rd, who had two daughters and John Alexander, who settled in Carolina.

An effort has been made to connect this John Alexander with the family to which Aaron Alexander belonged, but nothing further back than the record of Aaron has been definitely located. It is a fact that may yet be the means of establishing the origin of our Alexander family, that the coat of arms is identical with that of this John who settled in Carolina, and it will require more diligent research than the compiler of these records has been able to do, to fully establish the parentage of Aaron Alexander.

The settlers in Mecklenberg County, North Carolina, were largely composed of the Alexander and Harris families, and it may be that more than one Alexander family were among the early settlers.

From the foregoing, it is evident, that though we may claim descent from this John Alexander, we have no link to connect Aaron with him. Aaron Alexander had several brothers, and he was married twice.

AARON ALEXANDER and Jane Brown Ross, widow of Isaac Ross, were married in Charlotte, North Carolina, about 1763. They had two children, one dying in infancy, and the other, John Brown Alexander, born in 1765, near Charlotte, Mecklenburg County, North Carolina.

WILL OF AARON ALEXANDER.

(Original in the Court House at Charlotte, Mecklenberg County, N. C.)

In the name of God, amen, the 15th of November, 1771, I, Aaron Alexander, of North Carolina, Mecklenberg County, firm in perfect health and memory, thanks be given to God, therefore calling to mind and mortality of my body, and knowing that it is appointed to all men once to die, do make and ordain this my last will and testament, that is to say, principally and first of all, I give and recommend my soul into the hand of Almighty God that gave it, and my body I recommend to the earth, to be buried in a decent manner, at the discretion of my executor, and as touching such worldly estate wherewith it hath pleased God to give me, I give and devise and dispose of the same in the following manner:

First—I give and bequeath to my son, David Alexander, five shillings, sterling money of Great Britain.

Second—I give to and allow my beloved wife, Mary, her full third of my movable estate.

Third—I give to my son, Aaron Alexander, my real estate, and I order my son, Aaron Alexander, to pay to my son, John Brown Alexander, twenty pounds, current money of Pennsylvania, when of age, and if Aaron die under age or without heirs, then John is to be the heir.

I do hereby constitute, make and ordain my trusty friend, Zacheous Wilson, Sr., and William Alexander, my brother, my executors to this my last will and testament, and I deny all wills and testaments before the date of this above. I declare this to be my last will and testament.

In witness whereof, I have hereunto set my hand and seal this day and year above written,

AARON ALEXANDER.   eal.)

William Hayse, David Alexander.

JOHN BROWN ALEXANDER, whose mother died when he was young, was placed under the care of his uncle, Elijah Alexander, and learned the trade of a clothes dresser under his cousin, Daniel Alexander, son of Elijah. At age of 20 he married Barbara King, a native of Scotland, June 8, 1786, near Charlotte, North Carolina, and removed to the county of Elbert, Georgia, where he resided until 1804, when he temporarily removed to Nashville, Tenn., and afterwards settled near Fayetteville, the county seat of Lincoln Tennessee, in 1811, when that region was almost an unbroken forest. In 1818 he removed to Lawrence County, Alabama, and in 1820 to Illinois, and settled on the Little Vermillion River in November of that year. There was but one other family living on that stream at that time, that of Henry Johnson. In the spring of 1821 he temporurily left the Little Vermillion and settled six miles northeast of where Paris was afterwards located, joining Cambridge on his west line, and north of what is now Balwinsville. While residing there he was elected County Commissioner of Clark County, while the county seat was at Aurora. He was elected a member of the Legislature and attended the sessions st Vandalia, the capital of the state. At that time the members reached the capital on horseback, and in the eastern part of the State there were but two settlers on the trail to the capital, one near where Charleston is now located and the other near the present city of Shelbyville. These being missed, the wayfarer was subject to whatever fate might befall him.

Edgar County was organized at the session of the Legislature in 1825. Paris was selected as county seat. John B. Alexander was a member of the first Board of Commissioners in the county, and was the first postmaster at Terry. In 1825 he returned to the Little Vermillion, residing on his farm for several years, a post-office being established at his residence, called Carroll, after General Carroll of South Carolina.

The township in Vermillion County still bears the name of Carroll. He afterward sold his farm and removed to Danville, where he remained until the close of his life. His beloved wife and companion, Barbara King Alexander, died in December, 1847, and the sorrow of this event so affected this devoted man and husband, who had enioyed this unbroken companionship for three score years, that he survived her but a few years. The dust of these beloved ancestors rests quietly in the old cemetery at Danville, Illinois.

John B. and Barbara K. Alexander had twelve children, eight sons and four daughters, eight of whom were born in Georgia and four in Tennessee.

AARON ALEXANDER and Jean Brown Ross (widow of Isaac Ross—see p. 18) were married about 1763. Issue:
> Two infants, d young.

JOHN BROWN ALEXANDER, b in 1765, near Charlotte, N. C., m *Barbara King, June 8, 1786. Issue:

FIRST CHILD OF JOHN BROWN AND BARBARA KING ALEXANDER.

Josiah Alexander came with his family from Tennessee in the early 30's and seltled in Danville, Ill. He and his wife were charter members of the First Presbyterian Church of Danville, and were always faithful members, letting their light shine before the world.

JOSIAH ALEXANDER, b April 22, 1787, m March 14, 1811, to Elizabeth King, dau of Hugh and Mary A. King. He d Sept. 30, 1860. Issue:
> MARY ANN BROWN ALEXANDER, b in Maury Co., Tenn., Nov. 4, 1811, d May 2, 1864, m Sept. 12, 1837, to †James Ewing. Issue:

---

*Barbara King was a charter member of the Presbyterian Church at Paris, Ill., which was organized Nov. 6, 1824.

†James Ewing was born in Blount County, Tennessee, Nov. 3, 1804, and died March 1, 1889. He removed from Tennessee to Illinois in 1843, and located in Edgar County, where he remained for over twenty-five years, removing in 1854 to Cumberland County, where he resided till his death. He and his wife, Mary Alexander, were the parents of eight children, four sons and four daughters, only four of whom are living. He served in the Black Hawk war, and suffered many privations from want and disease. During a stampede by the Indians he was badly hurt, and carried the scars of his wounds throughout his life. He was for many years a member of the Presbyterian Church, and served for eleven years as elder of the church of Nooga, Ill. He had a good education, retentive memory, and possessed many virtues that made him dearly loved by a large circle of friends.

†Milton Augustus Ewing, b July 13, 1839, m Sept. 29, 1863, to Hannah E.
    Morrison. Issue:
        Carrie Estelle Ewing, b Aug. 31, 1866, m Rev. Mr. Brown.
        Grace Morrison Ewing, b March 17, 1872, m M. E. Kenilworth.
        Mary Florence Ewing, b July 13, 1874, m Arthur Sutton.
        ‡Charles Cyrus Ewing, b Oct. 7, 1877, m Cora L. Barclay.
    Martha Ewing, m John Blair.
    Flora E. Ewing, m E. F. Thayer.
    Linda J. Ewing, m Rev. Mr. Lyman.
      **Cyrus K. Ewing.
      **George F. Ewing, m Sarah Lewis.
§BARBARA JANE EVALINA ALEXANDER, b in Lincoln Co., Tenn., Jan. 26, 1814,
    m in Paris, Ill., Dec. 10, 1835, to §John Sheriff. She d in 1886. Issue:
    John Sheriff, d in infancy.
    Helen Sheriff, b Aug. 22, 1840, m A. Y. Magner. He d in 1862. Issue:
        Frank Ross Magner, d Dec., 1898, unmarried.
        Minnie Alice Magner, d Jan. 2, 1877, aged 17 years.
        §§Fannie E. Magner, m §§Charles E. Allen, May 25, 1886. No
        issue.
    Mary Sheriff, d in infancy.
    William Brown Sheriff, b Nov. 17, 1845, unmarried.
    Lucy Jane Sheriff, b Feb. 2, 1848, d Sept., 1901, unmarried.
    Edgar W. Sheriff, b May 7, 1852, d Nov., 1910, m Dec., 1882, to Edith
    Day. Issue:
        Helen Sheriff, b Sept. 18, 1883, m William Rogers, Sept. 19,
        1908. Issue:
            Edgar O. Rogers, b Jan. 10, 1910.
        Ruth D. Sheriff, b Aug. 7, 1885.
*CATHERINE ELIZA ALEXANDER, b in Lincoln Co., Tenn., Dec. 16, 1815, m March
    26, 1833, in Vermillion Co., Ill., to Joseph Bartley. Issue:
    Three children, d in infancy.
    Sarah E. Bartley, b March 17, 1834, m Carey A. Savage, 1856. No issue.
    Jennie B. Bartley, b Dec. 26, 1840, m John LeWarn, Jan. 17, 1861. He d
    July 23, 1907. Issue:
        George B. LeWarn, b Nov. 4, 1861, m Hattie Sanderson. No
        issue.
        Alice E. LeWarn, b Nov. 5, 1863, m March 23, 1882, to W. G.
        Gunnison. Issue:
            Olive Gunnison, b Feb. 28, 1883, m July 2, 1910,
            to Wallace J. Errickson.

---

†Milton Alexander Ewing enlisted as a private in Company B, 21st Reg. Ill. Vol., on April 7, 1861, and was promoted to Second Lieutenant and First Lieutenant, and on June 6, 1864, was commissioned Captain of Company I, 135th Reg. Ill. Inf. Vol.

‡Charles C. Ewing served in Company E, 4th Reg. Ill. Vol., Spanish-American war.

**Cyrus K. Ewing and George F. Ewing served three years in Company B, 97th Reg. Ill. Vol.

§John Sheriff and Jane E. Alexander were married in Paris, Ill., Dec. 10, 1835, and celebrated their golden wedding in Paris, where they had always resided, Dec. 10, 1885. There were five or six guests who had attended their wedding, among them Mrs. TenBrook, Milton Alexander's daughter, who was her bridesmaid. Among the remembrances was a beautiful cane, presented by the session of the Presbyterian Church. He had served as an elder in the church for fifty-four years.

§§They celebrated their silver wedding in March, 1911.

*"My mother was converted and united with the church when she was 9 years old, and grew up into a lovely Christian character. I do not know much about my father's family; that is, I do not know when they came to Illinois. They came from Pennsylvania. My grandfather, Bartley, was a genuine Pennsylvania Dutchman. He could scarcely speak English; but none of the children retained any of the brogue. They were staunch Methodists, and their children followed in their footsteps. My father went to California in 1859, with a train of emigrants from Danville and vicinity, but only lived a month after getting there.   JENNIE B. LeWARN."

Florence Gunnison, b May 7, 1888, m Elmer H.
Hill, Nov. 4, 1905. Issue:
Raleigh Hill, b July 10, 1907.
Mary Alice Hill, b Sept. 1, 1909.
William L. LeWarn, b Feb. 10, 1866, m Maud E. Reynolds,
July 14, 1888. She d June 8, 1888. Issue:
Two children, who d in infancy.
Genieve LeWarn, b Feb. 8, 1869, m June 12, 1895, to Charles
W. Hedge. He d Aug. 10, 1910. Issue:
Richard L. Hedge, b Aug. 30, 1897.
Emma J. Bartley, b Sept. 22, 1846.
†William J. Bartley, b Feb. 10, 1848, d during the war.
Joseph H. Bartley, b April 10, 1850, m Jennie Watth. Issue:
Frank Bartley, killed in an automobile accident, m. Issue:
Several children.
Leola A. Bartley, m J. A. Colquitt. Issue:
Two children.
Goldie Bartley, m Charles B. Keel. Issue:
Two children.
Hazle Bartley, m Mr. Schlicker. He is dead.
Harry Bartley.
MARTHA LAURENS ALEXANDER, b in Maury Co., Tenn, Dec. 29, 1817, d April
24, 1901, m at Paris, Ill., to Patric Caloway Tennery, Sept. 26, 1838. Issue:
Jane Angeline Tennery, d March 6, 1866, m Porter A. Savage. Issue:
Mary Alice Savage, m James Johnson. Issue:
Edna May Johnson.
Myrtle E. Johnson.
Francis P. Johnson.
Charles B. Johnson.
Louis L. Johnson.
Selma L. Johnson.
Lucius F. Johnson.
William McKinley Johnson.
Frederick E. Johnson.
Cyrus Edwin Tennery, m Mary E. Hale. Issue:
Frank Calloway Tennery, m Laura McMillan. Issue:
May A. Tennery.
Edwin R. Tennery.
Harmon Tennery.
Edwin W. Tennery.
Willet Richard Tennery, m Gertrude Trout. Issue:
Ruth Tennery.
Richard Tennery.
Katherine Elizabeth Tennery.
James Milton Tennery and
Mary Agnes Tennery, twins, d in infancy.
Florence Emmet Tennery, d May 2, 1907.
John Ross Tennery, d April 9, 1873.
Willet Judson Tennery, d Nov. 19, 1882.
Sarah Hellen Tennery, d Oct. 19, 1879, m A. J. Smith. Issue:
Henry Raymond Smith, m Florence Kirkland. He d March
17, 1898. Issue:
Harold Kirkland Smith.
Esther Smith, d in infancy.
Martha Laurens Tennery, m Richard J. Raymond. Issue:
Richardetta Raymond, d in infancy.
Charles Patric Tennery.
Cora Prentice Tennery.
Oscar Washington Tennery, d aged 9 years.

†William J. Bartley enlisted in the war when a mere boy, and, being very delicate all of his life, soon succumbed to
camp disease, and died at East St. Louis.

JOHN BROWN ALEXANDER, b in Franklin Co., Ala., Feb. 11, 1820, d June 19, 1904,
m Emily Bailey, at Danville, Ill., Nov. 14, 1848. Lived in Oregon.
HUGH KING ALEXANDER, b in Franklin Co., March 28, 1822, m Philinda Young,
near Pekin, Ill., February, 1849.
ISAAC ROSS ALEXANDER, b in Franklin Co., Ala., Aug. 29, 1824, d May 14, 1856.
WILLIAM N. ALEXANDER, b in Vermillion Co., Ill., Apr. 11, 1829, d Feb. 26, 1856.
SAMUEL E. ALEXANDER, b in Vermillion Co., Ill., Aug. 12, 1830, d Mch. 2, 1856.
EMMA J. ALEXANDER, b in Vermillion Co., Ill., Nov. 26, 1831, d Aug. 8, 1904, m
Daniel Bailey, at Pekin, Ill., Nov. 21, 1873.
HELEN M. ALEXANDER, b in Vermillion Co., Ill., Jan. 22, 1834, m William Shaw,
at Danville, Ill., Sept. 22, 1862. Issue:
    Bell Evaline Shaw, m Herbert G. Milliman. Issue:
        Herman E. Milliman, m Marion Powers, June 30, 1908.
        Raymond Prentice Milliman.
    Harry W. Shaw, m Cora Patmore. Issue:
        Frederick Shaw.
        Tracy Shaw.
        Marie Shaw.
Helen M. Alexander Shaw m 2nd David Miller, of Grand Haven, Mich.

SECOND CHILD OF JOHN BROWN AND BARBARA KING ALEXANDER

AARON ALEXANDER, b in Elbert Co., Ga., Aug. 17, 1789, lived in Tennessee, and reared
a large family there. Was a Cumberland Presbyterian minister. He died in 1850 with
typhoid fever, and at the same time several of his children succumbed to the same disease.
He married Mary Bell, dau of *John Bell and Nancy Wier. After the death of Mary Bell,
Aaron Alexander married a second time, to Mrs. Shoeton, and had one child, Bell Alexander, who died without issue. Issue by first marriage:
ELEANOR ALEXANDER, b in Lincoln Co., Tenn., June 30, 1825, m †Daniel Brazelton. Issue:
    Mary Brazelton, died without issue.
    Livia Brazelton, m W. Waterson. Issue:
        May Waterson, died.
    Livia Brazelton Waterson m 2nd to Jack Harris. Issue:
        Gertrude Harris, m Matt Cowan. Issue:
            Clarence Cowan.
            Jack Cowan.
            Evalyn Cowan.
            Infant.
        Thomas Harris, married. Issue:
            Two children.
        Mary Harris, m W. Hamilton. Issue:
            Dorothy Hamilton.
            Baby Hamilton.
    Marella Brazelton, died.
    Tommie Brazelton, m Benjamine Hayden. Issue:
        Eleanor Hayden, m Walter Smith. Issue:
            Hayden Smith.
            Nellie Smith.
        Letia Hayden, m Herbert Martin. Issue:
            Sara Martin.

---

*"John Bell came from Virginia, soon after the Revolutionary war. I think he fought under Andrew Jackson, in
the war of 1812; was wounded in the battle of Horseshoe. He was a friend of Jackson. Mother thinks he was his aide-
de-camp. John Bell was mother's grandfather. He married Nancy Wier. She died young, leaving two small children,
Mary and Elizabeth. Mary married Aaron Alexander, who was a Cumberland Presbyterian preacher, and lived near
Winchester, Tenn., and died there. Elizabeth Bell, my mother's mother, married Reuben Burrow, who was a Cumber-
land Presbyterian preacher and a great evangelist, also a professor of theology in the college at McLemoreville, Tenn.
Nancy Wier came from East Tennessee. John Bell lived near Franklin, Tenn., and died near Denmark, in Madison
County, Tenn. ELEANOR SMITH."
†He was a successful merchant of Winchester, Tenn.

Livia Hayden, m Ray Abernathy.

Benjamine Hayden, d when a young man.

Aaron Brazelton, m Fannie McGee. Issue:|

Infant, died.

Daniel Brazelton.

Frank Brazelton.

Eleanor Brazelton.

Edwin Brazelton.

Donald Brazelton.

JANE BELL ALEXANDER, b Oct. 9, 1827, m 1847 to Dr. Garrison.

MARTHA ALEXANDER, b Oct. 26, 1832, d 1850.

MARY ALEXANDER, b Oct. 26, 1832, m Robert Kinningham, Feb. 26, 1855. Issue:

Ellen Kinningham, m C. N. Kinningham. Issue:

May Kinningham, m John Marsh. Issue:

Eugene Marsh.

John Marsh.

Douglas Marsh.

Infant, died.

Robert Kinningham.

Walter Kinningham.

Finas Kinningham.

Thomas Kinningham, died.

George Kinningham, died.

Anna Kinningham, unmarried.

RUBEN BROWN ALEXANDER, died in infancy.

SARAH ALEXANDER, b Oct. 29, 1837, m Oct. 29, 1864, to Aaron McDonald, her first cousin. Issue:

May McDonald, died.

Bell McDonald, died.

*THOMAS ALEXANDER, killed in one of first battles of the Civil war, Oct. 12, 1861.

ANNA ALEXANDER, b July 25, 1841, m †William Crisman, Oct., 1860. Issue:

Nellie Crisman.

Willie Crisman, died.

Thomas Crisman.

Edward Crisman.

Robert Crisman, m Mary Smith.

FANNIE ALEXANDER, b 1845, m Wallace Kinningham, 1865. Issue:

Aaron Kinningham, died.

Mary Kinningham, m W. Mitchell. Issue:

Donald Mitchell, m Velma Friberger. Issue: .

Donald Mitchell.

Cain Mitchell.

Mary Kinningham Mitchell m 2nd to Ted Mullen. Issue:

Robert Mullen.

Joseph Mullen.

Edwin Kinningham, m Lola Davis. Issue:

Clarence Kinningham.

Eugene Kinningham.

Robert Kinningham, m Myrtle McCoy.

Bell Kinningham, m George Carson. Issue:

Wallace Carson.

Frank Carson.

Maxwell Carson.

Eleanor Carson.

Will Kinningham, m Eva Johuson.

Milton Kinningham, died.

Eleanor Kinningham, unmarried.

Bessie Kinningham, uumarried.

*He was captain in the Confederate army.

†William Crisman was known among his friends as "Billy" Chrisman. He was a large wholesale merchant o Memphis.

M. K. Alexander

GEN. MILTON KING ALEXANDER

Page 147

JOHN WASHINGTON SHIELDS ALEXANDER
Page 148

THIRD CHILD OF JOHN BROWN AND BARBARA KING ALEXANDER.

MARY, oldest daughter and third child of John B. and Barbara King Alexander, was born in Elbert County, Georgia, October 24, 1791. When she was quite young the family moved to Tennessee and later to Illinois, settling in Edgar County, where they remained until 1825, when they moved to Vermillion County, although the organization of the county was not effected until the following year, when her father was chosen one of three Commissioners empowered to organize it. He was also a member of the first Legislature of Illinois. December 1, 1825, she married Hezekiah Cunningham, who was born in Virginia, April 4, 1803, the son of David and Nellie Burnett Cunningham, both of Irish descent, his father being a farmer. Iu 1819 he and his mother, with the Murphy family, came from Virginia to Illinois in wagons, making the trip to the North Arm, in Edgar County, in seven weeks. The year of his marriage he moved, with the Alexander family, to Vermillion County, and in 1828 they moved to Danville, where they lived until their death. Mary Cunningham died September 5, 1867, her husband living until April 27, 1885. The following is quoted from Beckwith's History of Vermillion County: "While a resident here (Danville), he was interested in all affairs for the advancement of the town, and his name is written frequently in the history of the county." The same history gives his own account of an experience in the Winnebago war in 1827, when he, as a member of a company of about fifty men, went to the aid of the Chicago settlers, who were threatened with an Indian massacre, going on horseback all the way, swimming flooded streams, and provided with old and inferior fire-arms. He is remembered by one of his grandchildren as a man of a keen sense of humor simple directness of character, and a gentleness with children that made him loved by all.

MARY ALEXANDER, b ——, d Sept. 5, 1867, m Dec. 1, 1825. Issue:

*SARAH M. CUNNINGHAM, b in Vermillion Co., Ill., Sept. 3, 1827, d Aug. 4, 1892, m Dec. 5, 1844, to Oliver Lownes Davis. Issue:

Mary Olivia Davis, b Dec. 2, 1846, m Jan. 1, 1867, to Chas. J. Palmer, son of Lerin T. and Esther Gilbert Palmer. He was b Sept. 20, 1843. Issue:

Kate Jeanette Palmer, b Mch. 22, 1870, d July 1, 1870.

Esther Davis Palmer, b March 13, 1873, m Dec. 28, 1897, to Philip B. Voorhees, son of Peter and Mary Button Voorhees. He was b Jan. 8, 1875, d July 25, 1902.

†Carl King Palmer, b Oct. 21, 1876.

Janet Palmer, b Apr. 19, 1881, d June 23, 1902.

Sarah Barbara Palmer, b Jan. 7, 1886, m Nov. 30, 1909, to James E. Johnson, son of Charles B. and Maria Lewis Johnson. He was b March 10, 1879.

Lucy Ada Davis, b May 8, 1850, m Jan. 1, 1874, to Joseph Bonnell Mann, son of John M. and Eliza Bonnell Mann, of Somerville, N. J. He was b Nov. 9, 1843. Issue:

Fred Baldwin Mann, b March 26, 1875.

Oliver Davis Mann, b Dec. 10, 1877, m Sept. 21, 1910, to Jean McDonald, dau of Robert D. and Ellen Reshore McDonald. She was b Dec. 2, 1887.

---

*They made their home in Danville, Ill. He was born in New York City, Dec. 20, 1819, the son of William and Olivia Thompson Davis. He was educated in New York City and Cannandaigua, N. Y., and when a young man was connected with the American Fur Company in New York City. Coming from there to Illinois in 1841, he studied law with Judge Isaac P. Walker. In 1851 and again in 1857 he was elected to the Legislature of Illinois, and from 1861 to 1866 and from 1873 to 1885 he served as Judge of the 27th, 15th and 4th Judicial Circuits, and at the creation of the Appellate Court, in 1877, he was appointed one of its Judges, which office he continued to hold as long as he remained upon the bench, at the same time performing the duties of Circuit Judge. He was a friend, and an associate in his legal profession, of Lincoln David Davis, Leonard Swett, and many able lawyers connected with the circuit at that time. He was a delegate to the National Convention which nominated Mr. Lincoln for the Presidency in 1860. He died January 12, 1892, his wife surviving him until the following August. The spirit of true hospitality which always characterized their home made i a center for their friends from any distance, and the memory of it is loved and cherished not only by their children and grandchildren, but by all who came within its influence. Of the ten children born to them, four, Harriet, Nettie, William, and Gertrude, died in their childhood.

†Yale Class of 1899.

—145—

Nellie Davis Mann., b Aug. 8, 1881, m Feb. 27, 1906, to How-
ard Scott Shedd, son of William E. and Alice Scott
Shedd. He was b March 2, 1879, d Nov. 10, 1906.
Jennie Elizabeth Davis, b July 2, 1858, m Feb. 26, 1875, to Samuel M.
Millikin, son of William Hunter and Emily Gilkison Millikin. He
was b Nov. 25, 1855, d Jan. 12, 1895. Issue:
Donald Davis Millikin, b in Danville, Ill., Nov. 13, 1887.
Madeline Millikin, b in Birmingham, Ala., Feb. 1, 1890.
Gaylord Millikin, b in Danville, Ill., Oct. 29, 1891.
Nellie TenBroeck Davis, b April 25, 1863.
Henry Harmon Davis, b Nov. 17, 1865, m Dec., 1892, to Lulu Young, son
of William A. and Elizabeth Maddox Young. He was b in Dan-
ville, Ill., April 23, 1872. Issue:
Olive Lownes Davis, b Feb. 2, 1895.
Gene Davis, b Aug. 12, 1897.
Fannie Eliza Davis, b Nov. 16, 1867, m Aug. 23, 1893, to ‡David Walter
McCord, son of William B. and Mary Campbell McCord. He was
b in Paris, Ill., Sept. 13, 1865. Issue:
Dorothy Davis McCord, b in Riverside, Ill., July 23, 1894.
Janet McCord, b in New York City, June 2, 1903.
MILTON CUNNINGHAM, b July 9, 1829, d Jan. 3, 1897.
**WASHINGTON CUNNINGHAM, b in Danville, Ill., Feb. 8, 1834, m Jan. 4, 1859, to
Lucy A. Lamon, dau of John Lamon. She was b Dec. 5, 1834, d Jan. 8, 1876.
He d June 3, 1897. He m 2nd to Elizabeth Stansbury, in 1888. Issue by 1st
marriage:
Oliver Cunningham, d in infancy.
Charles Cunningham, b April 24, 1860.
Joseph McDonald Cunningham, b May 24, 1863, m May 24, 1883, to Mary
Boys, dau of Dr. Boys, of Portland. Issue:
Robert Cunningham.
Hobart Cunningham.
Lucy E. Cunningham, b Dec. 18, 1869, m Oct. 24, 1893, to Edward Beyer,
son of Peter and Julia Beyer, of April 1, 1869. Issue:
Peter Beyer, b Dec. 1, 1898.
Elizabeth Beyer, b Jan. 16, 1900.
Lucy Beyer, b October, 1903.
Ruth Dorothy Cunningham, b Aug. 21, 1875.

FOURTH CHILD OF JOHN BROWN AND BARBARA KING ALEXANDER.

JANE ALEXANDER, b Dec. 27, 1793, m Isaac R. Moores, in Lincoln Co., Tenn., removed
to Alabama in 1818, to Illinois in 1821, and to Oregon in 1853. They had three sons and
two daughters. (See Moores family, p. 98.)

FIFTH CHILD OF JOHN BROWN AND BARBARA KING ALEXANDER.

MILTON KING ALEXANDER removed from Giles Co., Tenn., to Paris, Ill., in 1828. He
served in the war of 1812-14. His discharge dated March 27, 1815, signed by Gen. John Coffee,
reads as follows: "I certify that Milton King Alexander, a third sergeant in my brigade of Tennessee volunteer mounted gun men, has performed a duty of six months in the service of the
United States; that his good conduct, subordination and valor, under the most trying hardships,
entitles him to the gratitude of his country, and he is hereby honorably discharged by his general." From the time of his coming to Illinois he took an active part in the affairs of his town

‡Princeton Class of 1889.

**Washington Cunningham received his education in Danville, and for several years was connected with the First
National Bank of the same place. He was a personal friend of President Lincoln, and received the appointment from
him to the office of Collector of Internal Revenue, Seventh District of Illinois. Later he filled the offices of Deputy Circuit Clerk and Master of Chancery.

and state. He was a successful merchant, was postmaster of Paris for twenty-five years, chairman of the State Board of Public Works. He was aide on the staff of Gov. Reynolds, and also commanded one of the brigades in the Black Hawk war. After his military service he was an invalid, and died in Paris, Ill., in 1856. He was survived by his wife and eight children. At this time (1911) there are only two of his children living, Mrs. Annie McMillin and Mrs. Lucy Lamon, both of Paris, Ill.

The old home of Gen. M. K. Alexander is still standing in Paris, and has never been owned except by members of the family since 1823. It is now occupied by Mrs. McMillin. The present house was built in 1840, and has been modernized by the addition of the twentieth century conveniences. It is a large, brick house, a wide hall extending through the house, with large rooms on each side. Many distinguished people have been entertained under its roof. Lincoln was dining there when Mrs. Luch Lamon took her first steps. Lincoln was a close personal friend of Gen. Alexander, and many letters from him are still kept in the family archives.

A peculiar circumstance attended the death of Mrs Alexander. A friend, Mrs. Gen. Stanford, hearing she was ill, went to inquire about her. As she stepped upon the threshold she fell dead, and in a few minutes Mrs. Alexander died, and the funeral of the two was held together.

MILTON KING ALEXANDER, fifth child of John Brown Alexander and his wife, Barbara King Alexander, b in Elbert Co., Georgia, Jan. 23, Jan. 23, 1796, m in Giles Co., Tenn., Dec. 16, 1819, to Mary Shields. She was b in Elbert Co., Ga., Feb. 12, 1800, and d in Paris, Ill., Jan. 1, 1866. She was the dau of Samuel and Jane Montgomery Shields. Issue:

*JANE CYNTHELIA ALEXANDER, b in Giles Co., Tenn., Dec. 12, 1820, m in Paris, Ill., to Dr. John TenBroeck, April 23, 1840. He was b in Northumberland Co., Pa., Dec. 21, 1808, d in Paris, Ill., Aug. 8, 1885. Issue:

John Milton TenBroeck, b Feb. 26, 1841, d in 1845.

†Ellen Mary TenBroeck, b March 5, 1843, m Nov. 26, 1868, to Stephen Bird. He was b in Cambridge, Eng., July 2, 1838. Issue:

John Clifton Bird, b in Lockport, N. Y., July 19, 1869, m July 1, 1897, to Florence S. Harner. She was b Sept. 24, 1871, in Valparaiso, Ind.

Thomas Alexander Bird, b Sept. 6, 1871, in Lockport, N. Y., m March 16, 1907, Isabella Vocke. She was b in Chicago, Jan. 20, 1878.

William Bird, b Aug. 10, 1873, in Lockport, N. Y., m Feb. 2, 1907, Mary O'Malley. She was b in London, Ky., Sept. 18, 1874.

Owen Stephen Bird, b June 10, 1876, in Lockport, N. Y., m Harriet Louise DeForest. She was b in Brownsville, Ind., July 15, 1880. Issue:

Eleanoro Mary Bird, b Aug. 17, 1908, in Des Moines, Ia.

John TenBroeck Bird, b Feb. 2, 1882, in Lockport, N. Y.

Jane Janet TenBroeck, b May 22, 1845, d 1870.

Zachariah Taylor TenBroeck, b April 19, 1847, d Mar. 3, 1860.

Dollie Ann TenBroeck, b in Paris, Ill., Jan. 4, 1849, m in Paris, Ill., Feb. 23, 1876, to Owen B. Jones. He was b in Athens, O., Jan. 5, 1843. Issue:

McMillan Jones, b in Paris. Ill., Feb. 7, 1877, m Caroline Gilbert, March 3, 1907. She wa b Feb. 1, 1879. Issue:

*When Jane Cynthelia Alexander's parents moved to Illinois, she remained in Tennessee with her maternal grand parents until her family were, in a measure, settled in their new home, and then her uncle, Col. Washington Alexander, brought her on horseback from Tennessee to join her family in Illinois. She was educated in Jacksonville, Ill., and Pulaski, Tenn. She married Dr. John TenBroeck, who graduated at Lafayette College and the Jefferson Medical College, of Philadelphia. He came to Paris, Ill., in 1840, and practiced his profession there till the time of his death. He was widely known in Eastern Illinois as a physician and a wholesouled, true Christian gentleman.

†Mrs. Ellen Mary Bird died in Lucern, Switzerland, July 11, 1904.

—147—

Gilbert TenBroeck Jones, b July 7, 1908.
Janet Clark Jones, b in Paris, Ill., June 1878, m June 20, 1901, to Allen Diehl Albert, Jr. He was b in Pa., Oct. 3, 1874. Issue:
Allen D. Albert 3rd, b April 27, 1902.
Owen Jones Albert, b Apr. 25, 1904.
John TenBroeck Jones, b June 8, 1880, m April 2, 1903, to Alice Conner. She was b in Springfield, Ill., May 6, 1883. Issue:
Owen TenBroeck, b at pringfield, Ill., Jan. 9, 1904.
Edward Conner TenBroeck, b at Springfield, Ill., Nov. 3, 1906.
Robert Clark TenBroeck, b at Peoria, Ill., June 5, 1909.
Nell Davis Jones, b in Paris, Ill., Sept. 22, 1881, m June 26, 1907, to her cousin, ‡Victor Leseure. Issue:
Janet Catherine Leseure, b March 17, 1910.
Cyrus Alexander Jones, b in Paris, Ill., Nov. 8, 1887.
Barbara Ann Jones, b in Paris, Ill., Jan. 4, 1893.
Elizabeth Pearson TenBroeck, b Oct. 23, 1851, d Dec. 21, 1853.
JOHN WASHINGTON SHIELDS ALEXANDER, b in Giles Co., Tenn., Dec. 10, 1822, m at Rockville, Ind., July 17, 1848, to Elizabeth Howard, dau of Gen. Tilgman Howard. He d in 1863. She d Sept. 22, 1855. Issue:
Howard Alexander, b in 1849, d in 1853.
Elizabeth Adelia Alexander, b Nov. 19, 1852, m Frank Field, of Boston. She d June 4, 1888. He d soon after. Issue:
Edwin Alexander. Nothing is known of him.
John W. S. Alexander m 2nd on Dec. 13, 1857, to Lucinda Canady, in Charleston, Ill. She d in October, 1858. Issue:
Infant, who died at the same time.

---

‡Victor Leseure was born in France. Was a successful merchant and a very fine character.

Judge Oliver Davis was a polished gentleman and a fine lawyer. Was a circuit and appellate judge for many years·

Mrs. McPherson's father, Col. Harmon, was a prominent attorney, a cousin of Mrs. Cleveland, and colonel of the 125th Ill. Vols.

John Washington Shields Alexander was carried to Illinois when an infant. He was graduated in 1845 at Wabash College, Crawfordsville, Ind., with the highest honors of his class, and with the degree of Bachelor of Arts. In 1848 his Alma Mater conferred on him the degree of Master of Arts. In 1846 he was made first lieutenant of company H, 4th Reg. Ill. Vols., when war was declared with Mexico. He was at the siege and capture of Vera Cruz and marched with the army under command of Gen. Scott to the City of Mexico, and remained in the service till the close of the war, participating in all the principal battles. At the close of the war he returned home, and was a successful merchant until the beginning of the Civil war. He was made captain of company F, 21st Reg. Ill. Vols., and entered the service in June, 1861. U. S. Grant was made colonel of the regiment and J. W. S. Alexander lieutenant-colonel. In August, 1861. Col. Grant was commissioned general, and Lieut.-Col. Alexander succeeded to the command of the regiment. The 21st Illinois was on duty in Missouri from July, 1861, until some time in 1862. At the terrible battle of Stone Hill, at Murfreesboro, Tenn., before going into this battle the 21st regiment mustered 866 men and after the battle only 363 answered to roll call. In this engagement Col. Alexander was severely wounded, was brought home, and under the skillful treatment of his brother-in-law, Dr. TenBroeck, he was able after several months to return to his command, but was compelled to use a crutch. At the battle of Chicamauga, when the Southern forces drove his men back, in his effort to restore order he was thrown from his horse and at the same time received a death wound. His body sleeps in an honored grave in the Edgar Cemetery. He was a strict disciplinarian, yet was always considerate of the welfare of his men. Gen. Grant in a letter to the adjutant-general, said: "When I was assigned to duty as brigadier-general I turned the regiment over to that gallant, Christian officer, Col. Alexander, who afterwards yielded up his life while nobly leading in the battle of Chicamauga." Col. Alexander's first wife was the daughter of General Howard, a prominent man of affairs in Indiana; at one time Minister Plenipotentiary to Texas.

—148—

*ANGELINE ALEXANDER, third child of Milton King Alexander and Mary Shields Alexander, was b in Paris, Ill., Oct. 10, 1824, m J. Wilson Ross, Sept. 1, 1846. He d Sept. 13, 1853. Issue:

Mary Ross, b May 20, 1848, d June 10, 1848.

Anna Ross, b and d May 21, 1850.

John Milton Ross, b July 2, 1851, d June 11, 1852.

Angeline Alexander Wilson m 2nd Uriah Griffith McMillan, Nov. 7, 1859, who was b in York Co., Pa., Jan. 21, 1826. He d in Paris, Ill., Sept. 16, 1880; she d in 1911. Issue:

Willet Enos McMillan, b Dec. 13, 1860, m Dec. 4, 1896, to Jessie Harding, who was b in Edgar Co., Ill., July 30, 1872. Issue:

Dudley Harding McMillin, b Oct. 27, 1897, in Paris, Ill.

Emma Alexander McMillan, b Oct. 14, 1902.

John TenBroeck McMillan, b April 26, 1863, d April 24, 1866.

Alexander McMillan, b Jan. 24, 1866, d Aug. 11, 1866.

Minnie Gertrude McMillan, b May 10, 1870, d Sept. 9, 1870.

*MARY ELIZABETH ALEXANDER, b in Paris, Ill., Jan. 7, 1827, m Sept. 14, 1843, to Oliver Jones Chestnut, who was b in Vigo Co., Ind., July 15, 1817, at Shocton, Cal., Sept. 8, 1850. She d in Washington, D. C., May 10, 1902. Issue:

Sarah Chestnut, b Sept. 16, 1841, d in Marshall, Ill., July 7, 1869.

John Oliver Chestnut, b and d June 9, 1846.

Elizabeth Alexander Chestnut, b Aug. 20, 1847, d Dec. 29, 1849.

Charles Oliver Chestnut, b Aug. 21, 1849, m Dec. 25, 1873, to Bell LeGore. She was b in Marshall, Ill., April 30, 1849. Issue:

†LeGore Chestnut, b in Cincinnati, O., July 21, 1875, m Aug. 19, 1879, to Adele Hastou. She was b Feb. 2, 1885. Issue:

Charles Oliver Chestnut, b July 28, 1899.

Emily Alexander Chestnut, b May 16, 1901.

Isabel Chestnut, b Nov. 1, 1903.

Mary E. A. Chestnut m 2nd to ‡Dr. Fleming Rice Payne, April 12, 1854. He was b near Lexington, Ky., Feb. 22, 1831, and d Dec. 2, 1873. Issue:

Vernon Alexander Payne, b Nov. 27, 1855, m Oct. 9, 1888, to Lou Alexander (not related), in Dudley, Ill. Issue:

Esther Mary Payne, b Sept. 21, 1889, in Paris, Ill.

Clara E. Payne, b June 13, 1792, in Paris, Ill.

Mary Gertrude Payne, b Feb. 26, 1861, d Aug. 13, 1861.

Lucy Jane Payne, b Sept. 12, 1862.

John Washington Payne, b Sept. 18, 1864, d in Phoenix, Ari., Dec., 1908.

JACINTHA ALEXANDER, b in Paris, Ill., Feb. 12, 1828, educated at Chitanango, N. Y., m Sept. 26, 1848, to §Willet Harmon Judson. He was b in Ithaca, N. Y., July 15, 1823, and d in New York, Dec. 29, 1890. She d in Cal. May 30, 1903. Issue:

---

*Angeline Alexander McMillan was the first white female child born in the town of Paris, Ill. She is living today, as one of its most honored citizens. She was educated in Bloomington, Ind., and Hillsboro, Ill. Her first husband, J. Wilson Ross, was a prominent lawyer, and practiced in Charleston and Sullivan, Ill. Dr. McMillan, her second husband, was a prominent physician, and practiced in Indiana until 1860, when he became a member of the firm of R. Macready Co., wholesale druggists of Cincinnati. Failing health forced him to retire from business in 1873. He with his family spent two years in Europe, and also traveled extensively in this country. He died in 1880, and Mrs. McMillan is now living in the house built by her father in Paris, Ill., and, while 87 years old, is bright and active, and a friend to many who feel honored to claim her as a friend.

*Mary Elizabeth Alexander was educated at Edgar Academy. Her first husband was a prosperous merchant of Paris, Ill., until he removed to California in the spring of 1850. His death followed soon after.

†Dr. F. R. Payne was a leading physician of Eastern Illinois. Their home was at Marshall, Ill., until the death of Dr. Payne.

‡LeGore Chestnut, a most promising young business man, accompanied by his wife, went to Europe in the summer of 1904, and died in Plymouth, England, Sept. 1, 1904.

§See note, page 150.

-149-

Jennie Shields Judson, b in Paris, Ill., July 30, 1849.

Russell Alexander Judson, b in Vicksburg, Miss., Dec., 1852, d in Colorado, Sept. 5, 1880.

Mary Elizabeth Judson, b in Vicksburg, Miss., July 30, 1857, d in a hospital in Indianapolis, Feb. 10, 1908.

Emma TenBroeck Judson, b in Vicksburg, Miss., Dec. 30, 1859, m to Counseler John H. VanWinkle, of Plainfield, N. J., June 18, 1891, d at Plainfield, Oct. 30, 1792.

Willet Alexander Judson, b April 6, 1861, m Mae McMahon, in Paris, Ill., Oct. 1, 1885. She was b Feb. 11, 1866. Issue:

Stanly McMahon Judson, b July 11, 1886, m Emma ———, in Indianapolis. Issue:

Mary E. Judson, b March 16, 1911.

Willet Ewart Judson, b Sept. 7, 1896.

Kathleen Judson, d in infancy.

Annie Rebekah Judson, b at Morton, Miss., March 6, 1863, d in Paris, Ill., Oct. 16, 1882.

Jacyntha Alexander Judson, b in Morton, Miss., Dec. 7, 1869.

MILTON KING ALEXANDER, m 2nd to Mary Shields. Issue:

*JAMES CYRUS ALEXANDER, m Emma Bodine Graydon, Aug. 24, 1859, in Indianapolis. She was b Aug. 24, 1840. He d in Paris, Ill., March 23, 1866. Issue:

Milton King Alexander, b in Clinton, Mo., Aug. 9, 1860, m Nov. 8, 1899, to Mary Gertrude Brown. She was b in Indianapolis, June 3, 1864. Issue:

Marjorie Gertrude Alexander, b May 22, 1909.

Willie M. Alexander, b in Indianapolis, May 9, 1862, d in infancy.

James Walter Shields Alexander, b in Paris, Ill., Feb. 22, 1863, d in young manhood.

†LUCY ALEXANDER, b in Paris, Ill., Jan. 29, 1843, m June 2, 1864, to Robert Bruce Lamon. He was b in Berkley Co., Virginia, Feb. 8, 1827; d May 19, 1899, in Washington, D. C. Issue:

‡Walter Shields Lamon, b Feb. 26, 1865, in Danville, Ill., m March 28, 1903, to Martha Woodward Varner. He was b Oct. 23, 1871.

Judson Alexander Lamon, b in Paris, Ill., Dec. 7, 1867, m June 18, 1900, to Emma Scott. She was b in Denver, Col., Dec. 21, 1878. Issue:

---

‡Willet Harmon Judson was a merchant of Vicksburg, Miss. At the breaking out of the Civil war he enlisted in the Southern army as quartermaster of one of the Mississippi regiments. At the time of the siege of Vicksburg Mrs. Judson, with a friend, Mrs. Dwight, four little children and her house servants, refugeed in Morton, Miss. During their stay both armies passed over that part of the country, and some of their experience there was at times very trying. Her recital of it all was most interesting and thrilling. Her slaves all followed the Northern army when it moved. Sherman's army, she said, was one of the grandest spectacles she had ever witnessed. with their uniforms and equipments, and the men strong and well cared for. The contrast between that picture and the one presented by Johnson's force, worn and haggard, with disordered uniforms and battered arms, was a sight which she wept over. Of the treatment accorded her in her unprotected situation by the officers of both commands, she had nothing but words of praise and gratitude. Their was no North and no South, simply the American soldier and gentleman At the close of the war the family removed to Selma, Ala., where Mr Judson resumed his mercantile business until his health failed, when they took up their residence in Paris, Ill., in 1875. He went to New York for treatment and died in a hospital there Dec. 28, 1899. Mrs. Judson died in San Diego, Cal., where she had gone for a temporary stay, May 30, 1903.

*James Cyrus Alexander was educated at Hanover College, and resided in Clinton, Mo., where he was a merchant.

†Lucy Alexander Lamon was educated at Oxford and Glendale. Judge Lamon was born in Berkley County, Virginia, Feb. 8, 1827; was educated at Wabash College, Crawfordsville, Ind. Went to California with the "forty-niners," and remained eight years. Served a term in the Legislature, representing the counties of Mariposa and Merced. While a resident of California he served as a volunteer under command of the noted Indian fighter, Captain Ben Wright, in the campaign of 1852, against the Modocs. He returned to Danville in 1857, and was admitted to the bar in 1858. Served one term as County and Probate Judge. He removed to Paris in 1866, and served two terms in the Edgar County Court. During the first administration of Cleveland he was appointed a member of the Board of Pension Appeals in the Interior Department. He and the family remained in Washington until he died, May 18, 1899.

‡Walter S. Lamon served as hospital steward in the 4th Ill. Vol. Inf. in the Spanish-American war. from April 26 1898, to May 2, 1899.

Lucy Elizabeth Lamon, b in Chicago, Nov. 25, 1904.
Robert Scott Lamon, b March 29, 1906.
GERTRUDE ALEXANDER, b in Paris, Ill., Aug. 14, 1845, m Sept. 16, 1869, to Jacoq
A. Ross. He was b in Edgar Co., Ill., Sept. 1, 1843. She d in Paris, Ill., in
March, 1871.

PORTION OF LETTER FROM MRS. *LUCY ALEXANDER LAMON.

Paris, Ill., June 22, 1911.

Dear Cousin:

My sister, Mrs. McMillan, is the other member of the family particularly interested in these family affairs, and she has been able to assist me but little. She and I are the only children living of my father's family, and she has been a wonder. Next October, if she lives, she will celebrate her 87th birthday, and, until this violent attack of jaundice, has been right up-to-date in everything—was perfectly erect in her carriage, never missed Sunday school or church services of any kind, and never declined an invitation. She has traveled a great deal, both here and abroad, and her accounts of her trips are most interesting. Her home was in Washington for some time, but she, some few years since, purchased our old home place from the grand-child, Mrs. Bird, who had inherited it, and has lived there since.

You may be interested to know that the ground upon which the house is built has never been out of the family since 1823. She was born there, as well as five others of us. The house she lives in, however, was built about 1840. I was the first child born in it. It, of course, has been modernized, with heat, bath and gas, but the brick house, with a hall in the center and large rooms on either side, stands as it was built, and a great many men who have made the history of this State have been entertained there. My sister tells me that Lincoln was dining with the family when I took my first steps. In later years I remember him at the house, and Douglas and many more. I have a personal letter to my father from Lincoln, and we had numerous others from a great many other men, but which were, unfortunately, burned.

There was a peculiar circumstance attending my mother's death. An old friend had heard she was seriously ill, and came to see her. As the friend (Mrs. General Sandford) stepped upon the verandah she fell dead, and five minutes later my mother died, and the funerals of these two pioneers, each leaving large families, were held together. The husbands of both were always addressed as "General."

In my uncle Washington's record I forgot to mention that there are no grand-children, and never have been. He was always called "Colonel Alexander."

You will notice that two of my sisters married men by the name of Ross. I know nothing of their ancestry, so do not know whether they came from your Ross family or not.

Mrs. Yeomans, of Danville, was here the other day, and said she and Mrs. Palmer had been communicating with you, but I saw them for so short a time that I did not hear what they had done. Mrs. Yeomans is Aunt Catherine McDonald's grand-daughter, and Mrs. Palmer is Aunt Mary Cunningham's grand-daughter. Their mothers and fathers were people that we were proud of. Mrs. Yeomans' father, Victor LeSeure, was born in France, was a very successful merchant and a fine character, and Mrs. Palmer's father, Judge Oliver Davis, was a most polished gentleman and fine lawyer; was a circuit and appellate judge for years.

Mrs. McPherson wrote me that she would get the data of her branch as soon as possible. Her father was a cousin of Mrs. Cleveland. Col. Harmon was a prominent attorney, and Colonel of the 125th Ill. Vols.; was killed at Kinesaw Mountain.

Yours sincerely,

LUCY A. LAMON.

*Mrs. Lamon has collected most of the records for her branch, and her interest in this work has greatly facilitated the labors of the compiler.

SIXTH CHILD OF JOHN BROWN AND BARBARA KING ALEXANDER.
JOHN NEWTON ALEXANDER, b Feb. 20, 1798, d Aug. 23, 1800.

SEVENTH CHILD OF JOHN BROWN AND BARBARA KING ALEXANDER.

In 1820 Katherine King Alexander, with her husband, moved to Illinois from Tennessee, first stopping in Edgar County, where they remained some years, then removed to the Little Vermillion, four miles south of Georgetown, Ill. Here she assisted her husband in making what was known to early settlers as the McDonald farm, on which she lived forty years, the best part of her life, enduring without a murmur the privations and hardships of a pioneer life and mother, manifesting the beauty of an unselfish life. No neighbor ever needed assistance but that she was ready to render it, if in her power. She was a faithful member of the Cumberland Church, for many years. In the early days of the settlement her house was open for church services, and all the neighborhood were invited to attend. It was also used as a hotel by travelers, where they were entertained with the best the house afforded, and nursed in sickness without money or price. One of the oldest grand-daughters remembers a traveler stopping one evening at twilight and asking for shelter for the night, as he was too ill to travel further. Al he asked for was a drink of water and a bed. In the morning it was found that he had the small-pox. The young people were sent away and the stranger nursed back to health and strength. He blessed that household as he went away. Her sympathy extended to all humanity. In matters of hospitality and charity she knew no class, no nationality, no religion. She aided the poor and lonely, as well as the rich and exalted; the Indian and negro trader as freely as the white man, and the heathen with the same generosity as she did the Christian. The writer knew her forty years, part of the time living in her family. He never heard her utter a harsh word to or of any person. Her whole life was void of malice toward any and full of charity to all.

KATHERINE KING ALEXANDER, b in Elbert Co., Ga., April 20, 1800, m Alexander
McDonald, who was b in Elbert Co., Ga., Feb. 14, 1796. She d July 6, 1880; he d Jan. 2, 1861. They were m in Lincoln Co., Ala., and removed to Illinois in 1820, and settled on Little Vermillion River, near Georgetown. Issue:
MARY JANE McDONALD, b in Franklin Co., Ala., Aug. 31, 1819, d Feb. 19, 1840, unmarried.
NANCY F. McDONALD, b in Edgar Co., Ill., March 12, 1822, m John Bailey, Nov. 22, 1840. She d April 20, 1904. Issue:
William Alexander Bailey, b in 1842, m in 1867 to Ann E. Baldwin. He d in 1884. Issue:
Laura M. Bailey, b 1867, m Mr. Becker.
Jesse Bailey, b 1869, d in 1878.
Mary Jane Bailey, b Aug. 10, 1844, m May 24, 1864, to Richard E. Ward, and live in Chicago. Issue:
Florence M. Ward, b June 18, 1865, d Oct. 3, 1865.
Charles Edwin Ward, b Nov. 6, 1866, m June 4, 1888, to Louise Fish. Issue:
Marion E. Ward, b Dec. 13, 1891.
C. E. Ward m 2nd Nov. 27, 1907, to Harriet Snyder. Issue: Ruth Ward, b Dec. 19, 1908.
William Ernest Ward, b March 1, 1869, m Jan. 1, 1896, to Carrie Brink. Issue:
Robert Ward, b July 20, 1897.
Harold Newton Ward, b Dec. 29, 1899, d Feb. 9, 1903.
Mary Jane Ward, b Sept. 4, 1901, d Jan. 2, 1903.
Harold Newton Ward, b Fec. 5, 1905.
Mary Jane Ward, b Feb. 9, 1907.
Dorothy Ward, b March 25, 1909.
Nellie L. Ward, b Feb. 2, 1873, d Mar. 17, 1892.
Ernest B. Ward, b Aug. 2, 1875, m May 12, 1897, to Josephine

Charney. Issue:
    Floyd Ward, b Sept. 27, 1898.
    Ernest Ward, b Jan. 22, 1900.
    Isabelle Ward, b July 3, 1904.
Alice May Ward, b Jan. 8, 1877, m July 12, 1899 to Will S.
Parks. Issue:
    Florence Louise Parks, b Aug. 26, 1900.
    Richard Charles Parks, b Nov. 11, 1903.
*Daniel S. Bailey, b Nov. 5, 1846, m Annette E. Teas, Sept. 3, 1868. Are
living at Ratouh, Ill. Issue:
    Arthur Teas Bailey, b July 20, 1870, m Nov. 18, 1897, to Fan-
    nie Fern Rose. Issue:
        Elizabeth Bailey, b Sept. 1, 1898.
        John Bailey, b Dec. 24, 1900.
    Oscar F. Bailey, b Oct. 17, 1875, m May 19, 1897, to Fannie
    Mae Dewey. Issue:
        Daniel Dewey Bailey, b March 9, 1898, d July 29,
        1898.
        Helen Bailey, b April 8, 1901, d Oct. 4, 1902.
        Frances Bailey, b March 18, 1905.
    Donald H. Bailey, b Jan. 1, 1879, m July, 1903, to Ruby L.
    Berry. He d Aug. 31, 1905. Issue:
        Donald Norburn Bailey, b Dec. 20, 1904.
Newton Hill Bailey, b Dec. 3, 1848, m Dec. 2, 1875, to Abbie F. Rugg.
He d Dec. 21, 1909. Issue:
    Archie Earl Bailey, b Sept. 11, 1879, m Feb. 2, 1901, to Lucre-
    tia Godard. Issue:
    Elton Rugg Bailey, b Jan. 2, 1883.
    Carrol Loren Bailey, b Dec. 21, 1895.
Martha F. Bailey, b 1851, d 1854.
Sarah Catherine Bailey, b April 19, 1853, m April, 1872, to Thaddeus C.
Knapp. They live at Wadena, Minn. Issue:
    Alice Olivia Knapp, b March 3, 1872.
    Phoebe Franklin Knapp, b May 7, 1877, m 1898, to Oliver
    Armstrong. Issue:
        Estelle Belle Armstrong, b Nov. 19, 1899.
        Beatrice Louise Armstrong, b May 3, 1901.
        Oliver Waldo Armstrong, b Dec. 20, 1908.
    Ruth Ann Knapp, b Jan. 27, 1881, m in 1900 to Clifton Gas-
    teller. Issue:
        Harold Vincent Gasteller, b Jan. 11, 1901, d
        March 1, 1901.
        Phillis Irene Gasteller, b July 7, 1904.
    Lucy Belle Knapp, b Jan. 15, 1886.
Donald W. Bailey, b 1855, d 1867.
Jeannette O. Bailey, b Aug. 10, 1858, m Dec. 24, 1892, to Seldon E. Hood.
They live at Hanlontown, Iowa. Issue:
    Ruth Hood, b Jan. 13, 1906.
Julia Alice Bailey, b March 1, 1863, m Sept. 5, 1889, to Dudley C. Rugg.
They live at Minneapolis, Minn. Issue:
    Lucile Marie Rugg, b Nov. 1, 1893.
    Dudley Gale Rugg, b June 9, 1899, d Jan. 5, 1905.
    Maynard Bailey Rugg, b Sept. 14, 1904.
    Donald Carlyle Rugg, b Sept. 11, 1906, d July 8, 1910.

---

*ELIZABETH CATHERINE McDONALD, 3rd dau of Catherine King Alexander and Alexander McDonald, b Aug. 16, 1823, m 1st to**Dr. Hardy Wallace Hill, in Georgetown, Ill., March, 1844, and returned at once to Cincinnati. She d Feb. 9, 1906   Issue:

    Eleanor Elizabeth Hill, b in Cincinnati, May 25, 1845, m in Danville, Ill. Oct. 18, 1866, to Alexander Short. Issue:

        Colmore Hill Short, b Sept. 29, 1867, d in Cal. in 1909.

        Nina Short, d 1873.

        Belle Alexander Short, b June 16, 1874, m in Cal. to Harry E. Butler. Issue:

            Alexander Short Butler, b 1894.

            Harmon Short Butler, b 1899.

        Edward Short, died.

        Donald Harmon Short, b Jan. 14, 1879, m Edith ——. Issue:

            Belle Eleanor Short, b 1906.

        Corinne Brooks Short, b July 23, 1884.

    Elizabeth Catherine McDonald Hill m 2nd in Danville, Ill., Feb. 22, 1854, to Oscar Fitzalan Harmon. Issue:

        †Lucy Belle Harmon, b in Danville, Ill., Feb. 18, 1855, m May 15, 1879, to §Rev. Simon John McPherson, of Munford, N. Y. Issue:

            Jeannette McPherson, b in East Orange, N. J., Nov. 7, 1880, m June 23, 1904, to Charles Harlow Raymond, in Lawrenceville, N. J. Issue:

                Jean Raymond, b Dec. 17, 1905.

                Charles Harlow Raymond, b July 5, 1909.

            ‡Oscar Harmon McPherson, b March 9, 1883.

            Elizabeth McPherson, b in Chicago, Ill., Aug. 26, 1883, m June 16, 1910, to Raymond Garfield Wright.

            John Finlay McPherson, b Jan. 15, 1888.

            Robert Crerar McPherson, b Jan. 15, 1893.

        Charles Augustus Harmon, b in Danville, Ill., Oct. 21, 1857, d March 19, 1875.

        †Fannie Davis Harmon, b in Danville, Ill., Sept. 10, 1860, m May 15, 1879, to Frank LeRoy Brooks. Issue:

SARAH EMILY McDONALD, b May 3, 1830, m **Dr. Hiram H. Hill, of Cincinnati, April 20, 1854. She d May 3, 1905; he d June 10, 1907. Issue:

    Rosa Bell Hill, b March 30, 1855, d Aug. 23, 1876.

---

*Elizabeth Catherine McDonald and Dr. Hardy Wallace Hill were first cousins. (See his line, p. 1—.) He was a successful electric physician in Cincinnati, Ohio, for some years. He fell a victim to the cholera scourge of 1849, and died there in March of that year. Mrs. Hill returned to her father's home in Illinois in the autumn of that year with her fatherless little girls, and lived at her father's home four years, and in 1858 she and her children moved to Danville and boarded with her aunt and uncle, Mr. and Mrs. Hezekiah Cunningham, until Feb. 22, 1854, when she became the wife of Oscar F. Harmon. Mrs. Harmon died at the home of her daughter, Mrs. McPherson, in Lawrenceville, N. J. Oscar F. Harmon was a successful lawyer.

†Lucy Belle Harmon and Fannie Davis Harmon were married the same night the double ceremony being performed by the father of the latter's husband, Rev. A. L. Brooks.

‡Oscar Harmon McPherson is a teacher at the school at Lawrenceville, N. J. John Finlay McPherson graduated from that school in 1906 and from Princeton 1910. He is in business in New York. Paul Crerar McPherson is a soph. in Princeton. He graduated at Lawrenceville, 1910.

§Rev. S. J. McPherson is a prominent Presbyterian divine. Has been pastor at East Orange, N. J., and on his wedding day received the call to the First Presbyterian Church of that place. He has for the past twelve years been head master of the school at Lawrenceville, N. J.

**See note, page 155.

—154—

Robert Harmon Brooks, b Aug. 31, 1881, m Sept.
6, 1904, to Ida Dunham, in Kansas City,
Mo. Issue:

Frank LeRoy Brooks, b Dec. 27, 1906, d Jan. 23,
1907.

Charles Dunham Brooks, b March 8, 1909, in
Kansas City, Mo.

Fannie David Harmon Brooks m 2nd Feb. 7, 1897, to Frederick Newman. No issue.

Corinne Alexander Harmon, b March 15, 1863, d in Emporia,
Kan., July 27, 1901.

Lilla Wallace Hill, b in Cincinnati, O., June 21, 1849, d in Danville, Ill.,
July 3, 1871.

JOHN NEWTON McDONALD, b in Vermillion Co., Ill., Jan. 17, 1826, d May 22, 1855,
m Mary J. Smith, March 29, 1855.

CAROLINE B. McDONALD, b in Vermillion Co., Ill., Feb. 28, 1828, m Victor LeSeure,
Dec. 20, 1849. She d August 3, 1872. Issue:

Kate LeSeure, b June 18, 1852, m Chas. T. Yeomans, Oct. 24, 1878. Issue:
Victor LeSeure Yeomans, m Nell Davis Jones, June 26, 1907.
Issue:
Janet Catherine Yeomans.
Nathaniel Tracy Yeomans, b Nov. 5, 1881.
Minnette Angeline Yeomans, b Aug. 31, 1886.

Minnette LeSeure, b January 23, 1862, m in 1896 to Thos. W. Elliott.
No issue.

Louise LeSeure, b Sept. 19, 1857, m in 1886 to William K. Palmer. Issue:
Frederick Palmer, b April 21, 1887.
Katherine Palmer, b April 2, 1889.
Dorothy Palmer, b Jan. 8, 1892.
Robert Palmer, b December 6, 1893.

Martha Caroline LeSeure, b Sept. 28, 1865.

Charles Franklin LeSeure, b Nov. 30, d June 10, 1884, m Jennie Sidell,
Oct. 5, 1881. Issue:
Callie Belle LeSeure, b Feb. 17, 1883.

†Mamye Hill, living at Doland, S. D.

Caroline Hill, m T. L. Durham, March 24, 1886. Issue:
Clarence Durham, b May 6, 1887, d Aug. 7, 1905.
Frank Hill Durham, b May 6, 1888.
Hiram Hunter Durham, b Sept. 1, 1889.
Mamye Durham, b Feb. 5, 1891, and
Josephine Durham, b Feb. 5, 1891, twins.
Robert Lincoln Durham, b April 9, 1892.
Kenneth William Durham, b June 29, 1895.
Dorothy Lois Durham, b Sept. 2, 1898.
Sydney Alexander Durham, b Nov. 4, 1905.

Wilbur McDonald Hill, m Sarah Allen, Dec. 4, 1892. Issue:
Sarah Ruth Hill, b April 8, 1904, d Feb. 5, 1910.

Charles Victor Hill, unmarried.

DONALD W. McDONALD, b in Vermillion Co., Ill., Jan. 16, 1833, d April 17, 1855,
unmarried.

---

*Dr. Hiram Hunter Hill and Dr. Hardy Wallace Hill were the sons of Isaac Hill and Margaret Cunningham. Dr.
H. H. Hill was born Jan. 29, 1836, died June 10, 1907. He was a wholesale and retail druggist of Cincinnati. His place of
business was at the corner of Race and Fifth streets. He was a lover of natural history, and was for a number of years
an officer in the Natural History Society of Cincinnati. He was a member of the famous Squirrel Hunters' Regiment in
service during the Civil war; and remained a member of that regiment till 1892, when he was honorably discharged. He
with his family removed to South Dakota in 1883, where his family still reside. He represented his county in the State
Legislature in 1891 and 1892.

†Miss Mamye Hill has given valuable assistance in compiling these records.

—155—

‡AARON A. McDONALD, b in Vermillion Co., Ill., Jan. 24, 1835, m Sarah Alexander, his cousin, Sept. 29, 1864. He d in California, in 1907. Issue:
>Two children, who d in infancy.

§MILTON ALLEN McDONALD, b. Nov. 11, 1836, in Vermillion Co., Ill., m Annie W. Jackson, of Terre Haute, Ind., in April, 1862. He d May 13, 1883. She was b July 17, 1840, d July 1, 1906. They married May 1, 1861. Issue:
>Oscar B. McDonald, b April 12, 1864, d June 17, 1910.
>
>Mary Gertrude McDonald, b Nov. 22, 1865, m Edwin L. Ebbert, Sept. 26, 1894. Issue:
>>Walter Edwin Ebbert, b Nov. 22, 1895.
>>
>>Robert McDonald Ebbert, b March 23, 1898, d June 4, 1899.
>>
>>Russell Samuel Ebbert, b. March 6, 1900.
>>
>>Corinne Emily Ebbert, b April 4, 1903.
>
>Martha McDonald, b April 7, 1871, m Geo. W. Shumway, Sept. 28, 1899. Issue:
>>Milton McDonald Shumway, b Sept. 7, 1903.
>>
>>Ronald Pixley Shumway, b April 8, 1906.
>>
>>Gertrude Shumway, b June 15, 1908.
>
>Walter Milton McDonald, b Nov. 4, 1874, m Mary Nelson, June 18, 1902. Issue:
>>Margaret Anna McDonald, b Jan. 11, 1904, d Feb., 1904.
>>
>>Helen Janet McDonald, b July 19, 1906.
>>
>>Mary Lucile McDonald, b Oct. 16, 1907.

ISAAC ROSS McDONALD, b in Vermillion Co., Ill., Dec. 1, 1838, d Dec. 23, 1838.

MARTHA ANGELINE McDONALD, b in Vermillion Co., Ill., March 6, 1842, d Nov. 2, 1859.

CHARLES DENISON McDONALD, only lived three weeks.

ERNEST McDONALD.

BESSIE McDONALD.

EDWARD McDONALD.

ROY McDONALD.

FRANK McDONALD—these died under 2 years of age.

EIGHTH CHILD OF JOHN BROWN AND BARBARA KING ALEXANDER.

CYRUS ALEXANDER, b Nov. 8, 1802, died at the residence of his brother, M. K. Alexander, Nov. 8, 1834. He never married.

NINTH CHILD OF JOHN BROWN AND BARBARA KING ALEXANDER.

ARTHUR NICHOLSON ALEXANDER, b March 20, 1805, d Jan. 14, 1825.

TENTH CHILD OF JOHN BROWN AND BARBARA KING ALEXANDER.

ISAAC HENRY ALEXANDER, b March 20, 1805, m Hattie Shaw, d May 10, 1827. Issue: Three children, none of whom are living.

---

‡Aaron A. McDonald was a soldier for the United States in the Civil war.

§Milton Allen McDonald was reared on his father's farm in Southern Illinois. When about 18 years of age he and his father's family removed to Georgetown, Ill., where he had previously been at school. In 1855 he united with the M E. Church, and was a faithful and consecrated Christian, and occupied many places of trust in the church. About 1862 he moved to Pontiac, Ill., and engaged in the mercantile business for a short time. Then removed to Danville, Ill., and engaged in the hardware business till 1883, when he sold out and moved to South Dakota. He reared his children in the fear and admonition of the Lord, and, while he went through the deep waters of trouble many times, he was so implied: in his trust of God that he was often heard to exclaim: "Though He slay me, yet will I trust Him." After his death, the church of which he had been a faithful member held a memorial service in his honor, and the proceedings of this meeting was printed in pamplet form.

NOTES.

Danville, Ill., Friday, April 12, 1871.

Dear Mother:

We remember that seventy-one years ago today, at the beginning of this eventful century, occurred the most important event of the century to us. On that day was born one who has lived to prove that the goodness and unselfishness we read of in books, are possibilities of every-day life. From her we have learned that, if we would have cheerfulness in our old age, we must live her unselfish and Christian life. To her we owe more than we will ever be able to repay.

Remembering these things, and remembering that this is our mother, who through three score years and eleven has scattered so much of sunshine along their way, we are mindful to send herewith a token of the affection we cannot express.

Our hope is that it may minister to our comfort until more than four score years have been lived out.   Affectionately, your children,

                     E. C. HARMON,   A. A. McDONALD,
                     C. B. LESEURE,   M. A. McDONALD.

(Written by A. A. McDonald and sent to our house at Cincinnati, where Grandmother Catherine King McDonald was at that time.   M. HILL.

Salem, Oregon, April 23, 1853.

Dear Brother:

Your good letter of Aug. 10 arrived here by last mail. I can truly say, as you do, that I was indeed truly glad to hear of your good health and spirits. I would like very much to be at home for a month or so while you are all enjoying life so fast, but as it is I have no reason for complaint, being surrounded with peace and plenty in a land that is famous for its mild climate and its lively "Coochmens." I've enjoyed life very well since last Spring. I have received letters nearly every mail from home, and learned by them that all was right in that quarter, and there has been nothing to prevent joy and tranquillity of mind in the immediate vicinity.

So my life has glided on, like the gentle summer breezes in comparison with its heaving and sighing last winter. Then I was surrounded with loafers and blackguards from dark till bedtime, and could not well get rid of them; but now they do not molest me at all, and if I have company in the evening it is either a book or newspaper, a friend or some person on business. I might add considerable more gas to my letter if I thought it would cause them to go any quicker or more direct to you, but, judging from the amount contained in your letters and their uncertainty and long delay on the way, I am fearful that if I should put it on too thick I might run it into the ground or ocean. In the attitude of deep humility, I lower myself in the eyes of the community by having to ask you a little advice. Now my advice to you is to get your mother to teach you a few lessons in apron-stringology before you take your final departure from the parental roor. I fear it would be rather a wild undertaking to start out from home, young and green as you are, inflated to corpulence with gas, and then, when that rooster would have dined on chicken feed, that superabundance of gas might find its way from your gasometer through that beautiful orifice just beneath that rosy probosis of yours. Then there would be one surveyor spoiled.

How would you like to come to Oregon and clerk for us? I do not know that we will want any other clerks yet, but I rather think we will after a while when I come home after my Coochman. There is not as much encouragement for a young man to come to this country as there was a few years ago. The best claims are taken up and wages are getting lower. There is not much regularity about wages yet. Some men get as much as $50 per month and others do not get more than $20 though about $30 is considered common wages, and there are many persons who would be glad to get that who can not. There are a great many persons dissatisfied, and are determed to leave because they can not do as well as they expected, but this is folly, and it is very evident that a young man can do better here now that can get regular wages, even at $25 per month, after he is here, than to go back there and get $20. I would not advise you to come here, but if you are determined on a wild goose chase, I would sooner have you come here than to go to Minnesota. You might do well in Minnesota and you might not. Remember, if you once leave the paternal roof you will have to depend entirely on your own merit and industry to gain a livelihood.

If you come to Oregon you must calculate on hardships and privations, and if you meet with them beyond your expectations, you must learn forbearance. If you do not find things as bad as you expect, you will feel good over it. If you conclude to come, try and get in with some good man like Stull, and start early and come through as quick as you can. I would be glad to see you here, but I do not advise you to come unless you are determined to leave home. If you are, I would as soon hear of your starting to Oregon as any other place. I may write you more on this subject soon, if you have any idea of coming to Oregon in the spring, and I will give you all I can on the subject. Tell pa I will probably write him a letter and send it by next mail. I do not know what to say about that land of mine now. I would be very glad to have the money for it, but I can get along without it. If I conclude to make this my permanent home, I will have it sold and the money laid out in goods for Moores & McDonald, Salem, Oregon Ter.

Our business for the three months just ended has paid us very well, and it is considered very dull times. I will write pa on this subject. Virginia sends her respects to you all, and complains that none of you write to her. Tell her sisters to write to her or to Ellen, just for variety. They say they have not received one from them since they have been here. Ellen is out at Roland's. It is thought, and I think with some reason, that Miss Plain R. will get married shortly. Mr. Atkison has just got in, with eight head of cattle. Macy and Watkins are in the valley some place. I have not seen them. Young Hooten is now in the store; he just came in. Charles Bailey and company have not got in, to my knowledge. I have not heard of Uncle Moores lately. They are above here. Alexander was well, the last account. I expect a letter from him soon. Tell his ma that I got a letter from her and Uncle John by last mail for Eleck, and will send them to him soon. John Brown's folks were in good health, the last account.

Your brother,   *NEUTE.
(Newton McDonald.)

Fountain Creek, Dec. 27, 1854.

My Dear Mother:

I take my seat this morning to let you know that I have not forgotten you yet, although I have not written to you as often as I ought. I have been looking for a letter from you for months, in answer to my letters. I have written two letters to you since I received my last.

Mother, we are all well at this time, and we have had very good health through the last year, for which I bless the God of all grace. Religion is at a very low ebb here at this time. We had a great many good meetings here last summer and fall. The Lord has done great things for us, wherefor we are glad. Mother, I have a great many difficulties to overcome. If it was not for the hope of a better future for all, I would be most miserable. Mother, pray for me that my faith may not fail.

Mother, I have strange news to tell you, and that is that I was at Sally's, and you may suppose I was glad to see the fat sister. I stayed with her ten days and eleven nights, and we talked a great deal about old times. You can't imagine how glad I was to find her so well satisfied with her situation, and to find the children doing so well. They have had a good school in the neighborhood for the last two or three years, and they are all pretty good scholars. The oldest was at college, and is a professor of religion, and a very civil boy. The second lives in Oxford, and he is behind the counter selling goods. He is a professor and a very smart boy and very civil, and the other children are smart and good looking.

James Newton is at Lebanon yet, and expects to graduate before he quits. He and Cousin William McKenzie were ordained last fall. I was at Hemsey's last week. Nancy's health was better than common. They were all well but Justinah. She had been sick for several days, but was better. Betsy's family was well when we heard from them, but in great trouble. Caroline died the last of October. Grandpa Henderson was there when she died, and he said he never saw such distress in his life. She begged grandpa to pray for her. Her sisters were crying around her bed. Mother, pray for us and them. The rest of the friends are well, so far as I know. Nothing more.   I remain, your little son,

ALLEN McDONALD.

P. S.—Write as soon as you get this.
To Catharine McDonald.

---

*John Newton McDonald. (See page 155.)

ELEVENTH CHILD OF JOHN B. AND BARBARA KING ALEXANDER.

WASHINGTON ALEXANDER, the 11th child of John Brown and Barbara King Alexander, was b June 3, 1808, in Williamson Co., Tenn., m in Paris, Ill., March 25, 1841, to Sarah Young. She was b in Cincinnati, Sept. 21, 1821, and d in Paris, Ill., Nov. 23, 1895. He d in Paris, Ill., Aug. 30, 1893. Issue:

RAVILLA COLINE ALEXANDER, b May 2, 1842, is living in Paris, Ill.

EDGAR ALEXANDER.

ANNIE ALEXANDER.

FRANK ROSS ALEXANDER, b July 30, 1856, m Mrs. Sue McCord, at Glenwood, Ala., Sept. 24, 1908. They reside at Morehead, Miss.

Washington Alexander occupied a high place in the esteem of his townspeople and acquaintances, and filled many places of honor and trust. He served in the Black Hawk war, and was colonel in the service of the State in other encounters between the whites and hostile Indians. He represented the county of Edgar in the Legislature. June 3, 1882, he was the only surviving member of the immediate family of John Brown Alexander, and this his 74th birthday was celebrated in Paris by 150 of his relatives, who, as a little token of the love they bore him, presented him with a silver service. On his 80th birthday the clan again assembled, showing the love and esteem in which he was held. (See picture.)

"Many years ago I visited Colonel Washington Alexander, brother of my grandmother, who was very old and mentally feeble, and lived in Paris, Ill. His daughter told me that he would not recognize me and that he was childish. I went in to see him, and when I came into the room his face lightened up and he said: "Why! it is Charlie Moores. Charlie, you don't look a day older than you did on the day you rode with us from Charlotte to the Tennessee State line. You remember that your wife, who was a Harrison, drove in a carriage with four horses and that you were on horseback, and when father said to you, 'Who don't you ride in the carriage with your wife?' you said, 'Carriages were made fo adies. Man's place is on the back of a horse.' MERRILL MOORES."

CHAPTER VIII.

THE KING FAMILY.

The King family under discussion were probably among the Scotish emigrants that settled in Ireland and reared families there, and were afterwards known as the Scotch-Irish. The following sketch of the family of Alexander King was furnished by Dr. **A. W. King, of California.

"Great-Grandfather Alexander King was born in the North of Ireland, and, when a young man, went to Scotland and married Catharine MacDonald, whom tradition says was his first cousin, and partly reared his family there. About the year 1770 he emigrated to this country and settled in Mecklinburg County, North Carolina, his family consisting of three sons and five daughters.　　　　　　　　　　　　　　　　　　　　　　　　　　A. W. KING."

ALEXANDER KING, b in the North of Ireland, m Catherine Macdonald. Issue:

　　　*HUGH KING, b in Argyle, Scotland, Dec. 17, 1754, m Mary (Polly) Montgomery, dau of Capt. Samuel Montgomery. Issue:

　　　　　　Samuel Montgomery King, m Isabella Shields. Issue:
　　　　　　　　Gideon B. King.
　　　　　　　　William M. King.
　　　　　　　　Eliza E. King.
　　　　　　　　Mary H. King.
　　　　　　　　Narcissa J. King.
　　　　　　　　Hugh P. King.
　　　　　　　　James S. King, died of cholera in 1833.
　　　　　　　　Anderson M. King, d of cholera in 1833.
　　　　　　　　A. W. King.
　　　　　　Alexander King, m Elizabeth (Betsy) Shields. Issue:
　　　　　　　　Jane Parker King.
　　　　　　　　William Harvey King.
　　　　　　　　Mary King.
　　　　　　　　Elizabeth A. King.
　　　　　　　　Addison H. King.
　　　　　　　　James H. King.

**"When I began the study of medicine Gen. M. K. Alexander, who was almost blind, wanted me to live with him during my medical course and aid him in tracing the various lines of our ancestry away back into the old country, He had unusual facilities for this, and I am sorry I did not grasp this opportunity. I am glad you are interested in the work and wish you great success. I anticipate great pleasure and profit in the perusal of your book when it comes. Only wish I could give you valuable material for it.　　　　　　　　　　　　　A. W. KING."

*During the Revolutionary war he served his country, with credit to himself and honor to his regiment.

Samuel B. King.
John L. King.
James C. King, died of cholera in Clayton, Ill.
Milton King, died of cholera in Clayton, Ill.
John King, m Rebecca Baldridge. Issue:
Jane King.
William H. King.
Margaret King.
John King.
Nancy King.
Claudius B. King.
Lyman King.
Ann King, m Leander Shields. Issue:
Rev. Hugh King.
Eliza King.
James M. King.
Louisa Ann King.
John King.
William King.
Isabella C. King.
Harriet King.
Samuel H. King.
Milton L. King.
Ruana King.
Jackson L. King.
Elizabeth (Betsy) King, m Josiah Alexander. (See his line.)
Catherine King, never married. Died at an advanced age.
†Hugh D. King, m 1st to Artemesia Codd, of Kentucky. Issue:
John Hugh King.
William G. King.
Abraham King.
James D. King.
Hugh D. King m 2nd to Margaret Keit, of Illinois. Issue:
Adeline King.
Sarah King.
Lucy J. King.
Alice King.
Henry Clay King.
NANCY KING, m A. Alexander. Issue:
Isaac Alexander.
Ruth Alexander, settled at Baton Rouge, La.
ANGUS McDONALD KING, m Miss King. Issue:
John King.
Alexander King, became an attorney.
BARBARA KING, m John B. Alexander. (See Alexander line.)
CATHERINE KING, m Donald McDonald, ancestor of the Illinois branch of the
family. Issue:
Nancy McDonald, m Holmes Baldridge.
Sarah McDonald, m Mr. Beauland, of Mississippi.
Archibald McDonald, m Elizabeth Henderson.
Alexander McDonald, m Catherine K. Alexander.
Allen McDonald, m Temperance Henderson.
Clan R. McDonald, m Nancy Baldridge.
John A. McDonald, m Miss McKinney.
PEGGY KING, m William McKinsey Issue:
Eldest daughter married Arthur Patterson.
John N. McKinsey, m —--. Issue:
Kenneth McKinsey.
Hugh McKinsey.
William McKinsey.
Grundy McKinsey.

†Hugh D. King was a prominent physician, and years ago was Secretary of the American Colonization Society, making many trips with emancipated slaves to Liberia, Africa. He moved to Texas and died there.

CHAPTER IX.

THE WADE FAMILY.

The progenitor of the Wade family of North Carolina was one of the lord proprietors that received lands from the crown. The given name of this first ancestor was John, Thomas or Benjamine. There is a division of opinion among members of the family, and no documentary proof to substantiate either theory. Not being able himself to take up the lands granted him, he sent two of his sons, Thomas Holden Wade and *Joseph Wade, who settled along the Dant river in Virginia.

Thomas Holden Wade married Jane Bogan, and afterwards moved to North Carolina and took a prominent part in the establishment of that colony. He settled in what is now Wadesborough, built the first houses there, and the place was named for him. He was a prominent figure in the early history of the colony of North Carolina, and his name is a familiar one to all acquainted with the history of that State. He commanded the minute men of the Salisbury district, was a member from Anson County of the first Provincial Congress of the State, a member of the Senate in 1776, 1783 and 1786. June, 1775, "Thomas Wade and two of the captains in the said committee made use of this interest to enlist men for the use of the †Congress, and enlisted vast numbers."

On the 20th of June, 1778, Thomas Wade said to the deponent that the King and Parliament has established the Roman Catholic religion in the Province of Quebec, and did intend to bring in Papist principalities to America, and that the King has forfeited his coronation oath, and that they, the Congress, intended to rule the people of America by way of a **Continental Congress. (P. 173.)

Thomas Wade was appointed by the Provincial Congress of North Carolina at Hillsboro, on the 20th of August, 1775, a member of a committee to confer with gentlemen who had lately arrived from the highlands of Scotland to settle

---

*Joseph Wade was imprisoned in Camden, S. C. He was a musician, and charmed the British by playing Yankee Doodle on his chains. This song was known as a British air at that time.

†See Colonial Records of North Carolina, vol. x, pages 126-8.

It was originally a hamlet called Newbern or Newtown. There is an old deed in Newbern or Newtorn from Patrick Boggan to Col. Thomas Wade, also a large body of land on Gould's book.

At the outbreak of the Revolution Col. Wade was appointed to the command of a regiment, which operated from Salisbury down through North Carolina against the Tories. The Wades were very rich, and the last of their money was lost during the Civil war.

in this province and to explain to them the nature of our unhappy controversy with Great Britain, and to urge them to unite with the other inhabitants of America in defense of their rights which they derive from God and the constitution.

WILL OF THOMAS WADE.

In the name of God, amen. I, Thomas Wade, of Anson County, in the State of North Carolina, a merchant, being in perfect health and senses, but knowing the mortality of the body and uncertainty of life, do ordain this my last will and testament.

First—I commit my soul to God, hoping, in his infinite mercies, through the merits of our Savior, a happy resurrection in the life to come, my body I commit to the grave, desiring the same may be buried in a decent, Christian manner.

Secondly—I desire that my estate, that God hath been pleased to bless me with, may be disposed of in the following manner:

Thirdly—As I have given my five living children by deed of gift apart of my estate, which, being left off to them, I hereby give and bequeath unto my five children, Holden Wade, Mary Vining, Thomas Wade, Sarah Wade and George Wade, ten pounds, to be paid by my executors administrators, and to them or their heirs, executors, administrators or assigns, also to my daughter, Sarah Wade, one feather bed, and furniture, and a brown mare, and two colts known by the name of her mare and colts, also two hundred acres of land on the Long Branch of Jones' Creek, now entered by lease to Peter Brown for one year. And to my son, George Wade, a bay mare and two colts known by the name of his mare and colts, and feather bed and furniture.

Fourthly—I lend to my beloved wife, Jane Wade, for her life-time, for her maintenance and support, London, Ben and Hannah, and their family, and the residue of my household and kitchen furniture of every kind, and at her death I desire my executors may divide the said negroes and household furniture amongst my five children or their representatives then alive.

Fifthly and lastly—I hereby appoint my beloved wife, Jane Wade, my executor, and my sons, Holden and Thomas Wade, together with my friends, Patrick Boggan and James Boggan, my executors to this my last will and testament, hereby authorizing them to sell my land, slaves and stock of every kind and all things belonging to my said estate not necessary for the support of my wife and younger children, and not otherwise disposed of, to pay my just debts, but when as much is sold on twelve months' credit as may amount to my just debts, together with the debts due to me, that then the residue of lands and slaves, etc.; not sold, and money arriving from such sales over and above the payment of my said debts, I hereby impower and direct that the slaves shall be last sold, if necessary, not otherwise disposed by deed or legacy or lent, and direct that the residue over and above my debts in lands, slaves or cash, etc., be equally divided by my said executors amongst my five children according to valuation.

In witness whereof, I, the said Thomas Wade, have to this, my last will and testament, set my hand and seal this second day of June, one thousand seven hundred and eighty-six.

THOMAS WADE. (Seal.)

Signed, sealed and acknowledged the day and date in the presence of Morgan Brown and Elizabeth Brown.

(Certificate of Clerk.)

State of North Carolina, Anson County

I, Thomas C. Robinson, Clerk of Superior Court in and for the County of Anson, State of North Carolina, do certify that the foregoing is a true and correct copy of the last will and testament of Thomas Wade, as the same is taken from and compared with the records in this office.

In witness whereof, I have hereunto set my hand and affixed my official seal.

Done at my office in Wadesboro, on the 10th day of June, 1907.

THOMAS C. ROBINSON,
Clerk of Superior Court of Anson County.

Benjamine Wade also settled on the Dant river, and his descendants claim relationship with the Wade family under discussion.

COL. THOMAS WADE, b about 1722, d in Anson Co., N. C., in 1787, m Jane Boggan, a sister of Capt. Patric Boggan. Issue:

HOLDEN WADE.
MARY VINING WADE.
‡THOMAS WADE.
GEORGE WADE.
SARAH WADE.

SON OF COL. THOMAS WADE AND JANE BOGAN.

GEORGE WADE was born in North Carolina, on Shoco Creek, May 29, 1747. There are two opinions in the families descended from him as to his descent. The will of Col. Thomas Wade gives his son George, and this line is claimed by a majority of the descendants of Capt. George Wade. George Wade married †Mary McDonald, daughter of *Donald McDonald, on Nov. 18, 1766. She died Aug. 22, 1779, and he remained a widower until Oct. 28, 1784, when he married Martha Center, widow of Major Nathan Center. By the first union he had three sons and two daughters; by the last, one son. George Wade died in Columbia, S. C., Nov. 24, 1824.

George Wade was a captain in the South Carolina militia, Col. Thomas Taylor commanding. He raised the first rifle from Lancaster, S. C., and marched with full number to the defense of Charleston when Tarleton passed there. He was wounded at the battle of Savannah, Ga., Oct. 9, 1779; was commissioned captain of the 2nd South Carolina Militia, February, 1776. He was taken prisoner by Tarleton at home at Dent's Mill. His home was burned, slaves taken from him, and horses and stock taken. From Capt. Wade's plantation, Wade's Island, Catawba river, supplies of corn, flour and meat were furnished to Gen. Sumpter's army.

*DONALD McDONALD was a scout under Sumpter, and the father of Sergeant Jasper McDonald, who was killed at Fort Moultrie.

†MARY McDONALD was the daughter of George McDonald and the wife of George Wade. Her home was burned and she, with her baby, was taken prisoner to Charleston by Tarleton, in retaliation for aid given by her to Sumpter, after he was wounded at King's Mountain. Both she and the child died of small pox while in prison, contracted while nursing fellow prisoners. Her body was afterward interred on the site of her old home, and a monument erected in loving memory by the citizens of Lancaster County. The child had been buried, with ten others, in a common grave, so it could not be recognized.

Mary McDonald, having General Sumpter ill at her home at McDonald's Ford, and being warned of the approach of the butcher, Tarlton, drove by night, with the General and her little daughter, to a place of safety in the swamps. Returning, she met Tarlton at the ferry landing on her own place. In an effort at delaying him, she possessed herself of his pistol and discharged it in the face of the irate red-coat. In the meantime, her little girl had cut the rope holding the ferry. This going adrift, the British were forced to make a detour of several miles to cross the river, swollen by recent rains. Thus ample opportunity was afforded Gen. Sumpter to make good his escape. As has been before stated, she was taken to Charleston, where she died in prison. Undoubtedly she was hated by Tarlton for some good cause, and beloved for like reason by her compatriots. The spot where she died is marked now only by a stone, as the monument erected by public subscription was destroyed by the Federal troops in 1864.

Another branch of the family claim that he was the son of one John Wade, who moved from North Carolina to South Carolina and settled on Lynch's Creek, in 1754.

‡The will of Thomas Wade is dated June 18, 1792, and records that he had the infection small pox, and would at once proceed to Caerow Hill for treatment. This will was probated late in the same year, small pox probably proving fatal.

My grandfather, George Wade, raised a company of sturdy men to teach the British that Americans intended to have liberty. In 1882 I visited the old Wade home, on the banks of the Catawba river, and went to the old camping ground, where I found the old pot still hanging from the poles, and forded the river where he and his men had erected a log hut to protect themselves from British bullets when the British would try to cross. Some months after his company went to Virginia the British attempted to cross the ford. Our few men had gone out foraging, but had left thirty-five old guns in the house. Old Aunt Betsy Wade Brown and her sisters went in and fired the guns through the holes so furiously that the British retreated. Another one of the family, Sarah, swam the Catawba to let the Colonists know that Tarlton and his men were again there in force.

My grandfather had a large fishery at the river at Wade's ford.

I had for years the following letter, but Gen. Wade Hampton borrowed it from me:

"Captain George Wade:

Dear Friend—I am going to make an inventory of all my losses during the Revolution and DEMAND pay for the same, and want to present your bill at the same time.

MAJOR WADE HAMPTON."

Capt. George Wade's reply was: "My country has gained her independence; that is al that I desire. Your friend, GEORGE WADE."

I glory in the patriotism of my ancestry. My uncle, Joe Wade, was a spy captured by the British and incarcerated in Camden, S. C. He released himself and a man named Franklin while the battle was raging. He was a man of indominable will and spirit. When the British guards carried him his meals, he invariably rattled the tune of Yankee Doodle on his chains to annoy them. Mrs. Elliot in her History of the Revolution mentions these facts, and also that he was whipped by the British a thousand lashes.

In 1882 I was invited and escorted to the Fair at Wadesboro. I was introduced by Dr. Battle, Chancellor of the University, as "Miss Wade, the grand-daughter of Captain Wade and the adopted daughter of North Carolina."

Moore County bears the name of my grandfather. He and his six brothers came to America and opened stores in New York, Savannah, Charleston and Columbia, S. C. My grandmother was the widow of Swanson Lunsford, who was raised by the Lees. She built the first granite house in Columbia, with iron steps and railings. It is still standing. She was a high church Episcopalian, and was noted for her charity. She met Grandfather Moore when on one of her charity visits. A year afterward they were married. He ran boats from Charleston to the old site of Columbia at Granby.

My grandfather, George Wade, was one of the incorporators of Columbia, and his sons were the first students of S. C. College. Grandmother Moore's husband, Swanson Lunsford, is buried in the old State Capitol yard in Columbia. His body lay in state there. He was a member of Lee's Legion in the Revolution There was no burying ground in Columbia at the time of his death save the potter's field, so the State laid him to rest in the Capitol yard.

MRS. JANE WADE CORLEW.

BIBLE RECORD.

From the old Scotch family Bible we get the following:

"Donald McDonald and Rebecca Middleton, his wife, were married in 1745. Their children were:

"Donald McDonald, who fought in the Revolution and was a patriot.

"Middleton McDonald, born Nov. 5, 1746, and Elizabeth, his wife, were married March 7, 1768. Middleton fought in the Revolution.

"Mary McDonald, born Jan. 15, 1748. She married George Wade, Nov. 18, 1760, and died Aug. 22, 1779. Geo. Wade was born May 5, 1847, married the sister of Gov. John Taylor of South Carolina 2nd, and died Nov. 24, 1823. He was a captain in the Revolution.

"William McDonald, born Nov. 21, 1749, and married Charlotte Massey, daughter of William Massey and Elizabeth Reeves (or Rives) of Virginia, in 1769. He died after 1804. He belonged to the Light Horse Cavalry troop during the Revolution.

"Sarah McDonald, born Oct. 7, 1751.

"Esther and Eleanor McDonald, twins, were born Feb. 1, 1758. Esther married John Woodward, of Revolutionary fame.

"Anne McDonald, born Oct. 1, 1760."

Donald McDonald came to America about 1720, and settled on the Catawba river.

FIRST CHILD OF CAPTAIN GEORGE AND MARY McDONALD WADE.

*THOMAS HOLDEN WADE, b in 1767, m Rebecca Center. Issue:

    JUDGE WILLIAM CENTER WADE, b 1791, m Olivia Ratliff, who was b in 1795. Issue:

        Ann Elizabeth Wade, b Aug. 18, 1812.
        Absalom Wade, b Nov. 25, 1814.
        Elizabeth Wade, b Nov. 5, 1815.
        Francina Rosaltha Wade, b Sept. 18, 1821.
        Martha Lane Wade, b July 15, 1823.
        William Center Wade, b May 3, 1826.
        Olivia Ruffin Wade, b Oct. 7, 1828.
        Mary Lane Wade, b Sept. 16, 1830.
        Joseph John Wade, b Jan. 15, 1832.
        Joseph John and Mary Lane, b Aug. 22, 1833.

  JOE WADE.
  NATHAN WADE.
  HAMPTON WADE.
  GEORGE WADE.
  WILSON WADE.
  SARAH WADE.
  AMY WADE.
  REBECCA WADE.

  THOMAS HOLDEN WADE, b in Lancaster Co., S. C., m Rebecca Moore, May 3, 1825. She was his first cousin. Issue:

    Rebecca T. Wade, m Dr. Martin Phillips, who was a professor in the University of Mississippi. No issue.
    Dr. Thomas H. Wade, mortally wounded at the battle of Chicamauga, Tenn. Unmarried.
    Rozena Wade, d in Marion, N. C., after the Civil war. Unmarried.
    Michael Douglass Wade, living in North Carolina. No children.
    Mart Fleming Wade, m Miss Gage. Left a widow with two children; one died in infancy. She is a resident of Columbia, S. C.
    Adaline Wade, died in early girlhood.
    Jane C. Wade, m Mr. Corlew. Now living in Waco, Texas.
    George Wade, killed in battle in the Shenandoah Valley.

SECOND CHILD OF CAPTAIN GEORGE AND MARY McDONALD WADE.

**DANIEL WADE, second child of Capt. George and Mary McDonald Wade, was born in 1768, m in Lancaster District, S. C., in 1807, to Jane Brown Ross, daughter of Captain Isaac Ross. (See page —.) In 1818 they moved from South Carolina to Mississippi. He d in Louisiana in 1820. Issue:

    LAWRENCE WADE, b July 8, 1808, d Jan. 26, 1879, m his cousin, Margaret Hannah Ross, Oct. 6, 1825. (See page 71.) She was b Feb. 16, 1810, d Sept. 23, 1868. Issue:

---

*Thomas Holden Wade was possibly married twice, as reference is made to his wife, Amy Tillinghast, and of his wife, Rebecca Center. He moved from Lancaster, S. C., to St. Mary's Parish, La., and is buried there.

**See note, next page.

Daniel Brown Wade, b Sept. 14, 1826, d Oct. 6, 1868.
Martha Jane Wade, b Jan. 4, 1826, d Oct. 6, 1854, m Oct. 1, 1848, to Wm.
    C. Guest. Issue:
        Sarah Adelaid Guest, b July 25, 1849, d July 23, 1852.
Elizabeth Adelaide Wade, b April 23, 1831, d Dec. 16, 1876, m †Robert C.
    Trimble, Feb. 21, 1850. Issue:
        Elizabeth Trimble, b April 27, 1851.
        Martha Jane Trimble, b April 5, 1853, d Sept. 28, 1901, m
            March 18, 1885, to Cicero Cogan. Issue:
            Maude Azalea Cogan, b Feb. 29, 1876, d Sept. 23,
                1905, m Jasper Luckett. Issue:
                Daughter.
            Ada Lucile Cogan, b Oct. 29, 1878, m Willingsby
                Hullom. He died.
            Earnest Trimble Cogan, b Oct. 7, 1880.
            Robert Wayne Cogan, b March 22, 1882, m Mary
                Compton, in 1903.
            Margaret Hellen Cogan, b Jan. 30, 1884, m Mr
                Lararus.
            Martha Jane Cogan, b June 10, 1891, m Jasper
                Luckett, her brother-in-law.
            Sarah Ellen Cogan, b Jan. 22, 1893.
        Sarah A. Trimble, b Feb. 25, 1855, m Feb. 24, 1878, to Russ
            Dennis, Feb. 24, 1876. She d Sept. 6, 1900. Issue:
            Elizabeth Adelaide Dennis, b March 3, 1877, m
                Willis Godwin. Issue:
                Wayne Godwin.
                Willie Godwin.
            Thomas Russell Dennis, b Aug. 11, 1879.
            Curren Wade Dennis, b Nov., 1861, killed by
                lightning.
            Nita Jane Dennis, b June, 1881. Died.
            Leon Kinsman Dennis and
            Lona Ruth Dennis, twins, b Nov., 1890.
        Matilda Adelaide Trimble, b Sept. 20, 1857.
Isaac Ross Wade, m Aug. 11, 1863, to Camelia Standard. Issue:
        Rhoda A. Wade, b Jan. 2, 1865, m 1st James Buckley, 2nd
            Arthur W. Dill.
Joseph Franklin Wade, b Aug. 24, 1833, d June 23, 1834.
Alexander Wade, b May 24, 1835, d May 18, 1847.
M. Agnes Wade, b Aug. 24, 1837.
Isaac Eoss Wade, b Feb. 3, 1840, d Aug. 26, 1867.
Allison Ross Wade, b Jan. 2, 1842, m Aug. 21, 1861, to Ellen Cogan. She
    d Sept. 11, 1905. Issue:
        David C. Wade, b Sept. 20, 1865, m Mary G. Rollins, June 24,
            1896. Issue:

**Daniel Wade was the son of George Wade and Mary McDonald, and, although a lad of 12, went out with his father following the fortunes of Sumpter, and was able to render him great service, after he was wounded at King's Mountain, by aiding him to escape Tarlton's men and by guiding him to the home of Mary McDonald Wade, where he was nursed back to health. For this service she was taken prisoner of war and her home burned. Daniel Wade and family moved from South Carolina to Mississippi in the spring of 1818. They came by land in carriages, buggies and wagons—family, slaves, household goods and stock—to the Mississippi river to the nearest or at that time the most convenient landing place below the Tennessee line. At that place Captain Isaac Ross and wife, Jane Allison Ross, met them in vehicles. They came from their plantation, Prospect Hill, Miss. He had all his slaves, stock, farming implements and household goods loaded on flat-boats on the Mississippi river and floated down to Rodney, Miss. From there everything came to Prospect Hill. Daniel Wade and family came from that point on the Mississippi river by a traveled road, in company with his wife's parents, to Prospect Hill, Miss., where they all stayed until he made the purchase of land in Louisiana and moved there.

†A member of Hinds' Troop in the war of 1812. Author of Account of the Battle of New Orleans, found in Claiborne's History of Mississippi.

Son, b Nov. 16, 1899.

Dela M. Wade, b April 13, 1867.

Mary E. Wade, b March 27, 1869.

Willie Jeff Wade, b May 18, 1870, killed accidentally, Jan.,
    1906, m Willie Rollins, Jan. 3, 1897. Issue:
        Willie Jefferson Wade, b Oct. 5, 1897.
        James Allison Wade, b Feb. 2, 1899, died.
        Lawrence Rollins Wade, b Feb. 23, 1901
        John Cogan Wade, b July 28, 1903, died.

Minnie A. Wade, b Nov. 22, 1872, m Annipias Killingsworth,
    Oct. 24, 1894. (See Killingsworth line.)

A. Ross Wade, b April 26, 1865, m Willie R. Wade, Jan. 18,
    1906. Issue:
        Stuart Dell Wade, b Sept. 30, 1906.
        Laura Ellen Wade, b June 6, 1908.
        Stanley Kurten Wade, b Feb. 9, 1910.

Daniel Brown Wade, b Jan. 13, 1878, m Mar. 27, 1900, to Mary
    Costley. She d March 22, 1900. Issue:
        Marion Penn Wade and
        A child, twins, b Nov. 22, 1900. Child died.

Helen Wade, b April 30, 1881, d April 24, 1883.

Bullard G. Wade, b April 28, 1883.

Sarah F. Wade, b Feb. 22, 1888, d Aug. 5, 1909.

Lawrence Wade, b Jan. 28, 1845, d April 9, 1891, m Dec. 28, 1869, to Kate
Tubbs Issue:
        Claude L. Wade, b Dec. 3, 1870, m Julia Harmon, Dec. 6,
        1891. Issue:
            Ernest Franklin Wade, b Oct. 15, 1900, d July
            22, 1902.

    Infant.

Margaret K. Wade, b Dec. 3, 1850, d June 3, 1852.

Sarah Hellen Wade, b Oct. 13, 1852, d Feb. 16, 1904.

WALTER WADE, b March 9, 1810, d July 12, 1862, m Dec. 1, 1841, to Martha Tayler
Wade, his first cousin. She was b Nov. 14, 1813, d Jan. 27, 1848. Issue:

James Taylor Wade, b Jan., 1843.

Martha Rives Wade, b Nov. 24, 1844, m Dunbar B. Wade, her first
    cousin. (See his line for issue.)

Sally Marshall Wade, b Oct. 23, 1846, m Wade Rives, in Lancaster, S. C.

Infant son, b and d June 27, 1848.

WALTER WADE m 2nd Mabello Chamberlain, widow, Dec 14, 1859. She was b
March 16, 1826. Issue:
        Walter Ross Wade, b May 26, 1861, m Jan. 8, 1890, to Cora Nesmith. Issue:
            Clara Nesmith Wade, b July 9, 1892.
    Robert Duncan Wade, b Dec. 15, 1862, d Dec. 25, 1907.

**ADELAID WADE, b Dec., 1811, m April 15, 1836, to John Crowley Richardson. Issue:
    *Martha Loss Richardson, b Jan., 1840, d April 15, 1845.
    ††Cabell Breckenridge Richardson, b 1840, m Mary Wade January, Dec. 6,
    1866. Issue:
        Mary Adelaid Richardson, b Sept. 14, 1867, m Nov. 27, 1889,
        to James Collins Cole. Issue:
            James Collins Cole, b May 2, 1898.
            John Richardson Cole, b Aug. 18, 1905.
        Wade Harrison Richardson, b March 22, 1869, m Mrs. Etta

---

*Burned to death in the old Wade home. (See account, page 72.)

**Adopted by her aunt, Mrs. Thomas B. Reed, and educated at Bethlehem and in Pennsylvania.

††Writer of letter in introduction to this volume.

Coleman Bean. Issue:
    Frank Richardson.
    Carrie Richardson.
    Ethel May Richardson.
Cabell Breckenridge Richardson, b April 7, 1870, m Josie
    Deale Jackson. Issue:
    Mary Louise Richardson.
    Hazel Richardson.
John Crowley Richardson, b Dec. 7, 1871, m Jan., 1899, to
    Anna Louise Montgomery, d March 11, 1899.
Carrie Drucilla Richardson, b Aug. 20, 1873, d Nov. 2, 1875,
    m Clarence Wade. Issue:
    Marie Meter Wade.
Philip January Richardson, b Aug. 20, 1875, d Nov. 2, 1907.
†Adelaid Richardson, unmarried.

MARTHA WADE, b Aug., 1818, d 1860, m Dr. Benjamin Farrar Young. Issue:
Margaret Allison Young, b 1836, d 1875. Never married.
Wade Ross Young, b 1842, d 1911, m in 1866 to Bertha Liddell.
William Conner Young, b June 3, 1843, m March 14, 1865, to Willie W·
    Evans. She was b Jan. 14, 1840, d 1883. Issue:
    Martha Margaret Young, b May 30, 1867, d June 20, 1879.
    Rebecca Tullis Young, b March 13, 1870, m March 18, 1891, to
        Alonzo S. Lewis. Issue:
        Willie Evans Lewis, b Aug. 12, 1892.
        Reeve Lewis, b March 27, 1894.
        Benj. Y. Lewis, b Nov. 26, 1902, d Aug. 11, 1903
    Bessie Young, b Nov. 15, 1872, m Sept. 8, 1891, to Robert Y.
        Newell. Issue:
        Jennie Yates Newell, b Aug. 19, 1892, d Oct. 9,
            1898.
        William Young Newell, b July 3, 1894, d Nov. 13,
            1897.
        Robert Yates Newell, b Nov. 27, 1898.
        Bessie Y. Newell, b Sept. 2, 1901.
        Rebecca Y. Newell, b April 16, 1904.
    Susie A. Young, b July 25, 1875, d Dec. 14, 1879.
    Isabelle M. Young, b Aug. 19, 1877, d May 21, 1906, m Oct.
        1, 1901, to E. Farrar Newell. Issue:
        Janie M. Newell, b July 22, 1902.
        Alberta Y. Newell, b May 25, 1905.
    William Conner Young. b Dec. 22, 1879, m Aug. 8, 1896, to
        Laura Annie Henderson. No issue.
    Willie Evans Young, b March 28, 1882, m Aug. 26, 1903, to
        James W. Whitaker. Issue:
        Willie May Whitaker, b Nov. 30, 1906.
        Sallie George Whitaker, b May 3, 1909.
    Blanche LeSassier Young, b Jan. 1, 1885, d Nov. 5, 1888.
    Janie M. Young, b May 26, 1887, m Elliot D. Coleman. Issue:
        Janie B. Coleman, b Jan. 10, 1908.
        Elliot D. Coleman, b Feb. 23, 1910.
*William Conner Young m 2nd to Alberta Bondurant, Nov. 26, 1891. She
    d Aug. 4, 1895. Issue:
    Alberta McNair Young, b Oct 5, 1893, d Dec. 8, 1896.
    May Bondurant Young, b Oct. 7, 1900.
*Samuel Charles Young, b 1838, m Dec. 4, 1860, to Blanche LeSassier.
    She d in 1894. Issue:

†Miss Addie Richardson is an authority on this branch of the family.
*Samuel Charles Young and his brother, William Conner Young, were Civil war veterans.

Louis L. Young, b Oct. 19, 1865, d Oct 15, 1900, m to Fannie
Smyth. Issue:
Samuel Charles Young.
Blanche Young.
Benjamine Farrar Young, b Oct. 15, 1863, m Jan.
25, 1888, to Catherine Whitney. No issue.
Benjamine Farrar Young, b 1840, d 1843.
**ISAAC ROSS WADE, b in Richland District, S. C. Feb. 7, 1814, m Catherine Dunbar,
April 15, 1840, at Belmont, on Pine Ridge. Issue:
Isaac Wade, b July 13, 1841, d at Oak Hill, Aug. 17, 1846.
*Dunbar B. Wade, b March 18, 1843, d March 24, 1908, m Martha R. Wade,
his first cousin. Issue:
Walter Bisland Wade, b Feb. 1, 1867, m Nov. 29, 1893, to
Sallie Stowers, daughter of Louis D Stowers. Issue:
Martha Bisland Wade, b Sept. 18, 1894.
Louis Dunbar Wade, b Dec. 6, 1895.
Eula Maud Wade, b May 1, 1897.
Walter Bisland Wade, b June 24, 1899.
Charles Edward Wade, b March 17, 1900.
Isaac Dunbar Wade and
Mary Stowers Wade, twins, b May 13, 1902.
Molly Stowers Wade, b Nov. 25, 1903.
Battaille Darden Wade, b March 25, 1905.
James Turner Wade, b Jan. 9, 1906.
Sarah Wade and
Elizabeth Wade, twins, b March 24, 1909.
Margaret Ross Wade, b Aug. 2, 1910.
Robert Emmett Wade, b Jan. 27, 1869, m July 20, 1910, to
Carrie Olive Baldwin.
Marshall Wade, b Jan. 8, 1871, m June 14, 1906, to Estelle
Cogan McCoy.
Charlotte Priscilla Wade, b Aug. 5, 1873.
Battaille Dunbar Wade, b Jan. 27, 1876, d Sept. 15, 1906.
Sallie M. Wade, b Feb. 27, 1878.
Infant.
Catharine Dunbar Wade, b Feb. 27, 1883, m Dec. 30, 1906, to
Wilson Ross. (See Ross line.)
Richard Wade, died.
Jack Ross Wade, b Jan. 9, 1881.
MARY BELTON WADE, d young.

---

†Dunbar Bisland Wade served during the war with Darden's Battery, from Jefferson County, Miss.

‡He was very young when the war commenced, but enlisted in the Tensas, La., Cavalry during the first year.

*Dunbar Bisland Wade was educated at Jefferson College, near Natchez, and at Oakland College. From the latter institution he resigned when in the senior class to enlist in the Jefferson Artillery, and was assigned to the Army of Tennessee. He served throughout the war, save a few months when on furlough suffering from a wounded foot. He was elected surveyor of Jefferson County in 1876, and served thirty years. He was a consistent member of the Presbyterian church.

**Judge Isaac R. Wade was one of the old-time Southern gentlemen. He is prominently mentioned in Claiborne's History and in the publications of the Mississippi Historical Society. His daughter, Mrs. Roger Killingsworth, gives many beautiful reminiscences of her devoted father   It was a common practice for him to lend his slaves to assist neighbors who for any reason were behind in their crops, and to send servants to wait on the sick.

"My father was simply the executor, the only one of a number who qualified, and all he received was his fees, which should have been in good gold.   But the estate had been so impoverished paying legacies and lawyers' fees (one fee to the celebrated S. S. Prentiss was $10,000), that he was glad to get the Prospect Hill plantation.   He had to appeal to the courts for that and for protection for his family.   He bought a few slaves after that, and my mother brought him a good number of very valuable slaves.   He bought and sold land, and was a very successful farmer in every sense of the word.   In my earliest recollection dear old Prospect Hill bloomed like a rose—really and truly a beautiful home.
MRS. JENNIE A. WADE KILLINGSWORTH."

Judge S. Charles Young and Hon. B. F. Young are prominent attorneys of St. Joseph, La.

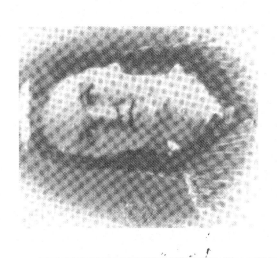

Catherine Adelaid Wade, b Nov. 13, 1844, m Edward Henry Newell, at
Prospect Hill, Feb. 2, 1870. Issue:
Adella Newell, b Jan. 15, 1871, m John Murdock. Issue:
Francis Louis Murdock.
Edward Dunbar Newell, b Feb. 2, 1873, m Mary McVea. Issue:
Marjorie Newell, b Jan. 16, 1900.
Bert Newell, b Oct. 9, 1901.
Ross Wade Newell, b April 28, 1874, m Irene McMillan, Oct.
28, 1902. Issue:
Mary Kirk Newell, b Oct. 29, 1903.
Irene McMillan Newell, b Feb. 4, 1905.
Roslyn Wade Newell, b Jan. 15, 1907.
Adele Murdock Newell, b April 12, 1908.
Benjamine Young Newell, b Aug. 13, 1876. Unmarried.
Allison Ross Newell, died in infancy.
Adele Newell.
Willie Dunbar Wade, b Sept. 9, 1846, d Sept. 3, 1893.
*Benjamine Young Wade, b May 16, 1848, m Feb. 1, 1869, to Cordelia Jane
Garrett, dau of G. G. Garrett. She was b July 12, 1846. Issue:
Eula Maude Wade, b Jan. 30, 1870, d April 15, 1896.
William Dunbar Wade, b Sept. 9, 1871, d Sept. 3, 1893.
Benjamine Young Wade, b Dec. 27, 1874.
Julius Gerard Wade, b Oct. 9, 1877.
Ross Wade, b May 18, 1882, d Sept. 16, 1882.
Allison Wade, b May 18, 1882—twins.
Anna Garrett Wade, b Sept. 29, 1883, m Jan. 22, 1911, to C.
B. Godbold.
Battaille Harrison Wade, m Dec. 20, 1882, to Carrie O. Wade. Issue:
John Tate Wade, b Feb. 7, 1885.
Robert Dunbar Wade, b Aug. 2, 1886.
Patrick Henry Wade, b June 11, 1889.
Edward Guy Wade, b Dec. 16, 1891.
Carrie Olivia Wade, b Jan., 1894.
Battaille Harrison Wade.
Thomas M. Wade, b Oct. 24, 1860, m Anna Magruder, Nov. 21, 1883. Issue:
Thomas Magruder Wade, b June 16, 1889.
WILSON WADE, son of Daniel Wade and Jane Brown Ross, b March 18, 1818, d Dec.,
1836, m Martha Jane Dunbar, dau of James Dunbar and Elizabeth Bisland,
Feb. 4, 1836. She was b April 1, 1819, and d Sept. 15, 1892. Both are buried
at Prospect Hill. Issue:
Walter Wade, b Dec. 31, 1836.
Girault Wade, b Dec. 17, 1838.
James Dunbar Wade, b Dec. 3, 1840.
Mary B. Wade, b April 3, 1842.
Jane Ross Wade, b Jan. 10, 1844, d Dec. 26, 1893.
Anna Garrett Wade, b Jan. 10, 1846, m Dec. 18, 1872, to ‡E. T. Compton.
Issue:
Son, b Oct. 27, 1872, d in infancy.
Annita Bertha Compton, b Sept. 20, 1874, m J. D. Mathy,
April 17, 1901. Issue:

Mrs. Catherine Wade Newell, the eldest child of Judge Isaac R. Wade and his wife, Catherine Dunbar, through
the death of her mother, was left with the care of her younger sisters and brothers, to whom she gave her best attention
and devotion as long as she was needed. She was educated in the best schools of the country and lived the life of a
devoted Christian, doing her duty by all that came within the precinct of her home.

*"Company A was formed of William Yerger's company K, as it had too many men at the time of division. I was
16 years and 4 months old when I enlisted. Only served eight months. Surrendered about April 12, 1865, at Gainesville,
Ala.   B. Y. WADE."

Albert D. Mathy, b March 25, 1902, died.
J. D. Mathy, Feb. 23, 1906.
Thomas Swann Compton, b Sept. 4, 1876, d Sept. 4, 1876.
Martha Dunbar Compton, b June 9, 1878.
Jennie McK. Compton, b June 2, 1881, m Eugene Enochs, Sept. 14, 1904.
Mary Edna Compton, b May 31, 1885, m Wayne Edgar, March 9, 1904.
Anna Laura Compton, b Nov. 3, 1887.
Alberta Young Compton, b Nov. 9, 1880, d June 9, 1891.
Martha Young Wade, b Dec. 13, 1847, m Feb. 26, 1889, to Albert L. Dorsey. No issue.
Robert Dunbar Wade, b Aug. 11, 1850.
Laura J. Wade, b Oct. 18, 1852; m Feb. 16, 1879, to Wm. E. Ross. Issue:
    Helen Perinne Ross, b Dec. 12, 1879, d Dec. 29, 1887.
    John Burch Ross, b June 6, 1881.
    Wilson W. Ross, b June 21, 1883.
    Percy Jeff Ross, b April 19, 1886.
Laura J. Wade Ross m 2nd, June 23, 1893, to M. B. Horton. She died Nov. 11, 1893.
Addie Richardson Wade, b April 26, 1856, m Nov. 19, 1889, to R. O. Davidson. Issue:
    Martha Annie Davidson, b Aug. 26, 1890.
    Sidney Ira Davidson, b Aug. 30, 1891.
    Orin Roberta Davidson, b Jan. 18, 1893.
    Berthal Randall Davidson, b Oct. 15, 1895.
    Laura Josephine Davidson, b June, 1899.
Wilson Walter Wade, b March 29, 1858.

THIRD CHILD OF CAPTAIN GEORGE AND MARY McDONALD WADE.

REBECCA WADE, dau of Capt. George Wade and Mary McDonald Wade, was b in Columbia, S. C., May 15, 1778, and d Nov. 4, 1851. She 1st m *Capt. Swanson Lunsford, of Petersburg, Va., Sept. 13, 1797. He d in August, 1799. Issue:
MARY LETHERED LUNSFORD, b Aug. 14, 1817, m to Dr. John Douglass. Issue:
    Swanson Lunsford Douglass, b in July, 1824, died in infancy.
    Dr. John Lunsford Douglass, b Dec. 25, 1825, d Dec. 4, 1856.
    Sarah Rebecca Douglass, b Sept. 1, 1827, d June 21, 1910, m Dr. James Cloud Hicklin. Issue:
        Mary Lethered Hicklin, b in 1848, m Dr. Robert Hall. Issue:
        Lizzie Hall, m Rev. Richard Thomas Gillespie. Issue:
            Richard Thomas Gillespie.
            Robert Hall Gillespie.
        Major James Hall, unmarried.
        Roberta Wade Hall, m Louis Williamson. Issue:
        Louis Williamson.
        Robert Hall Williamson.
        Annie Lou Hall, m Dr. William Sims. Issue:
        Mary Sims.
      Sarah Jane Hicklin, m J. E. Craig. Issue:
        James Craig, m Nettie Moore. Issue:
        Thomas Moore.
        Jean Moore.
        Swanson Lunsford Craig.
        Dr. Sylvester Douglass Craig, of North Carolina.

*Capt. Swanson Lunsford was also of Revolutionary fame. He was a native of Petersburg, Va., serving under Gen. Lee (Light Horse Harry.)

Alexander Bell Craig.
John Ed Craig.
Willie Lyles Craig.
Emelyn Craig, missionary Presbyterian Church
in Cuba.
Mary Rebecca Craig.
Susan Craig.
Sarah Craig.
Susan Wade Hicklin, m John Craig. Issue:
Two children, died in infancy.
Dr. Lawrence R. Craig.
Edward Craig, lawyer, Columbia, S. C.
Eli Robert Craig.
John Craig.
Wade Douglass Craig.
Neville Craig.
Zachariah Craig.
Johnny Lee Craig.
Mary Craig.
Emelyn Craig.
Frances Elizabeth Hicklin, m William Miller. Lives in Rich-
mond, Va. Issue:
Mable Lynwood Miller.
Lizzie Miller.
Roberta Miller.
Neely Miller and
James Cloud Miller, twins.
William Berry Miller.
Tommie Jessie Hicklin, m P. L. Langford. Issue:
Annie Lee Langford.
Rebecca Langford.
Louie Langford.
P. L. Langford.
Babe Langford
Emmie Walter Hicklin, twin of Tommie Jessie, m James E.
Douglass. Issue:
Alexander Douglass.
Jessie Bell Douglass.
Jane Douglass.
John Leighton Douglass.
Rebecca Isabel Hicklin, m Byers Douglass. Issue:
Byers Douglass.
Davis Douglass.
Zack Douglass.
Colvin Douglass.
Baby Douglass.
Elizabeth Fleming Douglass, b Feb. 15, 1829, m to Eli Hart Harrison,
Nov. 26, 1844, d May 7, 1901. Issue:
John Douglass Harrison, b Jan. 22, 1846, m Sallie Dikin,
March, 1867. Issue:
William Dikin Harrison, b 1868, m C. Dikin.
Issue:
Mary Harrison, m Mr. Ferguson.
Issue:
One child.
Mary Lunsford Harrison, m John Jones. Issue:
Marie Jones.
Sallie Jones.

Thomas Jones.
Two other children.
Viola Porcher Harrison, m Wm. Kennedy. Issue:
Sallie Kennedy.
Susan Kennedy.
Annie Harrison, m John Macearchem. Issue:
Several children.
Dr. Eli Hart Harrison, b Feb. 22, 1848, m Bettie Adams, d
several years ago. Issue:
Louise Harrison.
Rose Harrison, m Dr. Eli Hart Harrison.
Bessie Harrison.
David B. Harrison, married.
John Douglass Harrison.
Robert Wade Harrison.
Eli Hart Harrison.
David Thomas Harrison, b Sept., 1856, m Miss Rochelle.
Issue:
Two daughters.
Lawrence Sylvester Harrison, b 1858, m Minnie Bell. Issue:
Louise Harrison.
Lawrence Harrison.
Robert Wade Harrison, b 1863, married and died. Issue:
Two children.
Lucy Reeves Harrison, b Dec., 1855, m Dec., 1872, to Samuel
Dikin. Issue:
Eli H. Dikin.
Elizabeth Fleming Dikin.
Eugene Dikin.
Edna Dikin.
Mary Douglass Dikin.
John Lee Dikin.
Rebecca Lethered Harrison, b 1862, m 1886, to Robert B.
Lewis. Issue:
Robert B. Lewis, m Dec. 14, 1911, to Ruth
Othello.
Elizabeth Lethered Lewis.
Francis Reeves Lewis.
Marguerite Lewis.
B. Elmer Lewis.
Edgar Lewis.
Dr. Swanson Wade Douglass, b July 20, 1831, d Sept. 26, 1864, m May 3,
1854, to Susan C. Hemphill. No issue.
Mary Lethered Douglass, b May 5, 1833, d Oct., 1900, m W. H. H.
Moores, Sr.
Martha Adaline Douglass, b March 4, 1835, d April 13, 1845.
Dr. Lawrence Sylvester Douglass, b May 29, 1837, d Sept., 1897.
Dr. Thomas James Holden Douglass, b May 11, 1839, d Jan. 19, 1900, m
Lilly Mobley. Issue:
Seven children, all of whom died in infancy.
**Francis Petrena Porcher Douglass, b Dec. 9, 1841, m May 11, 1866, to
William Turner Thorn. He was b May 24, 1840, and d Jan. 12,
1879. Issue:
Mary Lunsford Thorn, b April 7, 1867, m June 19, 1888, to W.
H. H. Moores, Jr. (See Moores chapter.)

**Mrs. Thorn resides at the ancestral home, Mons Ascalapius, near Blackstock, S. C. She is, like the other members of this family, well educated and thoroughly posted on the many important issues of the times. She has a fine memory, and has furnished the above records.

Martha McC. Thorn, b Jan. 13, 1869, d Nov. 19, 189g.
Adaline Elizabeth Thorn, b Aug. 23, 1870, d June 14, 1911.
Susan Rebecca Thorn, b Sept. 22, 1872, a teacher.
Frances Douglass Thorn, b March 12, 1874, m Dr. James
    Adams Hayne. Issue:
        Theodore Brevard Hayne, b Aug. 7, 1838.
        Frances Douglass Thorn Hayne, b Dec. 27, 1900.
        Zillah Adams Hayne, b Oct. 5, 1902.
        Mary Lunsford Hayne, b Nov. 2, 1904.
        Isaac Hayne, b Dec. 12, 1906.
        Susan Wilhemina Hayne, b June 21, 1908.
        James Adams Hayne, b Aug. 12, 1910.
    Rosa Lethered Thorn, b Oct. 13, 1877, d Oct. 16, 1867.

REBECCA WADE LUNSFORD MOORE m 2nd to Michael Moore, on May 26, 1803. Issue:
    JOHN MOORE, m Nov. 13, 1832, to Mary Ann Carter. She and an infant both died
    soon after its birth. He then m, on May 25, 1836, to Jane Stewart. Issue:
        Capt. John Michael Moore, killed in battle before Richmond, 1862. Un-m.
        Sarah Elizabeth Moore, m Prof. W. Banks Thompson. Issue:
            Jane Thompson, m Mr. Patrick. Issue:
                Sarah Patrick.
                William Banks Patrick.
                Michael Patrick.
                Thomas Patrick.
                Mary Jane Patrick.
            Mary Thompson, m Joe C. McLure, a lawyer in Chester, S.
            C. Issue:
                Elizabeth McLure.
                Mary McLure.
                Maud McLure.
            Michael Thompson, died in young manhood.
            Robert Stewart Thompson, died in young manhood.
    SARAH ADALINE MOORE, b April 7, 1807, m Sept. 15, 1828, to Geo. W. Hill.
    She d prior to the Civil war. She had eleven children, all of whom pre-
    ceded her to the grave but two. Issue:
        Adaline Hill, m Mr. McGowan. Issue:
            Lizzle McGowan, died.
        Luella Hill, m Mr. Groves, of Mobile, Ala.
    *DR. THOMAS WADE MOORE, m 1st to Sarah Dabney Chisholm, in 1834, 2nd to
    Marian McDonald, of New York, about 1851-52. Issue by 1st marriage:
        Thomas W. Moore, killed in the Civil war in battle. Un-m.
        **Mary Rebecca Moore, m Wm. H. Hardin, of Chester, S. C. She d 1911.
        He d soon after. Issue:
            Sallie D. Hardin, m J. C. James; both dead. Issue:
                William Hardin James.
                Josephine A. James.
                Rebecca Capers James.
            Edmund Henry Hardin, m his cousin, Nancy Brice. Issue:
                Rebecca Moore Hardin.
                Nancy B. Hardin.

**Mrs. Rebecca Moore Hardin died in 1911, in her 76th year, in Chester, S. C. She was one of Chester's most excellent women, a kind and thoughtful friend and neighbor, and an affectionate wife and mother. She was born and reared in the Fishing Creek section. She and her husband celebrated their golden wedding anniversary several years ago.

*Dr. Thomas Wade Moore, one of the signers of the Ordinance of Secession, was born in Chester County, South Carolina, in 1809. His father, John Michael Moore, emigrated from Ireland after the Revolutionary war. He was educated for the ministry, but changed his plans and came to America and settled in Columbia, S. C. Dr. Moore was a man of broad culture, and wielded much influence in his neighborhood. He occupied a seat in the Legislature and was a member of the Secession Convention. During the war he rendered faithful service as District Funding Treasurer. He died in 1871. His son, Thomas Wade Moore, Jr., gave his life to the cause of the Confederacy.

Annie Hardin, unmarried.
Bessie Hardin, m her cousin, John Brice. He died. Issue:
    Nancy Boyce Brice.
    Thomas H. Brice.
    John W. Brice.

Susannah Moore, m Madison Ross. No issue.
Lydia Moore, m Madison Ross after the death of her sister. Issue:
    Thomas Ross.
    Madison Ross.
    Marion Ross.
Sarah Moore, m Mr. Hencaide, of Florida. She died. Issue:
    Several children.
Mary Ellen Moore, m Mr. King, of Florida. She died.
*Fanny C. Moore, unmarried.
Ida Moore, unmarried.
John Moore, d a few years ago in Alabama.
Marian Moore, m Mr. Larvis, of South Carolina. Issue:
    A large family.
EMELINE MOORE, m Dr. Walter Brice. Issue:
    Capt. Michael Jones Brice, killed in Civil war.
    John Moore Brice, killed in battle.
    Walter Scott Brice, d in Richmond from fever. Married. No issue.
    David Lunsford Brice, killed by falling tree after the war.
    Wade Brice, m 2nd Matilda Watson. Issue:
        Wade Brice, married and has children.
    Richard Watson Brice, m Miss Mobley. Issue:
        Several children.

DIARY OF MRS. REBECCA WADE LUNSFORD MOORE.

"Lost my mother when 15 months old. Was taken by my aunt (Mrs. Esther Macdonald Woodward), who was a mother to the motherless. She kept me till my father married again (Capt. Geo. Wade's second wife, Mrs. Martha Taylor Wade), which was over six years. Was raised by a step-mother who was kind and good to me. I married in my 19th year to (Capt.) Swanson Lunsford, a Virginian, native of Petersburg. He lived one year and eleven months after marriage, and left a child a year old, who is now Mrs. Douglass (Dr. John and Mary Lethered Lunsford Douglass, my parents.) My father's doors were opened to me and my fatherless child, and my mother was a mother indeed to the widow and fatherless. I stayed with them while a widow, which was nearly four years. I married Michael Moore (Major.) We had six children, but one the Lord took to Himself when he was only 10 weeks old. My husband lived nearly fifteen years after we were married. I was again left a widow, with five children, the oldest not 14 years old, and now they are all fathers and mothers. O, Lord! When I look back and see Thy upholding hand to one of the poorest of Thy creatures, the many trials and difficulties I have been brought through, I must say, my suffering was all of the Lord and not of myself. O, Lord! With lasting gratitude on my poor heart for the many benefits and blessings I receive from Thy all-bountiful hand. O, for the spirit of praise."

The words in parentheses in this quotation from my grandmother's diary are mine, not just written as she has it. This diary is full of interesting matter to me—letters to her family, texts of sermons, ministers mentioned, who preached to them, leading texts given, and how the minister tried to impress upon the hearts of his hearers' these truths, and gave hymns, songs, etc., at these services. Gives many daily meditations and prayers, prayers so fervently for her children and servants, and begs God's guidance in ruling all. Each day's writing ends in praise and thanksgiving to God, the Giver of all good.

My grandmother was a consistent member of the M. E. church. She and her last husband lie side by side in the old M. E. cemetery at Winnsboro, S. C. My grandfather, her first husband, Capt. Swanson Lunsford, is buried in our State Capitol grounds in Columbia. He then owned

*Fanny C. Moore has done a great work in rearing her motherless relatives.

that part of the grounds. His grave was put there in 1799, and years afterward a tombstone and substantial iron railing was placed there by my parents, Dr. John and Mary L. Lunsford Douglass. This lonely grave on our Capitol grounds, withstanding the devastation of Sherman's raids, attracts unbounded attention. It was a sacred spot to my mother, and she impressed the same deep feeling on her children.

I think I wrote you I had one of my great-grandfather's silver knee buckles (Capt. George Wade.) My mother also had her father's (Capt. Swanson Lunsford's) sword, used in the Revolution, but it has disappeared. I have one of the silver lapels from his coat.

FRANCES THORNE.

FOURTH CHILD OF CAPTAIN GEORGE AND MARY McDONALD WADE.

MARY WADE, was b in South Carolina, and died April 29, 1836, m David Fleming. Issue:
JAMES FLEMING, m Sarah Boatwright, of Columbia, S. C. Issue:
Malvina Fleming, m Marcus Brown and reared a family. One of their children was:
James Fleming Brown, m and had issue, of which Eleanor Scurry Brown is one.
Elizabeth Fleming, m Hugh McMerster. Issue:
Several children.
James Fleming, Jr., m and had children.
Dr. Edwin C. Fleming, m ond left children.
*Capt. David Fleming, died. No issue.
†Robert Green Fleming, m and had a large family.
‡Donald Fleming, m and had issue:
§ELIZABETH FLEMING, m Dr. Robert Green, of Columbia, S. C.

FIFTH CHILD OF CAPTAIN GEORGE AND MARY McDONALD WADE.

**GEORGE WADE, Jr., b in 1770, d 1853, in South Carolina, m Miss Mary McDonald.
BETSY DeMOSS WADE, b March 29, 1791.
MALERY WADE, b Jan. 10, 1793.
REBECCA WADE, b Dec. 12, 1795.
MARTHA WADE, b Sept. 12, 1797.
GEORGE WADE, b March 12, 1801.
MIDDLETON WADE, b Dec. 27, 1803.
THOMAS WADE, b Feb. 5, 1806.
TALLIE WADE, b April 24, 1808.
DANIEL WADE, b July 30, 1810.
GEORGE WADE married 2nd to Martha Taylor Center, sister of Gov. Taylor and widow of Major Nathan Center. Issue:
JAMES TAYLOR WADE, b Nov. 27, 1786, m his cousin, Martha Rives. Issue:
**DR. PATRICK WADE, m Miss Darden, of Mississippi. Issue:
James Darden Wade, b Nov. 7, 1858.
Carrie Olivia Wade, b July 21, 1861, m her cousin, Dunbar Bisland Wade.
(See his line.)

**Dr. Patrick Henry Wade was born in Richland District, South Carolina, on June 24, 1826. He was educated in the Male Academy in Columbia, S. C., and graduated in medicine in the Charleston Medical College, in 1849. In 1851 he came Mississippi and settled in the Red Lick neighborhood, where he practiced medicine till the time of his death, June 22, 1903. In 1857 he married Martha Darden, daughter of the late Jesse Harper Darden, of Jefferson County, Miss.

*Captain David Fleming was killed by the blow-up of Petersburg, Va., during the Civil war, at the beginning of which he was an officer in the U. S. army.

†Was a distinguished railroad official.

‡Donald Fleming was killed by a falling wall in his store after the Civil war.

§Died without heirs, leaving a large fortune.

**The above family was reared in South Carolina.

Blount Stuart Wade, b May 24, 1863.
Mattie Dunbar Wade, b Jan. 10, 1865.
Ernest Barnes Wade, b Nov. 26, 1868.
Jessie Blanche Wade, b March 24, 1870.
Helen Ross Wade, b Dec. 10, 1873.
GEORGE TIMOTHY WADE, m 1st his cousin, Anna Bookter, 2nd to Miss Perry.
Several children by the 2nd marriage.
JOHN RIVES WADE, m Miss Julia Stuart, of Mississippi.
MARTHA WADE, m her cousin, Dr. Walter Wade, of Mississippi. (See his line.)
CHARLOTTE WADE, and
††AGNES WADE, never married.

DAUGHTER OF COL. THOMAS WADE AND JANE BOGAN:

SARAH WADE, b Sept. 26, 1776, m Dr. Joshua Prout, Oct. 13, 1787. She d Jan. 1, 1819
Issue:
Hiram Augustus Prout.
Holden Wade Prout.
Patric Prout.
Lydia Prout.
Mary Prout.
Jane Wade Prout, b in Anson Co., N. C., May 4, 1789, m Feb. 4, 1804, to Capt. Robert
Coman. She d Jan. 1, 1816. Issue:
Margaret Williamson Coman, m Judge Matthew Brickell, of Huntsville,
Ala. Issue:
Robert Coman Brickell.
Richard Benjamine Brickell.
Eliza Morgan Brickell, d 1911, aged 81.
William Brickell.
Louisa Brickell (called Kitty.)
James Matthew Coman, m Elizabeth Mason. Issue:
Mary Coman, m Gov. John M. Stone, of Miss.
Lost two children.
Queenie Coman, m Jake Alexander.
James Coman.
Lucile Coman.
John M. Coman, m 1st to Miss Groesbeck, 2nd to Lula
Harrington. Issue by 1st marrage:
James G. Coman, m Miss Tillman.
Celia Coman.
James Coman, m Miss Oates. Issue:
Six children.
Sallie Coman, d 1911.
Rebecca Coman.
Sarah Jane Coman, m John McMeachan. Issue:
Robert McMeachan, m Ella Bean. Issue:
Robert Marshall McMeachan.
Erin McMeachan.
Will McMeachan, m Linnie W. Bridges. Issue:
Linnie Bridges.
Joshua Prout Coman, b April 4, 1912, m August 26, 1835, to Jane Heland
Lindley. Issue:
James Lindley Coman, b July 14, 1836, d Dec. 2,
1885, m Frances Jane Malone, July 18,
1860. Issue:
Louise Emmet Coman, m W.W. Beck,
of Seattle, Wash. Issue:

---

††Miss Agnes Wade was authority on the history of the Wade family.

—178—

Broussais Coman Beck.
Dillard Beck.
One dead.
Broussais Coman, m Boyd Baker.
    Issue:
        James Lindley Coman.
James Lindley Coman.
Frances Fawn Coman, m H. H. Clay-
    ton. Issue:
        Lawrence Clayton.
        Frances Clayton.
        Lindley Clayton.
Robert Brickell Coman.
Louise Coman, m William Mason. Issue:
        Ola Mason, m Dr. S. B Spickard.
            Issue:
                Evelyn G. Spickard.
Louisa Ann Coman, m Samuel DeWoody. Issue:
    Marion Eugenia DeWoody, m John M. Nelson.
    John M. DeWoody.
    Sarah DeWoody, m Emmet Reno.
    Louisa A. DeWoody.
    James Coman DeWoody, killed in Civil war.
    Samuel N. DeWoody, m Laura Moore. Issue:
        Betty DeWoody, m C. J. Petty. Issue:
            Laura Nell Petty.
            Charles Petty.
        Linnie Lyle DeWoody, m T. B. Lyle. Issue:
            Tom Brown Lyle.
            DeWoody Lyle.
            Richard L. Lyle.
            Elizabeth Lyle.
            Marshall Stone Lyle.
Children of Mary Lou DeWoody and J. B. Williams:
        Laura E. Williams.
        Louise Williams.
    Sammie DeWoody¶
    Laura DeWoody, died.
William L. DeWoody, m Mary Sorrells. Issue:
    Marion Louise DeWoody, m C. W. Pettigrew.
        Issue:
            C. W. Pettigrew.
    Rebecca DeWoody, m Earl W. Phillips.
        Issue:
            William W. Phillips, b 1902.
            Earl T. Phillips, b 1904.
            Robert E. Phillips, b 1906.
    Martha Alma DeWoody, m Newton E. Bright-
    well.
    Emma Virginia DeWoody.
    Florence A. DeWoody.
    T. Sorrells DeWoody.
    William L. DeWoody.
    Margaret Coman DeWoody.

CHAPTER X.

THE KILLINGSWORTH FAMILY.

The Killingsworth family were probably of English descent. Members of the family were found in New Jersey during the early history of this State. The name is found in a variety of forms, Keilingsworth being one, though Kielinsworth and Killingsworth are the most common.

This family are first recorded, as far as we have record, by the brothers, John, Jesse and Jacob, who lived in South Carolina in 1792, as shown by the United States census of that date. These brothers lived in Richland District, near Camden, or in what was termed the Camden District.

John Killingsworth had in his family one male over 16, one male under 16 and four females. He was a Revolutionary soldier, and his family lived near his brother Jacob and in the same neighborhood with Robert Hill, the father of John Hill, who married the daughter of Jacob Killingsworth.

Jesse Killingsworth had in his family, at the time the census of 1792 was taken, one male over 16 years of age, one male under 16 and four females. He was also in the Revolutionary war.

Jacob Killingsworth, the founder of the family that we devote this sketch to, had in his family two males over 16, four udder 16 and six females. Of his family we have record only of one son and one daughter. Nothing of his early life, the name of his wife, or other facts, come to us. His children were:
SARAH KILLINGSWORTH, who married John Hill (see his line for record.)
NOEL KILLINGSWORTH, m Jane Scott.
A DAUGHTER, who m Mr. Crockett.

In South Carolina there were Killinsworth families, and in North Carolina a number of Killingsworth families. We have no record of the relation these families bore each other. One of the characteristics that have come down through both the families of Noel and Sarah Killingsworth is the beautiful auburn hair, blue eyes and fair skin that predominates among the descendants. On one occasion the writer was introduced to a Mr. Killingsworth, and noticing his hair, which was of a golden, auburn color, remarked, "You are a cousin of mine." Mr. Killingsworth was somewhat surprised, but was told that the color of his hair was a family characteristic.

*Anon Killingsworth visited his uncle, Jesse Killingsworth, in South Carolina. Jesse Killingsworth was a very precise, particular man. His premises were kept in beautiful order. This characteristic is strong with the Killingsworth family.

SON OF JACOB KILLINGSWORTH.

NOEL KILLINGSWORTH, son of Jacob Killingsworth, of South Carolina, b in 1778, m
*Jane Scott, dau of Jane and Elizabeth Scott. He d July 3, 1831. She was b in 1792; d in
1857. He was the brother of Sarah Killingsworth, who m John Hill. Issue:
‡ANON WASHINGTON KILLINGSWORTH, b Feb. 18, 1814, d May, 1882, m Amelia
    Malinda Brashear, dau of Turner Belt and Catherine Brashear. Issue:
    Uncas B. Killingsworth, b May 28, 1838, d Sept. 24, 1840.
    Katherine N. Killingsworth, b May 28, 1840, d Sept. 25, 1871, m Benijah
        S. Ellis, Nov. 12, 1860. Issue:
        Estelle Ellis, b March 18, 1862, d Sept. 23, 1863.
        †Scott Killingsworth Ellis, b Feb. 27, 1864, married. Issue:
            Laura Katherine Ellis, b Jan. 21, 1894.
            Alice Vivian Ellis, b May 3, 1895.
            Leslie Fern Ellis, b Apr. 21, 1899, d July 31, 1899.
        †R. S. Ellis, b June 16, 1867, m 1st to Sarah S. Harris, who
            lived about nine months, and m 2nd to Mary E. Rich-
            mond. Issue:
            R. S. Ellis.
            Estell Ellis.
            Anon Ellis.
            Ernestine Ellis.
            Balmayne Mary Ellis.
    Noel Scott Killingsworth, b Aug. 5, 1843, d at Bowling Green, Ky., Jan.
        28, 1862, in the service of the Confederacy.
WILLIAM KILLINGSWORTH, d while an infant.
JOEL KILLINGSWORTH, died while an infant.
MARY E. KILLINGSWORTH, b Aug. 21, 1817, m T. J. Grafton. He was b in 1831
    and d in 1853. She d Jan. 19, 1847. Issue:
    **Sarah E. Grafton, b 1843, m Chas. B. McClaskey. He d in 1896. Issue:
        Charles McClaskey.
        Newell McClaskey.
        Thomas McClaskey.
        Hewitt McClaskey.
        Eddie McClaskey.
        Beulah McClaskey.
        Bessie McClaskey.
CATHERINE E. KILLINGSWORTH, b Oct. 23, 1822, d Aug. 25, 1886, m Richard
    Scott, son of Isaac Scott. Issue:
    Richard Killingsworth Scott, b Dec. 11, 1848, d Jan. 26, 1883.
    §Kate Scott, b July 17, 1851, m W. P. Darden, son of Geo. Darden. Issue:
        Elaine Darden, b Feb. 14, 1885. d March 8, 1902.
        Katsie Darden, b April 10, 1886.
        Willie Darden, b June 23, 1887, m Nov. 16, 1910, to Dr. C.
            W. Patterson.
    Scott Darden, b Feb. 16, 1894.
    Jane Ruth Scott, b April 20, 1853, d Oct. 23, 1865.

---

*Jane Scott was probably born in Scotland. She spoke the English language with a very decided Scotch accent. Both Mr. and Mrs. Noel Killingsworth are buried in Jefferson County, where they lived and reared their families and where many of their descendants now live. The old Killingsworth home is standing about two miles from Red Lick.

**Mrs. Sarah Grafton and her family reside at Bloomfield, Ky.

†The Ellis brothers live at Lorman, Miss. It was my pleasure to meet Mr. Scott Ellis recently, and have from him the records of his father's family.

§Mr. and Mrs. W. P. Darden live near Red Lick, Miss. Their beautiful daughter, Katsie, is with them. Willie is living at Rosedale, Miss., where her husband is a prominent physician.

‡See note, page 189.

ANAPIAS KILLINGSWORTH, b Dec. 30, 1820, m Matilda Trimble, Dec. 11, 1850.
    She was b March 7, 1830, and d Nov. 1, 1867. He d May 30, 1876. Issue:
        †Anon Ross Killingsworth, b Jan. 23, 1852, m Helen Perrine Ross, dau of
            John I. W. Ross and Hellen P. Beatty. No issue.
        Rodger Trimble Killingsworth, m **Jennie Wade, dau of Judge Isaac
            Ross Wade and Katherine Dunbar. (See page 170.) Issue:
                Benj. Young Killingsworth.
                Catherine Dunbar Killingsworth.
                Ross Wade Killingsworth.
                Rodger Trimble Killingsworth.
                Matilda Killingsworth.
                William Bisland Killingsworth.
        Sallie Killingsworth, m Jesse Darden, Jr. Issue:
                Stella Darden.
                Arthur Darden.
                Anon Darden.
                Jennie Varden.
                Martha Darden.
        Jennie Killingsworth, m Seaborn Ross, son of John I. W. Ross, April 26,
            1888. (For issue, see page —.)
        Matilda Jane Killingsworth, b Feb. 3, 1856.
        James C. Killingsworth, b June 24, 1858.
        Noel Killingsworth, b Jan. 4, 1860, m Edith Hall. Issue:
                Vivien Killingsworth.
                Louise Killingsworth.
                Mathilde Killingsworth.
        William W. Killingsworth, b Aug. 21, 1861, d Oct. 24, 1865.
        Scott Killingsworth, b Dec. 28, 1862, m Mattie D. Wade, dau of Dr. P. H.
            Wade. He d March 2, 1908.
        Kate Killingsworth, b Nov. 26, 1863, m James Wade, son of Dr. P. H.
            Wade, Dec. 1, 1887. Issue:
                Zula Wade, b Oct. 24, 1888.
                Willie Wade (dau), b Oct. 29, 1869.
                James D. Wade, b July 12, 1893.
        Beulah Killingsworth, b Aug. 16, 1866.
        Anapias Killingsworth, b Sept. 1, 1868, m Minnie Wade, Oct. 22, 1894.
            She was b Oct. 22, 1872. Issue:
                Anapias Killingsworth, b Oct. 22, 1895.
                Nina Rebecca Killingsworth, b Feb. 9, 1897.
                Minnie Aurelia Killingsworth, b April 28, 1898.
                Sarah Elizabeth Killingsworth, b Feb. 7, 1900.
                Anon Ross Killingsworth, b Aug. 18, 1901.
                Allison Wade Killingsworth, b March 26, 1903.
                Ellen Idella Killingsworth, b Nov. 29, 1905.
                Rosa Cogan Killingsworth, b May 13, 1909.
        Lula Killingsworth, b Oct. 15, 1870.
        Anita Killingsworth, b Aug. 16, 1872.
        Uncas Killingsworth, b June 25, 1876, m Oct. 30, 1901, to Lola Crosby.
            Issue:
                Uncas Killingsworth.
    SARAH KILLINGSWORTH, m Hamden Jordan McKey, son of Daniel and Rosa
        Harris McKey. (Sse McKee chapter.)

**Cousin Jennie Killingsworth has inherited the likeness of her Scotch ancestors, and many of their sturdy qualities. She is a lover of genealogy, and was one of the very first to give assistance to the writer. She could have added many incidents to this narrative if she had undertaken the task of compiling the family records. The benediction of her smile and the honest look from her blue eyes fully repaid the writer for a cold ride, facing a brisk north wind, to make her a call.

(Explanation.)—By an omission of the printer, Jennie Allison Wade is not given on page 170.

†Anon R. Killingsworth fills well the place of oldest child of his parents. His home is ever open to friends and relatives.

DAUGHTER, who m a Mr. Crockett. ssue:
  †WILLIAM CROCKETT, m Miss DeForest in Iowa. Issue:
      William Ashby Crockett.
      H: Clay Crockett.
      Uncas H. Crockett.
  MARY CROCKETT, m Eli T. Montgomery. (See letter.) Issue:
      Matilda Montgomery, m Malcolm Cameron. Issue:
          ††John R. Cameron, m Jennie Cheek. Issue:
              Malcolm Cameron.
              Lillian Cameron, m Dr. Staples.
              Virginia Cameron, m Mr. Martin.
              Pinquit Cameron, m Miss Purnell.
      Matilda Montgomery Cameron m 2nd to Sid Champion. Issue:
          Wallace Champion, m Miss Harvey. Issue: ,
          Ruth Champion.
          Sid Champion, m Olive Montgomery. Issue:
              Sid Champion.
          Mollie Champion, m ——. Issue:
              Several children.
      *Dr. Wallace Montgomery, m Miss Denson. Issue:
          Eli Montgomery, unmarried.
      Dr. Wallace Montgomery m 2nd to Cora Green. Issue:
          *Louise Montgomery, m to Joseph Foster Lipscomb, May 27,
              1886. Issue:
              Bertha Lipscomb, b Nov. 5, 1889.
              Sarah Rowland Lipscomb, b March 29, 1892.
              Robert Alexander Lipscomb, b May 15, 1896.
              Joseph Foster Lipscomb, b Sept. 5, 1899.
              Ruth Louise Lipscomb, b Nov. 7, 1904.
          William Alexander Montgomery, b Jan. 25, 1870, m Lillian
              Postel Smith, dau of Robert C. and Annie David.
              Issue:
              Lillian Anne Montgomery, b April 12, 1899.
              Annie David Montgomery, b June 18, 1901.
          Robert Estell Montgomery, b Nov. 20, 1872, in Yazoo County,
              Miss., m Jennie Jordan, of Alabama, Oct. 22, 1907.
              Issue:
              Robert Hamilton Montgomery, b April 2, 1909.
              William Jordan Montgomery, b Feb. 21, 1911.
          Talulah Montgomery, m Thos. Lipscomb. Issue:
              William Lipscomb, d age 2 years.

---

†William Crockett was an abolitionist and went North before the Civil war. He was reared by his uncle, Neel Killingsworth, and a picture of him hung for many years in the Killingsworth home, known as Holly Grove. His widow and two sons came to Mississippi after his death and she married Rev. Mr. Soreby, a Methodist minister, who had property and lived near Utica. One of the sons, Ashbey, lived in Jackson. Nothing further is known of this family.

*"My father was born on the centennial anniversary of Washington's birth, and died Jan. 10, 1910. He was a member of the 28th Mississippi, and was wounded in Alabama. He was more of a poet than a soldier, and although some things he wrote were very beautiful, he was so modest that, like my brother Eli, who is even a better writer, nothing has ever been published. They are in his possession in Camita, Sharkey County, Mississippi.
                                                    LOUISE MONTGOMERY LIPSCOMB."

CHAPTER XI.

THE HILL FAMILY.

Tradition has come down to the present generation, that this branch of the Hill family were of English descent, having first settled in Virginia and then removed to South Carolina before the Revolutionary war. Our first known ancestor, Robert Hill, was born in Virginia, about 1745, and died in South Carolina, in 1795. He was a Revolutionary soldier under Gen. Sumpter, and record of his service is on file in the Record and Pension Office in Washington, D. C. There were a large number of families bearing the name Hill in Virginia, some even among the earliest settlers, but our ancestor has not yet been identified with either of the Virginia families. He evidently moved to South Carolina before 1765, as he was married there in 1765 to **Margaret Allison, a daughter of Andrew and Margaret Allison, of whom notice was made in the sketch of Capt. Isaac Ross, page 69. The first census, dated 1792, gives the size of Robert Hill's family as ten, including himself and wife, and the record taken from the old family Bible tallies exactly with this census report. We know nothing of the life of Robert Hill, though there may be records of the family in South Carolina yet inaccessible to the public. A search has not been made by the writer, except to ascertain that many of the records of Richland County were destroyed during the Civil war. Robert Hill, as was stated in the Killingsworth chapter, was a neighbor of Jacob and John Killingsworth, and lived not a great distance from the Ross and Wade settlements.

There is an Oliphant relationship that has not yet been discovered, for records contained in the Hill Bible mention William Oliphant, born Sept. 21, 1759. From an old note *note book which was brought to Mississippi by John Hill, we find the record of the children of Robert Hill and Margaret Allison:

JANE HILL was born the 28th day of February, in the year of our Lord 1767.
JOHN HILL was born the 22nd day of February, in the year of our Lord 1769.
MARGARET ALLISON HILL was born March 5, 1871.
ANDREW ALLISON HILL was born Nov. 1, 1772, m Elizabeth Jenkins.

---

*This book also contained accounts of John Hill against Daniel Wade, Robert Knox, etc., also some accounts of Robert Hill against John McIanistry.

**There are members of the Ross family who claim he married a daughter of Isaac and Jean Brown Ross.

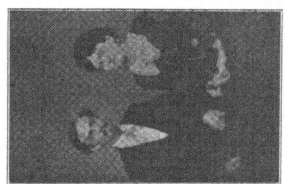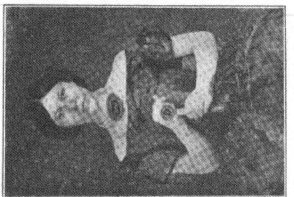

MR. AND MRS. ROBERT R. EXTER

DR. LOUIS HOBBS HILL
Page 192

JACOB KILLINGWORTHS HILL
Page 191

MR. AND MRS. JACOB KILLINGSWORTH HILL, SR.
Page 190

PIONEER HOME OF JACOB K. HILL, IN
COPIAH CO., MISS.   BUILT IN 1821.
Page 191

OLD HOME OF MRS. SARAH ANN McKEY
Page 221

ELIZABETH HILL was born Sept. 30, 1774, m Ely Kershaw Ross.
MARY HILL was born Oct. 20, 1776.
ROBERT HILL was born June 1, 1779.
JANE OLIPHANT HILL was born February 14, in the year of our Lord 1782.

FIRST CHILD OF ROBERT HILL AND MARGARET ALLISON.

JANE HILL, b Feb. 28, 1767, may have married William Oliphant.

SECOND CHILD OF ROBERT HILL AND MARGARET ALLISON.

JOHN HILL, the son of Robert Hill, lived in South Carolina until the general exodus of the family to Mississippi, about 1801. His wife, Sarah Killingsworth (see Killingsworth chapter), was also a native South Carolinian, and their children were born in that State, in Richland District. Arthur Brown Ross, in his diary, mentions visiting at John Hill's house, and of the many little children in his home, two of whom were orphan nieces. Sarah Killingsworth's sister, who married Mr. Crockett, died, leaving two children, one of whom was reared by Noel Killingsworth and the other, Mary Crockett, by John Hill.

John Hill was a favorite nephew of Captain Isaac Ross. After removing to Mississippi he was a frequent visitor to the Ross home, and was always an honored guest.

About 1817 John Hill entered a large body of land in Claiborne County, near his home in Jefferson County, where he resided until his death. There is still a bold spring on the old home place, known as "Sally Hill spring," called for Sarah Hill.

John Hill is buried in Jefferson County, and his grave bears the following inscription:

Sacred to the Memory of
JOHN HILL,
Consort of Sarah Hill,
Who was born in South Carolina,
Feb. 22, 1769,
And died Aug. 19, 1827.

Let the unknown peace of God
On the man of peace abide.

The Hill family were known as peacemakers and peaceable people. They were noted for their piety and temperate habits, for their learning and interest in everything of an uplifting nature.

WILL OF JOHN HILL.

In the name of God, amen. I, John Hill, of the State of Mississippi, but now sick in body but sound in mind, do will and bequeath unto my beloved wife, Sarah Hill, after paying my just debts, one negro woman, Grace, and one negro boy, Smart, and all my estate, both real and personal, for her sole use and benefit during her natural life, after that to be equally divided between her lawful heirs.

In witness, I have hereunto set my hand and seal this the 20th of August, 1827.

JOHN HILL.

A. Guardner, Isaac A. B. Ross.   (Book A, page 99, Jefferson County.)

FIRST CHILD OF JOHN HILL AND SARAH KILLINGSWORTH.

MARGARET ALLISON HILL, oldest dau of John and Sarah Killingsworth Hill, was b Jan. 19, 1793, m June 30, 1809, to Henry H. Cheek. Issue:

    SARAH AMANDA CHEEK, b April 23, 1810, m 1st to Mr. Gardner. Issue:
        Two children, d in infancy.
    SARAH AMANDA CHEEK GARDNER m 2nd to Mr. Walter. Issue:
        William Walter, m and had issue:
            Tom Walter.
            Beulah Walter.
            Daughter, m and had one child.
            Minnie Walter, b 1851, d 1912.
       *Dr. John R. Walter, m twice. Issue by 2nd marriage:
            John R. Walter.
        Mary Walter, m Mr. Thompson. Issue:
            Four children, d young.
        Margaret Walter, m Mr. Bennett. Issue:
            Sallie Bennett, m Dean Adams.
        Ella Walter, m Mr. Whites. Issue:
            John Thomas Whites, d young.
            George Whites.
            Luther Whites.
            Hiram Whites.
            Hunter Whites.
            Nora Whites.
  THOMAS OSBORNE CHEEK, m in Louisiana and had a large family.
  WINNIFRED HILL CHEEK, b Feb. 1, 1814, m John Robinett. Issue:
        Dr. John Robinett, m Sarah Bush. Issue:
            Bush Robinett, married. Issue:
                Two children.
            Ella Robinett, m Mr. Bankston. Issue:
                Jesse Bankston (son.)
                Lucile Bankston.
            Two children, d young.
            Annie Belle Robinett, m Dr. Tom Nelson. Issue:
                Several children.
            Marshall Robinett, m Miss Harris.
            Fred Robinett, m Miss Harris.
            John Robinett, m Sarah McCaleb.
  WINNIFRED HILL CHEEK ROBINETT m 2nd to Mr. Evans. Issue:
        Margaret Evans m Mr. Wells. Issue:
            Minnie Wells, died in infancy.
            Nannie Wells, died in infancy.

---

*John R. Walter was born in Mississippi in 1851, and moved to Arkansas when a small boy, and was reared on Grand Prairie. He graduated in medicine and located at Scott's Station, where he practiced for a number of years. He later moved to Little Rock, Ark., and engaged in the drug business at Capitol avenue and Main street. He served one term as Coroner of Pulaski County, and retired from active life about seven years ago, devoting his time to his farming interests.

On account of the recent death of Dr. John R. Walter, who had this branch of the family for compilation, it is not as complete as it would have been had he lived.

MAHALA CAROLINE CHEEK, b Dec. 20, 1816, m March 10, 1836, to John Gillespie Brown. He d in 1864; she d in 1874. Issue:

Arsenath F. Brown, b Jan. 6, 1837, m Henry Moody. Issue:

Burrell Moody, m Patsy Mahon. Issue:

Archie Moody, m Miss Kirkley. Issue:

Son.

Three infant sons, died.

Mahon Moody, married. Issue

Daughter.

Sallie Moody m Mr. Kirkley. Issue:

Lilly Kirkley, m Mr. Miller. Issue:

Several children.

Infant, died.

Sarah Elizabeth Brown, b March 9, 7838, d July, 1853, un-m.

Martha Ann Brown, b Aug. 21, 1839, m James Ainsworth. Issue:

Carrie Ainsworth, died, un-m.

Sallie Ainsworth, m Jesse Edwards. Issue:

Several children.

Annie Ainsworth, m Henry Evans. Issue:

Delia Evans.

Alma Evans.

Margaret Evans.

Archie Evans.

Ainsworth Evans.

Mullens Evans.

Daughter.

Archie Ainsworth, married and has issue.

Tom Ainsworth, married and has issue.

William Archibald Brown, b Dec. 2, 1840, d July 21, 1861.

Margaret Matilda Brown, b Jan. 11, 1743, m Furman Green. Both are dead. Issue:

Luna Bell Green, m Will Farmer. Issue:

Furman Farmer.

Margaret Farmer and

Jeannette Farmer, twins.

Neoma Green, m Allen Hicks. Issue:

Allen Hicks.

John Robert Hicks and

Mathilde Hicks, twins.

Mary Caroline Brown, b Oct. 14, 1845, m Feb. 13, 1866, to Rev. *Philip Augustus Haman. Issue:

Ada May Haman, b Feb. 12, 1867, m Chas. Duchesne. Issue:

Lunora Duchesne.

Lucile Duchesne.

Verde Duchesne.

Alma Duchesne.

P. A. Duchesne.

Alma Anna Haman, b March 15, 1869, d June 6, 1872.

Weenona Haman, b Jan. 30, 1870, m Vernon Hayden, April 11, 1909.

Weekona Haman, b Jan. 30, 1870, m Robert A. Perkins May 4, 1910.

---

*P. A. Haman was a member of Company B, 22nd Miss. Infantry, from July, 1861, to Nov. 30, 1864, when wounded at Franklin, Tenn. He marched on a pair of rough crutches from Columbia, Tenn., to Barton Station, Miss., about 100 miles, to avoid going to prison. He was ordained a Missionary Baptist preacher in 1871, by Harmony, now Learned Church.

Burks Glen Haman, b Jan. 8, 1874, d April 24, 1911, m Cora
Hillman, of Jackson, Tenn. Issue:
Thelma Haman.
Elizabeth Haman.
Elizabeth Haman, b March 9, 1876, d July 17, 1877.
William Brown Haman, b March 81, 1878, d July 5, 1902, m
Maud Fowler. No issue.
Lucy Ethel Haman, b Aug. 12, 1880, m Mose B. Lowe. Issue:
Mose B. Lowe.
Ethel Lowe.
Bernice Lowe.
Robert Allen Lowe.
Startford Pitt Haman, b Sept. 28, 1883, m Aug. 28, 1907, to
Mrs. Mary Ware.
Euelia Pearl Haman, b June 18, 1887, d Oct. 23, 1891.
Mahala Malvina Brown, b Nov. 21, 1847, d Nov. 31, 1847, and
Robert Henry Brown, twins, b Jan. 31, 1848, died, unmarried.
Narcissie Minerva Brown, b Sept. 15, 1850, died after maturity.
Jacob Hill Brown, b March 10, 1853, died, unmarried.
John Neil Brown, b March 17, 1853, m Belle Moore. Issue:
Rena Brown, m Charley Brady. Issue:
Brown Brady.
Thomas Shelby Brown, b June 25, 1855, m Maria Bell. Issue:
Mayrind Brown.
Caroline Brown.
Jacob Brown.
Luna Bell Brown.
Shelby Brown.
Maria C. Brown, b March 13, 1857, m Isaac Horn. Issue:
Three children, died in infancy.
Mathilde Horn.
MARGARET NARCISSIE CHEEK, daughter of Henry Cheek, b Nov. 27, 1818, m Rob-
ert Miller, who was b in 1810 and was the son of Robert Miller, a Presbyterian
minister, who came from Scotland as a chaplain in the British army. He m Miss
Pickens, a sister of Gen. Andrew Pickens, of South Carolina. Issue:
Irene Miller, b 1838, d 1882, m James R. Mallade. Issue:
Robert Mallade.
Joseph Mallade.
George Mallade.
*Geo. Miller, b 1842, d April 21, 1876, m Nov. 27, 1865, to Mary Bullock.
Issue:
Irene Miller, b Sept. 4, 1866, m A. R. Brashear. Issue:
Zola Brashear.
Bessie Brashear,
Rector Brashear.
Katy Brashear.
George Brashear
Russ Brashear.
†Bessie Miller, b Jan. 7, 1868, m Nov. 25, 1883, to Dr. T. S.
Walker. Issue:
Mae Walker, m Cecil Laughton.
Beatrice Walker.

---

*Served in the Confederate army, in the battles of Manassas and Gettysburg. After his death his wife, who is
now living, removed to Texas, and there her children have married and are occupying positions of esteem and trust.

†Mrs. Walker is now living in Texas. She is interested in genealogy, and has willingly assisted in compiling these
records.

Gladys Walker. (See picture.)
Sumpter Walker.
Robert Miller, b Jan. 21, 1870, d 1911, m 1st Pearl Lenier, 2nd
Florence Payne. Issue:
Florence Miller.
Emma Miller, b June 27, 1872, m G. L. Dupuy. Issue:
Murray Dupuy.
Dow Dupuy.
Olive Dupuy, d May, 1898.
Alice Dupuy.
George J. Miller, b Jan. 14, 1874, d March, 1909, m Miss
Reade. Issue:
Reade Miller.
Robert Miller.
George Miller.
Emma Miller.
Johnnie Miller, d March 8, 1885.
†Robert N. Miller, b 1850, m Emma Barr, dau of Judge Barr. Issue:
Hugh Barr Miller, b 1879, m 1904 to Miss Lewis. Issue:
Robert Miller, b 1905.
Hugh Barr Miller, b 1909.
JOHN HILL CHEEK, b Nov. 7, 1820, m in Louisiana.
MARY B. CHEEK, b Sept. 4, 1822, m Robert Miller. Issue:
Several children.
MATILDA M. CHEEK, b Aug. 25, 1823, d un-m.
WILLIAM KILLINGSWORTH CHEEK, b Nov. 15, 1825, m Jan. 1, 1857, to Frances
Speed Hill, widow of John Hill, Jr. She was b Feb. 28, 1831, and d Aug. 6,
1898. He d May 14, 1885. Issue:
Jennie Cheek, b Nov. 14, 1858, m Hamden J. Mackey. (See Mackey
line.)
Margaret Talula Cheek, b April 19, 1861, m James L. Moore, Jan. 19,
1885. Issue:
James C. Moore, b Oct. 20, 1885.
Charles Moore, b Sept. 20, 1886.
Etta May Cheek, b May 18, 1864, m William Love Lloyd, Jan. 22, 1884.
She d April 9, 1891. Issue:
John William Lloyd, b Feb. 9, 1885.
Edgar Cheek Lloyd, b July 18, 1886.
‡MARTHA JANE CHEEK, b Dec. 20, 1826, m Aug. 27, 1845, to William Strong Flowers,
son of Ignatius Flowers. He was b Dec. 25, 1817. Issue:
Richard Flowers, died an infant.
**Margaret A. Flowers, b March 16, 1848, m Nov. 7, 1867, to Geo. Bancroft
Nelson, Sr. He was b Aug. 11, 1846. Issue:
William Flowers Nelson, b May 7, 1871, m May 20, 1896, to
Birdie Shackle.
Elizabeth Kate Nelson, b May 7, 1871, d May 17, 1876.
Benjamin Franklin Nelson, b Sept. 6, 1873, m Oct. 3, 1897, to
Maggie Brittain.

---

†Hon. Robert N. Miller is one of the foremost lawyers of Mississippi. He has taken part in many of the most
noted criminal cases, and is now President of the Mississippi Bar Association.

‡Martha Jane Cheek was a real daughter of the U. S. D., 1812, her father having served in that war. She died Dec
17, 1909, beloved by all who knew her. She and her husband were large land owners, and their lovely home was always
open with a cordial welcome for friends of the family. Their children occupy high positions in the social and business
world. (See pictures.)

**"My great-grandfather, Henry Cheek, fought in the battle of New Orleans. I have often heard my mother tell
of his asking an old Indian woman, by the name of Minchie, to look after his family while he was away, and she was so
faithful to do so. She would stay with my grandmother at night, and when any of the children were sick would sit up
all night with them. MARGARET FLOWERS NELSON."

Elma Jane Nelson, b March 12, 1875, m Aug. 26, 1896, to
Jacob Adrian Ridgley.
Thomas Joseph Nelson, b Jan. 20, 1877, d Dec. 31, 1886.
Fannie Ethel Nelson, b April 13, 1879, d July 25, 1885.
Agnes Virginia Nelson, b Feb. 3, 1881, m July 20, 1904, to
Walter S. Dillon. Issue:
Jane Dillon, b Sept. 21, 1909, in Atlanta, Ga.
**Willie Nelson, b Aug. 26, 1883, d June 12, 1905.
Maida Alice Nelson, b Sept. 13, 1885.
George Bancroft Nelson, b Dec. 10. 1887.
Lewis Porter Nelson, b April 17, 1890
Maggie Belle Nelson, b June 7, 1894.
Joseph Bunberry Flowers, b Aug. 2, 1850, died March 30, 1904, m March
26, 1877, to Lucy Newman, dau of Albert Monroe and Minnie
Baldwin Newman. Issue:
Bessie Flowers, b Dec. 17, 1879, m Nov. 10, 1903, to Homer
H. Rhymes. Issue:
Emmy Lou Rhymes. b Aug. 26, 1904.
Homer Holden Rhymes, b Apr. 22, 1908.
Charles Flowers.
Ignatius R. Flowers, b Feb. 12, 1853.
Alice H. Flowers, b Jan. 26, 1856.
†Willie Jane, b Oct. 2, 1864, m Nov. 23, 1886, to Robert Patton, Jr., son of
Robert Patton Willing and Mary Ann Durr. He was b Oct. 8, 1863.
Issue:
Philip Mathias Willing, b Sept. 9, 1887, d Dec. 19, 1896.
Jane Willing, b March 4, 1890.
Mamie Stephens Willing, b April 6, 1894, d June 19, 1895.
Margaret Willing, b Feb. 25, 1896.
Vivian Willing, b Sept. 4, 1897.
Willie Flowers Willing, b March 28, 1903, d same date.
DR. STEPHEN HALE CHEEK, d after maturity, unmarried.
SUSAN HILL CHEEK, b Dec. 20, 1831, m Dr. Neil Brown. Issue.
Watson Brown, died young.
Kate Brown, died young.
Dodridge Brown, died young.
Archie Brown, m Miss Hamilton. No issue.
JACOB HILL CHEEK, b March 24, 1834, m Martha Jenkins. Issue:
Josephine Cheek, m Mr. Lollace. Issue:
A son and daughter.
Addie Cheek, m Mr. Knight. Issue:
Several children.
Mollie Cheek.
Jacob Cheek.

SECOND CHILD OF JOHN HILL AND SARAH KILLINGSWORTH.

*JACOB KILLINGSWORTH HILL, was b Jan. 9, 1795, in Richland District, S. C., and m
Rebecca G. Sims, daughter of Thomas and Elizabeth Ross Sims, May 16, 1816. He d May
17, 1855. (See Ross line for Rebecca G. Sims.) Issue:
THOMAS BROWN SIMS, b April 28, 1817, d Oct. 25, 1819.
HANNAH ELIZABETH ANN HILL, b April 12, 1819, m William Flowers, son of Igna-
tius Flowers. He afterwards married Martha Jane Cheek. She d about 1846.
Issue:

---

†Mrs. R. P. Willing is a member of the D. A. R. and U. S. D. 1812. She has three lovely daughters. Her husband
is one of the most prominent lawyers of Jackson, Miss.

**Just as the darkness of a summer evening stole over the land, the spirit of a good woman stepped into eternal life.

Appie Elizabeth Flowers, b in Covington Co., Miss., April 11, 1844, m
*Dr. William Lowe DeBerry, of Missouri, Feb. 7, 1868. She d July
30, 1875. Issue:
  Mary Belle DeBerry, b in Rankin Co., Miss., April 16, 1866,
    m Feb. 26, 1883, to George Wiley Harris. Issue:
      Kathleen Flowers Harris, b Dec. 3, 1885.
      George William Harris, b Oct. 27, 1888.
      Mary Elsner Harris, b July 2, 1897.
  Elsner DeBerry, M. D., b May 25, 1872, m Aug. 1, 1900, to
    Mattie Gaither Harris. Issue:
      Elsner Hobson DeBerry, b Oct. 24, 1901.
      Dorothy Rice DeBerry, b Sept. 28, 1908.
  Willie DeBarry, b May 9, 1870, d Oct. 2, 1874.
  Jennie DeBerry, m Edward Menefee Caperton. Issue:
      Elsner DeBerry Caperton, b April 26, 1893.
      Edward Menefee Caperton, b June 12, 1895.
      Joseph Woods Caperton, b July 20, 1897, d June
        23, 1898.
      Fitzgerald Flowers Caperton, twin of Joseph W.
      Richard Harris Caperton, b March 10, 1899, d
        July 12, 1899.
†SARAH ANN HILL, b 1821, m 1st to George Dorsey. (See McKey line.) Issue:
  Hill Dorsey, d aged 3.
SARAH ANN HILL m 2nd to Dr. Grant. No issue.
SARAH ANN HILL m 3rd to Hamden J. McKey.
**††JACOB KILLINGSWORTH HILL, b Feb. 19, 1826, m Emily Wells. He d about 1863.
Issue:
  Elizabeth Hill, m Dr. John Winn Hollingsworth. He d 1899. Issue:
      Bernice Hollingsworth, b 1884, m in 1903 to Willie Bunker.
      Issue:
          Nelson French Bunker, b 1904.
      Mary Thekla Hollingsworth, b 1888.

---

*Jacob K. Hill served in the war of 1812 as Sergeant in Capt. Robert Twilley's Company. He was a mere lad at the time, but did his duty for his country. He was an intelligent man, and one in whom his friends could commit any trust. He was temperate in all things, abhorred strong drink, and was one of the first members of the Sons of Temperance in Mississippi. He was a Methodist and one of the founders of the Pleasant Hill Church, which was near his home, and in the graveyard close by lies his body beside that of his wife, Rebecca Sims Hill. In his day office sought the man, and when he was urged to accept a seat in the State Legislature, he served with credit in this as in other positions he occupied. He was known as the peace-maker in his neighborhood. His friends often came to him for adjustment of questions, knowing that he was just in everything. His home sheltered many who were bereft of parents, and his home was truly theirs while they remained under its roof. The Pleasant Hill School near by was a popular seat of learning, and the Hill home cared for many students there. Jacob K. Hill and his wife reared their children to be good citizens, and the qualities they inherited added to their strength of character.

*A native of Robinson Co., Tenn., but when quite young his parents moved to Mississippi. At the beginning of the war he joined McIntosh's Cavalry as a private, but was soon promoted to the position of Regimental Surgeon and soon afterwards to the position of Brigade Surgeon for Gen. McNair's Brigade.

†Sarah Ann Hill, when a young girl, was happily married to William Dorsey, a prosperous planter. Their married life was very short, as he died in a few years, leaving one little son, Hill Dorsey, who died aged 3 years. Her second marriage was to Dr. Grant. This relation existed only a few years, and Sarah Ann Hill was again a widow. Her third marriage was to Hamden J. Mackey then a widower with two little children, Rosa and Noel. The mother of these children was a cousin of their step-mother, who never showed any difference in her attention to them and to her own children. She was the mistress of one of the typical ante-bellum homes, with slaves and all of the enterprises that made life in those days so different from the present day civilization. The trying years of the war changed the regime, but our grandmother was equal to this change and accepted the privations as did so many women of that time. She was left a widow for the third time and remained one until her death, many years later. She was a devout Christian, a member of the Presbyterian Church. Her home was ever open, with a hearty welcome, to all ministers who came within reach of it. She had a great fondness for flowers, and the beautifully kept beds in her yard were ever free with their choicest blossoms to her grandchildren, who also knew that there were tea-cakes in plenty and other good things always ready for them. She gave the inspiration to the writer of this work for its beginning, and though she has gone to her heavenly home, her presence seems ever near when writing of the people that she knew and loved in the long ago.

**See picture.

†† Was a Confederate soldier, and died while on a furlough home, given on account of his illness.

ROBERT A. HILL, b Feb. 19, 1829, died young.

*MARY REBECCA HILL, b March 25, 1833, d Dec., 1892.

**JOHN ANDREW ELLISON HILL, b Feb. 9, 1824, d Dec. 17, 1855, m Frances Speed. She m 2nd William Cheek. (See his line.) Issue:

John William Sanders Hill, d age 7 months and 21 days.

Kate Hill, m William Long. Issue:

William Hill Long, d aged 5 years.

Kate Hill m 2nd William Barnes. No issue.

**†DR. LOUIS HOBBS HILL, b July 6, 1835, in Copiah Co., Miss., m Oct. 25, 1865, to Nancy Susan Otterson, of North Carolina. He d at Long Beach, Miss., April 19, 1897. Issue:

Claude Victor Hill, b in Louisiana, Sept. 23, 1869, d in California, in 1899.

Louis Killingsworth Hill, b in Central America, Aug. 31, 1868, m Nov. 6, 1907, to Sara Berryville Wright, of Virginia.

Three children, who died in infancy.

Lillian Aurelia Hill, b in British Honduras, Feb. 13, 1878, m Aug. 31, 1904, to Charles Wyatt Beeson. Issue:

Ruth Evelyn Beeson, b June 7, 1905. (See picture.)

WILLIAM THOMAS HILL, b Nov. 18, 1837, d Aug. 18, 1838.

NOTES.

FROM SARAH ANN HILL TO HER MOTHER, REBECCA G. HILL.

Gallatin, July 30, 1838.

Dear Mother:

Knowing that you are very anxious to hear from me, I will write you a few lines to let you know that I am well and very well pleased with my school and board, though I want to see you all very much. I am almost home-sick. I want you to send for me Friday, if convenient; if not, Friday week sure. Cousin M. Vaughan and Cousin L. Miller want you to send word to Mr. Miller and Mr. Vaughan to send for them at the same time you send for us and E. Greenlee. I have nothing new or strange to write. Mrs. Johnson's child is very ill at present. We have sat up with it for a week.

The girls all join me in love to you all. Tell sister she has forgotten me. Give my love to all inquiring friends and no others. Tell the children I have not forgotten them.

SARAH ANN HILL.

Give my love to father. Tell him he must come and see me.

FROM J. K. AND R. G. HILL TO SARAH ANN HILL, THEIR DAUGHTER.

Peasant, Dec. 22, 1849—11 O'clock at Night.

My Dear Sarah Ann:

As Harry is going to start to Jefferson again in the morning, I write you a few lines by him (or Bill), as Mr. Hill speaks of letting Bill go down with him. If Bill does go I wish Mr.

---

*Mary Rebecca Hill never married. She lived to old age beloved by all who were fortunate enough to enjoy her acquaintance. Afflicted from birth, she was denied many pleasures that would have otherwise been hers; but she was never embittered on account of her afflictions, instead, she always felt that she had so much to be thankful for. Many lessons in the Christian life were learned by her nieces and nephews and great-nieces and nephews from her wonderful fortitude in suffering and joy through afflictions. She lived with her sister, Mrs. Sarah Ann Mackey, and the little grandchildren of that family always looked forward with pleasure to seeing Aunt Mary, and always found something for themselves in Aunt Mary's room. Her piety began when a young girl and ripened with her years until at last she was more spiritual than physical, and her entrance into the better world was no long step. She simply went quietly away, but her presence will ever live with her loved ones. (See portion of diary on page 196.)

†Dr. Louis H. Hill graduated from the medical department of the University of Louisiana in 1859. After the war he moved to British Honduras, and returned to Mississippi about 1880, remaining in Mississippi till his death. His wife is a highly educated and cultured woman. She is advanced in years, but is enjoying life in the home of her daughter in Texas.

**See picture.

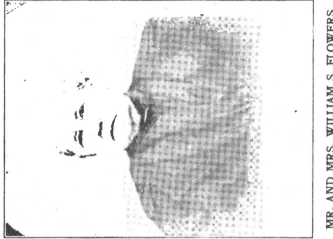

MR. AND MRS. WILLIAM S. FLOWERS
Page 189

McKey to take same care of him and his pony, as they may fare bad at some other place, as corn is scarce in some places and Bill's judgment is bad at best.

We are all well, and somewhat disappointed about Brother and Sister E. not coming, but will not be again without they do come. John and Fannie are here tonight, for the first time since she came from your house. We have had so much high water, or at least too high to ford. We had a call from some of our preachers as they returned from Conference—the Elder Wiggins and two Flyrs. They saw Brother L. on their way up, and said all were well. We are expecting Mr. Mackey to send his wagon up soon, and Mr. Hill says send a large wagon and strong team, so he may be paid for the trouble of sending it.

Smart has gone to Covington to help move Mr. Flowers, and we expected him back about this time, but he has not come yet. We are talking a good deal about traveling the road to Jefferson again before long. I hope it will not keep raining, so the roads will be too muddy to travel with comfort.

I hope if Aunt Middleton does come up she may come soon, or wait until I come back and then come and stay a long time, and I would like to have her company myself.

Mr. Hill and children join me in love to you and all your family.

We remain, ever your loving parents,

J. K. AND R. G. HILL.

Vernon, Miss., March 4, 1347.

Mr. J. K. Hill:

Dear Sir—I received yours from Jackson a few days since. I am glad to hear that you are well, for it is more than I can say. Mary has been ill all winter, and God knows whether she will ever get right well again, though she is now knocking about but looks badly. She talks of going up to Carroll this spring, and would be glad if you could go with her. I do not know what time she will start, but it will be sometime after the roads and weather become somewhat settled and before it gets too warm.

I shall start out to hunt me another place, as I am determined to leave next winter, well or not well. If I can succeed in making a good crop this year, I think we will get a good price for the next crop, which will enable me to purchase a place on the river or some of the bayous. There is too much hard work for but little profit.

I am in fine health and so are the children. Wallace is at Oakland College, where I rather think I shall keep him for four or five years. The little girls I have at school some seven miles from home, and I bring them home every Friday evening. They are doing well. Give my respects to your family, and keep a portion for yourself.

Yours, etc.   ELI T. MONTGOMERY.

(Portion of a letter from Eli T. Montgomery to Hon. Jacob K. Hill, received by him while he was a member of the Mississippi Legislature.)

PORTIONS OF DIARY OF MISS MARY REBECCA HILL.

This diary, written by Aunt Mary when she was a young girl, has been carefully kept, and gives a clearer insight into her beautiful Christian character than words of the writer could portray or picture of her lovely face:

TUESDAY, MAY 11, 1858.

So cool this morning that a good, big fire is required to make us at all comfortable, and, indeed, I wore my blanket shawl till 12 o'clock.

While at the breakfast table Ma received a note from sister stating that she had an idea of going as far with Mr. McKey (on his way to Raymond) as Utica, and wished her to go, too, requesting at the same time that I should stay with the children while she was gone, as Lizzie was quite sick last night. So as soon as Ma and I could make ready we were off with Rosa at full speed. R. and I had quite a quiet day. I read two Advocates through and sewed a little on Clara's dress.

When I read of such glowing accounts of revivals so numerous, I have an inexpressable feeling of joy and sadness—joy to know that others are being blessed, sadness to know that our church is so destitute of the spirit of revivalism, so little zeal among us. Oh! Divine Father, when will we awake? Grant that it may not be long till the good spirit that is abroad in the land may favor us with a gracious visitation of His power, which is able to "kill and make alive."

Mr. Scott (Uncle Bob) had intelligence that the life of Isaac Williams was despaired of, and his wife wished some of the relatives to go to Lexington immediately. So Ma, Aunt Ibbie and Jimmie S. start tomorrow.

SATURDAY, JUNE 20, 1858.

Have been so engaged all the week attending to the sick that I have scarcely had time to read any, much less to write. Ma and Mrs. Taylor are both better, much better, today.

I went to the hall, where I heard one of Bro. Johnson's best and warmest sermons. We had a good class meeting also. When we went to start home Aunt B. found that her horse was missing and proposed that we should take her in our buggy till she would meet or overtake her horse, as she was rather in a hurry that she might be able to get to the Tabernacle to attend 4 o'clock prayer meeting. We overtook her horse foraging in the big lane, and she got on it and we, that is Amelia and I, came around by Mr. McKey's, where I had promised to call on my way back. Found sister so much better that she was up stirring around, making preparation for the reception of Mrs. Cunningham on Monday.

THURSDAY, OCT. 7, 1858.

Was called out last night to take a view of the wonderful comet. How remarkably luminous it has become!

Finished a letter to Mrs. Josie Sims, then went to prayer meeting, where we met only about a dozen persons. The meeting was conducted by "Uncle Bob" this time, Bro. Barnes' family being so much afflicted he could not leave them.

FRIDAY, SEPT. 30, 1859.

Having been up last night till after 12, feel quite stupid. Rosa was married about 7 o'clock, and sat up till after 11, after having been sick in bed all the week. Astonishing!

Heard last night at the wedding some good news with regard to the Steel Chapel meeting, which quite revived me. Would that I could be there, too! But certainly I should be thankful for the privileges I have already enjoyed, for they have quite exceeded my expectations, far as it regards attending meetings. If I am so highly favored as to get to attend the camp meeting, how very grateful I shall be.

Today unbelief and Satan in various ways are disturbing my peace. but by the help of my great Redeemer I shall not give up my hold. What a frail, weak creature I am. My God, forbid that I should trust one moment to myself! How good and gracious the Lord is, to bear with one's so many infirmities with so much patience!

I felt astonished when I found myself actually nodding while reading the sacred truths even this day. O may I never read that blessed Word so carelessly again.

I go to Aunt Betsy's after Ma returns from Mr. McKey's.

SUNDAY, OCT. 16, 1859.

Had Mrs. Hilborne and Miss Turnley with us yesterday.

Today has been a blessed day of rest to my soul. Went with Ma to class, and our leader being absent, the duty of conducting the meeting devolved on Bro. Boren. It seemed such a cross to him; but there was but one way to do to avoid going around it, that was to take it up. We sung for his encouragement as well as our own

> "Shall Jesus bear the cross alone,
> And you and I go free?
> No, there's a cross for every one,
> A cross for you and me."

Resolved there to call in our servants tonight and read the Word of God to them, talk to them and sing and pray with them, in addition to my custom of catechising them; but the excessive badness of the weather seemed to render it impracticable this time. I feel that my talent is very feeble, but believe the Lord has given me one sufficent to reach the intellect and hearts of the poor negroes, and may God forbid that I should put it away in a napkin when poor, ignorant servants are starving for the Word of Life merely because they cannot read. I feel that there is an awful responsibility resting upon owners of servants with regard to their souls. In a degree it is as binding as that of parent and child—may I not say more so, for natural affection prompts the latter in many instances to make exertions for the spiritual benefit of the child. How awful to think of servants coming up at the last day of accounts and charging masters and mistresses with the fearful neglect of this duty! O, Father, awaken, enlighten us fully on this important subject and help us to do our whole duty irrespective of what "people say."

Took for my evening lesson the whole of Mark, and while reading how our Saviour surprised the disciples when He came in the ship, and how they had forgotten His past miracles, the thought came forcibly to my mind, How like Christians of the present day! How prone are we to forget past blessing till our hearts, too, become hardened. O, dear Saviour, increase in us a lively sense of Thy goodness to us and of our dependence upon Thee.

SUNDAY, MAY 20, 1860.

More than a month has elapsed since noting in my journal. O, the conflicts, the trials and afflictions I have endured in this short month! The chastening rod of my Heavenly Father has been laid heavily upon me, but at the same time His promise was verified in that He said, "My grace is sufficient."

My dear mother, whose health had been very poor for months, was taken violently ill on the night of the 25th and suffered on till the 8th instant at 12 o'clock. With what intense anxiety I watched by her bedside these two weeks!—hoping and praying that if consistent with the Divine will she might be spared to her devoted children yet a while longer, but He that is too wise to err and too good to be unkind saw fit to remove her from her suffering life here below to one of eternal happiness.

Before we thought she would die she drew me to her and kissed me, saying, "This is the last spell of sickness I shall ever have." This was more than a week before she left us. When I told her it seemed hard for me to endure the thought of her leaving us so soon, she said, "Yes, I know it is; but you must be resigned, for I feel that it shall not be long till we shall all meet again in heaven. The promise is, the grace of God is sufficient, and you must trust Him for that grace and say, 'Thy will be done.'" Said she had tried to live in reverence to eternity, and that the Lord had been so good in sparing her to raise all her children, and now her work was done. Speaking of her suffering, said, "It seems hard, but I know it is right." "Yes, Ma, said I, "Our Saviour was made perfect through suffering." "Yes," said she, "if He had to suffer in order to be made perfect, how much more need I to suffer to be made perfect?" She often spoke of rest. Said none knew how to appreciate the Word till brought where she was. Such expressions as these she was often heard to utter: "There is rest for the weary." "O heaven, sweet heaven, when shall I see, O when shall I get there," "My suffering will soon be over," etc.

Uncle Nixon came down on Thursday, as an angel of mercy. She conversed a little with him, though exceedingly low and weak. On leaving he promised to return Monday, which he did. Now Ma was too weak to converse, but answered his questions very satisfactorily by the motion of head and other signs. He remained with us till after preaching her funeral on Wednesday.

O, what an unspeakable satisfaction it was to have him here at such a time! After praying at her bedside I proposed that we should try to sing "O, Sing to Me of Heaven." This I did because she had years ago requested that that should be sung when she was dying. Though deprived of the power of speech, she seemed perfectly conscious of all that was going on around her, and seemed to enjoy both the singing and praying. Uncle Nixon preached her funeral to a large congregation, from Thess. 1:13-14.

How dreary and lonely home feels without a mother. Friends I have kind and true, but none of these can fill the place of that dear friend, yet all bow and kiss the rod that chastens, knowing that all the momentary afflictions shall work out for us a far more exceeding and eternal weight of glory. O, how could I endure this stroke had I not the precious promises on my side? At least, had I not strength granted me to rely upon them. O, for more faith! O for more of the Holy Spirit!

Have been at home alone most of this lovely Sabbath. Have been nearly sick enough to take my bed. Been reading in my Bible, guide and closet companion. The Old Testament I have just finished.

SATURDAY, NOV. 24, 1860.

Monday spent the day, with several others, at Mr. McKey's. Tuesday and Wednesday at home. Thursday at Mr. Hilburn's. Yesterday at home. This morning Bro. J. and Em, Sallie and Amelia went to Bethesda to church. How I wanted to go with them! but could not conveniently. Soon after they started in came Mr. Brown and Cousin Caroline, and spent the day with us.

What work I did this evening was preparing for tomorrow. Had yeast made of salt rising and made excellent bread—the first light bread we have had for months—the difficulty having always been to get the yeast to rise.

How glad I am that the approaching day is Sabbath. May it be a Sabbath of rest to my soul! Conscious am I of having been unfaithful, but blessed be God, I have the assurance that though my sins be as scarlet they shall be as wool. How thankful I am that I have an High Priest who can be touched with a feeling of my infirmity.

MONDAY, DEC. 3, 1860.

Started this evening to see poor Burnette die, but heard before leaving home that she was no more among the living, but numbered with the dead. It was hard, hard indeed for sister to give her up, and the children it seemed would go distracted. Never would she have lost a more valuable servant unless it would be Caroline. How uncertain is life; how certain is death! A few weeks ago poor Burnette was the very picture of health.

Uncle Nixon remained with us today till after 1 o'clock.

FRIDAY, DEC. 28, 1860.

Just now Bro. J. and Miss Sallie are scuffling for material to make an eggnog, it being against my principles to favor anything of the kind Would not give them eggs, so they playfully took them without permission

O, how I have wished it was convenient for me to attend some meeting during these holidays! How much better would I have enjoyed myself than I have.

Am trying to spend this day in self-examination, and as a means to help in the exercise have devoted it to fasting and prayer. But how hard it is tp get my mind composed when there is so much confusion of sound. Really, the cares of the day now somewhat distract and draw off my poor, unsettled mind.

O, for one hour's quietude! O, that more solemnity and humility pervaded all our hearts! I fear that our conversation is not such as becometh saints, but is mixed too much with the world.

I am determined to reprove sin more faithfully in future, if the Lord will help me. Heretofore I have been remiss in this respect, as well as in many others, but He who tryeth the heart knows that I have endeavored to live right. But

O to grace, how great a debtor
Daily I'm constrained to be.

CHILDREN OF JOHN HILL AND SARAH KILLINGSWORTH—Continued.

WINIFRED HILL, b March 19, 1797, m Mr. Vaughan. Issue:
BENNIE VAUGHAN, m three times. No issue.

WM. BROWN HILL, b Jan. 20, 1800.

MARY MALINDA HILL, b March 20, 1802, m ‡Judge William Y. Collins. Issue:
SARAH COLLINS, m Dr. W. W. Dabney. Issue:
Bartlett Dabney.
William Dabney.
**Cammie Dabney.
**THOMAS C. COLLINS, m Miss Neeley, of Bolivar, Tenn.
BETTIE COLLINS, m Reuben Baskin.
MOLLIE COLLINS, m Dr. W. L. Stovall. Issue:
Ann Stovall, m Mr. Veasey, of New Orleans.

---

*She never married. She lived with her sister, Sarah Ann Hill McKey, and her life was a benediction to all who knew her.

‡Judge William Y. Collins built a beautiful home at Middleton, Miss. He was a prominent man of affairs in Madison County. He reared his wife's orphan niece, Mary Newland, and her son, J. N. Lipscomb, now of Flora, Miss., was a frequent visitor to his home in childhood. An effort has been made to communicate with his descendants, but no answers have been received.

**Cammie Dabney and Thomas C. Collins once lived in Memphis. Mrs. Baskin lived at Winona, Miss.

FROM MARY COLLINS TO REBECCA SIMS HILL.

March 11, 1839.

Dear Mother:

We received a letter from Sister Rebecca, or rather Elizabeth, and sister stating that poor Brother Newland was dead. This was mournful intelligence to me on account of his little children, but thanks to the God of wisdom and goodness for the evidence of his having gone to rest, and O Lord grant that we may be prepared to meet him with all our friends that have gone before, where parting will be no more.

I hope you and your dear little children are well, although Elizabeth wrote me that you had been very much afflicted this winter with your face, which I am sorry to hear; but we can only hope for the best, that is, that all our afflictions may be sanctified to the good of our never-dying souls.

My dear mother, my weak prayer to God is that your last days may be your best days, and that you may have your lamp trimmed and burning, for we know not what hour He may come. May we be watchful and prayerful while we live in the world, and pray for your children, dear mother.

I think I mentioned in Elizabeth's letter that I would be down about the 20th of April, but I think it will be uncertain whether I can come down before the 1st of May. Our horse, Peter, is crippled; I fear he will not be fit for the road then. Mother, could you come up and spend the summer with me? I want you to think about it and see if you can reconcile yourself to come. We are going to have the old borouch dressed and a new harness got for it. I shall have my children at home, and can not stay long with my friends when I go down.

Now may the God of all peace be with you and bless you all.

Affectionately,   MARY. COLLINS.

My love to the little children, sister and family, Andrew and family. Adieu.

LETTER TO JACOB K. HILL FOR WM. Y. COLLINS, WHO MARRIED MARY HILL.

Vernon, Sept. 13, 1833.

Dear Brother:

Yours of the 3rd instant come duly to hand. I made one attempt to write, but failed.

I was glad to learn that our friends in your neighborhood who had been sick were beginning to mend. My family has been quite sickly. Malinda was unwell some time ago, but at this time is quite well; so also is her babe. Some of my negroes are still sick. Have given more medicine in the past two months than I have had occasion to give in the eight years that preceded. Our country is getting in better health. Cases are not so frequent nor are they so desperate. Many have fallen and many have quaked.

I intended sending down for Mother Hill about the 1st, but hearing she is not in very good health and thinking probably she would not be able to ride, have deferred it. Hope, however, she will come to see us as soon as she is able to ride.

Mrs. Bode is with us, and she and her child are well.

Corn crops with us are good; cotton not so good.

Give my compliments to your good lady, also to Mother Hill.

Respectfully,   WM. Y. COLLINS.

DAUGHTER OF JOHN HILL AND SARAH K. HILL.

SARAH MATILDA HILL, b Dec. 15, 1806, m John Newland. Both died young, leaving two little daughters. Issue:

MARY NEWLAND, b April 20, 1832, in Copiah Co., Miss., m Thomas A. Lipscomb, in 1859. He was b Dec. 31, 1828, and d in 1903. Issue:

*John Newland Lipscomb, b Jan. 24, 1862, m Nov. 28, 1888, to Mamie Lipscomb, dau of Joseph F. Lipscomb. She was b March, 1866. Issue:

---

*John Newland Lipscomb has given valuable assistance in compiling the above record. He has a fondness for family history, and besides being an active business man, is a popular and entertaining friend to many who enjoy his acquaintance.

John Newland Lipscomb, b Oct. 22, 1889, d Nov. 2, 1902.
Pat Henry Newland, b July 30, 1895, d June 14, 1902.
Frances Willard Newland, b Nov., 1897, d Sept., 1898.
Hellen Newland, b March 7, 1904.   (See picture.)
William Collins Newland, b Dec. 22, 1864, d 1897, m Jeanie Cook. Issue:
  Willie Lipscomb (dau.)
Margaret Lipscomb, b Aug., 1874, m R. A. Dakin, 1899. No issue.
  †Francis Lipscomb, b 1876, d 1900
JOHN NEWLAND, d in infancy.
MARGARET NEWLAND, b 1834, m 1860, to Dr J. W. Lipscomb, a brother of Thos.
A. Lipscomb, son of John Lipscomb and Emeline Andrews. He was b in 1836,
d 1901. Issue:
  Jack Hawkins Lipscomb, b Jan. 12, 1862.
  Emeline Lipscomb, b Jan. 17, 1864, d Aug. 27, 1904, m N. B. Howard, in
    1887. Issue:
      H. C. Howard, b Sept. 18, 1899.
      Percy Howard, b Feb. 8, 1901.
  Harry Andrews Lipscomb, b June 25, 1867, m Octavie Denson, in 1898.
    Issue:
      Maggie Lipscomb, b 1900.
      Ellen Lipscomb, b 1902.
  Maria T. Lipscomb, b Aug. 6, 1873, d Aug. 8, 1910, m J. N. McLeod, in
    Oct., 1902. Issue:
      J. N. McLeod, b Aug., 1903.
      Norma Marie, b March, 1905.
  Frank Montgomery Lipscomb, b July 17, 1876.
  Anna Lou Lipscomb, b July, 1878, m Frank Glick, Feb. 15, 1896. Issue:
    Elizabeth Monty Glick, b April 7, 1898.
    Frank Lipscomb Glick, b Dec. 6, 1907.
  Bessie Jane Lipscomb, b Nov. 29, 1880, m James Lamar Coon, June 30,
    1902. Issue:
      Alice Elizabeth Coon, b Jan. 8, 1904.

SON OF JOHN HILL AND SARAH KILLINGSWORTH HILL.

ANDREW JACKSON HILL, b in Jefferson Co., Miss., April 14, 1814, d 1855, m Elizabeth
Jenkins, Dec. 11, 1834. Issue:
  SUE M. HILL, m Dec. 20, 1866, to William West Johnston. Issue:
    Mary Hill Johnston, m Charles D. Walcott. Issue:
      Charles DeWitt Walcott.
      Willie Mae Walcott.
      Keneth Myles Walcott.
    Pearl Rose Johnston, b 1872, m 1894 to William Adeson Walker. Issue:
      W. A. Walker, b 1898.
  ‡FRANCES CORINNE HILL, b Aug. 8, 1838, m **DeWitt Clinton Vaughan, Jan. 10,

---

‡Frances Corinne Hill, b Aug. 8, 1838, m DeWitt Clinton Vaughan, Jan. 10, 1856. Was left a widow August 6, 1872,
with five children, the oldest 13 years old. She struggled to rear her children right. Her last days were days of bodily
suffering, but were borne with fortitude. She was a timid and shrinking woman, never wanting any praise for what
she did.

**"I will write you a little incident that occurred while he was in Dr. Dudley Jones' company. Dr. Dudley Jones
told Mama that once they were thinking of being in battle. He asked his men if there was one who would wear his
uniform, as he was nervous, and said my father came forward readily and told him he would take his place. He answered,
'No, Clint, you are too good a man to take it. I'll wear my own clothes.' My father was first in the infantry, but on
account of delicate health was transferred to the cavalry.

ZILPHA VAUGHAN TOWNSEND."

†Enlisted in the Spanish-American war, contracted tuberculosis and died.

1856. He d Aug. 6, 1872. Issue:

    Ella Vaughan, b March 29, 1857, m R. H. Hudson, Jan. 13, 1876. Issue
        James George Hudson, b Nov. 10, 1876.
        Richardson Vaughan Hudson, b Dec. 11, 1887.
        Welch Bolton Hudson, b Jan. 28, 1892, d Sept. 29, 1910.
        Alice Corinne Hudson, b Oct. 29, 1893.
        Sarah Belle Hudson, b June 3, 1898.
    Ida Vaughan, b July 16, 1861.
    Margaret Elizabeth Vaughan, b Nov. 1, 1864, m L. A. Holliday, Jan. 20,
      1885. He was b Oct. 24, 1861. Issue:
        T. DeWitt Holliday, b Nov. 9, 1885.
        Lottie Holliday, b March 14, 1887, m Earl Ainsworth, Nov. 16,
          1908. Issue:
            Clayton Earl Ainsworth, b Aug. 27, 1909.
            Doris Elizabeth Ainsworth, b Nov. 18, 1910.
        Mamie Zilpha Holliday, b April 7, 1891.
        Annie Peyton Holliday, b Dec. 16, 1899.
    Andrew Hill Vaughan, b July 25, 1867, d March 17, 1896.
    Zilpha Ann Vaughan, b Dec. 31, 1871, m Jan. 13, 1903, to John E. Town-
      send. He was b Feb. 14, 1852. Issue:
        Carrie Lee Townsend, b Feb. 2, 1904.

OTHER CHILDREN OF ROBERT HILL.

JANE HILL, b 1767.

MARGARET HILL, b 1771, possibly married William Oliphant.

ANDREW ALLISON HILL, b 1772.

ELIZABETH HILL, b 1774, m Ely K. Ross. (See page 40.)

MARY HILL, m Dr. *Robert Knox and settled in Tennessee, near Newport.

ROBERT HILL, b 1779. No records.

JANE OLIPHANT HILL, b 1782, m Isaac Arthur Brown Ross. (See page 47.)

*Dr. Robert Knox is mentioned frequently in the diary of Arthur Brown Ross.

CHAPTER XII.

THE HARRIS FAMILY.

The Harris family originated in Weltshire, England, from whence members of the family emigrated to Ayrshire, Scotland, and later to America.

Tradition current in the family is that Samuel Harris, the progenitor of the branch of the family under discussion, had *five sons, Col. Robert, James, Samuel, Charles and Thomas; that three of these sons came to America and after locating, sent for their father and two brothers, and that Samuel, the father, died at sea, in sight of land, in 1728, and was buried on Manhattan Island by his two sons.

This family first settled in Pennsylvania and remained till about 1730, when possibly on account of the persecution then inflicted by strict religious laws, they decided to change their abode. North Carolina offered a suitable home for the persecuted, and the Harris brothers were among the first settlers in the region in and around Mecklenberg County.

Samuel Harris is said to have been the first settler in what is now Mecklenberg County. The following is told of his coming to this part of North Carolina: He married Martha Laird, who had come over on the same vessel to America. After he had married Martha in Pennsylvania he came to his brothers in North Carolina, about Poplar Tent. They recommended that he go on to what is now Rocky River Congregation and settle there. The tradition is that he went and selected a location for his house and cut down a tree for boards. When he had cut off a log he could not split it. He went back to his brothers and reported that he could not find any board timber that would split. They told him that this could not be the case, and went with him to help build his house. They showed him a board tree right in his yard. After they had cut off a cut they went to his former board tree to get a wedge, and found it was a sweet gum tree. They soon built his house, and he moved his family there. He is said to

*Mr. J. W. Slaughter, of Goodwater, Ala., says that in 1865 Edwin Wiley, a grand-son of Samuel and Martha Laird Harris, told him that three brothers, Robert, James and Charles, came first from Ireland and then from Pennsylvania and settled in North Carolina, and that afterwards the balance of the family came to Pennsylvania, the father having died when in sight of land and having been buried on shore, and after landing Samuel married Martha Laird, who came over on the same ship and went to his brothers in North Carolina. This Edwin Wiley died in 1865 at an advanced age. This makes it appear that at least three of the brothers came ahead of the father. The uniform tradition in my own family (which is from James), and in the family of Charles of Poplar Tent, is that the sons came first and after them the father. REV. J. C. HARRIS.

—200—

have been the first settler in what is now Mecklenberg County, N. C. The third day after he had moved in he heard an axe, and on going to it found that a Mr. Alexander had moved in on the previous day. He was the second settler in what is now Mecklenberg. The two families formed the nucleus of Rocky River Church, and were the ancestors of the large number of Harrises and Alexanders of Mecklenberg County, North Carolina.

The Harris family in North Carolina is descended from the brothers above mentioned and from Robert Harris, who was born in the County of Donegal, Province of Ulster, on August 26, 1702. About 1745 he came to America and settled in Lancaster County, Pennsylvania, where he lived until 1766, when he settled on Rocky River, where the church now stands. He died Dec. 26, 1788. He brought three children with him to North Carolina, viz.:

WILLIAM, born in Pennsylvania, Jan. 1, 1755, married Ann Maddly.
ROBERT, married Elleanor Ross.
MARY, married Alexander Ferguson.

Dr. Charles Harris, "the Surgeon" of Poplar Tent, called this William Harris (above), "Cousin Billy."

Robert, Jr., lived about ten miles from Harrisburg, in Cabarrus County, near Clear Creek. This Robert and his brother William corresponded with relatives in Pennsylvania. Some of their correspondence is in the hands of their Rocky River descendants today.

Confusion naturally arises in distinguishing the members of these families who lived in the same sections of the country about the same time. There are at present three distinct Harris families in Mecklenberg County, and many detached members of other families that bear the name.

FIRST CHILD OF SAMUEL HARRIS, WHO DIED AT SEA.

ROBERT HARRIS, known throughout the family as Col. Robert and Robert of Reedy Creek, was possibly the most prominent of the five Harris brothers. He was one of the officers appointed by Gov. Tryon and participated in the battle of the Regulators; and his name is attached to the report of the officers declining to fight when they reached the Yadkin River. (See Wheeler's History of North Carolina.) "On May 20, 1776, when the delegates had met to declare independence, Robert Harris, a member of the convention, arose and addressed the chair, saying: 'If you resolve on independence, how shall we all be absolved from the obligations of the oath we took to be true to King George the Third, about four years ago, after the Regulation battle, when we were sworn, whole militia companies together? I should be glad to know how gentlemen can clear their consciences after taking that oath?' The speaker referred to the blood shed by Gov. Tryon on the 16th of May, 1771, on Almance Creek, when he dispensed the Regulators, men driven to open resistance of his Majesty's officers by their tyranny and exactions; and to numerous executions that followed in Hillsborough and the neighboring country; and to the oath of allegiance forced on the people by the Governor, to save their lives and property, after that bloodshed. The question produced great confusion, and many attempted to reply; the chairman could with difficulty preserve order. The question did not imply fear, or want of patriotism; it simply revealed the spirit and tone of the man's conscience, and that he was one of those blessed of the Lord, 'who sweareth to his own heart, and changeth not.' The excitement that followed evinced the fact that the speaker had struck a chord that vibrated through the assembly." (Taken from Foote's Sketches of North Carolina.)

This occurrence caused Col. Robert Harris to be spoken of as a Tory, although he was not a Tory in an obnoxious sense, as was proved by the fact that he held office throughout the Revolutionary war.

He was appointed Register of Deeds of Mecklenberg County in 1763, and served till 1793. This was possibly the first office held in Mecklenberg County, and the records of the county between those dates show in many instances the bold, clear handwriting of Col. Harris.

Col. Robert Harris's wife's name has not yet been found. She was possibly dead at the time of making his will, as no mention is made of her in the will. He died about 1798. as the will was made in 1796 and codicil in 1798.

WILL OF COL. ROBERT HARRIS.

In the name of God, amen. I, Robert Harris, being in my ordinary state of health, blessed be God for all His mercies to me, calling to mind mortality of my body, do make this my last will and testament:

First—I order all my just debts to be paid, with funeral expenses.

Second—I bequeath to my son, Robert Harris, my negro Harris, and admise my son to sell said negro in this neighborhood so that he may live near his parents. I also bequeath to my son my watch and one bed and clothes, also my book, M. S. Baxter, and Shaw's two books, and Milton's Paradise Lost and Gained, and my body cloth and my new saddle. Secondly, I bequeath to my daughter Elizabeth my negroes, Dublin, Cloe, Prince and Charles. I order my negro Sal to go with Cloe, so that my daughter may take care of her, as she has the fits, the said negroes to continue in her possession during her life, and at her death she may dispose of them as she thinks proper. I bequeath to my grandson, Major James Harris, my negro Melinda. I bequeath to my grand-daughter Grizel one bed and clothes and two cows and two calves, and also my little negro, Liney, daughter to Malinda. I also bequeath to my grand-daughter, Dorcas John Cochran's wife, 40 lbs, to be paid in two years after my death. I will and bequeath to my son-in-law, Samuel Harris, one English shillings. I order my executors to pay the heirs of Robert McMurry 15 lbs, the remainder of William Campbell's estate. I bequeath to my daughter Elizabeth the remainder of what furniture is in my house not mentioned above, the oval table excepted, which I order to be sold. I order all my land to be sold and every part of my property not mentioned above, and after paying the above legacy the money arising from the sale and what may be in my hands at my death to be equally divided between my son Robert and my daughter Elizabeth, to be by them possessed and enjoyed. I ordain and appoint my whole and sole executors my grandson, James Harris, and Edward Giles, Esq., revoking all former wills by me made.

In testimony whereof, I set my hand and seal this 25th day of January, 1796.

Signed, sealed and delivered in the presence of Charles Harris, Robert Cochran, William Harris.　　　　(Signed)　　　　　　ROBERT HARRIS. (Seal.)

---

*"I feel pretty sure that Col. Robert Harris lies in old Coddle Creek Cemetery. I think he was the oldest of the five brothers. The descendants of his in North Carolina were much agrieved over his so-called adherence to the King, and let his name drop from their records. The discovery of the will was a revelation to me. I cannot find out where it is recorded in court, but I am going to try to find out. In my own father's day I used to hear them talk about 'the Tory.' and then about the fortune in Jamaica left by his son. Robert, and the old cousin, who used to tell me so much, said that it was believed he would have divided it between his sister's children, Levi and Rosa, but they were in the Far West, and then he left no will, and nobody seemed to know how to establish the claim for any of the connection. Nor did they know where his father was buried. and no one knew the name of the ship upon which Samuel died and which brought the brothers to America. I think two of the brother, Robert and James, came over first. It is clear that two of Samuel Harris's sons (Samuel, who married Martha Laird, father of Matthew, etc.), James and Samuel (called Sr.), married sisters, daughters of Col. Robert, but in the records of their children the names of the mothers are not mentioned "

　　　　　　　　　　　　　　　　　　　　　　　　　　　　　LYDIA HARRIS CRAIG.

ISSUE OF COL. ROBERT HARRIS, OF REEDY CREEK.

ROBERT HARRIS, died unmarried. He went to Jamaica and amassed a large fortune. He visited his relatives in North Carolina and Mississippi about 1816.

ELIZABETH HARRIS, m a cousin, Mr. Harris, and had issue:

**ROSANA HARRIS, m Daniel Mackey, in Mississippi. (See his line for issue.)

*LEVI CUNNINGHAM HARRIS, brother of Rosanna Harris and son of Elizabeth Harris, m Lucy Anne Green Carpenter, April 20, 1833. Issue:

Marie Louise Harris, b 1834, d 1834.

Levi Cabell Harris, b 1836, d 1836.

Elizabeth Savage Harris, b Dec. 25, 1837, d in Vicksburg, Miss., May 25, 1873, m to John Templeton Green, of Vicksburg. He died Oct. 9, 1892. Issue:

Thomas Marston Green, b at White Hall, Claiborne Co., Miss., May 27, 1864.

Elizabeth Harris Green, b in Clinton, Miss., Sept. 30, 1865, m April 11, 1888, in Selma, Ala., to §Junius Moore Riggs, of Montgomery, Ala.

Sidney Stewart Green, b 1868, d 1871.

Harris Green, b at Goodrich Landing, La., Sept. 5, 1870, d January, 1899.

Frank Templeton Green, b 1872, d 1874.

Mary Bradford Harris, b May 14, 1843, m †H. M. Coulson, of Port Gibson, Miss. Issue:

Lucy Hughes Coulson, b March, 1872, m July 20, 1893, to W. G. Millinder.

Lucy Anne Harris, b July 9, 1845, m May 4, 1872, to ‡Daniel Partridge, of Mobile, Ala. Issue:

Daniel Partridge, b March 3, 1873, m Nov., 1903, to Grace S. Solomon, of Maryland. Issue:

Daniel Partridge, b July 16, 1906.

Preston Hughes Partridge, b Sept. 27, 1874, m Bessie Du-Laney, of St. Louis, Mo., Aug. 13, 1902. Issue:

Preston Hughes Partridge, b June 2, 1903.

Charles Stevens Partridge, b July, 1906.

---

‡Daniel Partridge enlisted in the 3rd Ala., and served three years as 1st lieut. of his company. The balance of the war he was Inspector and Ordnance Officer of Battle's Brigade, Rodes' Division, Army of Northern Virginia.

*Levi C. Harris was in the war of 1812. Cavalry, under Major Thomas Hinds. Was shot through the right shoulder in the battle of New Orleans, Jan. 8, 1815, and lost the use of his right arm and hand. He was a successful merchant, an elegant gentleman and devoted Christian. He moved to Clinton, Miss., to educate his children, and died there Jan. 28, 1863. His wife died nine years before, Jan. 12, 1854.

**Daniel Mackey and wife, Rosana Harris, his brother, Hugh Mrekey, and wife, came to Mississippi about 1810. The census for that year contained their names. Levi C. Harris, the brother of Rosa, might have come at the same time, but his name was not on the records of that year as contained in the Hall of History of Mississippi. The mother of Rosa and Levi Harris married a second time, and had two sons that lived to be grown. Her husband was named Snider, and may have been Adam Snider, who came to Mississippi at the same time Daniel Mackey came, and in 1810 this Adam Snider had three males under 21, one female over 21 and three females under 21 in his family. Of the children of Rosa Harris's mother by the Snider marriage only two sons were known by our family. One Ranson, always known as Uncle Ranson, made his home with Grandfather Hamden Jordan Mackey, and never married. My mother has a very pleasant recollection of this old uncle, and his daguerreotype shows a very neat, pleasant-faced old gentleman, too good for the sad fate that was his. During the Civil war he went with a number of wagons to Louisiana for salt, and was captured by the Yankees while he was trying to cross the river near Natchez, put on a gun-boat, and never heard of any more. I have often wished that I knew what his fate was. The other Snider son was named Alonso, and I do not know what became of him.

Members of the family in North Carolina visited the Mississippi relatives, and one cousin of Levi Harris, who taught school near him, used to write back to North Carolina of Levi and his family. This school teacher cousin used to say that Jamaica Bob intended leaving his fortune to the children of Levi and Rosanna.

§Junius Moore Riggs is State Supreme Court Librarian of Alabama.

†H. M. Coulson served through the war as a private in company K, 12th Miss., C. S. A., and was severely wounded at Frasier's Farm, June 30, 1862.

Lucy Green Partridge, b May 4, 1876, m June 1, 1907, to Frederic McRae Hatch, of Greensboro, Ala.

Charles Stevens Partridge, b June 30, 1879.

Mary Winslow Partridge, b April 29, 1881,

Mildred Cabell Partridge, b 1883, d 1884.

Martha Augusta Harris, b Feb. 9, 1847, d July 17, 1872, m Oct. 12, 1870, to **Dr. W. C. McCaleb, of Adams Co., Miss. Issue:

Lucy Augusta McCaleb, b May 10, 1872, m Nov. 22, 1898, to C. A. Morris. Issue:

Elizabeth McCaleb Morris, b Oct. 29, 1899.

Charles E. Morris, b Nov. 6, 1900, d May, 1901.

Lucy Augusta Morris, b Nov. 15, 1901.

Eugenia Cristler Morris, b Oct. 15, 1903.

Pearly May Morris, b Aug. 22, 1905.

William Collins Morris, b Sept. 23, 1909.

JAMES, SECOND SON OF SAMUEL HARRIS, WHO DIED AT SEA.

Nothing is known of James Harris expect that he lived and died at Poplar Tent or in that region. The Anson County records show him to have been one of the first and one of the largest land owners about the forks of Rocky River.

WILL OF JAMES HARRIS.

State of North Carolina, Mecklenburg Co., Oct. 14, 1778.

In the name of God, amen. I, James Harris, of the county and state aforesaid, being in perfect health and sound mind, in the exercise of my reason and judgment, but considering the mortality of my body and knowing it is appointed for all men once to die, I do hereby constitute and appoint this my last will and testament (hereby do revoke, make void and disannul all former wills and testaments made by me.) Imprimis: I commit my soul into the hands of a merciful Creator.

Item—I commit my body to be decently interred in the earth, at the discretion of my dear wife and executors.

Item—I order all my lawful debts and funeral expenses to be paid.

Item—I bequeath to my dear wife four half ichanuas in gold money and likewise 40 pounds proclamation money, her bed and bed clothes. I also bequeath to my dear wife during her lifetime the use of the plantation I now live on, together with all the implements, improvements and appurtenances thereunto belonging, likewise one negro fellow Lewis and one horse, she shall make the choice of, belonging to my estate. Also three cows and one 2-year-old steer and four sheep and one set of plow-irons. Also my household furniture, except what shall hereafter be bequeathed. And at her demise I order that the said articles (except one bed out of the above, which bed I order to be given to my daughter, Jennett's, son Baptiste) be sold and equally divided among all my children.

Item—I bequeath to my son Robert all my wearing apparel.

Item—I bequeath to my daughter, Jennett, 15 pounds lawful money of the state, her bed and bed-clothes, her saddle and spinning-wheel. I also order 100 pounds to be put to interest, and the interest arising from said 100 pounds to be paid to her annually as long as she lives, and at her demise the said 100 pounds to be equally divided among all the children.

Item—I bequeath to my daughter Mary 15 pounds, her bed and bed-clothes, her saddle and spinning-wheel. I also order that 100 pounds be put at interest, and that the interest arising from the said 100 pounds be paid to her annually as long as she lives, and at her demise the said 100 pounds be equally divided among all my children.

Item—I order that 100 pounds be put to interest, and that the interest arising from said 100 pounds be paid to my daughter Jennett's son, Baptiste's, use, for his maintenance as long as he lives, and at his demise the said 100 pounds to be equally divided among all my children.

Item—I order that what is over and above, or remains, of my estate after the above legacies are paid off, be sold and equally divided among all my children, viz: Robert, Samuel, Jennett, John, James, Elizabeth, William and Mary, and if any one of my children herein named should die before the above legacies are their property, I order that their children shall be heirs of the part of my estate herein bequeathed to their parent by me.

I constitute and appoint Robert Harris, son of Charles Harris, and my two sons, Samuel and James, to be my executors of this my last will and testament, and I constitute and appoint Charlie Harris, Robert and my two sons, Samuel and John, to be guardians for my two daughters, Jennett and Mary, and for my daughter Jennett's son, Baptiste.

In witness whereof I have set my hand and seal this 14th day of October, A. D. 1778.

JAMES HARRIS. (Seal.)

Witnesses: Adday Gingles and Margaret Gingles.

JAMES HARRIS, son of Samuel Harris who died at sea, settled in Poplar Tent neighborhood, on Rocky River. Issue:

*ROBERT HARRIS, m Margaret Harper, on Oct. 19, 1757. She was b Aug. 17, 1737. He was private in Capt. Charles Polk's company, in Gen. Rutherford's campaign against the Indians. (See Hunter's Sketches of Western North Carolina, page 178.) Issue:

> SAMUEL HARRIS.
>
> MARGARET HARRIS.
>
> JAMES HARRIS.
>
> †OLIVER HARRIS, b Sept. 28, 1763, d Jan. 25, 1835, m Margaret Shelby, Sept. 4, 1788. She was b Dec. 16, 1772, d Oct. 11, 1844. Issue:
>
>> Dorcas Harris, b Oct. 28, 1789, d April 9, 1814, m John Sheppherd, May, 1807. Issue:
>>
>>> Dorcas Harris Sheppherd, m July 25, 1835, to Daniel Cline.
>>
>> Robert W. Harris, b May 8, 1791, m Rachel Harris, Oct. 13, 1818.
>>
>> Jane Harris, b Feb. 2, 1793, m Cyrus Henderson, Jan. 2, 1818.
>>
>> Isabella Harris, b June 24, 1895, m William Johnson, Feb. 13, 1817.
>>
>> Moses Harris, b Feb. 9, 1798, m M. A. K. Harris, April, 1828.
>>
>> ‡Hezekiah Price Harris, b May 5, 1800, m Matilda Sadler, in Nov., 1828. Issue:
>>
>>> Wade Hampton Harris, and others.
>>
>> Thomas S. Harris, b June 18, 1802.
>>
>> Bernice Harris, b April 16, 1804, Thomas Jahiel Sloan, Nov. 17, 1825.
>>
>> Charles A. Harris, b Jan. 9, 1807.
>>
>> Narcissus S. Harris, b April 20, 1809, m David C. Hope, Nov. 8, 1831.
>
> JOHN HARRIS.
>
> MARY HARRIS.
>
> HANNAH HARRIS.

SAMUEL HARRIS, b about 1735, in Pennsylvania, and came with his father's family to the Rocky River section, about Poplar Tent. He m 1st Rebecca Morrison, dau of William Morrison, who came from Pennsylvania in 1751 and settled on Third Creek, in what is now Iredell County, N. C. She d Aug. 11, 1776. Issue:

> JAMES HARRIS, b Aug. 24, 1759.
>
> WILLIAM HARRIS, b Oct. 5, 1760, m a dau of Fergus Sloan.
>
> MARGARET HARRIS, b Jan. 20, 1762, m Wm. Roseborough and moved west. No further records.
>
> EDWARD HARRIS, b May 5, 1763, m Sarah Kollock.
>
> ANDREW HARRIS b Oct. 26, 1764, m Ed Perrin, in Kentucky. She was of the Virginia Perrin and Clopton families. Had a large family.
>
> MARY HARRIS, b March 11, 1766, m James McCollum. Had a large family.
>
> REBECCA HARRIS, b Sept. 20, 1767, m Andrew Province. Had issue.

---

*This Robert Harris was called "Robert Harris, Junior," because he had a cousin, "Robert Harris, Senior," the son of Charles Harris, of Poplar Tent.

†Moved to Cape Girardeau County, Missouri, in 1818.

‡Hezekiah Price Harris, born in the neighborhood of Bethphague Presbyterian Church, in North Carolina, in about 1818 moved with his father's family to Missouri, returned and read medicine under "Dr. Charles Harris, the Surgeon," m Matilda Sadler, in November, 1828. He had a son, Richard Sadler Harris, who died recently in Concord, N. C., and who was the father of Wade Hampton Harris, the distinguished editor of the Charlotte Chronicle, in Charlotte, N. C.

**Dr. W. C. McCaleb was a Surgeon, C. S. A., 4th Miss. Cavalry, and was promoted Chief of the Medical Board of Brandon Post. (See preceding page.)

MARTHA HARRIS, b Feb. 12, 1770, m Robert Sloan, son of Fergus Sloan, March 13, 1788. Had a large family.

SAMUEL HARRIS, b Oct. 27, 1772, m 1st Sarah Province, Sept. 4, 1795. She d in 1803. He m 2nd, in 1805, to Jane Devir. She d in 1819. He m 3rd to Mrs. Lydia J. Silliman, in 1819. He d in 1841.

PAMILLA HARRIS, b Nov. 14, 1775, m Robert McCord, Dec. 31, 1795.

SAMUEL HARRIS m 2nd on April 8, 1786, to Mrs. Mary Dixon Wilson. She d Sept. 7, 1833. Issue:

ABNER HARRIS, b Jan. 15, 1787, m Mary Stevenson. He m 2nd to Mrs. Mary Wilson, nee Wilson. He d May 31, 1845. Issue:

William Harris, the father of Rev. J. C. Harris, of Tocan, N. C.

ELI HARRIS, b Aug. 22, 1789, m Cynthia ———, April 26, 1815, d Sept. 27, 1821, in Lawrence Co., Ill. She d Aug. 31, 1821. Issue:

Rufus K. Harris, b June 1, 1816, d Feb. 5, 1856, m Minerva Nichols, Dec. 20, 1841. Issue:

Edward Silliman Harris, b Jan. 5, 1853, d Dec. 30, 1791, m Elizabeth McAfee, of Kentucky, in 1874. Issue:

George Edward Harris, b Sept. 24, 1876.

Virgil Lee Harris, b Jan. 17, 1879.

Amanda McAfee Harris, b May 3, 1882.

Anna Minerva Harris, b Sept! 14, 1888.

LYDIA HARRIS, b Dec. 22, 1791, m Thomas Stevenson, May 7, 1812. Issue: Twelve children.

SKETCH OF CHILDREN OF SAMUEL HARRIS, BY REV. J. C. HARRIS.

SAMUEL AND REBECCA MORRISON HARRIS settled one-half mile due north of Loray, on the south fork of Fourth Creek. Their children were:

JAMES—Went west, to Tennessee, perhaps. Was still alive in 1815, and shared with the brothers and sisters the estate of their brother, Edward Harris. I have not found him or his descendants.

WILLIAM—Moved for a time to Bourbon Co., Kentucky, then to Wilson Co , Tennessee, where he raised a large family and died.

MARGARET—Moved west. I have not found her family.

EDWARD—Married Sarah Kollock, daughter of a Princeton, N. J., professor. He was a graduate of Princeton. Settled at Newberne, N. C., where he practiced law and engaged in land entry business in Hyde Co., around Lake Mattamuskeet, also in Cabarrus Co., North Carolina and in Tennessee. He entered in all, from first to last, not less than 100,000 acres. In 1811 he was elected Judge of the Superior Court of North Carolina, which office he continued to fill until July, 1813, when he died while holding court at Lumberton, in Robertson Co., N. C., where he is buried and where he has a monument to his grave. He had no children. His widow married Samuel King, of Iredell Co., North Carolina, but died without heirs.

ANDREW—Went west to Kentucky, in company with Daniel Boone, shortly after the close of the Revolution, and took an active part in the Indian warfare of that country. He resided at Point Lick, in Madison Co , Kentucky, until the year 1806, when he removed to Williamson Co., Tenn., where he died in 1812. He left a large family.

MARY—Lived and died in what is now the Loray neighborhood, Iredell Co., North Carolina, on a place that adjoined the place of her father, Samuel Harris, and that of her grandfather, William Morrison. She raised a large family. Her three sons and one of her daughters moved to Tennessee, where they lived and died.

Other children of James Harris as mentioned in his will were:

JENNETT HARRIS.

JOHN HARRIS.

JAMES HARRIS.

ELIZABETH HARRIS.

WILLIAM HARRIS.

MARY HARRIS.

REBECCA—Married Andrew Province, in Madison Co., Kentucky. They removed to Carroll Co., Tennessee, where they lived and died. Their descendants live in Tennessee and Arkansas.

MARTHA—Married to Robert Sloan, son of Fergus Sloan. They moved to the vicinity of Nashville, Tenn., in 1802, and on to Washington Co., Mo., in 1804, where they had nuerous descendants.

SAMUEL—Married 1st to Sarah Province (a niece of Andrew above), in Madison Co., Kentucky. He removed to Tennessee in 1800, where he lived (in Wilson and Sumner Counties) until 1815, when he removed to Edwards Co., Illinois, in 1815. His wife Sarah died in 1803, and in 1805 he married 2nd Jane Devir, a kinswoman of his first wife, in Madison Co., Kentucky. Jane Devir Harris, his second wife, died in 1810, and he married 3rd Mrs. Lydia Silliman, nee Jarvis, of Sullivan Co., Indiana, in December, 1819. He removed to Parke Co., Indiana, and settled at Rochville in 1837, where he lived and died in 1841. He left numerous descendants.

PAMILLA—Married Robert McCord, in Madison Co., Kentucky. Removed to Rochville, Parke Co., Indiana, where they died and are buried and where they left a large family.

ABNER—Removed to Tennessee. Lived for a time in Wilson Co., and later removed to Obion Co.

ELI—Moved to Tennessee. Had 500 acres of land in "Western District of Tennessee, on Obion River." He moved on to Lawrence Co., Illinois, where he owned 800 acres of land.

LYDIA and her husband lived and died in the old Samuel Harris home at Loray, in Iredell Co., North Carolina. They raised twelve children.

SAMUEL HARRIS, the father of these thirteen children, died of typhoid fever Oct. 5, 1796. His first wife, Rebecca Morrison, died Aug. 30, 1776. His 2nd wife, Mrs. Mary Wilson, nee Dixon, died Sept. 7, 1833.

SAMUEL, SON OF SAMUEL HARRIS WHO DIED AT SEA.

SAMUEL HARRIS, son of Samuel Harris who died at sea, married Martha Laird in Pennsylvania. They had come to America in the same ship, and doubtless their courtship was the result of their long voyage together. They moved to North Carolina and later to Georgia with their son Matthew, who married Hannah Ross, and are buried under the tree that gave shelter to their first camp in Green County, Georgia. (For Hannah Ross, see page 109.)

WILL OF SAMUEL HARRIS.

In the name of God, amen. I, Samuel Harris, of the State of Georgia and County of Greene, being weak in body but of sound memory (blessed be God), do this 10th day of March, 1789, make this my last will and testament in the following manner, that is to say:

First—I will and bequeath to my son, Robert Harris, 40 pounds, and my wearing apparel.

Also I bequeath to my son, James Harris, 15 pounds.

I give and bequeath to my son, Thomas, one negro man named Sanco, and one negro woman, named Dinah, and that my son Thomas pay 10 pounds to the other legatees.

Also I give and bequeath to my son, Samuel Harris, the sum of 30 pounds.

Also I bequeath to my son-in-law, William Wylie, 30 pounds and my desk.

Also to my son-in-law, Thomas McCaul, the sum of 5 pounds.

Also I give and bequeath to my son, John Harris, the sum of 10 pounds.

Also I give and bequeath to my son, William Harris, the sum of 20 pounds.

Also I give and bequeath to my grand-son, Samuel Ross, the sum of 15 pounds.

Also I give and bequeath to my son, Laird Harris' (deceased), son, Laird, the sum of 10 pounds and a horse worth 10 pounds, and if he should die before he comes to the age of 21 years, the property to return to my own children, to be divided among them on the same principles that my other bequeathments are made.

Also I give and bequeath to my son, Matthew, 200 acres of land, whereon he now lives, and a negro girl, Ruth, and a negro man, Peter, to be his property after the decease of my wife, Martha Harris.

Also I give and bequeath to my sons, Thomas and Matthew, and my son-in-law, William Wylie, all my plantation, tools and implements of husbandry and kitchen furniture, to be equally divided among them by lot after the decease of my wife, Martha.

Also I give and bequeath mp library of books to my children, to be equally divided by lot to all except Thomas McCaul.

Also I give and bequeath to my grand-son, Moses Wylie, a negro woman named Mary Ann, to be his after the death of my wife, Martha, providing he acquit my heirs of a sum of money I am indebted to Moses, deceased, which is about 14 pounds, principal and interest thereon due and if the said Moses should die without issue, the negro to revert to my own children, to be divided on the same principles as above mentioned.

Also I give and bequeath to my son, Matthew Harris, a negro man named March, in place of the negro Peter, who he is to get as aforesaid, and March is to be sold for the use of my other children, to be divided as before mentioned.

Also my land to be sold to the highest bidder after the decease of my wife, together with my wagons and horses and cattle, and all such articles as are not bequeathed to any one of my legatees.

Also I will and bequeath to my wife, Martha Harris, all that pertaining to the dwelling house, orchards, buildings, cleared land (all that is on the same side of the branch on which the buildings stand.)

Also the use of two horses fit for service and three milch cows, kitchen furniture, household plumishon, and after her decease to be observed that the kitchen furniture and household plumishon to be only divided among my children, Thomas and Matthew Harris and Wm. Wylie.

All my property that is not divided, willed or bequeathed to any one of my legatees is hereby ordered to be exposed for sale, and the net products to be divided in proportion to the above legatees mentioned to my own children only.

I hereby ordain Thomas Harris, Samuel Harris and Andrew Reid my sole executors of this my last will and testament, to take care and see the same performed according to my true intent and meaning, and I do hereby renounce all former wills and bequeathments whatsoever.

In witness whereof, I have hereunto set my hand and seal the day and year above written.

Schedule: It is to be remembered that March is to be in Matthew's service during the life of my wife, Martha, then to give up March and take Peter, and March to be sold and the neat products to be divided as above to my own children.

Also I appoint and constitute Andrew Baxter one of my executors.

Signed, sealed and executed in the presence of James Flanigan, Elizabeth Baxter and Martha Harris.   SAMUEL HARRIS.   (Seal.)

SAMUEL HARRIS, b in Scotland, son of Samuel Harris who died at sea, married Martha Laird. (See p. 207.) Issue:

SAMUEL HARRIS, son of Samuel Harris and Martha Laird, m Martha Harris, dau of Col. Robert Harris. They were cousins. (See p. 202.) Issue:

    SAMUEL HARRIS, m Miss Cochran.

    ROBERT HARRIS, m 1st Miss Robb, 2nd to Miss Glass.

    LAIRD HARRIS, m 1st Theresa Alexander. Issue:

        Samuel Harris.

        Nathaniel Harris.

    LAIRD HAKRIS m 2nd to Mrs. Harriet Alexander.

    PEGGY HARRIS, m Mr. Johnson.

    JANE HARRIS, m 1st McCamey Alexander, m 2nd Andrew McConnell. Issue:

        Francis McConnell (son.)

    MARY HARRIS, m John Gilmer.

    DORCAS HARRIS, m John Cochran.

    LINNIE HARRIS, m Wiley Harris.

JAMES HARRIS, son of Samuel Harris and Martha Laird. Issue:

    WILLIAM HARRIS, m Martha Cochran, March 3, 1795. Issue:

        Elizabeth Harris, b March 25, 1796.

        James Harris, b Jan. 22, 1798.

        Tirzah Harris, b April 16, 1800.

        Robert Cochran Harris, b Oct. 8, 1802, m March 16, 1829, to Mary Orr Alexander. Issue:

            Martha Jane Alexander, b Dec. 18, 1831.

            Mary Hunter Harris, b Oct. 24, 1833.

Warren Cunningham Harris, b Jan. 16, 1836, m Mrs. Annie
(Alexander) Query, Oct. 18, 1866. Issue:
    Robert Newton Harris, b July 22, 1867.
    Thomas Sidney Harris, b Oct. 29, 1869.
    Marcus Layfayette Harris, b June 5, 1872.
    Nathaniel Baxter Harris, b April 3, 1874.
    William Pringle Harris, b Feb. 28, 1876.
    Manlius Orr Harris, b Feb. 5, 1878.
    John Henry Harris, b April 18, 1880.
    Irene Caroline Harris, b June 22, 1883.
    Annie Lessye Harris, b Sept. 19, 1885.
    Fred Warren Harris, b July 1, 1888.
Moses Manlius Harris, b Feb. 16, 1838, m Martha Harris, dau
of William Pringle Harris. Issue:
    Martha Harris.
    Jane Harris.
Katherine Elizabeth Harris, b June 12, 1841.
Charles Cunningham Harris, b May 4, 1806.
Jesse Whitaker Harris, b May 25, 1809, m Adeline Alexander. Issue:
    Nathan Harris.
    Charles Harris.
    Adaline C. Harris, b May 8, 1836.
    Mary Jane Harris, b Aug. 13, 1837.
Margaret Mariah Harris, b Nov. 11, 1811, m Mr. Alexander.
William Pringle Harris, b March 7, 1815. Married, name of wife not
given. Issue:
    Martha Harris, b May 15, 1835.
    William Brice Harris, b Nov. 3, 1837.
Martha Ann Harris, b Nov. 15, 1817.
Nathan Charles Harris, b June 26, 1827.
Major Harris, signer of the Mecklenberg Declaration.
"Tailor Billie." See above.
Major Thomas Harris, m Miss Carouth.

*ROBERT HARRIS, son of Samuel Harris and Martha Laird.

*LAIRD HARRIS, son of Samuel Harris and Martha Laird.

MARTHA HARRIS, m Moses Wylie. He was drowned in the Tiger River, S. C. Issue:
    MOSES WYLIE, progenitor of the Wylie family in Charleston, S. C.

MARY HARRIS, m William Wylie and settled in Hancock Co., Georgia.

JANE HARRIS, m Rev. Thomas McAule and d in Winnsboro, S. C. He and family went to
    Florida.

WILLIAM HARRIS, settled in Georgia.

THOMAS HARRIS, settled in Georgia.

†MATTHEW HARRIS, son of Samuel Harris and Martha Laird, m Hannah Ross, in 1784.

---

*Reared families and died in Mecklenberg County, N. C.

†Matthew Harris was allowed a pension on his application executed Oct. 39, 1832, at which time he was a resident of Greene County, Ga. and 73 years old. He alleged that he resided in Wilkes County, Ga., when he enlisted in 1776, in Capt. Hutton Middleton's Second Company, Major Leonard Marbury's First Regiment of Horse Brigade, was in engagements with Indians at Marbury's Fort and on the Tougaloo River, and discharged about the first of 1778, having served 18 months.

‡William and Thomas Harris settled in Hancock County, Ga., where they raised families and died. The Baxters of Georgia are descended from this Thomas Harris on the mother's side. Eli Harris, of Georgia, descended from Thomas. The youngest son, Matthew, settled in Greene County, Ga., where he reared his family. He was a member of the Bethany Presbyterian Church. His wife, Hannah Ross, was buried there. He was buried in Tallapoosa County, Ala., in April, 1845, with military honors. Robert must have been 45 or 50 years old at the time of the Revolutionary war; Samuel and James between 40 and 45. The family as a rule were very intellectual and moral, and made good citizens. The above is from J. W. Slaughter, of Goodwater, Ala., whose mother was Temperance Harris, a daughter of Matthew and Hannah Ross Harris. He obtained it from Edwin Wylie, of Hancock County, Ga., a son of Mary Harris and William Wylie, who was a well-posted and intelligent gentleman, who knew personally all the parties and relatives mentioned. He gave the above sketch in 1865, just before he died at an advanced age.

He was b in North Carolina and died in Georgia in 1845, aged 102. Issue:

ROSS HARRIS, born in Georgia, unmarried. Killed by Indians in the Seminole war.

SAMUEL HARRIS, b in Georgia, m Euphemia Pealer. Issue:
        Ross Harris.
        Mary Harris.
        Sarah Jane Harris.
        Martha Harris.
        Narcissa Harris.

JOHN NICHOLAS HARRIS, b in Georgia, unmarried.

JAMES HARRIS, b in Georgia, m Lucretia Jones. Issue:
        Matthew Harris.
        McCamey Harris.
        Margaret Hrrris.
        Sarah Harris.
        Jane Harris.
        Priscilla Harris.
        Jessie Harris.
        Martha Harris.

CHARLES HARRIS, m Tabitha Gibbs. Issue:
        Lucy Harris.
        Ann Harris.
        Elizabeth Harris.
        Matthew Harris.
        James Harris.
        John Wesley Harris, d in Mexican war.

ELIZABETH HARRIS, m Justus Lake. Issue:
        Joseph Early Lake.
        Martha Miller Lake.
        Richard Lake.
        Lannen Lake.
        Matthew Harris Lake.
        Sarah Jane Lake.
        Margaret Ana Lake.
        Marion Hannah Lake.
        Cynthia Caroline Lake.

MARTHA HARRIS, m Dickinson Jones. Issue:
        Ephraim Harris Jones.
        William Aibert Jones.
        Temperance Ana Victoria Jones.
        Seymour Millie Jones.

JANE HARRIS, m William S. Orr. Issue:
        Hannah Jane Orr.
        James Orr.
        John Nicholson Orr.
        Kate Orr.
        William A. Orr.
        Justus Orr.
        Jack Orr.
        Martha Orr and
        Mary Orr, twins.

TEMPERANCE HARRIS, m John Slaughter. Issue:
        John Nicholson Slaughter.
        Alfred Slaughter.
        Harris Slaughter.
        Miles Slaughter.
        Matthew Slaughter.

Radamanthus Slaughter.
Ann Eliza Slaughter.
Richard Ross Slaughter.
SARAH ROUNSAVILLE HARRIS, m Zack Jones. Issue:
Martha Hannah Jones.
Alex Smith Jones.
Marcellus Jones.
Henry Jones.
Louisa Jane Jones.
Mattie Georgiana Jones.
Sarah Elizabeth Jones.

MATTHEW HARRIS' PENSION CERTIFICATE, (p. 209.)

Commissioners' Office, Washington, D. C.

In reply to your letter of Feb. 10, 1911, in case of Matthew Harris, war of Revolution certificate 12279, Savannah, Ga., Agency, you are informed that the records of this office show that last payment was made at $75.00 per annum to March 4, 1845, to Anthony Porter, attorney for the pensioner, who was alive and resided in Tallapoosa County, Alabama, for four years, and previous to that time had resided in Greene County, Ga.

H. C. SHOHER, Audtor,
Treasury Dept., Washington, D. C.

CHARLES, SON OF SAMUEL HARRIS WHO DIED AT SEA.

CHARLES HARRIS is called "Charles of Poplar Tent" and "Charles of 1732," as if he came to N. C. then. Tradition makes him to be the youngest of the brothers and the first to come to North Carolina. He was one of the first bench of Elders of Poplar Tent Church. The given or maiden name of his first wife is not known. The will shows that her people lived here at the time of the making of his will, as he says "Is to be paid to James or whoever takes care of him, and that must be any of his mother's people he chooses to live with." Charles' second wife was the Widow Baker nee Elizabeth Thompson, daughter of the celebrated Rev. John Thompson, the pioneer Presbyterian preacher who preached in N. C. in 1751-1754. Elizabeth was married to Baker at that time, for Rev. John Thompson had a cabin of his own in Baker's yard, and when he died, in November, 1753, they lifted the floor and buried him underneath. That was the beginning of Baker's graveyard, in the vicinity of old Center Church, in Iredell County, North Carolina. Elizabeth was married to Charles of Poplar Tent some time between this and 1763, for his son, "Dr. Charles Harris, the Surgeon," was born in 1763. She was yet not too old to exclude the possibility of a third marriage when Charles made his will in 1776, for he made provision for her in case she did marry again. It is likely that Samuel (who taught the Poplar Tent School and was a graduate of Princeton College and a tutor in Princeton College and who died and was buried at Princeton, N. J., while a student of theology there) was older than "Dr. Charles the Surgeon," although this is not certain. "Dr. Charles the Surgeon" was a noted physician and surgeon in his day, and conducted a medical school in Popular Tent, from which he graduated as many as ninety doctors, many of whom were leaders in their profession. "Dr. Charles the Surgeon" was an Elder in Poplar Tent up to the time of his death, in 1825. When he died mention was made of his death in some of the leading journals of London.

—211—

WILL OF CHARLES HARRIS.

Mecklenburg Co., North Carolina, May 3, 1776.

In the name of God, amen. I, Charles Harris, of the county and state aforesaid, being in good health of body and sound mind and memory (thanks be to God), calling to mind the mortality of the body and that it is appointed to all men once to die, I do make and ordain this to be my last will and testament. That is to say, first of all I give and bequeath my precious soul unto God who gave it, and my mortal body to the earth, to be buried in a decent manner, at the discretion of my executors, nothing doubting that at the general resurrection I shall receive the same reunited to my soul by the Almighty God, and as touching such worldly goods as God has been pleased to bless me with in this life, I give, devise and bequeath the same in the following manner and form:

First—I allow all my lawful debts to be paid.

Second—I give and bequeath to my oldest daughter, Martha, five shillings.

Third—I bequeath to said Martha's oldest daughter, Jane Harris, twenty-five pounds proclamation currency, to be paid to her as soon as she is married, and also I bequeath to the above Martha's second son, Charles Edward Harris, twenty-five pounds, proclamation currency, to be paid to him as soon as he comes of age.

Fourth—I give and bequeath to my oldest son, Robert, all that tract of land on the west side of Broad River, on both sides of Brown's Creek, in South Carolina, and 150 acres joining said tract, and the negro boy Jack, with one-half my wearing apparel.

Fifth—I bequeath to my two daughters, Margaret Alexander and Jane Reese, to each of them, five shillings sterling.

Sixth—I bequeath to my son James 100 pounds proclamation currency, to be kept in the hands of my son Samuel, and he to pay the interest of it yearly to James or to whoever takes care of him, and that must be any of his mother's people he chooses to live with, and when he dies I order said 100 pounds to be equally divided among all my children to my first wife.

Seventh—I bequeath to my sons Samuel and Charles all that tract of land on which I now live, with that tract or lot called the Rich-Hill, and also 150 acres on the Big Run, west of said land. Likewise that land I purchased from John Mitchel on the Milky or Back Run, and that forty acres I bought from Adam Meek.

Eighth—I give and bequeath to the issue of my son Thomas, lawfully begotten, all that tract of land I bought of Robert Brevard, on Beaver Dam Creek, containing 600 acres, to be equally divided among them all when the youngest comes of age according to law, their mother to have her maintenance of it during her lifetime or widowhood.

Ninth—I bequeath to my well-beloved wife, Elizabeth, one-third of all my personal estate during her life or widowhood, and if she marries I order that she have one good feather-bed and necessary clothing and her choice of all the horses belonging to the estate (Samuel's mare and her issue being excepted), and twenty pounds proclamation currency, and the negro wench, Dinah, during her lifetime, and when she dies the said Dinah and her issue to go to my two sons, Samuel and Charles.

Tenth—I give and bequeath to my two sons, Samuel and Charles, all and every part of my estate not before mentioned, and if either of them dies before they come of age, their part to go to the surviving brother, and if they both die during their non-age, their part is to be equally divided amongs t all my children.

And, lastly, I do hereby nominate and appoint my well-beloved wife, Elizabeth, and my well-beloved sons, Robert Harris and George Alexander, as executors of this my last will and testament, ratifying this and no other to be my last will and testament.

In witness whereof, I have hereunto set my hand and seal this 3rd day of May, 1776.

Signed, sealed and delivered by the above named Charles Harris as his last will and testament, in the presence of James Gardner, William Gardner and Adam Meek.

CHARLES HARRIS.	(Seal.)
ELIZABETH HARRIS.	(Seal.)

*CHARLES HARRIS, son of Samuel Harris who died at sea, married 1st Jane ————: Issue:

---

*Charles Harris, the father of Jane, was a member of the Mecklenberg Militia under Col. Adam Alexander.

COL. ROBERT HARRIS, m Mary Wilson. Issue:
    ROBERT HARRIS, m Abigail Hackett. Issue:
        Dr. Charles Wilson Harris, m Mary Barringer. Issue:
           ††Lydia Harris, m Rev. J. N. Craig.
MAJOR THOMAS HARRIS, m Miss Caruth. Issue:
    SARAH HARRIS, m Major James Harris.
***JANE HARRIS,** m †Rev. Thomas Reese, in 1773.

    Thomas Reese was the son of David Reese, a signer of the Mecklenberg Declaration of Independence, Elder of Poplar Tent Church, and a prominent man in his day. His descendants are numerous, and to this day are people of intelligence and closely identified with prominent interests, social, business and spiritual, in their communities. Susan Polk, the wife of David Reese, was a descendant of Robert Polk, of Maryland, and related to the large family by that name in North Carolina. The Reeses intermarried with many prominent families in Mecklenberg County, North Carolina, the Harris, Alexander, Ross, etc., and are therefore related to many people mentioned in this volume. Issue:

    EDWIN TASKER REESE, b March 24, 1774, d unmarried.

    THOMAS SIDNEY REESE, b Oct. 30, 1775, killed in a duel.

    ELIHU REESE, b Feb. 22, 1777, graduated in medicine and died with yellow fever, unmarried.

    LEAH REESE, b Dec. 1, 1779, m Major Samuel Taylor, of Pendleton, S. C., son of Major Samuel Taylor, of Revolutionary fame. Major Taylor, Jr., was b March 1, 1777, d Sept. 30, 1833. Both he and wife are buried at Eutaw, Ala. Issue:
        Harriet Taylor, m Edmund Bacon. Issue:
           Henry Bacon, m Miss Skinner.
           Waddy Bacon.
           Harriet Parks Bacon, m Mr. Dickson, of Tupelo, Miss. Issue:
               Leila Dickson.
               Anna Dickson, m Mr. Gardner.
               Norma Dickson, m Mr. Leyslen.
               Walter Dickson, m Mary Roberts.
        Thomas Reese Taylor, m Hannah Longmire. Issue:
           Jane Taylor, m Mr. Weir. Issue:
               Mary Weir, m Mr. McCafferty.
           Frances Taylor, m Mr. Taggert. Issue:
               Jane Taggert.
           Marie Taylor.
           Edwin Reese Taylor, killed in the Confederate army.
           William Dobson Taylor, killed in the Confederate army.
           Aquilla Taylor, killed in the Confederate army
           Thomas Taylor, killed in the Confederate army.
        Samuel Taylor, m Narcissa Watkins. Issue:
           Lide Taylor, m Robert Hibbler.
           Mary Taylor, m Mr. Edwards. Issue:
               Aurelia Edwards, m 1st Mr. Long, 2nd William
                  Gill. Issue:
                  Willie Gill, m Mr. Staunton.
           Harriet Taylor, m Samuel Barnes. Issue:

**Col. Robert Harris was wounded at Guilford Court House, in the right arm. His wife brought him from the battle field.

†Dr. Thomas Reese, besides being an eminent preacher was also an ardent patriot, and was appointed by the authorities to assist his aged father, David Reese, in collecting arms for the American cause. "Though too old to take the field, he (David Reese) was appointed by the Provincial Congress of April, 1776, with Thomas, to procure, purchase and receive arms for the use of the troops of Mecklenberg."   LYMAN DRAPERS, Signer of the Declaration. (See Mecklenberg Declaration of Independence, by Graham, page 130.)

††Mrs. Lydia Harris Craig is authority in the Harris family, and has rendered valuable assistance in the preparation of these records.

***Material for this branch taken by permission from "History of the Reese Family," by Miss Mary E. Reese.

Willey Barnes.

John Barnes, m Miss Richardson.

Hattie Barnes.

Drusilla Taylor, b March 9, 1808, m Grief Richardson, Oct. 22, 1830. She
d Jan. 10, 1884. Issue:

Mary Richardson, m Mr. Higginbotham, d young.

Lieut. William Hull Richardson, killed in the Confederate
army.

John Taylor Richardson, m Cornelia Brown, of Mississippi.
He was a Confederate soldier. Issue:

Mary Richardson, m Mr. Queen.

John Richardson.

Reese Taylor Richardson.

Leonore Richardson, m Chambers McAdory.

Ida Richardson, m John Rockett. Issue:

William Richardson Rocket.

Percy Rockett.

Ida Rockett, m Mr. Burgess.

Sallie Richardson, m Amos Horton. Issue:

William Taylor Horton, d un-m.

Hugh Clifford Horton.

Chas. Horton, m Belle Jones.

Reese Taylor, m Virginia Clarico, of Virginia. Issue:

Walter Taylor, m Mary Roberts. Issue:

Sallie Taylor, m Rev. Richard Holcomb. Issue:

Walter Holcomb.

Virginia Holcomb.

Armstead Holcomb.

Dr. William Taylor, m Lide White. Issue:

Hattie White Taylor.

Lida White Taylor.

John Taylor, m Eleanor White. Issue:

John Taylor.

Sallie Taylor.

Mary Taylor.

*LYDIA REESE, m 1st to Mr. Findley, of South Carolina. Issue:

William Findley, killed, unmarried.

Jane Elvira Findley, m Dr. Peyton King. Issue:

Dr. Hamden Sidney King, m 1st Pinkie Gates, of Miss. Issue:

Peyton King.

Sidney King.

Corinne King.

Marietta King, m Mr. Lewis, of North Carolina. No issue.

LYDIA REESE FINDLEY m 2nd to John Martin. Issue:

Lewis Martin, m Miss Marshall. Issue:

Lida Martin, m Mr. Montgomery.

Sarah Martin, m Thomas Rockett. Issue:

John Richard Rockett, m Ida Richardson.

Eliza Rockett, m William Brown. Issue:

Claudia Brown.

Benjamine Brown.

Julia Rocket, m John Dean. Issue:

---

*Educated at the Academy at Pendleton, S. C. Her first husband, Mr. Findley, was accidentally killed while out
hunting by his brother-in-law, Samuel Cherry, who cared for the widow and their children in his home until her second
marriage.

Henry Dean.
Jessie Dean.
Harriet Martin, m William Rockett. Issue:
Leonora Rockett, d unmarried.
Julian Rockett, killed in Civil war.
Margaret Rockett, unmarried.
Lydia Reese Rockett, unmarried.
Sarah Rockett, unmarried.
Sidney Rockett, unmarried.
Frank Rockett, unmarried.
Rosa Rockett, unmarried.
Hattie Rockett, unmarried.
Julian Martin, m Alfred Dupuy. Issue:
Harriet Dupuy, m Robert McAdory.
Elizabeth Dupuy, m John Reid. Issue:
Dr. Robert Reid.
Hallie Reid, m Mr. Riddle.
Jane Reid.
Jane Elvira Reid, m Mr. Todd. Issue:
Kate Todd, m Mr. Blair.
Julia Todd.
Cora Todd.
Katherine Dupuy, m Noah Todd. Issue:
Lewis Dupuy Todd.
Samuel Todd.
John Dupuy, m Miss Ware.
†HENRY DODSON REESE, m Rebecca Harris, dau of Robert Harris, a Revolutionary soldier, who lost one eye in that war, and grand-daughter of Gen. Andrew Pickens, of South Carolina. Issue:
Sidney Harris Reese, m late in life.
Frank Reese, b April 11, 1807, m and had issue:
Maria Reese, b Nov. 20, 1809, m Washington Knox. Issue:
Ella Knox, m Mr. Archibald, killed in the Civil war.
Mary Knox, m John Baskins. No issue.
Dobson Reese Knox, m Miss Richey. Issue:
Homer Knox.
Fannie Knox, m Mr. Chiles. Issue:
Ruth Chiles.
Catherine Chiles.
Ethel Chiles.
Walter Chiles.
John Andrew Knox, m Angeline Egerton. Issue:
Catherine Knox.
George Knox.
John Knox.
Lafayette Knox, killed in the army in 1861.
Edwin Reese, b Oct. 29, 1812, m Charlotte McKinstry. Issue:
Florence Reese, unmarried.
Carlos Reese, m Mary Clinton. Issue:
Nannie Reese.
Charlotte Reese.
Clarence Reese, unmarried.
Fred Reese, m Maria Steele. Issue:
Maude Reese.
Ella Reese.
Fred Reese.

---

†Was of a mechanical turn, having a remarkable talent in this line. He and his wife were cousins.

Flora Reese, m Mr. Rowland.
‡Carlos Reese, b Nov. 30, 1815, m Mary Crenshaw. Issue:
　　††Joseph E. Reese, b Dec. 18, 1841, un-m. Confed. soldier.
　　§Carlos Reese, b May 13, 1843, captain in the Civil war, m
　　　Virginia Jones. Issue:
　　　　Sidney Reese, died young.
　　　　Fannie Reese, m J. A. Stephens.
　　　　F. Carlos Reese, unmarried.
　　Margaret Reese, m Dr. Samuel Lewis, of Lexington, Ky
　　　Issue:
　　　　Mary Lewis, d in infancy.
　　　　Margaret S. Lewis, m Rev. L. O. Dawson. Issue:
　　　　　Andrew Lewis Dawson.
　　Catherine Reese, m Theodore Lewis. Issue:
　　　　Mary H. Lewis, d in infancy.
　　　　Annie Reese Lewis, unmarried.
　　　　Higgins Lewis, m Lillian Petit.
　　J. Pickens Reese, m Miss Sullivan.
Harriet Reese, m W. Smith.
Elihu Milton Reese, b July 10, 1820.
Jane Reese, m W. W. Scott. Issue:
　　Walter Scott, unmarried.
　　Winfield Scott, unmarried.
　　William Scott, m Miss McCafferty.
　　Robert Scott.
　　Mary Scott, unmarried.
　　Georgiana Scott.
Thomas Reese.
Mary C. Reese.
**SUSAN POLK REESE, m Samuel Cherry, of South Carolina, Nov. 5, 1807, at Pendle-
ton, S. C. Issue:
　*Robert Madison Cherry, b 1808, m Caroline Crenshaw, in 1840. Issue:
　　†Charlotte Elmore Cherry, m Geo. N. Croft, Oct. 11, 1865.
　　　Issue:
　　　　Robert Madison Croft, unmarried.
　　　　Mary Crenshaw Croft, m Mr. M. Askew, d soon
　　　　　after.
　　　　‡‡Caroline Elmore Croft, m William J. Nelson, of
　　　　　Mississippi. Issue:
　　　　　　Charlotte Christine Nelson.
　　　　　　Robert Mayo Nelson.
　　　　　　Two sons.
　　　　Lulu Croft, m Claude Melton, Sept., 1900. Issue:
　　　　　Stanley Croft Melton.

---

‡Was a soldier in the Seminole war, a man of affairs in Alabama, to which state he removed from South Carolina.

††Private in the 9th Ala. Reg., C. S. A.

§Captain in the Civil war, in the Western Army, C. S. A.

**Youngest daughter of Rev. Thomas Reese. Her husband, Samuel Cherry, was of the distinguished Cherry family of South Carolina. Their home was one of cordiality, and its atmosphere of love and good will to all mankind. Twelve children were the priceless possessions of these parents, all of whom filled places of usefulness in life.

*He moved from South Carolina to Alabama, where he was a successful lawyer and consistent Christian. His wife's memory was held sacred by him till his death, and no one ever came into his life to take her place.

†This family owe much to the training of their mother and father, Mr. and Mrs. Geo. N. Croft, and to their heritage from ancestors who loved the right and have held the love of God the greatest gift that they could possess.

‡‡Mother of an interesting family, and herself a devoted wife. She is active in every movement for the good of her home, state and country, is interested in the patriotic societies, women's clubs, and her church work is second to none.

MRS. ROSA McKEY FULGHAM
Page 220

NOEL KILLINGSWORTH McKEY
Page 220

JAMES McKEY
Page 221

MRS. MARY REBECCA FULGHAM
Page 221

CLARA MIMS WRIGHT

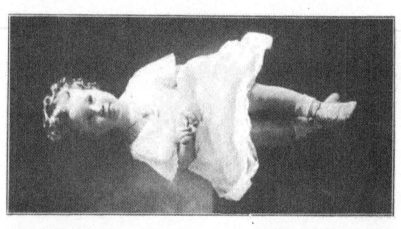

WILLIAR PATRICIA WRIGHT

ANNE ROBERT WRIGHT

ANNE MIMS WRIGHT
(MRS. WILLIAM R.)

MRS. ELIZABETH ANN McKEY JONES
Page 221

MRS. CLARA FRANCES McKEY MIMS AND CLARA MIMS WRIGHT

HAMDEN J. McKEY, JR.
Page 221

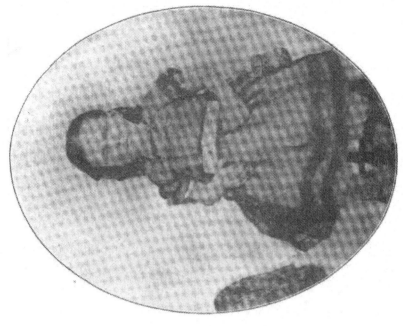

CLARA FRANCES McKEY
See McKey Chapter

ELIZABETH ANN AND MARY REBECCA McKEY
See McKey Chapter

HAMDEN J. McKEY
Page 220

HAMDEN J. McKEY AND HIS SECOND WIFE
SARAH ANN HILL McKEY
Page 220

Lillian Croft, twin to Lulu, unmarried.
Sallie Croft, m George Smith. Issue:
Mary Lewis Smith.
Lillian Louise Smith.
George Croft, unmarried.
§Thomas Reese Cherry, b Feb. 9, 1810, m Mary Reese Harris, his cousin,
Nov. 8, 1837. Issue:
Edward B. Cherry, m Helen Quinn, of Connecticut. Issue:
Ives Cherry, died young.
Mary Story Cherry, m Robert Prior. Issue:
Wilton Burton Prior.
Annie Cherry, m Mr. Mitchell.
Thomas Reese Cherry, m Belle Harris, of Baltimore. Issue:
Edwin Harris Cherry.
Laura Cherry, m James Headrick. Issue:
Glennie Headrick.
Lilly Headrick.
James A. Headrick.
William Headrick.
Nathaniel Harris Cherry, unmarried.
Lilly Bee Cherry, m Prof. William Emerson. Issue:
Cherry Emerson.
Austelle Emerson.
Kate Cherry, m Mr. Bowden. Issue:
Mary Frances Bowden
James Alvin Cherry, m his cousin, Mary Elizabeth Reese, Aug. 9, 1832.
Issue:
Five children.
Samuel Sidney Cherry, b Jan. 6, 1814, lived a long life, unmarried.
William Backley Cherry, D. D. S., d Dec. 24, 1901, aged 87, m Sarah
Lewis. Issue:
Lortie Cherry, died young.
Samuel David Cherry, m Minnie Johnson. Issue:
Frank Lorton Cherry, b 1878.
Mary Bates Cherry, b 1800.
William Reese Cherry, b 1885.
David Edward Cherry, died young.
Thomas Johnson Cherry, b Sept 26, 1894.
Fannie Lewis Cherry, m Warren R. Davis. Issue:
William Cherry Davis, b Dec. 7, 1889.
Warren Ransom Davis, b Feb. 21, 18.2.
David Sidney Davis, b 1894.
Sara Lorton Davis, b 1898.
James Adelaide Cherry, b April 14, 1817, m her cousin, Dr. A. H. Reese,
May 27, 1834.
Edwin Augustus Cherry, b Feb. 10, 1819, died unmarried.
Sarah Ann Cherry, b March 31, 1821, m Jonathan Smith, who died in the
service of the Confederacy. Issue:
Susan Cherry Smith, m Mr. Wright. Issue:
Charlotte Smith Wright.
Mary Cherry Smith, m Mr. Pressley. Issue:
A son.
David Elihu Cherry, b Feb. 19, 1823, m Edmonia Schull. Issue:
Rufus Schull Cherry.
John Calhoun Cherry, b April 1, 1825, d unmarried.
Mary Elvira Cherry, m Elijah McKinley. Issue:

Susan Cherry McKinley, m Luther Turner. Issue:
Frank Turner, unmarried.
Julia Turner.
Mary Turner, m Thomas DeLemar. Issue:
Luther Frank DeLemar.
Edward Turner.
Samuel Cherry McKinley, m Tommie Fear. Issue:
Mercer Elijah McKinley.
Charles Henry Cherry, d unmarried. Soldier in the Confederate army.

SAMUEL HARRIS, died unmarried. Was professor at Princeton.

JAMES HARRIS, supposed to have died young.

CHARLES HARRIS, m 2nd Mrs. Elizabeth (Thompson) Baker. Issue:

CHARLES HARRIS, M. D., m 1st Sarah Harris, 2nd Lydia Houston. Was known as "Dr. Charles, the Surgeon."

ADDENDA.

The following, by mistake, was left off of page 204, and is a continuation of the record of Col. Robert Harris of Reedy Creek:

ELIZABETH HARRIS m 2nd to Mr. Snyder (possibly Adam Snyder), and removed to Mississippi and settled near Port Gibson. Issue:
RANSOM SNYDER, captured by the Union soldiers when on a trip to Louisiana to buy salt. He was an old man, and was never again heard of.
ALONZO SNYDER. (No record.)

DAUGHTER, m Major James Harris, son of Samuel and Martha Laird Harris. Issue:
"TAYLOR BILLIE" HARRIS.
GEORGE HARRIS.
HOUSTON HARRIS.
GRIZEL HARRIS.
JANE HARRIS.

MARTHA, m Samuel Harris, son of Samuel and Martha Laird Harris. Issue:
(See page 208.)

EXPLANATION.

It has not been the purpose of the compiler of these records to give, in this one chapter devoted to the Harris family, a full account of the descendants of the five brothers who first came to America, but to show the descent from each brother and fill in the lines that are of most interest to the relatives that have been reached through correspondence.

From the foregoing, the reader will be able to have a general view of the various branches of the family, and interest may, thereby, be aroused in a completion of the records.

There is an effort being made by members of the family, more experienced in Harris lore than the writer, to publish a full history of all of the descendants of the five brothers, and your assistance in their undertaking is asked.

CHAPTER XIII.

THE MACKEY FAMILY.

The progenitors, as far as are known, of the Mackey family were Daniel and Jonathan Mackey, two brothers, who came to Mississippi before 1810 and settled in Jefferson and Claiborne Counties. These brothers came from North Carolina, about Mecklenberg County, it is thought, and it is probable that they were not the emigrant ancestors, but were born of parents or grand-parents who came to the Colonies from Scotland along with the early tide of emigration.

In Bertie County, N. C., in 1730, a William Mackey made a will and mentioned a son Daniel and daughter Margaret, but an effort has not yet been made to connect this family with the Mississippi family. A will of more ancient date was that of Daniel Makee, of North Carolina, which was probated July 15, 1695, which mentioned sons Daniell and John, and daughters Catherine and Eleanor, and wife Elinor.

There was a large family connection in Salisbury District, N. C., bearing the name Mackey in its various forms when the census of 1792 was taken.

In South Carolina the name is found principally in Edgefield, Pendleton and Newberry Districts, and it is probable that the brothers who settled in Mississippi first emigrated to South Carolina and from thence to Mississippi along with the number who took up lands in the new territory soon after it was purchased. We find the Mackey family under discussion closely associated with other families with whom various members intermarried and are treated of in this volume.

Daniel Mackey lived in Jefferson County, Mississippi, until his death, and occupied the position of County Clerk for many years. His home was near Fayette, and he is buried there. He was born about 1770 in North Carolina, died in Mississippi about 1839, married in North Carolina about 1808, to Rosana Harris, daughter of Elizabeth Harris. (See page 204.) Issue:

HAMDEN J. McKEY was born in Jefferson County, Miss., where he resided till some time after his third marriage, when he removed to Copiah County and settled at Burtonton, where his lands lay in a very fertile valley between White Oak and Bayou Pierre Creeks. His home was equipped with all of the usual ante-bellum necessary machinery for the maintenance of the large number of slaves that tilled the lands and attended his family. A typical picture of Southern life before the war could have been taken from this home. He and his family were Presbyterians, and he an elder in that church, with all of the beliefs that are fostered by the true churchman, made his home one where piety and godliness were nurtured and where God was held supreme

On Sundays, the family with a retinue of servants rode sometimes many miles to church, oftentimes to Port Gibson or to the Brick Church at Red Lick. (See picture.)

The children of this home were educated by governesses, and later sent to college. The boys served their country in some of its hardest fought battles, in the service of the Confederacy. Hamden J. Mackey, on account of his age and being disabled, did not enter active service, but furnished corn and other provisions to the soldiers, and his home was an asylum for the wounded and sick and any who chanced to pass his door.

After the war, he accepted the privations that came to all Southerners, and determined to establish once more his estate as it had been, but before he saw the accomplishment of the end his death occurred, and his family left the old home and moved to Crystal Springs, where they lived till removed by death or for business reasons, Mrs. Robert Jones being the only daughter now living in Crystal Springs.

(For Mrs. Hamden McKey, see page 191.)

HAMDEN JORDAN McKEY, b Jan. 11, 1811, in Jefferson Co., Miss., d June 1, 1871, at Burtonton, Copiah Co., Miss. He m 1st Hibernia Margaret Hughes, dau of Felix and Margaret Hughes and niece of General Andrew Pickens, of South Carolina, on Aug. 13, 1835. She was b Feb. 7, 1810, d April 27, 1837. Issue:

Martha Virginia McKey, b May 15, 1836, d Nov. 17, 1836.

HAMDEN J. McKEY m 2nd Sept. 19, 1838, to Sarah Jane Killingsworth, dau of Noel and Jane Scott Killingsworth. She d Sept. 19, 1845. (See Killingsworth line.) Issue:

Jane Scott McKey, b Aug. 15, 1836, d May 15, 1840.

Rosa Ann McKey, b July 30, 1840, d Aug. 2, 1883, m in 1858 to Lucius Wells. He d in April, 1866. No issue.

*Rosa Ann McKey m 2nd April 28, 1870, to Dr. Fenton Lafayette Fulgham. Issue:

John Henry Fulgham, M. D., b Dec. 8, 1872, m Ottillie Pesold. Issue:

Beatrice Fulgham, b June 27, 1902.

Rosa McKey Fulgham, b Aug. 2, 1883, m Dec. 24, 1908, to James Harry Wells, of South Carolina. Issue:

Rose Fulgham Wells, b April 5, 1911.

†Noel Killingsworth McKey, b Feb. 24, 1842, d Feb. 19, 1902, m 1st Sept. 7, 1865, to Mary Ophelia Shelby, dau of Dr. William Love Shelby and Martha Barnes. Issue:

William Hamden McKey, b July 25, 1867, unmarried.

---

*Rosa Ann McKey married Lucius Wells and removed to Arkansas for several years, and afterwards returned to Mississippi and lived in Copiah County till her death. She was a woman of remarkable executive ability, of an amiable disposition, and popular with all who knew her. She was a fine manager, and had many womanly gifts that made her a kind friend and congenial companion for those of her own class. Her second husband, Dr. F. L. Fulgham, survived her many years. He was a Confederate soldier, and to his death a veteran with all of the devotion to the cause which is so characteristic of the ex-Confederate soldiers. He was a successful physician, and his big heart responded to many calls that were made just for love's sake. His association as physician of the Baptist Orphanage of Jackson, Miss., gave him an opportunity to hold in affection the many little children that he cared for just for charity's sake. He was a writer of prominence in his state, and lent this talent to causes that he espoused. He is survived by his second wife, Mary Mims Fulgham, who has been a devoted mother to his two children.

Noel Killingsworth McKey served in the Confederate Army in some of the hardest fought battles. He lived at Burtonton, in sight of his father's old home, where he reared a large and promising family, who have entered the business life of their respective homes and are rearing families with the same high ideal before them. (See picture.) His second wife has lived a useful life, and been a mother to his children.

—220—

Noel Killingsworth McKey, b Jan. 20, 1869, m Sept. 1, 1909, to
    Bessie Whitfield.
James Anon McKey, b Oct. 27, 1871, m Dec. 22, 1902, to An-
    nabell McWilliams, of McKinney, Texas. He d Jan. 10,
    1911. Issue.
        Rosabell McKey, b Sept. 29, 1903.
        James Anon McKey, Jr., b Sept. 4, 1910, d June
           5, 1912.
Idaline McKey, b 1873, unmarried.
Love Shelby McKey, b March 9, 1876, m Oct. 15, 1903, to
    Virginia Weeks. Issue:
        LeNoel McKey (daughter), b Oct. 21, 1904, d
           Nov. 24, 1904.
        Daniel Shelby McKey, b Nov. 14, 1905.
        Virginia McKey.
Rosa May McKey, m Sept. 14, 1904, to Dr. Clarence Butler.
    Issue:
        Rose Mary Butler, b May 2, 1910.
Noel Killingsworth McKey m 2nd to Sally Shelby, sister of his first wife,
    Oct. 9, 1887.
HAMDEN J. McKEY m 3rd to Sarah Ann Hill, on Aug. 25, 1846. She was the dau of
Jacob Killingsworth Hill and Rebecca Gibson Sims. (See Sims and Killings-
worth lines.) Issue:
    *Hamden John McKey, b Dec. 5, 1845, d March 5, 1906, m Lida Moore, in
    1873. Issue:
        Elizabeth McKey, b Feb. 9, 1876 m Wm. Love Lloyd, son of
        John and Maria Love Lloyd. Issue:
           Ruth Lloyd.
           William L. Lloyd.
           Lida Moore Lloyd.
           Infant, died young.
        Lida McKey, m James Y. Jones. No issue.
Hamden J. McKey m 2nd Jennie Cheek, daughter of William Cheek and
Fannie Speed. (See Hill line.) Issue:
        Francis McKey, b Nov. 17, 1879, m Nov. 24, 1897, to Earl Rob-
        inson. Issue:
           Albert McKey Robinson, b Aug. 22, 1898.
        William Robert McKey, b Sept. 18, 1881, m May 23, 1906, to
        Nellie Stubbs. Issue:
           Francis McKey, b March 26, 1908.
†Elizabeth Ann McKey, b Feb. 9, 1850, m Dec. 16, 1869, to Dr. Robert Elam
    Jones, son of Dr. Robert Jones and Mary Robertson. Issue:
        Rena Robertson Jones, b Aug. 30, 1876, m July 2, 1902, to
        John Meridith Wood, son of William Rilcrest Wood
        and ——. Issue:

---

*Hamden J. McKey lived at Utica, Miss., until a few years ago, when he removed to Fort Worth, Texas, and engaged in the stock business, and where his wife and son and daughter are now living. He served in the Confederate Army, though a mere youth at the time. Was educated at Oakland College and married early in life, and was soon left a widower with two little daughters, Lizzie and Lyda. Lyda, the younger, was reared bo her Grandmother McKey. His second marriage was to his cousin, Jennie Cheek, who survives him, and adds great pleasure to her children's lives.

†Elizabeth Ann McKey Jones and her husband, Dr. Robert E. Jones, are the parents of a very attractive family, who, with the exception of two, are married and established in the social, religious and business life of their homes. They have reared their children in a beautiful Christian atmosphere, and developed them along high ideals of life. She is a gifted writer, and has been prominent in church and club circles of her town and state. Her administration as President of the Mississippi Federation of Women's Clubs was marked by great progress of the organization of the state. She has been identified with all movements for the advancement of her community, and unselfishly gives her talents for the betterment of society and the pleasure of her friends. Dr. Robert Jones served with distinction during the Confederate Army, and has since devoted his time to the practice of medicine, having held many responsible positions in the profession, and is a recognized power in the medical world of the South.

Elizabeth Wood, b July 2, m 1908.
Charles Meridith Wood, b Aug. 8, 1910.
Robert Hill Jones, b July 10, 1879, m Nov. 12, 1902, to Ada
Elizabeth Cook. Issue:
Robert Cook Jones, b May 23, 1904.
Louise Jones, b Feb. 14, 1906.
Clara Mims Jones, b Sept. 4, 1882, m Oct. 27, 1903, to Wm.
B. McCluney. Issue:
Mellville Jones McCluney, b June 27, 1905, d
Sept. 26, 1905.
Wm. Jones McCluney, b Oct. 22, 1910.
Eva Jones, b Aug. 30, 1886, d Nov. 3, 1889.
Elizabeth Jones, b Feb 2, 1889, m Dec. 15, 1909, to Charles
Hazlitt Parsons. Issue:
Rena Cornelia Parsons.
Elma Jones, b Nov. 3, 1881.
Wyeth Jones, b July 16, 1894, the youngest grandchild of
Hamden J. and Sarah Ann McKey.
*Mary Rebecca McKey, b Feb. 5, 1852, d Aug. 3, 1898, m Nathan Lott
Fulgham, son of John Fulgham and Eliza Craig and brother of
Dr. F. L. Fulgham. Issue:
Hamden McKey Fulgham, b Jan. 7, 1873, m Ethel Beamon,
of Yazoo City, Miss.
Mary Eliza Fulgham, b Oct. 26, 1876, m Theodore Hastings
Kendall, son of Theodore and Sarah Stackhouse Ken-
dall. Issue:
Theodore Hastings Kendall, b Jan. 12, 1905.
Nathan Fulgham Kendall, b Nov. 28, 1908.
Henry McKey Kendall.
Henry Craig Fulgham, b in Oct., 1879, m Mary Howell, dau
of Solon and Mignonne Russell Howell.
*Clara Frances McKey, b Aug. 20, 1854, m Nov. 6, 1872, to Robert Burr
Mims, son of Henry Mims and Augusta Nagel, of South Carolina.
Issue:
††Anne Julia Mims, b April 10, 1876, m Nov. 14, 1900, to William
Richard Wright, D. D. S., son of Patrick Henry Wright
and Anna Clark. Issue:
Clara Mims Wright, b June 5, 1902.
Anne Robert Wright, b Feb. 16, 1906.
William Patricia Wright, b Aug. 3, 1909. (See
pictures.)

*Mary Rebecca Mackey Fulgham, more affectionately called "Pet," was a woman of the most lovable nature, one of God's choicest creatures so filled with meekness, kindness, gentleness and unselfishness, that her life, though touched by adversity and not free from trouble, was one sweet song, that has given inspiration to all who were fortunate to have known her. Her husband, Nathan Lott Fulgham, was of like nature, and their home was one that was tempting to the friends and strangers who were often entertained there. It was often the subject of comment by their friends that no two better people were ever mated in this world. Nathan L. Fulgham was a brother of Dr. F. L. Fulgham, and was one of the youngest Confederate soldiers.

†To write a note on one's parents is an extremely difficult task, yet it is one that any loving daughter delights in. Clara Frances McKey Mims inherited many of the noble traits of her ancestors. She is especially like the Killingsworth family in physical characteristics, love of order and industry. "She looketh well after her household and eateth not the bread of idleness." Her special delight is in her three little grand-daughters, and she is never too tired to spend an hour or so amusing them. Robert Burr Mims entered the Confederate army when but 14 years old, and although the youngest member of his company, served as Orderly Sergeant for several years. He is a retired business man, having had in his charge the affairs of the New York Life Insurance Company in Mississippi for twenty-five years. He is a great and patient sufferer of rheumatism for eleven years, but is able to drive and visit and attend church, being the senior Deacon of the First Baptist Church of Jackson, Miss.

††At 408 North State street, Jackson, Miss., is the beautiful home where Mrs. Robert Burr Mims and her daughter, Mrs. Anne Mims Wright, dispense the liveliest hospitality. Every corner of this home shows forth the refined taste of two splendid, cultured women; and while the long illness of her husband has claimed the attention of the mother, the daughter has been forced, often against her will, into positions of prominence and responsibility, which she has filled

FROM HAMDEN J. MACKEY TO JACOB K. HILL.

July 24, 1850.

Dear Father:

As Robert is going to spend a part of his vacation with his friends, I have an opportunity of writing to you and letting you know how we are. The health of our place is very good except Ann, and she has not been entirely well since she was at your house. My general health has been better this spring and summer than it has been in several years, having had nothing the matter with me but a sore toe, from which I am suffering a good deal at present, not being able to walk without a good deal of pain. The rest are all well.

I wrote to New Orleans to Mr. Roseau about ten days ago to find out if he was in New Orleans and if he intended to come to Jackson this summer, and to know about the land, when I could be sure to see him in New Orleans if he did not intend to come to Jackson. To this letter I ought to get an answer in another week, and if he writes to please me I may come up to see you some time next month, as I shall want to see Mr. Lloyd.

I wrote to Roseau to know what he would take for all the Lloyd land near Burtonton, embracing the old residence and land lying on both sides of Bayou Pierre and White Oak. As I did not know how to describe the land in any better way, I thought it best to say we would take the whole of the land in that township.

My cotton crop is a bad stand, but corn tolerably fair. I did not plant to make much. Hail Cheek was in my cotton yesterday, and said it was the best cotton he had seen. I have not seen any but my own for some time, and do not know how it will compare with other crops. I shall get it in good order in a few days more, if the weather remains as it now is.

We would be glad to see you and mother and any of the family that can come to see us Nothing more.   I remain, your affectionate son,

H. J. McKEY.

DANIEL McKEY m 2nd on Jan. 15, 1824, to Jane Pickens Hughes, dau of Felix Hughes and Margaret Miller and niece of Gen. Andrew Pickens, of South Carolina. She was born April 24, 1792, and died July 29, 1836. Issue:

JOHN SHANKS McKEY, b Jan. 27, 1825. He never married. Was in the war with Mexico, in 1846. (See picture)

CLARINDA HARRIS McKEY, b Jan. 27, 1825, twin sister of John S., m Richard Lawless. Issue:

Richard Lawless.

EDWIN McKEY, b Sept. 30, 1829, d Oct. 23, 1853, m Rebecca Nixon. Issue:

Charles Clark McKey, b Oct. 23, d April 6, 1852.

Samuel Nixon McKey, d Dec. 10, 1842, aged 6 weeks.

Eddie McKey, d June 8, 1883, aged 29 years.

Amelia McKey.

Thomas D. McKey, d Sept. 15, 1909.

Mary Eliza McKey, b May 1, 1846, d Nov. 28, 1908, m Jan. 24, 1871, in Chicago, to †Harry C. Moore, son of Judge William G. Moore and Nancy Hogan. Issue:

Glessner Moore, b Feb. 9, 1873, m June 18, 1895, to Henry C. Brady. He d Dec. 2, 1906. She m 2nd Dec. 26, 1907, to *George S. Few.

ROBERT EMMET McKEY, b Dec. 25, 1827, m Miss Price. He died soon after. No issue. His widow married again.

FELIX PICKENS McKEY, b April 1, 1830, died unmarried.

WILLIAM LEMUEL McKEY, b Oct. 22, 1832, died unmarried.

JNNATHAN MACKEY, b about 1775 in North Carolina, m Mary Montgomery. She was b about 1780 and d in 1837, in Mississippi. Issue:

§SAMUEL MACKEY, m March 5, 1841, to Eliza Ann Griffing, d in Feb., 1877. No issue.

JOHN MACKEY, m John Hannan. Issue:

‡Emily Jane Hannan, b May 25, 1827, m Henry Heisenbouttle. He d in 1853. Issue:

**Samuel Mackey, b Sept. 18, b 1846, d May, 1910, m 1869 to Laura Jane Jett, dau of Capt. and Mrs. J. T. H. Jett. She d in June, 1910. Issue:

Emily E. Mackey, b Oct. 18, 1870, m H. E. Milner.

††Henry H. Mackey, b Jan. 5, 1872, m Mable Glass, June 27, 1900. Issue:

J. B. Mackey, b Dec. 17, 1901.

Henry E. Mackey, b Oct., 1903.

Lucille Mackey, b Feb., 1905.

Clarence H. Mackey, b Aug., 1908.

---

††Henry H. and Samuel E. Mackey enlisted in the United States army at the beginning of the Spanish-American war. Both contracted typhoid fever and barely escaped death.

†Harry C. Moore, a prominent merchant of Nevada, Mo. His father, Judge Moore, was of Irish descent. His mother was a Duncan, of Scotch descent, daughter of Thomas Duncan, of Nelson Co., Kentucky. The Duncans were prominent people of Kentucky, connected with the McElroys, the Knotts, the Russells, the Davises and Simpsons, of Nelson and Washington Counties, Bloomfield, Bardstown and Lebanon, Ky.

*George S. Few served under General Funston in the 20th Kansas Volunteers in the Philippines in the Spanish-American war, and was given an honor medal for bravery by Congress.

§Captain in the Mexican war.

**After the death of their mother, who was a merchant and planter of Warren, Miss., they were reared by their uncle, Samuel Mackey, and their names changed, by act of the Legislature, to Mackey.

‡Emily Jane Hannan was considered a very beautiful woman. She was cultured and of a lovable disposition. Her second marriage was to Charles H. Fontaine, a prominent attorney.

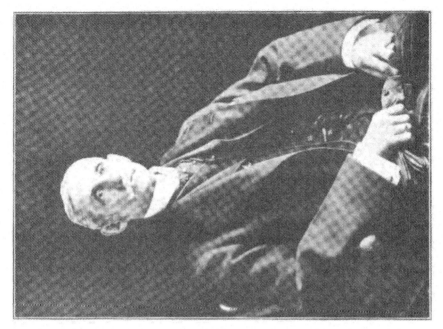

THOMAS D. MACKEY
See Mackey Chapter

JOHN S. MACKEY
See Mackey Chapter

Thomas J. Mackey, b Aug. 26, 1874, m Mrs. Stout,
Sept., 1900.
Laura Lucille Mackey, b Sept. 5, 1876, m A. H.
McMorris, Sept., 1902. Issue:
Four children.
††Samuel E. Mackey, b Jan. 5, 1879, m Louise Bur-
chardt, Sept., 1901.
Robert L. Mackey, b March 11, 1881, m Maggie
Valley, Jan., 1904. Issue:
Daughter, aged 4 years.
Daughter, aged 7 years.
‡‡Charlie Mackey, b 1848, m Florence Grimes, in Sept., 1876.
Issue:
Charles Macky, b 1877, unmarried.
Emma Mackey, m Henry Schlottman. Issue:
Henry Schlottman.
Bertha Mackey, b 1883, m Claude Allen.
Rosabel Mackey, b 1886, m Charles Seay. Issue:
Maurice Seay.
Charlie Seay.
Henry Seay.
Susie Mackey, m G. G. Bowen.
Eugenia Mackey.
John W. Mackey.
Dolly Mackey, m J. J. Parker.
Annie Mackey.
Emily Jane Mackey Heisenbouttle m 2nd to Charles H. Fontaine. Issue
Walter S. Fontaine.
May Fontaine, m Dr. Surghuor, of Monroe, La.
*HUGH MACKEY, m Sally Caroline Hughes, Feb. 4, 1819. She was b Feb. 5, 1800,
and d Aug. 8, 1831, and was the dau of Felix and Margaret Miller Hughes and
a sister of the second wife of Daniel Macky and the first wife of Hamden J.
Mackey. Issue:
Daughter, m John Henderson. Issue:
Frank Henderson.
Felix Henderson.
And others.
*JONATHAN MACKEY, m ———. Issue:
Daughter, m Gabe Fowler. Issue:
Olivia Fowler, m Mr. Whittington. Issue:
Three children.
§BALSORA MACKEY, b in Jefferson Co., Mississippi, Aug. 5, 1815, d Jan., 1869, m
George Williams, Oct. 29, 1837. He died in Aug., 1869. Issue:
Four sons, died in infancy.
†Florence Williams, b in Warren Co., Miss., Sept. 13, 1845, m Nov. 16,
1871, to William Whitney Spielman. Issue:
Charles Mackey Spielman, b Dec. 25, 1872, d July, 1873.
William Whitney Spielman, b Jan. 7, 1874, d 1874.

---

§I was at Port Gibson, Miss., going to school, boarding at my Uncle Samuel Mackey's, when New Orleans fell.
School closed and my mother came and took me home to Louisiana. We lived on the Ouchita River, below Monroe, about
five years. My mother died there in January, 1869, and my father died in August the same year. Then I was left alone,
and came to make my home my home with Uncle Samuel Mackey, and was married there, though we lived in Ohio many
years.   BALSORA MACKEY.
†We always lived in Warren County, near Vicksburg, until during the war my parents moved to Louisiana, thinking to avoid meeting with the Norhtern soldiers, but we got right among them, for they landed at Vicksburg and scattered through the country and destroyed everything as they went. They placed my father and mother under guard and
threw everything out of the store-room to the negroes. They saddled one of the carriage horses, rode it off, and that
was the last seen of it.   MRS. FLORENCE SPIELMAN.
*Both died in Louisiana, on the Ouachita River.

Cora Mackey Spielman, b Sept. 29, 1875, m Frank Marshall
March 25, 1897, at Greenville, O. Issue:
Carl Marshall, b March 9, 1898.
Irene Marshall, b Nov. 17, 1902.
Esther Marshall, b March 1, 1904.
Blanche Montgomery Spielman, b June 20, 1878, m Leo Haas,
at Dayton, O., July 28, 1896. Issue:
Florence E. Haas, b Feb. 18, 1898.
Elwood Haas, b Dec. 3, 1901.
Joe Neibert Spielman, b Aug. 29, 1880, m Martha Schenck,
at Dayton, O., Aug. 23, 1903.
James Arthur Spielman, b Aug. 28, 1883.
Daughter, born and died in March, 1886.

HARMOM PUBLISHING CO.,
Jackson, Miss.

REVOLUTIONARY ANCESTORS.

ALEXANDER, AARON—Constable in Mecklenberg County during the Revolutionary period. (Pages 18, 136, 140.)

ALLISON, ANDREW—North Carolina Militia.

CONGER, JONATHAN—Quartermaster Sergeant, 4th North Carolina Reg. (Pages 105, 107.)

CONGER, JOHN—Commissioned as Ensign by the Committee of Safety of Rowan County, Nov. 11, 1775. (Page 110.)

HARRIS, ROBERT—(Page 201.)

HARRIS, ROBERT—(Page 205.)

HARRIS, CHARLES—Mecklenburg Militia. (Page 212.)

HARRIS, MATTHEW—Captain, Middleton's 2nd company. (Page 209.)

HILL, ROBERT—Fought under Sumpter. (Page 184.)

KING, HUGH—(Page 160.)

KILLINGSWORTH, JESSE—North Carolina Troop. (Page 180.)

KILLINGSWORTH, JOHN—Musician. (Page 180.)

LUNSFORD, SWANSON—Captain. (Page 172.)

MOORES, HENRY—(Page 78.)

McDONALD, DONALD—Scout under Sumpter. (Pages 164, 165.)

McDONALD, MARY—(Pages 164, 165.)

McDONALD, WILLIAM—(Page 168.)

ROSS, ARTHUR BROWN—No official record. (Page 19.)

ROSS, ISAAC—Captain. (Pages 69, 72.)

REESE, DAVID—(Page 212.)

REESE, REV. THOMAS—(Page 212.)

WADE, DANIEL—(Page 167.)

WADE, GEORGE—Captain. (Page 164.)

WADE, JOSEPH—Imprisoned at Camden. (Page 162.)

WADE, THOMAS—Member of Committee of Safety, Colonel, etc. (Page 162.)

Records of the following were found in the Capitol at Raleigh:

ALEXANDER—Joseph, private, 3 years, William, private, 1 year; Charles, lieutenant; Benjamin, private, 3 years; Anthony, private, 1 year; John, private, 9 months; Ezekiel, private, 1 year; Benjamin, private, 1 year; William, ensign.

CONGER—Stephen Conger was sergeant major in 1st regiment, enlisting Oct. 10, 1776, and serving 3 years; Jonathan Conger, quartermaster sergeant 4th regiment, enlisted Jan. 25, 1777, promoted Sept. 11, 1777. (Page 105.)

HARRIS—John Harris, private; Peter Harris, Agt. Armr.; William Harris, private, 3 years; John Harris, private, 3 years; George Harris, private, 2 1-2 years; Thomas Harris, captain; Jas. Harris, private; Stephen Harris, private, 2 1-2 years; Goodman Harris, private, 2 1-2 years; Edward Harris, private. 3 years; Harry Harris, private, 3 years; Hugh Harris, private, 3 years; Thomas Harris, corporal, 2 1-2 years; Abraham Harris, private, 9 months; Abner Harris, private, 9 months; Jesse Harris, private, 9 months; Robert Harris, private, 1 year; Nelson Harris, sergeant, 1 year; Elijah Harris, private, 1 year; Henry Harris, musician, 1 year; Thomas Harris, private, 1 year; Jesse Harris, private, 18 months; Henry Harris, private, 18 months; Benjamin, private, 18 months; David Harris, private, 18 months; Edward Harris, sergeant; Geo. Harris.

McKEY—Dougal McKey, quartermaster sergeant, 10th regiment; time out, Feb. 1, 1783. John McKey, private Hadley's Co., 10th Regt., enlisted Aug. 1, 1782, served 18 months.

ROSS—John Ross, private, James Ross, private, 10th Regt., Lytle's company, enlisted 1781, left service Aug., 1782. John Ross, private, 4th Regt., Williams' company, enlisted 1777. Chas. Ross, private, 10th Regt., Quinn's Co., enlisted July 20, 1778, served 9 months. Thos. Ross, private, 10th Regt., Montfort's Co., enlisted Mar. 1, 1779, served 9 months, discharged Dec. 1, 1779.

OFFICES HELD BY THE HARRISES.

James Harris, Clear Creek, captain, 1777, 1779; collector, 1778. James Harris, Rocky Creek, captain, 1777-82; major, 1782. Robert Harris, Jr., justice of the peace, 1778. Robert Harris, Sr., Col., 1774. Samuel Harris, constable, 1785; assessor, 1777. Thomas Harris, Rocky River, sherif, 1782. Thomas Harris, Providence, sheriff, 1774.

ADDENDA.

The following information was received too late for classification:

Indianapolis, Ind., April 22, 1912.

Mrs. William R. Wright, 406 North State Street, Jackson, Miss.:

Dear Mrs. Wright—I have been anxious for a long time to find out something with regard to my great-grandfather, Henry Moores, and knowing that his son, my grandfather, had been born in Madison County, Kentucky, I went Friday last to Frankfort and Richmond, Ky., to see what I could learn in the Virginia branch in the Kentucky Land Office.

I found a patent from Henry Lee, Governor of Virginia, to Henry Moore, of which I send you a copy. I also found the orignal survey upon which the patent issued. In this survey the name is spelled "Moores," but it is not signed by the Henry Moores for whom it was made. It is signed by the surveyor, Hugh Ross, and by the chain men, Robert Kincaid and Ambrose Ross. At the time of the survey there were but three counties in Kentucky, and the land was in Madison County, but by reason of an increase in the number of counties, the land granted is now in Clay County, near Manchester, on the left bank of the Kentucky River, just below the mouth of Goose Creek. It is in the mountains, and presumably of very small value.

I was not able to examine the records of Clay County, but I searched carefully through the records of Madison County, and found that from the time this patent was granted until Clay County was cut off there was no conveyance recorded. There is no conveyance by or to Henry Moores or Henry Moore recorded in Madison County, nor does his name appear on the county records except in this patent.

I found the will of James M. Moores, of which I procured an attested copy, of which I send you a copy made in my office. I am not certain who this James Moores was, but think he was probably an elder son of Henry Moores, unless possible he was a brother. The names Charles, Isaac and Henry are family names.

I drove from Richmond out to Waco, some eight miles, and talked there with George Burrell Moores, who runs a small shop in which is located the post office. Mr. Moores told me that he was the son of the Henry Moores named in James Moores' will. He had the impression that his grandfather came from Virginia, and was of a family which had originally come from England, but he knew very little about the family, and referred me to his cousin, John Alexander Moores, the oldest member of the family now living, who is a farmer near Union, in Madison County.

I talked with John Moores and his wife, who was his step-sister, his father, a widower with six children, having married his mother with six children. John A. Moores is 77 years old, deaf, rheumatic and feeble, but very intelligent. He looks strikingly like my uncle, John Henry Moores, of Salem, Ore. He told me that his uncle, Isaac Moores, had gone to Oregon before he, John, was married, his marriage having been in 1855. I could not learn the year nor the part of the state to which his Uncle Isaac had gone. I think it possible that this Isaac was a great-uncle and my grandfather, who went to Oregon in 1854.

I was told by many people that within the last five years Charles K. Moores and John W. Moores had died, and that either one of them could have given me much more information.

I found, as might be expected, many of the name in and around Richmond and in and around Lexington, Ky. They are not wealthy people, but I was told, without exception, they were people of exceptional education and intelligence. This James Moores married Sarah Ann Kavanaugh, and there are many Kavanaughs in the northeastern part of the county. There are many Rosses in the southwestern part, but there is not a single tradition of any relation with the Alexanders, except a daughter of James Moores married a man of that name. John A. Moores told me that his impression was that his grandfather had come to Kentucky from South Carolina. I found from an examination of the records that James Moores had owned several thousand acres of land, none of which was really a good character. I am inclined to believe that the supposition of John Moores that his grandfather came from South Carolina is correct.

If I can give you any further information, I shall be glad to do so.

Very truly yours,   MERRILL MOORES.

The following rrecod is taken from a manuscript in the handwriting of Charles W. Moores, and was written about 1854 from records given him by his father. The records were recently discovered by Merrill Moores, of Indiapolis, and sent to the compiler of these secords. It gives some new light on various connections of the family, and corresponds with the records given in this book.

The record of marriages of the children of Isaac Ross and Jean Brown corresponds to mention made of the brothers and sisters of Arthur Brown Ross by him in his diary, and bears out the author in the statement that Robert Hill (page 134) did not marry one of the daughters of Isaac Ross, as believed by some members of the family:

"WILLIAM MOORES and HENRY MOORES were brothers, whose father came from Ireland and settled in New Jersey."

WILLIAM MOORES, a brother of Henry Moores, m Elizabeth Ross. (See page 76.)
Issue:

    HENRY MOORES, m Winny Whitaker, and in 1854 she lived in Nashville. He was killed by a fall from a horse. Issue:

        William Moores.
        Elizabeth Moores.
        Martha or Martin Moores.
        Nancy Moores.
        Brown Moores
        James Moores.

    ISAAC MOORES, m Martha ——. Lived in Tennessee. Issue:

        Mrs. Dr. Betsy.
        McGowan Moores.
        Martha Moores, drowned.

    JAMES MOORES, Kentucky, married. Issue:

        Elizabeth Moores.

    ARTHUR MOORES, Tennessee.

    WILLIAM MOORES, m Miss Hawkins. Lived in Tennessee. Issue:

        Rhoda Moores, m Mr. Bowman.
        Harriet Moores.
        William Moores.
        Brown Moores.
        A. B. Moores.
        Henry Moores.

    JOSIAH MOORES, m Margaret ——. See page 76. Issue:

        Lanner Black Moores, killed in Mexico.
        Rev. William Moores. See page 76.
        Hannah Moores.

    JOSHUA MOORES, lived in Illinois and had issue:

        James Moores.
        Josiah Moores.
        Nancy Moores.

    DANIEL MOORES, lived in Tennessee and had issue:

        William Moores.
        Eliza Moores.
        Otho Moores.
        James Moores.
        Evaline Moores.
        Jane Moores.

The memorandum is in pencil and undated, and is in my father's handwriting. He died in 1854. My gress as to the date of the writing is that it was written in December, 1854. My father was married December 24, 1854, and his father, Col. Isaac Ross Moores, who had gone from Danville, Ill., to Eugene City, Ore., in the spring of that year, returned overland to the wedding. I think that, as that was the last time my father saw him, the memorandum was probably made at that time. I am sorry it gives such few dates. It does, however, tell who was the original immigrant and the colony to which he came, so that it seems probable that we can secure future data when I am next in New York. It is amusing to me to see how often the Ross, Conger and other families have intermarried with members of the Moores family.   MERRILL MOORES.

PHOBBE MOORES, m Mr. Petty and lived in Virginia.
JANE MOORES, m Mr. Rouncifer.
ELIZABETH MOORES, m James Berry. Issue:
    John Berry.
    William Berry.
    Alfred Berry.
    Jane Berry.
    Eveline Berry, m Mr. Davis.
    Rachel Moores, m Mr. Lamkins.
    Hannah Moores m Mr. Moore.

HENRY MOORES. See page 78. Issue:
CHARLES MOORES, Texas. See page 80.
JOHN MOORES, Tennessee, m Jane Conger. See page 90. Issue:
    Eli Moores.
    Alexander Moores.
    Charles Moores.
    Mary Moores, m Mr. Hines.
ELIZABETH MOORES, m Joel Payne. Page 92. Issue:
    Hiram Payne, Arkansas.
    Culbertson Payne. Page 93.
    Marilla Payne, m Mr. Manning. Page 93.
    Harriet Payne, m Mr. Cobb. Page 93.
    Jane Payne, m Mr. Cobb. Page 93.
    Henry Payne.
    Margaret Payne, m Mr. Stephens. Page 93.
    William Payne, Arkansas. Page 93.
    Julia Payne. Page 93.
    Mary Ann Payne, m Mr. Lewis, of Arkansas. Page 93.
MARY MOORES, m Isaac Conger. Page 93. Issue:
    Sion M. Conger.
    Melinda Conger.
    Delilah Conger.
    Felix Conger.
    Matilda Conger.
PHOEBE MOORES, m Lazel, of New Jersey, m 2nd to Thomas Sheridan Stilwell.
    Page 93. Issue:
    William McKendree Stilwell.
    Henry Stilwell, of Clinton, Miss.
    Margaret Amanda Stilwell, m Mr. Jones, of Indiana.
    Jane Brown Stillwell, m Mr. Brown.
    Mary Elizabeth Stilwell, m Mr. Burke.
    Phoebe Rachel Stilwell, m Mr. Neely, of Indiana. Buried near Medora.
ISABELLA MOORES, m David Nott. Page 93. Issue:
    Alexander Nott.
    Jane Nott, m Mr. Rice.
    Matilda Nott, m Mr. Wood.
    Mary Nott, m Mr. Rutledge.
    Henry Nott.
    James Nott, Texas.
    David Nott, Lawrence County, Tenn.
SARAH WINNINGS MOORES, m James Higgins. Page 93. Issue:
    Nancy Jane Higgins, m Geo. Whitaker.
MARGARET THAXTON MOORES, m John Norvell. Issue:
    Henry Norvell. Page 94.
    Jane Norvell, m Mr. Fugit.
    William Brown Norvell.
    Sarah Norvell, m Thomas or Theodore Moony.

HENRY MOORES, of Tennessee, m Fanny Reese. Page 94. Issue.
    William Moores.
    Mary Moores, m Mr. Beanland.
    Jordan Reese Moores. Page 96.
HENRY MOORES m 2nd to Fanny Cole. Page 96. Issue:
    Charles Moores.
    John Moores.
    Frances Moores.
    Jane Moores.
    Henry Moores.
ISAAC ROSS MOORES, of Oregon. Page 97.
JANE BROWN MOORES. Page 99.
WILSON ALEXANDER MOORES, of Tennessee. Page 99.

ELIZABETH MOORES, sister of William Moores and Henry Moores, m Mr. Scudder, of Kentucky.

To be added to the Ross family record:

ISAAC ROSS and JEAN BROWN ROSS. Pages 17, 18. Issue:
    EUPHEMIA ROSS (daughter of the first marriage of Isaac Ross), m —— Conger
      See note, page 22. Issue:
        Isaac Conger.
        Jane Conger, m Mr. Byles.
        Zephyra Conger, m Mr. Todd.
        Euphemia Conger, m Mr. Tingle or Lingle.
        Abigail Conger.
        Effie Conger.
        Sarah Conger.
        Phebe Conger.
ISAAC ROSS, of South Carolina, son of the first marriage. Page 17.
ARTHUR BROWN ROSS, son of Jean Brown Ross. Page 18.
ABIGAIL ROSS, m Mr. Sutton, of North Carolina.
NICHOLAS ROSS (a brother, not son, of Isaac Ross, A. M. W.), m Miss Conger.
    Page 18.
ELIZABETH ROSS, m William Moores. Page 18.
JANE ROSS, m Henry Moores. Page 18.
POLLY or MARY ROSS, m John Conger. Page 110. Issue:
    Jonathan Conger.
    Joshua Conger.
    Eli Conger.
    Isaac Conger, m Miss Moores.
    Josiah Conger.
    John Conger.
    Elizabeth Conger, m Mr. Cole.
    Jane Conger, m Mr. Moores.
    Hannah Conger, m John Railsback, of Ohio.
    Polly Conger, m Mr. Elson, of Mississippi.
ISABELLA ROSS, m Mr. Davis, of North Carolina. Page 18. Issue:
    Jane Byles Davis.
    Euphemia Davis.
    Eliza Davis.
    Thomas Holland Davis.
    John Davis and
    Arthur Davis, twins.
CAPTAIN ISAAC ROSS, of Natchez.

The foregoing statement of the children of Isaac Ross accounts for each child, and tallies with the diary of Arthur Brown Ross and the previous information.

The following letter was sent by Mrs. Frances Thorn, of Blackstock, S. C., and was written by Mrs. Elizabeth Wade Fleming Green, a daughter of Mary Wade and David Fleming:

Columbia, S. C., Aug. 11, 1818.

Dear Aunt (Mrs. Rebecca Moore):

I take this opportunity of writing to you to inform you that we are all well, and to ask you to come down next week to a young camp-meeting that is expected to last from Thursday to Sunday or Monday morning. There are a good many preachers and teachers expected to attend in Columbia at that time. It is hoped that the luke-warm state of religion in this church will experience a revival with which it has not been blessed in some years.

If you will come you will meet Uncle D. Wade probably for the last time, as I am informed that he intends moving away.

By the time you receive this I shall have a sister ready to present to you on your arrival. Love to friends. Yours truly, E. W. FLEMING.

Irwinton, Bourbon County, Ala., 2nd February, 1841.

Dear Cousin:

Your letter of the 8th of last month is before me. It was quite a pleasure to me to receive your letter, as I had not been able to account for not getting an answer to my letter, not having any doubt that all that friendly feeling that is peculiar to our race was in your heart, leaving out of view that near relation that exists between use.

But to answer your inquiries, as near as I can, as to my Georgia relations, etc. I have not seen my brother John for four years. I received two letters from him during the past summer. I am sorry to say to you that he has been extremely unfortunate. My sister, Mrs. Wilkins, lives in Coweta County, Ga., and still remains a widow, with six children, most of whom are grown up. She is doing tolerable well Uncle John King and Aunt are still living, and reside at a village called Culloden, Monroe County, Ga. Their eldest son, Augustus D. King, is living in Forsyth, Monroe County, Ga., and a man of high standing in the State of Georgia. He is Judge of the Superior Court in the county in which he lives. Cousin James has never married. He has been for many years a member of the Legislature from Crawford County, Ga. Cousin Hugh is a Judge of the County Court in Sumpter County, Ga. Two of Uncle John King's daughters have married and are doing well.

I had the great misfortune to lose my only son in this place on the 12th of March, 1837. He was in his 19th year. This has greatly blighted all my prospects in this life. I have at this time an only daughter living. She lives in the County of Elbert, Ga., and is married to a gentleman by the name of Harper and is doing well. He is a merchant. I have a great desire for them to settle in this place, which I hope they will do. I formerly practiced law in Georgia, but have not attended to the practice in this state. I have a valuable property in town and a plantation four miles out. Our town is on the western bank of the Chattahutchie, thirty miles below Fort Michael and twenty-four above Fort Gaines. We have one of the most beautiful locations for a town in the United States. We have a population of about three thousand souls. There is a considerable town at Fort Gaines, and near the spot where the fort was built there is a splendid female college in successful operation. You would be delighted with our climate. In the four years I have lived here we have not had a particle of snow. Our summers are long and very hot.

I have a great desire to go and visit all my western connections, and spend two or three summers with them. When you go to New York come and see us, if possible. When in New York, by calling on Peter Johnson, No. — Mulberry street, you will be able to find out something about Brother James' oldest son. The youngest was in an orphan asylum the last account. I would be under great obligation if you would be so kind as to hunt them up, if they are alive. The oldest son is named Criswell and the youngest John. I would be very glad for one of them to come and live with me.

I have a desire for us to keep up a correspondence, therefore I hope you will write me often. Give my kindest respects to Uncle and Aunt, when you see them, and all my connections. Send me some of your newspapers and I will forward you some of ours.

Your friend and relative,

ALEXANDER McDONALD.

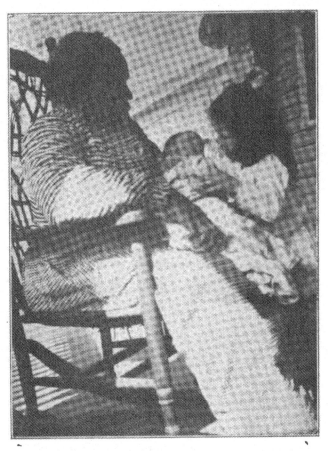

"MAMMY" BETSY WITH CLARA AND ANNE WRIGHT

In memory of the many faithful mammies who
have ministered to these families

To be added to page 123:
    Myrtle Corley was born Sept. 11, 1878, died Nov. 22, 1889.
    Minnie E. Corley was born June 9, 1882. Unmarried.
    Elisha Roy Corley was born Feb. 17, 1884. Unmarried.
    Lillian Corley was born Sept. 7, 1886. Unmarried.
    Floyd L. Corley was born March 16, 1889. Unmarried.
    N. L. Corley died March 10, 1910.

To be added to page —— :

Zuella B. Porter, b Oct. 25, 1870, d Jan. 11, 1903, m Mr. Ashworth. Issue:
    Harold L. Ashworth, b Feb. 6, 1893.
    Nellie R. Ashworth, b Feb. 15, 1895.
    Jordan F. Ashworth, b Apr. 24, 1897.
    Bernice M. Ashworth, b July 2, 1899.
    James M. Ashworth, b Sept 26, 1901.
W. Frank Porter, b Jan. 14, 1872, m Ida Armstrong, Aug. 2, 1891. Issue:
    Mary D. Porter, b June 11, 1892.
    W. Henry Porter, b Apr. 26, 1895.
    George D. Porter, b Oct. 28, 1898.
    John W. Porter, b 1904.
    Rosie Lee Porter, b Mch. 22, 1906.
    L. Leon Porter, b Feb. 25, 1912.
    Baby, b Feb. 25, 1912.
W. Wesley Porter, b May 11, 1878, m Josephine Lineberger, Nov. 5, 1905.
J. Terry Porter, b Apr. 20, 1880, m Bell Mason, Dec. 24, 1908.

ERRATA.

Jennie Allison Wade, dau of Judge Isaac Ross Wade, should appear on page 170.

Edmonton, on page 16, should read Edenton.

Date of letter on page 22 should be Feb. 3, 1834.

John S. O'Quin, born 1876 instead of 1896, page 36.

Illustration of Nannie Wilson Smith, instead of Nannie Wilsue Smith.

Hellen Ross is a sister instead of child of Percy J. Ross. Page 50.

Marilla Payne and sisters and brothers, page 93, should be in one space to the left in same position as Hiram Payne, their brother, on page 92.

On page 148, Victor Leseure should read, Victor Leseure Yomans. He was born in Danville, Ill.; his grandfather, Victor Leseure, was born in France.

On page 148, Janet Catherine Leseure should read, Janet Catherine Yomans.

Foot note on page 148, Stone Hill.should read, Stone River..

Page 133, John Newton Conger died young, and James Harvey Conger m Emma S. Lockwood, and had issue as given.

Page 33, Elizabeth Conger married Barney W. Huffman, May 30, 1865.

William H. H. Moores, instead of Monros, in illustration.

MARRIAGES.

NAMES.

DATE.

BIRTHS.

NAMES.	DATE.

NAMES.

DEATHS.

DATE.

CORRECTIONS AND ADDITIONS

Please give below, any corrections to the records contained in this volume also any additions giving pages where additions, etc., should be added.

INDEX

THE ALEXANDER FAMILY.

THE CONGER FAMILY.

THE HARRIS FAMILY.

THE HILL FAMILY.

THE KILLINGSWORTH FAMILY.

THE KING FAMILY.

THE MACKEY FAMILY.

THE MOORES FAMILY.

THE O'QUIN FAMILY.

THE ROSS FAMILY.

THE SIMS FAMILY.

THE WADE FAMILY.

ILLUSTRATIONS.

CPSIA information can be obtained at www.ICGtesting.com
Printed in the USA
BVOW06*0921270516

449563BV00003B/5/P